CU00656122

London Topographical Record

London Topographical Record

VOL. XXXII

EDITED BY
SHEILA O'CONNELL, B.A., F.S.A.

Publication No. 184
London Topographical Society
2021

©

LONDON TOPOGRAPHICAL SOCIETY
312 Russell Court, Woburn Place
London WC1H 0NG
2021

ISBN
978-0-902087-71-2

PRODUCED IN GREAT BRITAIN BY
SCORPION CREATIVE

CONTENTS

EDITOR'S MESSAGE

This volume of the London Topographical Record has been produced during a year when much of the United Kingdom has, like other countries across the world, been closed for business. The Editor has not been able to meet authors to discuss their articles and has had to resort to lengthy email exchanges. Illustrations have had to be sourced far and wide while the photographic departments of the major institutions have been closed (Ashley Baynton-Williams deserves special thanks for his help with tracking down digital images of maps). Authors have worried that they have not been able to access archives and libraries to check references and records and, more than ever, we have appreciated the value of the internet in making so much material available in our homes. As always, we have to thank Linda Fisher and Steve Hartley of Scorpion Creative for dealing efficiently with all matters concerned with production.

At a late stage in preparing the *Record* we heard the sad news of the death of our Patron, His Royal Highness Prince Philip, Duke of Edinburgh. His Royal Highness had been Patron since 1952, following our former Patrons Their Majesties King George VI and King George V. Long-standing members will remember the 100th Annual General Meeting held at St James's Palace in June 2000 when Prince Philip gave a short talk on the history of the Palace in his typically humorous style.

SHEILA O'CONNELL

NOTES ON CONTRIBUTORS

IAN DOOLITTLE has written widely on the City of London and its Livery Companies. As well as his work on the Fire Court decrees and the property market at that time, he is writing a history of the City of London Corporation. He is a consultant (previously a partner) at the law firm Trowers & Hamlins, where he specializes in public sector housing.

DAVID ELIS-WILLIAMS lives in Bangor, Gwynedd, where he was a pupil of Friars School. He is retired from a career in local government finance and now — in his words — 'dabbles' in local history and archaeology. In 2017 he fulfilled a long-held ambition to walk the length of the historic A5 from London to Holyhead. He is currently chair of trustees at Gwynedd Archaeological Trust.

AMELIA FAIRMAN holds a BA (Hons) and MA in Egyptian Archaeology from University College London and has worked on fieldwork projects in Egypt and the UK. She has been employed as a Project Manager by Pre-Construct Archaeology and is so currently by Museum of London Archaeology. She has co-authored a monograph on the archaeology and history of medieval and post-medieval Southwark and has published various archaeological papers.

Dorian Gerhold is an independent historian, and was formerly a House of Commons Clerk. He has written about carriers and stage-coaches, the history of industry, Westminster Hall, London's suburban villas, urban cartography, old London Bridge, Chancery records and Putney (where he lives). He is a member of the Council of the London Topographical Society.

Elizabeth Hallam Smith is an Academic Research Consultant attached to the Architecture and Heritage Team, Houses of Parliament, and holds honorary posts at the University of York and UEA. She served as Director of Public Services at The National Archives and from 2006 to 2016 was Director of Information Services and Librarian at the House of Lords.

Vanessa Harding teaches London history at Birkbeck, University of London. Her research and writing focus on the city's social history, c. 1500–1700, with a particular interest in the built environment and how it was inhabited. She is currently working on a book-length study of seventeenth-century London, and developing a project to map London on the eve of the Great Fire.

Malcolm Jones retired from the English Department of Sheffield University in 2010 with the publication of *The Print in Early Modern England*. He has long been interested in non-religious iconography, the subject of *The Secret Middle Ages* (2002), and is currently working on the wealth of such imagery to be found in early modern students' *alba amicorum*, an important class of manuscript that is, however, little known to British art historians.

The late Ann Saunders was one of the leading figures of the London Topographical Society for more than forty years. Her obituary on pp. 312–17 gives an account of her career.

Richard Stephens is an independent art historian, interested in prints and drawings and the history of the art trade. He edits *The Art World in Britain 1660–1735* website and the *Walpole Society* journal. His catalogue raisonné of the landscape painter Francis Towne (1739–1816) was published online by the Paul Mellon Centre in 2016. His love of London topographical prints was sparked by childhood visits to the Guildhall Library.

Guy Thompson holds a BA (Hons) in English History and Landscape Archaeology and an MA in Early Modern English History. Guy worked as an archivist for Pre-Construct Archaeology and is currently employed as a historic landscape specialist. He co-authored a well-received monograph on the development of King's Cross Station and has contributed to various other monographs on the history of Glasgow and the British Museum among others, as well as publishing and co-writing numerous articles.

Rosemary Weinstein BA, PhD, FSA was a curator at the former London Museum at Kensington Palace and at its successor, the Museum of London, where the Cheapside Hoard is held. In 1985 she acquired for the Museum the City section of the *Copperplate Map* which joined that of Moorfields already in the collection. A member of the LTS since 1979, she contributed to volumes xxiv and xxv of the Record, and to *London Parish Maps* (2020). Other publications include *Tudor London* (1994), *The History of the Worshipful Company of Feltmakers* (2004) and, with Ian M. Betts, *Tin-Glazed Tiles from London* (2010).

I. FROM THE KING'S BRIDGE TO BLACK ROD'S STAIRS: THE PALACE OF WESTMINSTER AND THE THAMES, 1189–2021

By ELIZABETH HALLAM SMITH

Introduction: Bridges, Stairs and Landing Places in London and Westminster in 1743

A POCKET *Map of the Citties of London & Westminster and the Suburbs thereof … to this Present Year 1743* (Fig. 1) provides a vivid visual snapshot of the extent of London in the eighteenth century. Westminster is to the west, and the River Thames runs right across it, as its main artery. At the centre of a network of navigable rivers from Roman times,[1] and later of canals, the Thames would remain crucial for the transport of heavy goods and freight from the Middle Ages until the mid-twentieth century.[2] For passengers, too, the river was vital, and the *Pocket Map* helpfully includes the main docks, wharves and stairs, and lists the fares charged by the watermen between the main staging points, as set by the Court of Aldermen back in 1671. Also shown are the rates for the faster and more costly Hackney coaches, which had by this time been plying their trade for more than a century.[3] A journey by coach from St Paul's to Westminster Hall cost 1*s*. 6*d*., but the slower route by water from London Bridge to Westminster Stairs cost 6*d*. by oars and 3*d*. by sculls.

Passenger access to and from the river was via landing places, or jetties, which the map describes as stairs, although an alternative term, used from the Middle Ages until the nineteenth century, was bridges. All these jetties gave the public free access to the river, a right upheld by the Crown from the Middle Ages onwards.[4] There were also numerous lesser, private stairs (not depicted on the map) belonging to people with houses along the river. The steps down to the river were often timber built, with stone for those in heavy use, and, from many, wooden causeways stretched into the river to allow embarkation and disembarkation at low tide.

Why were these bridges, which were by any modern definition piers or landing stages, so called? Although largely lost today, this was long a well-understood usage, particularly on the tidal Thames. The old Norse/ Scandinavian word *bryggja*, reflected in place names such as Brigg, Lincolnshire, originally denoted a jetty or quay.[5] The Latin word *pons*, usually translated as bridge in the modern sense, was used for a gangway or causeway from classical times and could be deployed to denote jetties from the eleventh century onwards. This use was found at Westminster from the twelfth century.[6] In English, one obsolete or dialect reading of 'bridge' as

Fig. 1   Robert Hulton (publisher), William Roades (engraver), *A Pocket Map
of the Cities of London & Westminster and the Suburbs thereof ... to this
Present Year 1743*. The map shows all the main landing-places, including those at

Westminster; Westminster Bridge, completed in 1750, has been added indicating that this is a later edition of the map. Courtesy of Jonathan Potter Ltd.

a fixed or floating landing stage, jetty, or pier, occurs between about 1425 and 1879.[7]

The old Palace of Westminster had several private sets of stairs and two main bridges or piers, providing public access from the river: the King's Bridge or Westminster Stairs and the Queen's Bridge or Parliament Stairs. These principal landing places, and their Victorian successors, are the focus of this article. Their topographical setting, the tidal Thames, flows south to north past the Palace of Westminster. The King's Bridge was at its downstream, northern end, near to where the Elizabeth (Clock) Tower and Speaker's Green are today located, while the Queen's Bridge was towards its southern end, now beneath Charles Barry's Royal Court.[8] Although important, neither the King's Bridge nor the Queen's Bridge was the main crossing point for this stretch of the river. That was the Lambeth Horse Ferry (running roughly along the line of modern-day Lambeth Bridge), which appears at the south-eastern edge of where the 1743 map ends. Established by 1189, it ran until 1862, and was operated from 1514 by the Company of Watermen.[9]

The King's Bridge and the Queen's Bridge, 1189–1509

The medieval Palace of Westminster, magnificent centre of English royal power, directly abutted the Thames, and much of its site lay on low and marshy land.[10] In 1179–80, Ailnoth the Engineer made or remade its stone river wall and quay, the earliest documentary evidence identified for a landing place here. That was in response, perhaps, to rising high-tide levels, identified as a concern since the eleventh century and exacerbated by the effects of London Bridge, work on which began in 1176. Not long after Ailnoth's repairs are documented, there is a specific mention of repairs to the *pons regis*, the King's Bridge, in the 1189 pipe roll. Some presumed remains of this work were found in archaeological excavations under Bridge Street. These suggest a gateway in the river wall leading to a landing stage with access to New Palace Yard and adjoining it a wide dock with stone retaining walls and a sloping floor of stout wooden planks.[11] This dock enabled flat-bottomed sailing barges (known in the later Middle Ages as shouts) bringing building materials, food and other provisions to Westminster to be borne up the river on the incoming tide and to be unloaded at low tide.[12] Sail-less lighters, flat-bottomed freight 'workhorse' boats with high sides and rounded ends, were used to bring up heavy cargoes transferred from the great sailing barges below London Bridge. These were reliant on the tides to carry them up and downstream and were steered with oars.[13]

For long-distance trade such as wine imports from Gascony, cogs, much larger and more robust vessels, were used.[14] Smaller vessels were deployed to catch and land fish — cod, whiting, haddock, herring, flounder, salmon, even sturgeon — of which the tidal Thames was a vital source right up to the early nineteenth century. A fish market was well established near Westminster Abbey by the fifteenth century and catches regularly came ashore at the King's Bridge.[15] So, too, did the monks.[16] For the kings' subjects, regular ferry services from Westminster along the Thames were available from the thirteenth century and perhaps earlier. For private hires, licensed watermen plied their trade in their wherries: a form of water taxi. In 1372, the mayor and aldermen of London fixed the prices of such journeys: the one between London and Westminster was set at 2*d*., rising to 3*d*. for a full boat.[17]

As later, the gateway and landing stages at the King's Bridge were in frequent need of repair in the Middle Ages: they appear in several accounts of the twelfth and thirteenth centuries, and again in 1308–09 when the pier was damaged by ice.[18] From 1292 to 1348 successive kings rebuilt St Stephen's chapel to the south-east of Westminster Hall in magnificent style. Records show that building materials for the new chapel were brought into the *pons regis*. This was followed by the construction of a fine complex of buildings to house its wealthy college of canons, founded in 1348, which was endowed with substantial estates including much of the palace's riverfront. Although in the mid-fourteenth century the dock was demolished, heavy materials needed for the construction or maintenance of the palace or for government business continued to arrive at the landing stage at the King's Bridge.[19]

Access was controlled by a watergate, whose keeper is mentioned in the patent rolls for 1349.[20] Edward III's foundation charter for St Stephen's college, in 1354, gave the canons and vicars toll-free access though the gateway at the King's Bridge by day and night, and possession of a set of its keys.[21] This was a valuable exemption, for a typical charge per boatload of goods from London to Westminster was 8*d*.[22] In addition, tolls were payable to maintain the pier and dock and to raise funds for other purposes. For example, in 1355–56, duties from the King's Bridge on wool and leather were granted to fund the building of a further and separate bridge or pier to serve the King's new wool staple, created in 1353, which lay just to the north of the King's Bridge.[23] The King had acquired this site from the college of St Stephen in return for rents, but these would in the event prove an erratic and unstable source of income.[24]

The Queen's Bridge, towards the southern, upstream end of the Palace of Westminster, was evidently so-called because of its proximity to the Queen's palace, by the end of the Middle Ages much of which was encompassed within the royal privy apartments.[25] This complex first emerges in the accounts in 1237–38, underwent major repairs in 1307–11, and was further extended in 1342 when a new chapel and chamber were built close to

Figs 2 (above) and 3 (facing page).   Lucas Cornelisz. de Kock (attributed to),
Westminster Abbey and the Parliament House from the Thames, c. 1515–32, pen and
ink. These two drawings are the earliest depictions of the waterfront of the Palace;
they are believed originally to have formed a single sheet, and show both the Queen's
Bridge, on the left, and the King's Bridge, on the right. © London, Victoria and Albert
Museum, E 128-1924, and Paris, Musée du Louvre, inv. no. 18702, verso.
Photo © RMN-Grand Palais (musée du Louvre)/Adrien Didierjean.

the Queen's Bridge.[26] It had a watergate: a room in it, known as the red
chamber, was used in 1371 to transfer the great seal to new Chamberlain Sir
Robert de Thorp.[27] The Queen's Bridge underwent major repairs in 1396.[28]
Like the King's Bridge, it could handle goods as well as public passengers:
for example, in 1322 the royal coinage from the Westminster treasury was
taken from here to the Tower of London. Fifty-two barrels of coins each
containing £500 were transported in two barges and four boats at the cost
of 2.*s* 9*d*., a reduction on the normal rates of 8*d*. per boat.[29]

The earliest known depictions of the waterfront of the Palace, 1515–32
(Figs 2–3),[30] show the Queen's Bridge as a modest watergate within the
privy palace (on the left). The King's Bridge (on the right) is by contrast an
elegant entrance. In the later fifteenth century it began to be used for grand
royal and civic cavalcades: the Lord Mayor's annual water procession
from London to Westminster, which soon became a renowned spectacle,
and landed here, started in 1453.[31] The Crown was not far behind: in 1486
Henry VII, met and accompanied by a magnificent flotilla of barges from
the City of London, landed at the bridge after his triumphal royal progress
to York.[32] In 1501, in preparation for the nuptials of his eldest son Arthur

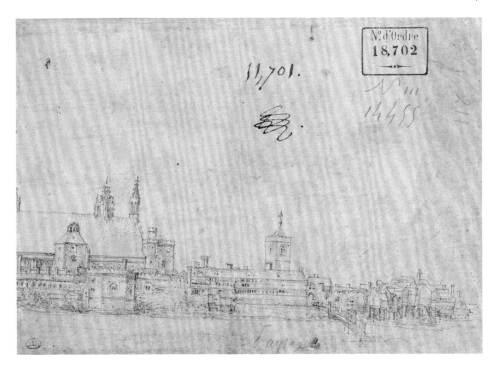

and Catherine of Aragon, Henry VII spent lavishly on the palace, including mending and repairing the carved and painted heraldic beasts set on posts by the King's Bridge. From here, a grand procession of barges travelled upstream from the King's Bridge to Richmond Palace.[33] Over the next two centuries, most major royal events would be celebrated with magnificent water processions.[34]

The King's Bridge and the Queen's Bridge, 1509–1660

Westminster's magnificent medieval royal palace underwent a profound transformation during the sixteenth century. Following a major fire at its southern end in 1512, Henry VIII relocated his quarters first to Lambeth and then in the 1530s to his impressive new palace of Westminster, known as Whitehall and built from stone from his ruined privy palace to the south, which was now demolished. But the central and northern sections of the old palace round Westminster Hall and adjoining the Abbey remained the hub of royal ritual. Here were housed the bulk of the royal administration and the law courts, Elizabeth's reign seeing a major expansion in their functions, space and buildings.[35] The two bridges feature prominently in the 'Agas' map of about 1561.[36]

After the dissolution of the college of St Stephen in 1547–48, its former chapel was granted to the House of Commons as its meeting place, conveniently close to the House of Lords which had since the fourteenth century occupied the Queen's or White Chamber.[37] The former college's riverside lands at Westminster, stretching from the King's Bridge to the Queen's Bridge, were from 1550 to 1572 held by three well-connected courtiers in succession, but reverted to the Crown in 1572. The northern portion from the King's Bridge to the House of Commons, encompassing many of the former college's buildings, was now granted to the Auditors and Tellers of the Receipt of the Exchequer as offices and dwellings.[38]

The rest of the site, to the south of the House of Commons, and including the land round the Queen's Bridge, had after its clearance been left by the Crown and its succession of private owners in a poor state. The Lady Pew tenement directly to the south of the Commons was in 1566 described as being in a state of 'great ruin', with much of its bank washed away by the violence of the river. A demise was granted on the basis that the new holder, Edmund Sexton MP, would repair it.[39] The area round the Queen's Bridge would subsequently be parcelled out in a complex and apparently haphazard way.[40] Described by a contemporary as the 'back yard' of the palace,[41] this area was in use for trade and residential purposes and subject to complex tenurial disputes. Wealth and poverty were starkly juxtaposed and the risks of crime and disorder were constant.[42] A commission of trespasses in 1597 criticized John Wynyard, who held land round the Queen's Bridge, 'for a great nuisance made [by] his tenants in the making of stalls at the bridge of the lady queen on both sides of the way'.[43] Yet the Crown ensured that all relevant grants included the obligation to maintain the sewers and drains of the House of Lords, and reserved both an access route to the House of Lords and a public right of way to Old Palace Yard from the Queen's Bridge.[44]

To the north, the King's Bridge remained the grand ceremonial entrance to New Palace Yard and Westminster Hall. Its river side was remodelled in 1517,[45] and a drawing made in 1543–44 depicts not just the posts, rails and heraldic beasts, but a stylish Renaissance arch to the watergate, set in a great wall (Fig. 4).[46] There was a further rebuilding in 1548, and some more significant work on the structure in 1568, when thirteen new piers were built from Kentish hardstone and ashlar brought downstream from Reading Abbey. The edifice was further adorned with the royal arms, painted in gilt, and four new heraldic beasts together with a stone lion.[47]

The King's Bridge thus provided a suitably grand stage for the many Tudor and Stuart royal water ceremonies and processions, with their ornate and colourful barges.[48] On the way to their Coronation vigils in Westminster Hall, sovereigns from Mary to James II took the short river journey by barge from Whitehall Palace to Westminster Stairs.[49] From the

Fig. 4.
Anthonis van
den Wijngaerde,
*Panorama of
London, c.* 1543–
44, pen and ink.
Detail depicting
the King's Bridge
as a ceremonial
watergate entrance
to the Palace
of Westminster.
© Ashmolean
Museum Oxford,
WA1950.206.1.

1540s onwards, the King's Bridge also played a role in the State Opening of Parliament: for example, Edward VI returned from here to Whitehall by barge in 1547 while the Commons were electing their Speaker; and Charles I landed with a large entourage in 1640. So, too, perhaps surprisingly, did Oliver Cromwell in 1658.[50] To assist with all the necessary arrangements, under Elizabeth I and James I the Crown retained the services of about forty watermen, including the eccentric and self-appointed water poet, John Taylor, who during the Civil War was to become Charles I's official water bailiff at Oxford.[51]

The Thames evidently offered a lively and colourful spectacle: sixteenth-century visitors to the capital expressed their admiration for the numerous passenger wherries with decorative canopies and upholstered cushions skimming across the river.[52] Such craft were able to land at Westminster, for the King's Bridge was not just for royalty and their entourages: in 1603, John Stow wrote that it was 'a fair landing-place for all men that have occasion'.[53] The earlier wherry fares of 2*d.* to ply between London and Westminster, rising to 3*d.* for a full boat, were still in operation in the early sixteenth century but were increasingly hard to maintain, and were reiterated by an Act of Parliament in 1514. This also set up the Company of Watermen as an early attempt to regulate the trade;[54] in 1555 the watermen plying between Gravesend and Windsor were given a more formal organization and their regulation was vested in the City of London and in JPs in the counties adjoining the Thames.[55]

Maintaining the King's Bridge in the face of tides, currents and flooding and heavy use was, as earlier, a major engineering and maintenance challenge: numerous repairs and improvements were needed during the last quarter of the sixteenth century, with a more substantial reconstruction taking place in 1604–05.[56] The Watergate, too, was seemingly again remodelled when in 1599–1602 an important range of medieval Exchequer buildings, including the Star Chamber, was extended and redeveloped in New Palace Yard, at right angles to Westminster Hall.[57] Further major work to the bridge and river wall took place in 1609–11, followed up with more minor maintenance. In 1629–30 the piers were repaired in ashlar to take the weight of the planking, while in 1631–32 new planks were set in to replace those washed away by the 'rough tides'. The planking was replaced yet again in 1647–48.[58]

As a contemporary image by Wenceslaus Hollar shows (Fig. 5),[59] by the mid-seventeenth century the King's Bridge was starting to lose many of its ceremonial trappings and was becoming a busy no-frills landing stage for people and goods. This was evidently in part a response to commercial pressures. But, at the same time, whilst Westminster's waterside retained its significance for major royal and mayoral set-pieces, Whitehall Palace, with its magnificent regal watergate, had by this time become the centre of royal pageantry.[60]

Given its squalid surroundings, it seems improbable that the Queen's Bridge or Parliament Stairs also had a significant ceremonial function.[61] Yet it was here that the sovereign landed when attending the House of Lords, the difficulties overcome by a portable landing stage or landing table. In 1532 carpenters were employed to make a 'bridge for the dry landing of the king, for the barge to go, in the parliament chamber'.[62] A 'new landing bridge' is also mentioned in the accounts for the 1590s, enabling the ageing queen Elizabeth I — an aficionado of the newfangled coach for royal processions — to reach dry land when attending to some of her parliamentary duties.[63]

Fig. 5. Wenceslaus Hollar, *The Thames below Westminster Pier*, c. 1638, pen and ink. Seen from the north in this mid-seventeenth-century drawing, the King's Bridge is now a busy landing-place for people and goods. © The Henry Barber Trust. The Barber Institute of Fine Arts, University of Birmingham/Bridgeman Images, *BIRBI-54.3.*

Although its causeway underwent a number of repairs,[64] the Queen's Bridge was disparaged in a crown survey of 1612 as 'a common landing place from the said River Thames called and graced only with the bare name of the Parliament Stairs (for, indeed, there are no stairs at all). But the said landing place … serves for his majesty to land at, when he comes by water to the Parliament, which landing place being very mean and very inconvenient for his highness'.[65]

The private stairs on this stretch of the river, although receiving far less traffic, were generally better maintained: examples may be seen in a drawing of the central part of the waterfront from the 1660s (Fig. 6). An example, on the left, is the stairs in the garden of Sir Robert Cotton, who in 1622 had acquired the Lady Pew tenement to the south of the Commons for his house and library.[66] In 1626 these were lavishly prepared for the ceremonial landing of Charles I on his way to his coronation, in preference to the normal landing place at the King's Bridge. But at the last minute, as a political rebuff to Cotton, the flotilla failed to land there, diverting to the 'dirty and inconvenient' Queen's Bridge or Parliament Stairs nearby. The new King had to leap ashore when the royal barge stuck in the mud.[67]

For his planned visits to the House of Lords the King would use the royal landing-table,[68] but so degraded was the condition of the Queen's Bridge in 1645 that six watermen petitioned the peers about the decayed state of the 'cawsey' or jetty there. They were unable to land their passengers at low water and they asked that the Office of Works should survey and rectify the problems.[69] Any resulting activity is not reflected in the accounts.

Fig. 6. Michiel van Overbeek, *Westminster*, c. 1663–66, pen and ink and wash. This detail from a drawing of the 1660s shows the waterfront of the central part of the Palace, including several private landing-stairs. The Cotton Garden stairs are on the far left. © Trustees of the British Museum, G,3.245.

Westminster Stairs and Parliament Stairs, 1660–1740

In the years around 1700, Westminster Stairs (the King's Bridge) and Parliament Stairs (the Queen's Bridge) remained important access routes into Westminster (Fig. 7). Westminster Stairs were significant for public passenger traffic, and, in recognition of rising prices, by 1671 the price of a passenger wherry arriving here from London Bridge was — as already noted — set at 6*d*. by oars and 3*d*. by sculls.[70] Substantial quantities of freight were also landed. This was done by the lightermen, whose livery company emerges fully-fledged in 1667 and merged with the watermen in 1700. In 1707 the ancient rights of the Thames watermen were formally recognized when they were licensed to ply their trade from both the King's Bridge and Queen's Bridge.[71] This ordinance also regulated and licensed them to carry corn and malt and similar goods to and from the King's Bridge.[72] A visiting diplomat admiringly estimated in the 1720s that the

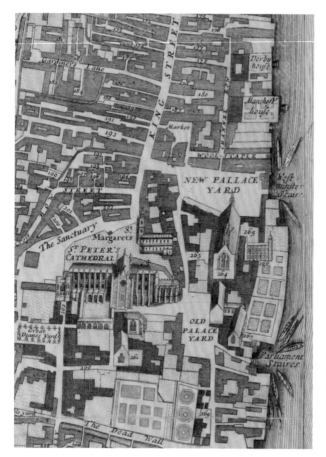

Fig. 7.   William Morgan, *London &c. Actually Survey'd*, 1682. Detail showing Westminster with the Westminster Stairs and Parliament Stairs featuring prominently. © The British Library Board *Maps Crace Port. 2.58.*

river could boast 15,000 colourful passenger wherries and a further 15,000 boats to transport goods.[73] This was still an era of great water processions, too, amongst them the Lord Mayor's flotilla, with its painted, carved and gilded ceremonial barges,[74] which continued to land at the King's Bridge or Westminster Stairs.

More prosaically, after 1660 the Office of Works accounts continue itemize frequent repairs to the King's Bridge to keep at bay the ravages of commerce, storm and tide. Many of the interventions were required simply to maintain the oak piles and boards above; but in 1693 seven stone piers under the bridge were repaired.[75] The timber superstructure was often dislodged, for example in 1683, and again in 1690 when measures were taken to secure 'a beame and two Squares of the bridge that was blowne up by the stormy winds and high tide'.[76] By 1733 the bridge had become very dilapidated, its 'ruinous condition' being attributed to coals and malt being brought in here rather than at the former wool staple site, 'to the great interruption of the Members of Parliament and others landing there'. It transpired that this was because the wool staple dock had been leased out to a carpenter, Hercules Taylor, who was storing deal boards there. The Office of Works having declared that the King's Bridge was unfit to pass over, it now underwent yet more major repairs at a cost of £250.[77]

As shown in contemporary depictions (Figs 8–9), the area round the Parliament Stairs, cutting both Houses off from the river, remained a jumble of buildings and waste ground.[78] The rights to these were frequently contested and the surroundings remained crime-ridden and lawless. Here as elsewhere the Thames itself was notorious for theft, violent behaviour

Fig. 8. Anonymous, *Lambeth Palace and the Horseferry from Westminster, c. 1720,* oil on canvas. The jetty leading to the Parliament Stairs and its busy surroundings are depicted from the Thames shore in this early eighteenth-century painting. © Government Art Collection, *GAC 10000.*

Fig. 9.   Samuel Scott, *Westminster Abbey and Hall*, 1739, watercolour. This drawing shows the buildings behind the Parliament Stairs in the foreground; the jetty with its boats extends into the river. © Trustees of the British Museum, *1865,0610.1323*.

and piracy, and offered a rapid escape from the crime scene.[79] Some of the miscreants were caught: in 1736 prolific burglar John Maxworth, 'otherwise Paddy, otherwise Parliament Jack', was sentenced to death for stealing silverware from a house in Cotton Garden, near the Parliament Stairs.[80]

Substantial works were still needed to maintain the Parliament Stairs: for example, in 1689 fifty piles were driven into the riverbed and 80 feet of causeway repaired, while in 1697 seventy piles were driven in and 240 feet of railings put in.[81] This was not least to enable the bishops to access the House of Lords via their own entrance,[82] and the monarch to attend Parliament. To ease the king's way through the morass, in 1692 Christopher Wren provided 'a more convenient and safe passage … by her Majesties' command for the King, from the landing place to the House of Lords … [and] the passage from Westminster Hall to the Parliament Stairs [was] made more lightsome'.[83]

The sovereign continued to rely upon the royal landing table to disembark here from the royal barge. Frequently deployed between 1660 and 1702, it emerges from the accounts as a heavy, though collapsible, upper structure mounted on four robust wheels on two axles, and expensively decorated by a coachmaker or royal painter. Once brought out of storage and assembled, it was moved into place across the boards and gravel which had been laid around the causeway and chained to the Parliament Stairs to prevent it

from floating away.[84] Its final appearance was in 1702, when the new Queen, Anne, attended the House of Lords on two consecutive days: thereafter the Queen came by coach from St James's Palace.[85]

A further hazard right along the palace's waterfront was flooding. In 1678 Allan Probard was paid 45s. not just for his normal job of emptying the Commons stool room but also for 'ramming up the draine with horse litter to keep out the Tyde'. In 1692 he was instructed 'to hang a wooden flap to the mouth of the great Shore' at the King's Bridge, to prevent the water from backing up here.[86] From 1714–29 it fell to Mrs Deborah Reding and her workmen to operate 'the two flaps at the King's Bridge to prevent the tide from overflowing'. A wealthy widow, she had taken over and ran very effectively her late husband's extensive scavenging and maintenance operations, including clearing rubbish, drains and gutters for Parliament.[87] Such operations would become increasingly challenging, for in the eighteenth century, as high tide levels continued their slow but inexorable rise, London experienced some forty major inundations.[88]

A Time of Transformations: The Westminster Stairs and the Parliament Stairs, 1740 –1834

By the middle of the eighteenth century, the King's Bridge or Westminster Stairs had begun its long slow trajectory of decline, a significant reason for which was the advent of the first Westminster Bridge (Fig. 10). Opened eventually in 1750 after a long and painful genesis, it was much admired by contemporaries both for its design and as an emblem of public improvement.

Fig. 10.   Antonio Canaletto, *View of the Thames and Westminster Bridge*, 1746–47, oil on canvas, detail. This painting shows the new Westminster Bridge with the downgraded Westminster Stairs adjoining it, and the Parliament Stairs jetty at the centre; Westminster Abbey is on the left. © Lobkowicz Palace, Prague Castle, Czech Republic/Bridgeman Images.

Its surroundings were rapidly transformed, the King's Bridge or Westminster Stairs falling victim even before its completion.[89] Thus it was reported in the press in September 1742 that 'the bridge to the Thames in New Palace Yard, call'd the King's Bridge, was begun to be pulled down, boats being to land for the future at the foot of the new stone bridge on Westminster side'. The new public landing stage next to the new bridge was to be known as the Westminster Bridge Stairs.[90] Grand ceremonial flotillas, most notably the Lord Mayor's procession, continued to follow the time-honoured way to Westminster, but now embarking and disembarking here.[91]

The former King's Bridge was not entirely destroyed, though — it was simply downgraded to a pier known as the 'wooden bridge' (Fig. 11). The wherrymen still plied their trade from here, and it was one of several staging points for the popular regattas staged by the watermen from the 1770s onwards, involving rowing races from Westminster to the Rotunda at Ranelagh.[92] The area to the north of it, formerly the wool staple, saw numerous changes, being developed for houses in the 1740s and then in 1785 taken over by His Majesty's Stationery Office (HMSO).[93] The substantial premises here included a stone tenement and houses next to the river, and a dock adjoining New Palace Yard.[94] To the south of it lay waterside houses occupied by Exchequer and parliamentary officials.[95] Behind the wooden bridge lay the medieval and Elizabethan timber-framed Exchequer range, by now in a ramshackle state, with the watergate through it, and in 1789

Fig. 11. W. M. Fellows after John Thomas Smith, *The Water-Front of the buildings on the eastern side of New Palace Yard*, 1808, etching and aquatint. This print from Smith's *Antiquities of Westminster*, 1807–09, depicts the watergate and the 'wooden bridge' pier from the river side. © Parliamentary Art Collection, *WoA 2981*.

housing several government offices, including the Lottery Office and the tellers for the payment of American claims.[96]

The area was well recorded by contemporary antiquaries,[97] immortalizing a world that was gradually to vanish. As part of the Westminster improvements the northern end of the Exchequer range, including the watergate, was pulled down in 1808. That created an open area fronted by a new embankment bordering the river, and opened up a magnificent vista of Westminster Abbey from Westminster Bridge (Fig. 12). Those changes would be followed in 1822 by the demolition of the southern end of the former Exchequer terrace, including the building known as the Star Chamber.[98] During the course of the improvements, HMSO moved out to Scotland Yard in 1812.[99] In 1834, the area it had occupied contained a drilling shed

Fig. 12.   Daniel Havell after John Gendall, *Westminster Hall and Abbey*, 1819,
aquatint with etching and hand-colouring. This print from Rudolph Ackermann's
series *Views of London* shows the prospect from Westminster Bridge after the
demolition of part of the Elizabethan Exchequer range and of the watergate.
The 'wooden bridge' pier, formerly the King's Bridge, is visible near the
parapet of the Bridge. © London Metropolitan Archives, City of London,
SC/GL/PR/W2/HAL/EXT/p5419376.

for the Metropolitan Police, and another carpenter's workshop.[100] A grand
hotel had been constructed nearby, next to the Bridge.[101]

To the south, near the Parliament Stairs, improvements also cleared out
some of the impoverished and crime-ridden properties round Old Palace
Yard, the footprint of which was extended.[102] Off it, running west to east
towards the Thames, still lay a narrow street at this time known as Parliament
Place, which marked the southern end of the old Palace. Here, closest to
the river and to the Parliament Stairs, was the residence of distinguished
inventor Edward Hussey Delaval.[103] After a fire had destroyed his house
near Westminster Abbey in 1768, Delaval had acquired from the Crown the
lease of the now-vacant corner site, and funded by a mortgage built a new
house here. Into this, he and his wife Sarah had moved by 1772.[104]

This attractive and compact confection, with its charming bay window,
is a distinctive presence in panoramas of the old Palace from the river (Fig.
13).[105] Described by John Carter as 'a curious modern house in the gothic
style',[106] it marks an early arrival of the gothic revival within the precincts
of Parliament. Here the Delavals entertained leading scientists of the day
as well as writers and poets,[107] extending their lease in 1799, seemingly

after John Soane's first set of plans to redevelop this end of the old Palace were shelved.[108] In 1784 a party of burglars arrived here by water and broke in, but failed to get through the stout iron door to Mr Delaval's chamber, departing from the Parliament Stairs with some silver and cash from the kitchen.[109]

After Delaval's death in 1814, at his house,[110] Sir Thomas Tyrwhitt, Black Rod since 1812, took it as his official residence and moved in, remaining here until his death in 1832.[111] It fell to Tyrwhitt's servants to lock and unlock the gates to the Parliament Stairs,[112]

Fig. 13. Samuel Leigh, *View of the banks of the Thames from Westminster Bridge to Richmond*, 1829, etching and aquatint. This detail of Leigh's panorama shows Parliament Stairs, on the left, with Edward Hussey Delaval's former house adjoining them. © London Metropolitan Archives, City of London, *SC/GL/LEI/001*.

evidently installed in case of public disorder, but closing off public access from the river. By this time the northern side of Parliament Place had been tidied up to allow the building of Sir John Soane's Royal Entrance to the House of Lords (1822–23),[113] and the public right of way to the river had been blocked. People of note who were permitted by the Crown to use this access included the exotic foreign witnesses for Queen Caroline's trial in 1820, much criticized by the press,[114] and peeresses and some other dignitaries attending the coronation of George IV in 1821.[115]

So, too, were the boys of Westminster School, to enable them to practise 'the manly and healthy exercise of rowing'. Theirs was claimed to be the oldest amateur rowing club in the world, dating from the late eighteenth century, its main boathouse at this time situated on the shore opposite, where today St Thomas's Hospital stands.[116] The School saw itself as the main user of the passage to the Parliament Stairs, in 1815 co-opting the Commons Speaker, Charles Abbot, a Westminster School alumnus, to support the removal of a temporary brick wall built across it to deter rioters — which necessitated the scholars in going round through a coal yard and over some barges to reach their boats.[117] This initiative was only partly successful, for in *c.* 1820 the School demanded that Charles Bacon,

Clerk of the Works at Westminster, should remove the stones and rubbish obstructing the gates, that he should keep the gates unlocked between 7.00 am and 9.00 pm, and that some piles be fixed at the end of the stairs to prevent encroachment by barges.[118]

By this time, despite the claims of eminent authorities to the contrary, the health benefits of the river were clearly minimal. Since 1815 it had been legal to use the river as a sewer, exacerbating the already-high levels of pollution from raw sewage and industrial effluent, not to mention the threat of disease, and wiping out the remaining fishing trade.[119] The prevailing theory of miasma — that contagion was airborne — served only to impede any hopes of improvement.[120] Further hazards to the rowers must soon have been offered by the expanding fleet of small paddle steamers, from the 1830s carrying regular ferry services upriver past Westminster and back.[121]

After the Fire: The New Palace of Westminster and the Stairs Re-Imagined, 1834–58

By 1834 the Palace of Westminster, its entrances on the west side grandly remodelled by James Wyatt and John Soane, was already turning its back on the river;[122] and the fire in October that year which destroyed many of its finest surviving buildings would in its turn sweep away the last remnants of its colourful riverside life. Numerous depictions of the conflagration provide us with a final stark view of the jumbled and picturesque outline of the buildings, as they entered a wholly new chapter.[123]

In the aftermath, most of the still surviving parts of the old Palace of Westminster — save Westminster Hall, St Stephen's cloisters and the chapel of St Mary Undercroft — were swept away as Charles Barry's new Palace began to rise on the banks of the Thames. Work on the cofferdam, needed to reclaim land from the river, started in 1837,[124] to the dismay of the watermen who had had plied their trade from the Westminster Bridge Stairs and the wooden bridge (known by this time as New Palace Yard Stairs). In 1838 they petitioned the Office of Woods and Works for recompense, and although the City of London supported their claim for a temporary landing stage, nothing came of this.[125] By now the river was teeming with steamers, the new form of transport for goods and people. Their fares from Westminster to London Bridge were 4d., compared with 3d. for a wherry, but the public increasingly favoured the faster steamers.[126] Eventually in 1841 this burgeoning, if challenging, market would draw the watermen themselves into ownership of new steamships.[127]

The riverfront range of the new Palace was the first section to be built. Plans for it clearly mark the locations of both the old Parliament Stairs (Queen's Bridge) and the Westminster Stairs (King's Bridge).[128] At the north end of Barry's new Palace, the garden of the Speaker's House was to occupy the footprint of the former King's Bridge, with the base of the Clock Tower not far from where the watergate had once been. Towards the southern end of the site, Barry's Royal Court and the adjoining areas of the House of Lords would be constructed over the former site of the Queen's Bridge and Parliament Place (Fig. 14). Adjacent to these, land where the medieval privy palace had stood was purchased and cleared of its wharves. Here would stand Barry's Victoria Tower and southern façade of the new Palace, along with what became Black Rod's Garden to their south.[129]

First, in 1837, came work on the cofferdam, to push the footprint of the site further out into the river so that work could begin on the river wall and the foundations for the great eastern front of the new Palace.[130] The first contract for the work specified that 'the watermen's stairs are to be entirely taken down',[131] and the second that good quality stone from all existing structures should be used for infilling prior to laying the foundations of the new building.[132] By 1839 the cofferdam was complete and operational, and the distinctive and haphazard riverfront of the old Palace had largely disappeared.

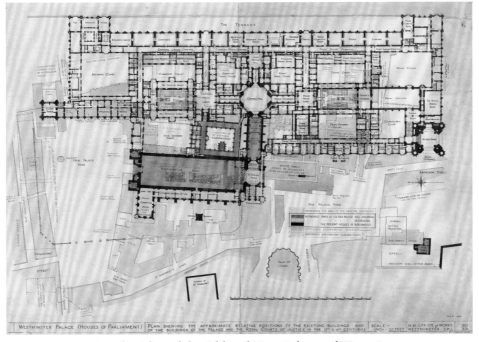

Fig. 14. *Overlay Plan of the Old and New Palaces of Westminster*, 1932.
The Westminster Stairs are on the left, beneath Speaker's Green, and the Parliament Stairs under Royal Court on the right. © Historic England Archive, Swindon, *PSA01/08/00003*.

During the excavations three stone piers from the former King's Bridge at the north end of the site were discovered and were recorded by Barry's assistant, the young William Hayward Brakspear, prior to their destruction. His drawings (Figs 15–16)[133] suggest that these were the piers of the bridge as it had existed up to 1742, but that they had been cut right down to 6 ft 3 in. below high-water level and used to support stout wooden struts and planking: the wooden bridge. Given the number of times that the original King's Bridge (Westminster Stairs) had been repaired, any dating of the stonework as depicted is not feasible. Yet the piers with their cutwaters designed to withstand storms and tides hint at a continuity of design with the medieval stone and timber landing stages of the tidal Thames.[134]

At the south end of the site, Black Rod's quirky gothic residence had after the fire been pressed into service as a temporary accommodation, but in 1839 Barry insisted that it must be cleared so that the site could be levelled. Along with the Parliament Stairs and Parliament Place it disappeared without trace to enable the construction of the river wall, terrace and footings for the riverfront range of the massive new building.[135] One influential user of the old Parliament Stairs was not, however, to be deterred by the vast changes taking place. In 1836 the Headmaster of Westminster School petitioned Home Secretary and School alumnus Lord John Russell, requesting that a safe access for his boys to their boats should still be provided, in the form of

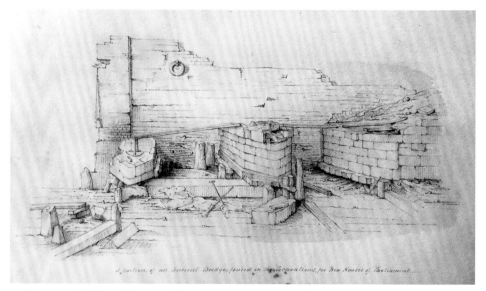

Fig. 15. William Hayward Brakspear, *A portion of an Ancient Bridge, found in the Excavations, for New Houses of Parliament*, 1839, pen and ink over graphite. The drawing records Brakspear's identification of three cut-down piers of the King's Bridge/Westminster Stairs. © RIBA Drawings Collection, *Brakspear PB852/3(1)*.

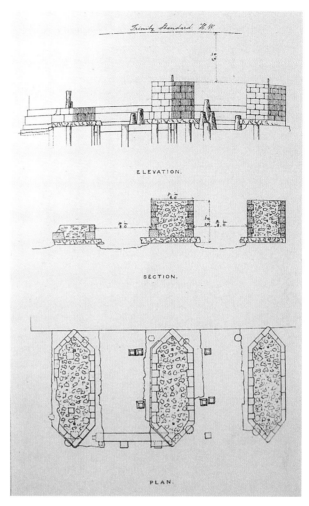

Fig. 16. William Hayward
Brakspear, *Elevation,
Section and Plan from
the former King's Bridge*,
published by George John
Vulliamy, 'Proceedings of the
Archaeological Institute',
Archaeological Journal, 6
(1849), p. 71. A record of the
bridge footings.

a floating quay attached to the coal barges from which they were currently
boarding their craft. Barry expressed strong reservations about the safety
of such an arrangement and fended them off.[136] But this was not for long:
in 1840 fixed steps were provided for them instead, near the site of the
planned southern river entrance to the Palace.[137]

   Nor were the Lord Mayors of London deterred by the condition of
the Thames, the cofferdam and the hazards of the vast building site from
continuing to land their annual water processions at the Westminster
Bridge Stairs, a custom which continued right up to 1856 when the Thames
Conservancy took over the management of the river from the City and the
procession moved to an overland route. This change was long overdue: the

Lord Mayor's barge had often in latter years been towed, incongruously, by a steam tug.[138] The incongruity of the gilded barges set against the backdrop of the industrial landscape of the building site at Westminster during these final years is vividly captured in a watercolour of about 1841 by Richard Henry Nibbs (Fig. 17).[139]

The terraces, embankments, river stairs and new landing places for Barry's Houses of Parliament were not completed until the last phase of the massive building project. At the north end of the site, Westminster Bridge, now almost a century old, was increasingly unstable, and was costly and complex to maintain.[140] Yet the tender for its much-needed successor was not finally let until 1854, and took until 1862 to complete.[141] Whilst this work was in progress, in 1855 Barry produced a plan for landing stairs at both ends of the Palace, and an estimate of costs for those at the northern end, adjoining the new Westminster Bridge, of £7,000. Including a public landing place and decorative stone features supporting lighting, this northern landing stage was agreed in 1856, and constructed by lead contractor John Jay to dovetail with the new bridge.[142] The elegant design of its steps (Fig. 18) was recorded in a photograph of 1897 by Sir Benjamin Stone MP, and has been largely preserved in subsequent repairs.

Fig. 17. Richard Henry Nibbs, *Arrival of the Lord Mayor at Westminster*, c. 1841, watercolour. The Lord Mayor's barge is shown about to land at Westminster; the smoking chimney on the left debouches from the heating system for the temporary House of Commons. © London Metropolitan Archives, City of London, Guildhall Art Gallery *no. 1239.*

Meanwhile at the southern end of the Palace, the wharves where the Victoria Tower Gardens now stand were still in use to bring in many of the building materials needed for the new Palace.[143] Consequently, the grander and more elaborate southern waterfront access was not put into design until July 1858. This was to feature a carriage drive along the side of the Victoria Tower leading to a stone staircase, initially to be known as 'The Queen's Landing Place'. It was to be for the use of 'Her Majesty and suite, Great Officers of State, Peers of the Realm, the Westminster scholars ... and others who may be specially privileged' and was to be protected from the river by iron gates under the control of the police, for whom a small lodge would be built. John Jay estimated the budget at £12,500.[144]

This phase of the plan coincided with the 'Great Stink' when a particularly hot, dry summer in 1858 reduced the Thames, already notorious for filth and pollution, to a noxious sewer. Relief, in the shape of Sir Joseph Bazalgette's magnificent system of intercepting sewers, would come in 1865, returning

Fig. 18. Benjamin Stone, *Westminster Bridge and Parliamentary Landing Steps*, July 1897, photograph. View of the House of Commons' Landing Stairs near Speaker's Green. © Parliamentary Archives *HC/LB/1/111/9/9*.

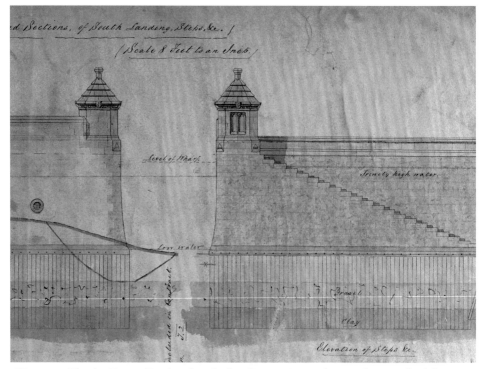

Fig. 19.   Charles Barry, *Design for the landing stairs at the southern end of the new Palace*, 1858, pen and ink and watercolour, detail. © TNA *WORK 29/1997*, south terrace, plan, September 1858.

the river to a better condition.[145] Barry's staircase down to the water, with its distinctive lodge (Fig. 19), was designed and then built according to plan at the height of the dramas, and by September 1858, just prior to its construction, was being described in a far less grandiose way: merely as a 'private landing place'. It was subsequently to be known as Black Rod's Stairs.[146]

Parliament's Stairs and Bridges Forgotten, 1858–2021

Over the next century, the final vestiges of the access routes from the Palace to the river gradually fell away. Heavy flooding in the 1870s, culminating in a record inundation in 1881 that was 5 ft above the Trinity high water mark, resulted in both sets of stairs being raised with additional granite steps.[147] Another record high tide followed in 1928, adding a further foot to the 1881 levels, overflowing the landing place at Speaker's Green and inundating the basements of the Palace, including the vital sewage ejector chamber. Sandbags were provided as a temporary measure and then the terrace walls were raised by one foot.[148] Although less harm was done at the southern end of the estate, a temporary brick wall was built here at Black Rod's Stairs, cutting off access to and from the river.[149] In 1933 the way to the stairs was reinstated, and Westminster School's right of access was reconfirmed.[150] In addition, the Speaker's steps were raised and reconfigured, so that they might still give satisfaction to 'the occasional member of Parliament who desires to reach the Palace of Westminster by water (there is apparently at least one such)'.[151] It is not, however, clear how often this right has been exercised in practice — and a recent attempt to revive it was not successful.[152]

The rebuilding of the Houses of Parliament after the Second World War brought the basement level of the Palace into far greater use. The new heating and electrical systems located here, as well as the area under the House of Commons occupied by members, were by the early 1950s again deemed to be at considerable risk from flooding. At the same time, high-tide levels had once again increased: a surge in 1953, which disastrously breached the flood defences down the east coast of England, caused particular concern. The river terrace walls of the Houses of Parliament only just held back the water, and flood prevention measures were rapidly put in place here, including the provision of many sandbags, pending a more strategic solution.[153] That was first envisaged in 1954 by the Waverley Committee in the form of a Thames Barrier,[154] but it took almost three decades to complete, finally becoming operational in 1982.

Meanwhile there was a major strengthening of London's flood defences in 1972, when the parapet walls of Parliament's terrace were raised and reinforced by 18 in. to a height of 6 ft — as was also the wall at Black Rod's Garden. The level of the terrace itself was heightened by the addition of a concrete deck 2 ft 9 in. high. That major work was completed just in time for a further tidal surge in 1978, although this did not in the event affect London and Westminster as much as anticipated.[155] But the threat from flooding was seen as very real. Detailed contingency plans were made to relocate both Houses in the event of floods, and even after the advent of the Thames Barrier in 1982, Parliament continued to view the river as a major hazard.[156]

Today, a highlight of any visit to the Palace of Westminster is the great panorama of the Thames as viewed from its river terraces. Barry's elegant river stairs at each end of the Palace, repaired and raised against the ever-higher tides, are still there, along with the decorative lampstands at Speaker's Green and the little police lodge in Black Rod's Garden. But they are blocked off and are barely visible: and apart from during special events such as the Parliamentary Boat Race,[157] access to and from the river itself is normally barred — for very understandable reasons of security. Their predecessors, the King's Bridge and the Queen's Bridge, have fared worse still. They have, undeservedly, been almost entirely forgotten by Parliament and the public. So, too, has the vital part that they played for over seven centuries in linking the Palace of Westminster with the River Thames, but this story can now start to be more fully known and understood.

Acknowledgements

The author would like to thank Professor Tim Ayers, Dr Elizabeth Biggs, Dr Mark Collins, Dorian Gerhold, Dr David Harrison, Professor Susan Irvine and Tim Tatton-Brown for their helpful advice on many aspects of this paper.

1. Peter Marsden, *Ships of the Port of London*, English Heritage Archaeological Report, 5 (London, 1996), p. 222.
2. Claire A. Martin, 'London: The Hub of an English River Transport Network, 1250–1550', in *Roadworks: Medieval Britain, Medieval Roads*, ed. by Valerie Allen and Ruth Evans (Manchester, 2016), pp. 249–76.
3. Julia F. Merritt, *The Social World of Early Modern Westminster, Abbey, Court and Community, 1525–1640* (Manchester, 2005), pp. 169–70.
4. E.g., John Stow, *A Survey of London Reprinted from the Text of 1603*, ed. by Charles L. Kingsford (Oxford, 1908), p. 122.
5. David Harrison, *The Bridges of Medieval England, Transport and Society 400–1800* (Oxford, 2004), pp. 25–26; Kenneth Cameron, *English Place-Names*, 2nd edn (London, 1963), p. 170.
6. *Pons*, Perseus Classical Collection, http://logeion.uchicago.edu/pons [accessed on 19 August 2019].
7. *Bridge*, Oxford English Dictionary, https://www.oed.com/ [accessed on 19 August 2019]; see also R. J. B. Walker, *Old Westminster Bridge, the Bridge of Fools* (Newton Abbot, 1979), pp. 31–32.
8. *Plan of London (circa 1560 to 1570)*, *Agas Map of London 1561* ([s.l.], 1633), British History Online, http://www.british-history.ac.uk/no-series/london-map-agas/1561/map [accessed on 30 January 2019]; Historic England Archive, Palace of Westminster Collection, *Overlay Plan of the Old and New Palaces of Westminster*, commissioned by G. H. Checkley, 1932.
9. Walker, *Old Westminster Bridge*, pp. 31–32; Joan Tucker, *Ferries of the Lower Thames* (Stroud, 2010), pp. 88–91.
10. John Crook, 'An Introduction to the Topography of the Medieval Palace of Westminster', in *Westminster II. The Art, Architecture and Archaeology of the Royal Palace*, ed. by Warwick Rodwell and Tim Tatton-Brown, British Archaeological Association Conference Transactions, 39 (2015), II, pp. 1–21 and map on p. x.
11. John Thomas Smith, *Foundation Plan of the Ancient Palace of Westminster*, in *idem*, *Antiquities of Westminster: The Old Palace; St Stephen's Chapel* (London, 1807–09), facing p. 125 notes that in 1803 piles were found adjoining the river side of the east cloister, intended 'to keep off the craft'. *The History of the King's Works*, ed. by Howard M. Colvin, Joseph Mordaunt Crook and Michael H. Port, 6 vols (London, 1963–82) [hereafter *KW*], I, p. 493; Gustav Milne, 'The Changing River Thames: Some Thoughts from an Archaeological Perspective', *The London Journal*, 40 (2015), pp. 211–27, esp. p. 213; Stuart Gilbert and Ray Homer, *The Thames Barrier* (London, 1984), pp. 2–3; *The Great Roll of the Pipe for the First Year of the Reign of King Richard the First, A.D. 1189–90*, ed. by Joseph Hunter

(London, 1844), p. 223.

12. Christopher Thomas, Robert Cowie and Jane Sidell, *The Royal Palace, Abbey and Town of Westminster on Thorney Island*, MOLAS Monograph no. 22 (London, 2006), pp. 61–63, 68–69.

13. Marsden, *Ships of the Port of London*, pp. 156–57.

14. Marsden, *Ships of the Port of London*, pp. 23, 30–37.

15. Gervase Rosser, *Medieval Westminster, 1200–1540* (Oxford, 1989), pp. 141–42; Markman Ellis, 'River and Labour in Samuel Scott's Thames Views in the Mid-Eighteenth Century', *The London Journal*, 37 (2012), pp. 152–73, esp. p. 153.

16. E.g. Joseph Burtt, 'Some Discoveries in Connection with the Ancient Treasury at Westminster', in George Gilbert Scott, *Gleanings from Westminster Abbey* (Oxford and London, 1863), pp. 282–90, at pp. 285–86.

17. Martin, 'London: The Hub', pp. 266–67.

18. *KW*, I, pp. 493, 508, 548.

19. For example, during the 1330s: *The Fabric Accounts of St Stephen's Chapel, Westminster, 1292–1396*, ed. by Tim Ayers, 2 vols (Woodbridge, 2020), I, pp. 775, 973; Thomas *et al.*, *The Royal Palace*, p. 106.

20. *Calendar of Patent Rolls, Edward III, vol. 8, 1348–50*, ed. by Henry C. Maxwell Lyte (London, 1905), p. 270.

21. *Calendar of Charter Rolls, vol 5, 1341–1417*, ed. by Henry C. Maxwell Lyte (London, 1916), pp. 133–39, esp. pp. 133–34. See also *Calendar of Close Rolls, Edward III, vol 13, 1369–74*, ed. by Henry C. Maxwell Lyte (London, 1911), p. 398, grant to the college of a room in the King's Bridge gateway, 1372.

22. Martin, 'London: The Hub', pp. 263–64.

23. Thomas *et al.*, *Royal Palace*, p. 97; Crook, 'Topography of the Medieval Palace', p. 17; *KW*, I, p. 552. The former location is shown in *A Groundplott of part of the city of Westminster*, in Francis Sandford, *The History of the Coronation of the most High, most Mighty and most excellent Monarch James II* (London, 1687), following p. 64.

24. Elizabeth Biggs, *St Stephen's College Westminster, A Royal Chapel and English Kingship, 1348–1548* (Woodbridge, 2020), pp. 53, 131.

25. *The Medieval Palace of Westminster, KW, Plans*, no. III.

26. *KW*, I, pp. 501–02, 534–35; *KW*, II, pp. 1041–44.

27. *Calendar of Close Rolls, Edward III, vol. 13*, p. 287; *KW*, I, p. 535n.

28. *Fabric Accounts*, II, pp. 1391–92.

29. Martin, 'London: The Hub', p. 264; *KW*, I, p. 508.

30. The connection between these two drawings and the identification of the view was made by Ann Saunders, 'Westminster Hall: A Sixteenth Century Drawing?' *London Journal*, 12.1 (1986), pp. 29–35.

31. *The Lord Mayor's Show, 800 Years, 1215–2015*, ed. by Dominic Reid (London, 2015), pp. 64–65; Tucker, *Ferries of the Lower Thames*, p. 70.

32. *Johannis Lelandi Antiquarii de Rebus Britannicus Collectanea*, ed. by Thomas Hearne, IV (London, 1774), p. 202.

33. 'The Voyage etc of the Princess Catherine of Aragon to England …', in *The Antiquarian Repertory*, ed. by Francis Grose, II (London, 1808), pp. 248–330, esp. pp. 312–13; *KW*, IV, p. 287.

34. David Starkey, 'London, Flower of Cities All: Royal Ritual and the River', in *Royal River: Power, Pageantry and the Thames*, ed. by Susan Doran (London, 2012), pp. 10–17; Simon Thurley, *Houses of Power, the Places that Shaped the Tudor World* (London, 2017), pp. 340–41.

35. *KW*, IV, pp. 287–88; Mark Collins, 'The Topography of the old Palace of Westminster, 1510–1834', in *Westminster II*, pp. 206–56, esp. pp. 216–17.

36. *Plan of London (circa 1560 to 1570)*, produced in *c.* 1633, depicting the City of London in the 1560s, in *Agas Map of London 1561* ([s.l.], 1633), British History Online, http://www.british-history.ac.uk/no-series/london-map-agas/1561/map [accessed on 30 January 2019].
37. *KW*, IV, pp. 286–87, 299–300.
38. TNA, C 66/834, m. 22, enrolled letters patent; Elizabeth Biggs, *St Stephen's College Westminster, A Royal Chapel and English Kingship* (Woodbridge, 2020), pp. 206–08.
39. TNA, LR 1/46, fols 35–35d, enrolled lease, 1566; Nora M. Fuidge, *Sexton Edmund (d. c. 1589), of Westminster and Uxbridge, Mdx*, www.historyofparliamentonline.org/volume/1558-1603/member/sexton-edmund-1589 [accessed on 21 June 2020].
40. For a full tenurial history and plans, see Dorian Gerhold, *Victoria Tower Gardens. The Prehistory, Creation and Planned Destruction of a London Park* (Putney, 2020), pp. 11–17.
41. James O. Halliwell, *The Autobiography and Correspondence of Sir Simonds d'Ewes, Bart.*, I (London, 1845), p. 292.
42. Merritt, *Social World*, p. 191.
43. TNA, LR 1/44, fols 261–62; C 66/1313, mm. 32–33.
44. British Library [BL], Cotton Charters I 11; TNA, C 66/1313, mm. 32–33; T 1/118, no. 102, pp. 386–87, report by Sir Christopher Wren, 1706. For access to the drains, see e.g. TNA, C 66/1529, mm. 30–39, 1600; LR 1/53 fols 43–44, 1610.
45. *KW*, IV, p. 288.
46. *The Panorama of London circa 1544*, ed. by Howard M. Colvin and Susan Foister, London Topographical Society publication No. 151 (London, 1996), pp. 5–7, 17; Crook, 'Topography of the Medieval Palace', p. 15.
47. TNA, E 351/3203; E 351/3204, works accounts; *KW*, III, pp. 77–78 and *KW*, IV, p. 295. For construction techniques, see Harrison, *Bridges of Medieval England*, pp. 106–08.
48. Thurley, *Houses of Power*, pp. 340–43; Henry Humpherus, *History of the Origin and Progress of the Company of Watermen and Lightermen*, 3 vols (London, 1887), I, p. 87.
49. TNA, E 323/4, m. 95; E 351/3326; *KW*, IV, p. 292; *Acts of the Privy Council, vol 2, 1547–50*, ed. by J. R. Dasent (London, 1890), p. 222; Roy Strong, *Coronation: A History of Kingship and the British Monarchy* (London, 2005), pp. 195, 213, 246, 261, 289, 327; William John Passingham, *A History of the Coronation* (London, 1937), pp. 191, 219.
50. Harry Cobb, 'Descriptions of the State Opening of Parliament, 1485–1601: A Survey', *Parliamentary History*, 18 (1999), pp. 303–15, esp. p. 308; Humpherus, *History of the Watermen*, I, p. 233; TNA, SP 16/471, fol. 21; *Calendar of State Papers Domestic, Charles I, 1640–41*, ed. by William Douglas Hamilton (London, 1882), p. 640; Jason Peacey, 'The Street Theatre of State: The Ceremonial Opening of Parliament, 1603–1660', in *Managing Tudor and Stuart Parliaments: Essays in Memory of Michael Graves*, ed. by Chris R. Kyle (Chichester, 2015), pp. 155–72, esp. pp. 162, 170–71.
51. Merritt, *Social World*, p. 169; Bernard Capp, *The World of John Taylor the Water Poet* (Oxford, 1994), esp. pp 1–4, 8–10, 55–57; Art News, 'William Dobson: A Portrait Revealed', *Cassone: The International Online Magazine of Art and Art Books*, September 2011, http://www.cassone-art.com/art-news/2011/09/william-dobson-a-portrait-revealed/ [accessed on 16 July 2020]. I am grateful to John Chandler for this reference.
52. *The Journals of Two Travellers in Elizabethan and Early Stuart England: Thomas Platter and Horatio Busino*, ed. by Thomas Platter (London, 1995), pp. 10–12, 134–35.
53. Stow, *A Survey of London*, p. 122.
54. Tucker, *Ferries of the Lower Thames*, p. 97.
55. Martin, 'London: The Hub', pp. 253–56, 267–68.
56. E.g. TNA, E 351/3211, 3217, 3219, 3221–22, 3240–41.
57. *KW*, I, pp. 545–46; *KW*, IV, pp. 297–98.
58. TNA, E 351/3244–45, 3250, 3252, 3254, 3263, 3265, 3267, 3269, AO 1/2431/79; *KW*, IV, p. 300.

59. Wenceslaus Hollar, *Civitatis Westmonasteriensis pars*, 1647; *The New Hollstein: German Engravings, Etchings and Woodcuts, 1400–1700* (Amsterdam, 1996 onwards), cat. no. 950.

60. Simon Thurley, 'The Vanishing Architecture of the River Thames', in *Royal River*, pp. 20–25.

61. These are idealized in a further Hollar image: BM Prints and Drawings, 1935,0608.3, Wenceslaus Hollar, *London, Westminster Abbey*, drawing, 1637–43.

62. Oxford, Bodleian Library, MS Rawlinson D. 775, fol. 169.

63. TNA, E 351/3225. For Elizabeth's use of coaches, see Thurley, *Houses of Power*, pp. 343–47.

64. E.g. TNA, E 351/3215 (1580–81); E 351/3237 (1601–02); E 351/3267 (1622–23).

65. TNA, LR 1/54, fols 94d–95.

66. BL, Cotton Charters I. 6; see also Colin Tite, 'The Cotton Library in the Seventeenth Century and its Manuscript Records of the English Parliament', *Parliamentary History*, 14.2 (1995), pp. 121–38, esp. pp. 122–26.

67. *Autobiography of Sir Simonds d'Ewes*, I, pp. 291–92; BL, Harl. MS 383, fols 24–25; Kevin Sharpe, *Sir Robert Cotton, 1586–1631: History and Politics in Early Modern England* (Oxford, 1979), p. 140.

68. E.g. TNA, AO 1/2429/71 (1639).

69. Parliamentary Archives, HL/PO/JO/10/1/190, petition, 25 July 1645.

70. Hulton, *A Pocket Map of the Cities of London & Westminster* (Fig. 1); Tucker, *Ferries of the Lower Thames*, p. 94.

71. Walker, *Old Westminster Bridge*, p. 32; William H. Manchée, *The Westminster City Fathers (The Burgess Court of Westminster)* (London, 1924), pp. 78–82.

72. Humpherus, *History of the Watermen*, II, pp. 81–82.

73. *A Foreign View of England in 1725–29: The Letters of Monsieur César de Saussure to his Family*, ed. by Madame van Muyden (London, 1995), pp. 58–59.

74. E.g. Royal Collection Trust, RCIN 402608, British School, *The Lord Mayor's Water-Procession on the Thames*, c. 1683, oil on canvas.

75. TNA, WORK 5/13; WORK 5/14; WORK 5/21, works accounts.

76. TNA, WORK 5/37, fol. 149; WORK 5/44.

77. TNA, WORK 6/16, fols 2–3, 20, 28–29; *Calendar of Treasury Books and Papers, vol. 2, 1731–34*, ed. by William A. Shaw (London, 1898), pp. 372, 375; Walker, *Ferries*, p. 32. For Hercules Taylor, tenant up to his death in 1740, see Westminster City Archives, City Rate Books, Highway Rates 1730–33, fol. 11d.

78. E.g. TNA, C 6/44/98, 1658; C 6/506/51 and C 8/437/36, 1692, Chancery pleadings; WORK 8/51, no 2 (1710), deed.

79. E.g. *May 1725, trial of John Alloway* (t17250513-53); *February 1747, trial of Henry Lovat* (t17470225-4), Old Bailey Proceedings Online, www.oldbaileyonline.org, version 8.0 [accessed on 27 April 2019].

80. *July 1736, trial of John Maxworth, otherwise Paddy, otherwise Parliament Jack* (t17360721-13), Old Bailey Proceedings Online, www.oldbaileyonline.org, version 8.0 [accessed on 27 April 2019].

81. TNA, E 351/3286, 3305, 3319; WORK 5/43, 45; AO 1/2452/161.

82. Smith, *Antiquities of Westminster*, p. 251; *KW*, v, p. 399.

83. *Calendar of State Papers Domestic Charles I, 1625–49, Addenda*, ed. by William D. Hamilton and Sophie C. Lomas (London, 1897), p. 305, 19 December 1628; TNA, WORK 6/2, fol. 31.

84. TNA, WORK 5/1–4, 46–48; E 351/3275, 3280.

85. TNA, WORK 5/53, fol. 177; *KW*, v, pp. 127, 237, 239.

86. TNA, WORK 5/30, fol. 171; WORK 6/2, fol. 140; 'shore' in this context is clearly used in the sense of 'sewer'.

87. TNA, E 351/3320; AO 1/224/150; Westminster City Archives, Will no. 2037, April 1729, fol. 48; SMW/1944, fol. 122, Westminster Scavengers Rate Book, 1728; SMW/E/1/109–110, burial record, 1728–29.

88. Carry van Lieshout, 'Floods and Flood Response in Eighteenth-Century London', in *Tides and Floods: New Research on London and the Tidal Thames from the Middle Ages to the Twentieth Century*, ed. by James A. Galloway (London, 2010), pp. 29–43; Milne, 'The Changing River Thames', pp. 213–14; Gilbert and Homer, *The Thames Barrier*, p. 4.

89. Walker, *Old Westminster Bridge*, esp. pp. 32–33; Ellis, 'River and Labour in Samuel Scott's Thames Views', pp. 165–70; BL, Maps Crace XIX, no. 18, John Rocque, *An Exact Survey of London, Westminster, Southwark and the Country near Ten Miles Round*, 1746, engraving; BL, Maps Crace XI, no. 39C, John Major, *Ground Plan of Part of the City of Westminster as it appeared at the Coronation of King George III*, 1761, engraving.

90. *Ipswich Journal*, 18 September 1742, p. 3.

91. *Lord Mayor's Show*, pp. 64–65.

92. Sarah Murden, 'The First Thames Regatta, 23rd June 1775', *All Things Georgian*, https://georgianera.wordpress.com/2018/06/23/the-first-thames-regatta-23rd-june-1775/ [accessed on 19 August 2019]. The earliest professional rowing race on the Thames was Doggett's Coat and Badge, running since 1715: Tucker, *Ferries of the Lower Thames*, pp. 67–69.

93. Parliamentary Archives HC/LB/1/119 (Britten portfolio), fol. 18, C. Fourdrinier, *A Plan of Part of the Ancient City of Westminster*, c. 1770; Walker, *Old Westminster Bridge*, pp. 88, 91, 168–69; Collins, 'Topography of the Old Palace', p. 229; Horace Barty-King, *Her Majesty's Stationery Office: The Story of the First 200 Years, 1786–1986* (London, 1986), pp. 4–10.

94. TNA, STAT 7/1, pp. 1–25, lease.

95. Westminster City Archives E 137 (001), 'J. Shelton' [*recte* Jonathan Skelton], *Westminster Stairs*, watercolour, 1755.

96. 'Report from the Committee Appointed to Inspect the Several Houses and Buildings Adjoining Westminster Hall, 22 July 1789', *House of Commons Papers*, 1790 (66), esp. pp. 6–7.

97. E.g. Parliamentary Art Collection, WoA 2983, W. M. Fellows after John Thomas Smith, *Buildings on the eastern side of New Palace Yard*, engraving, 1808; Parliamentary Art Collection, WoA 2025, William Capon, *New Palace Yard about 1805–08, Water Gate Entrance*, watercolour, c. 1808.

98. *KW*, VI, pp. 515–16.

99. TNA, CRES 2/907, Westminster improvements; Westminster City Archives E133 (107), William Capon et al., *Plan of the ancient palace of Westminster by the late Mr William Capon measured and drawn between 1793 and 1823*, watercolour, 1793–1823 with annotations up to 1851; Barty-King, *Her Majesty's Stationery Office*, p. 15.

100. TNA, WORK 29/3288, Charles James Richardson, *Plan of the Parliamentary and other Public Buildings adjacent to Westminster Hall*, 1835.

101. [Samuel Leigh], *Panorama of the Thames: A Riverside View of Georgian London, [1829]*, ed. by John R. Inglis and Jill Sanders (London, 2015), pp. 114–15.

102. TNA, WORK 6/16, p. 135, Works memorial.

103. William H. Brock, 'Delaval, Edward Hussey, 1729–1814', *Oxford New Dictionary of National Biography*, www.oxforddnb.com/view/article [accessed on 19 August 2019]; Charles Taylor, 'Biographical Memoranda Respecting Edward Hussey Delaval Esq.', *The Philosophical Magazine and Journal*, 45 (1815), pp. 29–32.

104. *Stamford Mercury*, 28 January 1768, p. 2; TNA, CRES 2/558, Cotton Garden, leases; Westminster City Archives, Westminster Rate Books Watch Ledger 1770–72, fol. 71; Westminster City Archives, indenture 0374, *re* Delaval's mortgage, 1769–81.

105. Parliamentary Archives HC/LB/1/119 (Britten portfolio), fol. 49, Philip Wyatt, *View of the buildings adjoining Westminster Hall*, engraving, 1827.

106. Frances Lehman Loeb Art Center, Vassar College, Poughkeepsie, 1864.2.2787, John Carter, *Plan of the remains of the old Palace of Westminster*, 1788, drawing.

107. TNA, CRES 2/558; Martin Green, *The Delavals: A Family History*, 3rd edn (Newcastle-upon-Tyne, 2014), pp. 117–18.

108. TNA, CRES 2/558.

109. *Reading Mercury and Oxford Gazette*, 18 October 1784, p. 1.

110. *Stamford Mercury*, 19 August 1814, p. 3.

111. TNA, WORK 1/23, letterbook, p. 60.

112. John Thomas Smith, *A Book for a Rainy Day* (London, 1845), p. 162.

113. Westminster City Archives, Gardner Box 56 no. 6, [John Soane], *Houses of Parliament: plan of the Parliament Buildings adjoining Westminster Hall* [n.d.]; Michael H. Port, *The Palace of Westminster Surveyed on the Eve of the Conflagration, 1834*, London Topographical Society publication No. 171 (London, 2011), no. 1, General Ground Plan.

114. *Salisbury and Winchester Journal*, 21 August 1820, p. 1.

115. Parliamentary Archives, LGC/5/2/121, letter from Lord Sidmouth to the Deputy Great Chamberlain re persons travelling to and from Westminster Hall, 17 July 1821.

116. Smith, *A Book for a Rainy Day*, p. 162; Samuel John Wilde, *Recollections of S. J. Wilde* (London, 1913), p. 9.

117. TNA, WORK 11/151, Right of boys of Westminster School to use steps to river for boating, 1815–38.

118. Parliamentary Archives LGC/5/1/215, Letter to Mr Bacon from the King's Scholars Westminster re the keeping clear the passage to Parliament stairs, *c.* 1820; for Bacon, see *KW*, VI, p. 114.

119. 'Report of the Commissioners appointed by His Majesty to inquire into the state of the supply of water in the metropolis', *House of Commons Papers*, 267 (1828), esp. pp. 9–10; Bill Luckin, *Pollution and Control, A Social History of the Thames in the Nineteenth Century* (Bristol and Boston, 1986), pp. 12–19.

120. Stephen Halliday, *The Great Stink, Sir Joseph Bazalgette and the Cleansing of the Victorian Metropolis* (Stroud, 1999), pp. 17–18; Rosemary Ashton, *One Hot Summer, Dickens, Darwin, Disraeli and the Great Stink of 1858* (New Haven and London, 2017), pp. 15–16; Joseph Hillier and Sarah Bell, 'The "Genius of Place": Mitigating Stench in the Palace of Westminster before the Great Stink', *The London Journal*, 35 (2010), pp. 22–38.

121. John Armstrong and David M. Williams, 'London's Steamships: Their Functions and their Owners in the Mid-Nineteenth Century', *The London Journal*, 42 (2017), pp. 238–56, esp. pp. 249–50.

122. E.g. TNA, WORK 29/20, Thomas Chawner and Henry Rhodes, *General Ground Plan of Westminster Hall [etc]*, 1834, published in Port, *The Palace of Westminster*, no. 1.

123. E.g. Museum of London Paintings Collection, no. 63, British School, *The Palace of Westminster from the River after the Fire of 1834*, oil on canvas, 1834; UK Parliament, *The Fire of 1834*, Art in Parliament, https://www.parliament.uk/worksofart/collection-highlights/buildings/the-fire-of-1834 [accessed on 18 July 2020].

124. Caroline Shenton, *Mr Barry's War: Rebuilding the Houses of Parliament after the Great Fire* (Oxford, 2016), pp. 71–74.

125. TNA, WORK 11/5/17, contracts for cofferdam; WORK 1/23, pp. 106, 165.

126. *The Times*, 18 October 1838, p. 6.

127. Dix, *Royal River Highway*, p. 77; Armstrong, 'London's Steamships', p. 249.

128. E.g. TNA, WORK 29/1857, riverfront plan drawing, undated; WORK 29/2356, embankment wall, plan, 1837.

129. Historic England Archives, Swindon, Palace of Westminster Collection, *Overlay Plan of the Old and New Palaces of Westminster*, commissioned probably by G. H. Checkley, 1932; Gerhold, *Victoria Tower Gardens*, pp. 22–24.

130. Shenton, *Mr Barry's War*, pp. 71–74.

131. 'Copy of Several Contracts with Builders or other Persons for the Construction of the Palace of Westminster', *House of Commons Papers*, 1847–48 (46-II), esp. p. 4.

132. 'Copy of Several Contracts with Builders', esp. pp. 4, 17; TNA, WORK 11/5/18, fol. 7, contract for foundations; *The Houses of Parliament*, ed. by Michael H. Port (New Haven and London, 1976), p. 197.

133. My thanks to Catherine Wilson at the RIBA Library and Information Centre's Study Room for her advice on it.

134. Harrison, *Bridges of Medieval England*, p. 206; Stuart E. Rigold, 'Structural Aspects of Medieval Timber Bridges', *Medieval Archaeology*, 19 (1975), pp. 48–91, esp. pp. 52–53.

135. TNA, WORK 1/23, pp. 380, 417; WORK 1/24, pp. 147–48; *The Houses of Parliament*, p. 197; Shenton, *Mr Barry's War*, p. 94.

136. TNA, WORK 11/151; WORK 1/23, p. 93, 26 March 1838 and index.

137. TNA, WORK 1/24, p. 196; WORK 11/344, Rights of boys of Westminster School to use steps to river for boating, 1934.

138. *Lord Mayor's Show*, pp. 64–65.

139. For a better-known and more attractive view, see Guildhall Art Gallery no. 1246, COLLAGE: London Picture Archive ref. 11315, David Roberts, *The Lord Mayor's Show at Westminster*, watercolour, 1830.

140. TNA, WORK 11/5/17; Walker, *Old Westminster Bridge*, pp. 270–73.

141. Walker, *Old Westminster Bridge*, pp. 271–78.

142. TNA, WORK 11/6/7, contract for completion of works, 1855–58; WORK 29/2361–62, plans of north terrace and river steps.

143. See the contemporary depiction in *The Houses of Parliament*, p. 215.

144. TNA, WORK 11/6/7.

145. Ashton, *One Hot Summer*, pp. 179–87, 226–28, 283–85; Halliday, *The Great Stink*, pp. 77–107.

146. TNA, WORK 29/1998, section, September 1858; Museum of London PLA Archives, folder 5 sheet 37, Jules Arnout, *The New Houses of Parliament and Westminster Hall c. 1860*, print.

147. TNA, WORK 11/171, River Wall parapets: Thames flood prevention, 1877–81; Gilbert and Homer, *The Thames Barrier*, p. 4.

148. TNA, WORK 11/305, River Wall parapets: Thames flood prevention, 1928–37; WORK 6/404, Flooding: 7 January 1928, 1928–38; Parliamentary Archives, OOW/39, Plan for proposed Thames flood protection works to the terrace, January 1931.

149. TNA, WORK 11/344.

150. TNA, WORK 11/305; WORK 11/344.

151. TNA, WORK 11/305; Parliamentary Archives, PWO/20/99, flood precautions, 1933–56.

152. By the late Jo Cox MP: see Kate Allen, 'Where Do Politicians Live?', *Financial Times*, 13 April 2016, https://www.ft.com/content/ [accessed on 19 August 2019].

153. TNA, WORK 11/538, Prevention of flooding, 1951–61; Gilbert and Homer, *The Thames Barrier*, p. 4.

154. *House of Commons Hansard*, 5th ser. vol. 258, 3 June 1954, cc 104–05; 'Report of the Departmental Committee on Coastal Flooding', *Command Papers 1953–54*, vol. 13, no. 9165, esp. pp. 23–25.

155. 'Eighth report from the Select Committee on House of Commons (Services). Raising of the level of the terrace, session 1970–71', *House of Commons Papers*, 1970–71 (576); TNA, CM 23/161, Thames Flooding: interim flood measures, 1967–71; Parliamentary Archives, PWO/2/14, Houses of Parliament: prevention of flooding including raising level of the terrace, 1968–71; Gilbert and Homer, *The Thames Barrier*, pp. 4, 24–25, 52–56, 79–80, 105, 122.

156. Parliamentary Archives, HC/CL/CO/EB/5/68, Flooding, draft action plan, 1978–82; TNA, STAT 14/5322, Thames tidal flood plan to ensure parliamentary printing supplies reach the Palace of Westminster, 1982–87.

157. E.g. Tim Koch, '(Legislative) Bodies Between Their Knees: The 2016 Parliamentary Boat Race', Hear the Boat Sing, 17 September 2016, https://heartheboatsing.com/2016/09/17/ [accessed on 19 August 2019].

II. FROM ASSELYNE'S WHARF TO WIGGINS' KEY, OR, WHATEVER HAPPENED TO BROWNE'S PLACE?

By VANESSA HARDING

R EADERS of the map of early Tudor London published in the British Historic Towns Atlas volume III, *The City of London from Prehistoric Times to c. 1520*, edited by Mary D. Lobel (Oxford University Press, 1989), or of the single-sheet map based on the Atlas published for the Historic Towns Trust by Old House Books in 2008, may well have noticed the representation of a substantial property on the waterfront east of Billingsgate, labelled Browne's Place. Readers of the revised map of early Tudor London published by the Historic Towns Trust in 2018 (with generous financial support from the London Topographical Society), and reissued with minor amendments in 2020, may have noticed that Browne's Place is absent, and wondered why.

The representation of Browne's Place in the Atlas was based on the reconstruction of the property in the fifteenth century by C. L. Kingsford and W. H. Godfrey, published in *Archaeologia* in 1923–24.[1] Kingsford traced the descent of the property from Asselyne's Wharf of the fourteenth century to Gibson's or Draper's Key of the late sixteenth, and drew on two texts of 1384 and 1463, one a draft rebuilding lease and the other a schedule of the widow's share in the property by way of dower, to reconstruct the layout of a substantial riverfront property, Browne's Place, with a sizeable hall and domestic buildings. Godfrey drew an elegant and persuasive plan, based on the documentation presented by Kingsford. However, Kingsford was slightly astray in his location of the property, and more so in his interpretation of the texts to reconstruct its overall size and shape: as is shown below, the buildings must have fitted into a much smaller plot than he believed, though they would still have formed an impressive complex.[2] The Historic Towns Trust's cartographer, Col. Henry Johns, followed Kingsford's expansive reconstruction for the 1989 Atlas, but corrected the location so that the property lies where it should, near the middle of the stretch of waterfront in the parish of St Dunstan in the East. The name 'Browne's Place' does not seem to be recorded after 1463, nor does 'Browne's Key' after 1478. The revised map of London *c.* 1520 therefore omits both the reconstruction and the names, replacing the latter with 'Gybson's Key', reflecting the then tenant.

The following discussion aims to establish the descent of Kingsford's 'Browne's Place' into the eighteenth century, and to draw together some of the evidence for how it was used at different times. It is quite a long story, but it illustrates change over time, from a city where domestic and commercial spaces, and land ownership and occupation, were integrated,

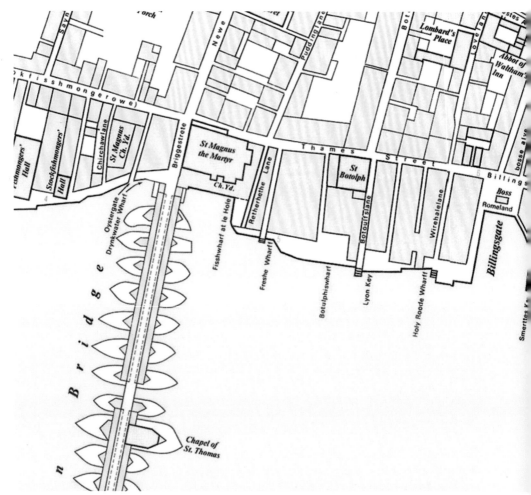

Fig. 1.   The waterfront showing Browne's Place, from the British Historic Towns
Atlas volume III, *The City of London from Prehistoric Times to* c. *1520*, edited by
Mary D. Lobel (Oxford University Press, 1989; http://www.historictownsatlas.org.uk/
atlas/volume-iii/city-london-prehistoric-times-c1520-volume-iii), Map 4. Cartography
by Henry Johns. Reproduced by permission of the Historic Towns Trust.

to one where functions were specialized and separated, and several layers
of ownership and interest separated the owners of property and capital
from everyday workers and residents. The complexity of the story and the
evidence means it is clearest to trace first the descent of the freehold, then of
the leasehold and uses from the sixteenth century. This enables the property
to be located with reference to the earliest reliable maps. The discussion then

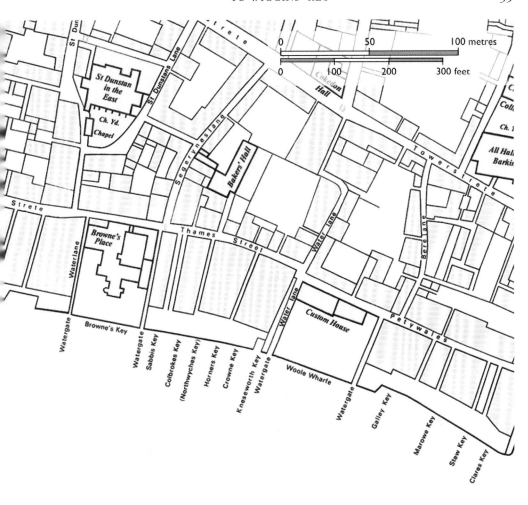

revisits the detailed information given in the medieval texts to reconsider how the buildings might have been laid out on the much smaller plot they actually occupied, and traces other evidence for how the plot was occupied and developed up to and after the Fire of 1666.

The Descent of 'Browne's Place'

The waterfront between Billingsgate and the Tower seems to have been developed later or more slowly than some areas further upstream, and Thames Street, along the line of the Roman riverside wall, may have marked the shoreline well into the twelfth if not the thirteenth century. Owners of properties on the north side of Thames Street seem to have

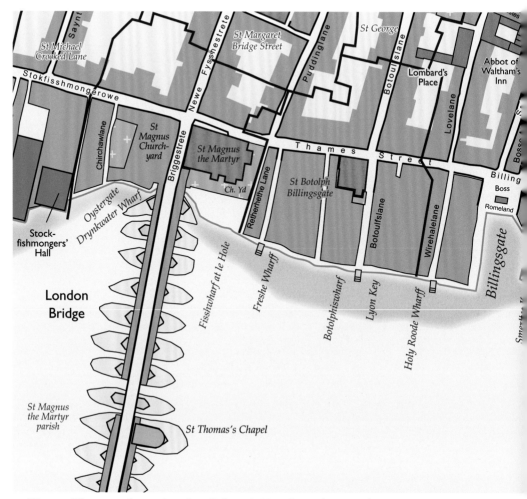

Fig. 2.   The waterfront showing Gybson's Key, from the British Historic Towns Trust, 'Map of the City of London *c.* 1520' (Historic Towns Trust Town and City Maps, 2018). Cartography by Giles Darkes. Reproduced by permission of the Historic Towns Trust.

taken possession of land to the south, pushing the waterfront further out as they did so, though eventually ownership of the properties on either side of Thames Street became separated.[3] By the fourteenth century the waterfront between Billingsgate and the Tower comprised a string of privately owned properties stretching from Thames Street to the river, most abutting east and west on other properties, some adjoining public lanes or watergates leading to the river.[4]

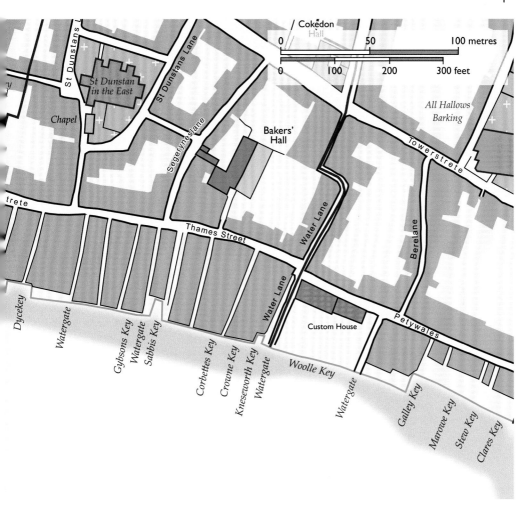

Kingsford traced the history of the property known as Asselyne's Wharf from the early fourteenth century, but it is possible to take the story a bit further back. The earliest known holder was Reginald le Sipwritche or Shipwright, some time before the later thirteenth century.[5] He might have been practising his trade here: there is evidence of boat- or ship-building further down the waterfront, in the parish of All Hallows Barking, but it had probably been displaced by the early fourteenth century, as the city's overseas trade expanded and the collection of the export custom on wool became a major undertaking.[6] The wool merchant William de Coumbe acquired this property, described as a messuage and wharf, in 1269/70. In the fourteenth century it passed successively though the hands of John de Coumbe; Richard Asshele of Berners Roding, Essex, and his wife Agnes;

John Asselyn; Ralph Kneveton of Aveley, Essex; and John Cherteseye of Hertford, gentleman.[7]

Cherteseye leased the wharf (as 'Pakemannys Wharf') to Richard Willysdon, chandler, in 1384, for a hundred years, and in 1396 left the rent and reversion to the priory of Holy Trinity Aldgate, otherwise known as Christchurch. The transfer was secured by one of several wills made by William Sevenoke proved in 1434. In the meantime Richard Willysdon's lease had passed to Stephen Browne, Grocer and alderman, who in 1444 obtained a new eighty-year lease from Holy Trinity. Browne died in 1462 or 1463, leaving 'Asshelyns warff', formerly 'Pakenams warff', to his son John, who appears to have died within the year. In December 1463 Stephen Browne's executors, including his former servant Thomas Bledlowe, made an agreement with John's widow Agnes, now married to Piers Pekham, specifying her dower rights in 'Browne's Place' and 'Brownes Key' by listing the rooms she was to enjoy. Bledlowe, like Browne, was a prosperous Grocer, serving both as master of his company and as alderman. In his own will of 1478 he left 'all the grete messuage wherein I nowe dwelle with all the celers Wharff or keye grete gate and Entre [...] called Browneskey' to his son Thomas, with provision for his own widow Anneys to occupy the house in exactly the same words as the agreement with Agnes Pekham. Anneys Bledlowe lived till at least 1502, though whether she occupied the property for the rest of her life is not known.[8]

The lease of 1444 seems to have been surrendered early. In 1505, Holy Trinity Priory granted a new lease for ninety-eight years of 'Ashelyngs warffe formerly Pakenams warffe and then Crychurche warffe' to Sir John Cutte, under-treasurer of the chamber. Cutte granted his interest in 'Bledlowes Key' to Roger Halle, Grocer, in 1516.[9] It was next acquired by another prosperous trader, Nicholas Gibson, master of the Grocers' Company, and sheriff in 1538–39.[10] He died in 1540, leaving his estates to his wife Avice. Another of his properties in this area, the Old Wool Quay, became a principal endowment to the Coopers' Company, to endow Gibson's school at Ratcliffe.[11] Avice Gibson acquired the freehold in 1541, and, following her marriage to Sir Anthony Knyvett, granted it to a group of feoffees, from whom it passed in 1555 to Christopher Draper, Ironmonger and later alderman, for £840, suggesting an annual value of between £40 and £70.[12]

Draper occupied the property himself, perhaps rebuilding or refurbishing it.[13] He and his family were closely associated with the parish, buried or commemorated in the church.[14] In 1571 Draper settled Asheling Wharf, alias Gibson's Key, on his three daughters, Bennett, Bridget and Agnes.[15] Following his death in 1581 his daughters each continued to hold an undivided one-third share or interest in Gibson's Key, by this time let to William Wiggins. All three made good first or second marriages to men high in civic circles. Bennett (d. 1604) married (Sir) William Webbe

(d. 1599), Salter, Lord Mayor 1591–92; Bridget (d. 1588) married first Stephen Woodroffe, Haberdasher (d. 1575x1577), and then (Sir) Henry Billingsley (d. 1606), Haberdasher, later Lord Mayor; Agnes (d. 1600) married first (Sir) Wolstan Dixie (d. 1594), Skinner, Lord Mayor 1585–86, and then William Hickman, esquire.[16] Bridget had a son, Christopher Woodroffe, born *c.* 1569, who inherited her share on her death in 1588 and sold it in 1589 to his uncle-in-law Sir William Webbe.[17] Webbe left this to his infant grandson, also William Webbe, in 1599.[18] Agnes Hickman, who had no children, died in 1600, leaving all the property that had come to her from her father, including her one-third share of 'a wharf commonly called Drapers Key or Gibson's Key in Thames Street [...] now or late in the tenure of William Wiggins', to her cousin Robert Draper 'the Apprentys'.[19] Bennett Webbe, the eldest sister, was the last to die, in 1604; she left all her lands and tenements to her grandson William Webbe, including the 'key or wharf called Drapers Key or Wharffe'.[20]

In 1614, William Webbe the younger, now Sir William Webbe of Thornton Bridge, Yorkshire, sold Gibson's Key, of which he now apparently possessed the whole, to Barnard Hide of Little Ilford, Essex, for £1,000.[21] Robert Draper contested this sale, but it appears that Hide remained in possession.[22] Webbe had also inherited Dyce Key and Haddock's Key, further west in the same parish but not adjoining Gibson's Key, from his grandfather, and sold them, too, to Barnard Hide in 1614, for £4,350.[23]

Kingsford traced the history of the property up to 1614 and its sale to Barnard Hide. Although he had noted Wiggins as tenant of Draper's Key in the 1590s, he failed to identify Gibson's/Draper's Key with the seventeenth-century Wiggins' Key, believing it instead to have become Porter's Key.[24] However, as Wiggins' Key it can be traced into the nineteenth century.

The freeholds of the three quays, Gibson's or Wiggins', Haddock's and Dyce Key, remained in the Hide or Hyde family through the seventeenth and eighteenth centuries. Barnard Hide the elder was a citizen and Salter, fining for alderman in 1614, and involved in the farm of the London customs. He lived in Mincing Lane, and left benefactions to the parish of St Dunstan in the East, where he was buried in 1631, and to other charitable uses in London and Essex.[25] His son Barnard Hide lived in Kent, but was also buried in St Dunstan in the East, in 1656.[26] The freehold of Wiggins' Key passed to his younger son Humphrey, who was in possession at the time of the Fire,[27] and remained in the hands of his descendants to the later eighteenth century.[28] By 1800 Wiggins' Key, along with Ralph's and Young's Keys, was occupied by the lightering and shipping firm of James and Edward Ogle, who may by then have acquired the freehold, too.[29] Wiggins' Key or Quay was one of the legal quays acquired by government in *c.* 1812 in order to build a new Custom House to the west of the existing

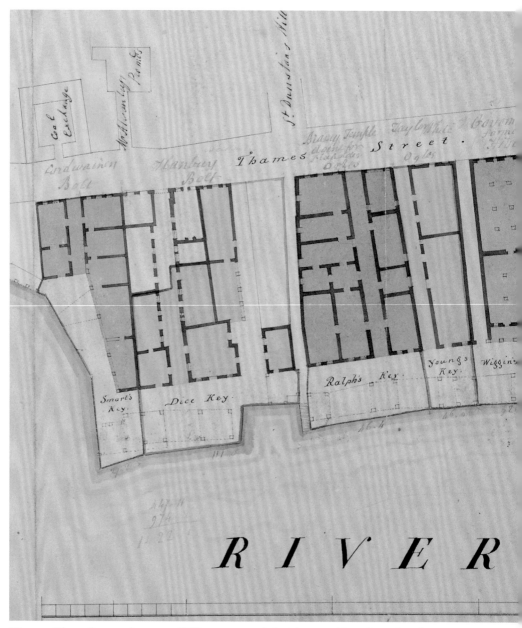

Fig. 3.   Plan of quays between Billingsgate and the Tower of London (detail), *c.* 1800.
© London Metropolitan Archives, City of London, *SC/GL/PR/VGP/LA/07/p7499758*
(COLLAGE: The London Picture Archive, ref. 28206).

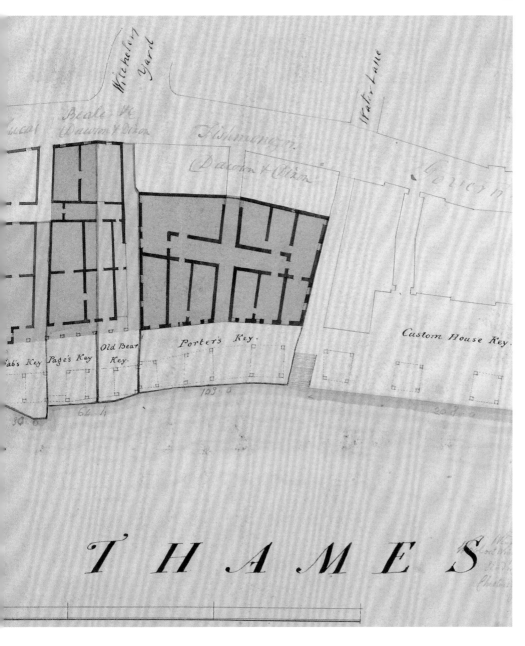

one, extending across almost the whole of the waterfront of the parish of
St Dunstan in the East.[30]

The descent of this freehold illustrates the trend over time for ownership
and occupation of London properties to diverge. Of course, wealthy

Londoners were rentiers in the fourteenth and fifteenth centuries, but they were also resident in the city themselves. The mid-sixteenth century saw a lively property market as former religious and chantry properties came up for sale, and the mid-Tudor aldermen and wealthy merchants moved promptly to acquire them. There was obviously interest in waterfront properties as the cloth trade, and the corresponding general import trade, boomed.[31] Nicholas Gibson occupied both Gibson's Key and Old Wool Quay; Sir William Webbe the elder held Old Thruston's or Haddock's Key and part of Dyce Key, and later, through his wife Bennett, a share of Gibson's/Draper's Key. In 1582 quays between the bridge and the Tower were owned by Aldermen Henry Amcotts, William Webbe, James Bacon, Henry Herdson, Ralph Warren, Christopher Draper, William Page and William Roche, or their heirs.[32] In the mid-seventeenth century, freeholds were owned by institutions in and outside London, and by private individuals and families, in several cases gentry families descended from prosperous Londoners of an earlier generation. The descendants of Roche, Page and Warren, and of Alderman Henry Hubberstey, still owned freeholds here at the time of the Fire.[33] By the early eighteenth century, it is clear that the Hyde family regarded Wiggins' Key as a transferable investment or security akin to their holdings of South Sea stock or government annuities.[34] Leaseholders were also investors and rentiers in their own right, but were more likely to be involved in the use or exploitation of the property, whether for residential or commercial uses. Both freeholders and leaseholders engaged in mortgaging and borrowing against their assets, and the arrangements for rebuilding after the Fire of 1666 reveal a tangle of freehold, leasehold, tenancy and reversionary interests in the waterfront wharves.[35]

Occupants and Uses from the Sixteenth Century

Christopher Draper appears to have been the last person to both own and inhabit the property. At or not long after his death in 1581, the commercial part of Gibson's Key was leased to William Wiggins or Wickins for £50 a year. Wiggins, a Skinner, was a parishioner of St Dunstan in the East from at least 1575; as William Wyckyns, he witnessed Draper's will on 21 July 1580.[36] 'Wm Wickines' was described as 'firmar' (farmer, lessee) of Gibson's Key to Alderman Draper's heirs in 1582.[37] Though the property continued to be referred to as Draper's Key for some time, a reference in 1606 to the burial of 'a child found at Mr Wiggens his key' suggests that this name was becoming attached to it.[38] After Wiggins' death in 1614 the lease passed to his widow Maud, and then, following an acrimonious lawsuit with her second husband, to Thomas Matthew or Matthews, citizen and Skinner.[39]

In 1638, Thomas Matthew is listed as a householder at Wiggins' Key, for a property valued at £40 per annum. Matthew also occupied Bare (Great

Bear) Key, next but one east of Wiggins Key, valued at £100.[40] In his will of that year he mentions having assigned £50 a year from his lease of 'Wiggens Key' to his elder son Thomas.[41] The Matthew family continued to reside in the parish, recording the baptisms or burials of several generations in the parish register.[42] In March 1666 John Matthew, grandson of the elder Thomas, occupied a house on 'Wigonses Key'.[43] By the time he made his will in 1676, John Matthew held a two-thirds share in a thriving partnership that leased Wiggins' Key together with Young's and Ralph's quays adjacent to the west. His uncle Mark Mortimer held the other one-third.[44] At John Matthew's death in 1680, the net annual value of the three quays and eleven houses, after payments of rent to ground landlords, was stated to be £758 13s. 10d. Matthew left his share of the leases of the three quays and other tenements there, and of his ships and lighters, to his three children, all under age.[45] Mark Mortimer, his uncle, partner, and one of his executors, died in 1686; Mark's son John was his heir and executor.[46] Peter Cartwright, John Matthew's brother-in-law and another of his executors, and John Mortimer granted sub-leases of their respective shares in Wiggins' Key in the later 1680s and 1690s at a rent of £1,200 in all.[47]

The complex layers of interest in Wiggins' Key and its neighbours make it hard to pin down its actual occupants and users, and the terms on which they held the property, for most of the eighteenth century, though several names can be associated with it. Joseph Phillips, citizen and Cooper, and John Phillips, citizen and Grocer, were lessees of two-thirds from 1687; Anthony Job, wharfinger, was lessee of one-third from 1695.[48] James Butlin, wharfinger (d. 1739), 'late of Wiggons Key', was mentioned in 1754.[49] In 1800 Wiggins', Young's, and Ralph's Keys were held by Messrs Ogles,[50] identifiable as James and Edward Ogle, variously described as brokers, shipbrokers, lightermen and merchants. They occupied Ralph's Key (and probably Young's and Wiggins') by 1790, and in 1795 applied to license nine barges operating between Ralph's Key and Deptford.[51] Edward Ogle was chairman of the Committee of Proprietors of the Legal Quays and the author of a 1796 proposal to organize the mooring of ships along the Thames.[52] He described himself in 1801 as having been a wharfinger for fourteen or fifteen years.[53]

As the foregoing suggests, the property once known as Asselyne's wharf evolved over the years from one that was largely residential — a capital messuage with wharf — to a busy and highly commercialized wharf property, equipped for handling large and valuable cargoes, though still with a number of inhabited houses. The cloth export boom of the later fifteenth and first half of the sixteenth centuries no doubt played a part in the beginning of this transformation, as London commanded a growing share of a rapidly increasing trade. Several of the lessees of the property — Browne, Bledlowe, Gibson — were Grocers, traditionally more associated with the import trade, but this, too, was increasing in volume and value.

A key moment in this evolution was the designation in 1559 of a number of 'legal quays' for overseas trade, part of the reform of the customs administration under Lord Treasurer Winchester. Having 'searched surveyed and vywed [...] all the open places kayes and wharfes and other ladinge and discharginge places for the chardge and dischardge of merchandizes within the porte of London', the commission designated twenty-one quays, including 'Gybsons Kaye', as legal for overseas trade.[54] Almost the whole of the waterfront between the Bridge and the Tower, most of it in private ownership, was now formally associated with the oversight of trade and customs collection, to which all ships leaving or arriving in the port had long been subject. In the short term it probably made little difference to existing activities, but in the longer term it conferred an important monopoly right on the owners or lessees of the 'legal quays', and created a shared interest in defending the monopoly. A subsequent attempt by the lessee of the Custom House Quay to confine all trade in cloth and 'mart wares' to that quay was strongly resisted by the wharfingers and 'key keepers' in 1582, on the grounds that the volume of business was increasing and this would cause major delays, to the cost and detriment of merchants, not to mention their own investment in leases, rents and improving facilities.[55] While there was some official concern that too many quays had been licensed, making effective supervision impossible, a proposal to limit overseas trade to six quays, not including Gibson's/Draper's, does not seem have been implemented.[56] While trade was not growing rapidly in the 1580s, given the problems in the Spanish Netherlands and the loss of the Antwerp cloth mart, over the next decades there was certainly a major increase in the volume and value of trade.[57]

There is little information on commercial activities on Gibson's/Draper's/Wiggins' Key before the later seventeenth century. Sir Christopher Draper only appears twice in the portbook for 1567–68, in both cases importing *poldavis*, a coarse canvas, from Antwerp.[58] It may be, if he was an ironmonger by trade as well as by company, that his principal business was with English ironmasters: in 1584 Gibson's Key was said to be used for 'lead and tynne and other cost [coastal] wares'.[59] The first Barnard Hide was involved in customs farming, but his interest in Wiggins' Key was probably as investment only.[60] The term 'wharfinger', which first appears in the mid-sixteenth century, and is used along with 'key-keepers' in the 1582 report on the legal quays, was by the seventeenth century coming to denote a specialized occupation and interest group, the owners or lessees of the legal quays who ran wharfage, warehousing and lighterage businesses, rather than being themselves import or export merchants.[61] William Wiggins' activities are obscure, but he may in practice have been a wharfinger; he must have been sufficiently active and prominent for his name to become permanently attached to the quay. In 1636 a note of the rates for lighterage at Wiggins' and Young's Keys suggests that a wide variety of wares was being handled there, including wine, (olive) oil, raisins, currants, figs, sugar and molasses, wool, yarn and iron, many of which may have come from or via Spain, but also more mundane goods such as corn, wheat, rye and flax. The report was made by Francis Kestian, listed as a householder on Mason's Key (another name for Young's Key) in 1638, who may have been operating a lighterage business from both quays.[62]

The Matthew–Mortimer partnership, however, is well documented, thanks to a Chancery suit brought after Mark Mortimer's death in 1686. The business clearly combined shipping and lightering with wharfage and warehousing, owning shares in twenty-one ships and eight lighters; John Matthew also had shares in three more ships. Wiggins' and adjacent quays were used both for coastal grain and the West Indian sugar and tobacco trades. While they handled a high proportion of the former trade, earnings from handling transatlantic and East Indian imports made up nearly 50 per cent of the partnership's income, and the partners appear to have secured a highly lucrative agreement for wharfage services with the East India Company. Matthew also had other partnerships and interests, including a quarter share in a sugar house in Dunghill Lane.[63] Wiggins' Key evidently continued to be used for landing sugar through the eighteenth century, as well as 'wood' (fustic, a dye) and tea, as several Old Bailey prosecutions show.[64] In 1801 Edward Ogle, wharfinger, the current occupant of the quays, was called to testify at the Old Bailey on the usual allowances for 'drainings' and 'scrapings and sweepings' when sugar was imported and handled, presumably because of his expert knowledge of such matters.[65]

In 1809 a fire devastated the waterfront, burning east from Billingsgate:

> the range of warehouses, filled with sugars, tar, oil, hemp, turpentine, tallow &c. were all successively consumed [...] The extensive warehouses of Ralph's Key, Smart's Key, Young's Key, and Dyce's Key, with their valuable contents, are entirely destroyed; Wiggon's Key is partly so.[66]

The destruction may have facilitated the replacement of these quays and warehouses by the new Custom House in 1813–17; by this period, the movement of trade to wet docks further down river was well under way.[67]

Locating the Property

The deeds and surveys that allow us to trace the descent of interests in the property through to the seventeenth century also confirm its exact location. Like most other waterfront properties in this area in the Middle Ages, it comprised a roughly oblong plot, fronting on Thames Street to the north and the river to the south. To the west it abutted on another privately owned property with a wharf; to the east, on a watergate or lane giving public access to the Thames, on the other side of which was another privately owned wharf property.[68] Kingsford thought this watergate was the one forming the parish boundary between St Dunstan in the East and All Hallows Barking, but reconstruction of all the properties along the waterfront locates it as the watergate in the middle of the waterfront of St Dunstan in the East. Once this is established, some topographical problems or inconsistencies are resolved, and it confirms that Asselyne's Wharf or Gibson's/Draper's Key is identical with the later Wiggins' Key, not Porter's Key, as Kingsford suggested.[69]

The watergate was something of a landmark for several centuries. Located opposite the medieval lane or street known as Segerymeslane, later Harp Lane, running up from Thames Street to Tower Street, it may represent an early element in the street pattern, established between the ninth and eleventh centuries.[70] Like other watergates, it was a point of public access to the Thames, and therefore of some concern to the City. In the late thirteenth century it was known as Olvendebrigge or Holvedebrigge, names that indicate the existence of a 'bridge' — a jetty or stairs — to the Thames, though later it was simply referred to as a watergate.[71] A survey of the lanes leading to the Thames in 1343 reported that, though the gate (*porta*) called 'le Watergate' between the tenements of William Box and Richard Asshelyn used to be common or public, it had been impeded by the gutter from a latrine, and by a paling put up within the last two years.[72] Further problems arose in the early sixteenth century, when a frame or bridge of timber at Sabbe's Wharf (the property on the east side of the lane) was said to obstruct the common ground of the City as well as the wharf of its own neighbour to the east.[73] In 1566 the lane was described as 'the Cyties ground and sewer', when Christopher Draper was allowed to encroach marginally on it to build his kitchen chimney.[74] Leake's plan after the Fire indicates an inlet in the waterfront between Wiggins' Key to the west and Sabb's Dock to the east. This inlet may represent the watergate, left behind, as it were, as the private properties on either side advanced into the river.[75] The inlets at Queenhithe, Dowgate and Billingsgate, all public access points to the river, may similarly represent an early medieval shoreline. An undated sketch plan in Oliver's book of post-Fire foundation surveys seems to show the lane leading to Sabb's Dock.[76] In 1667 it was noted that the stairs at Sabb's Dock, probably the watergate, were specifically excluded from use for overseas trade.[77] There was still a 'sewer against Sabbs dock' in 1676.[78] A plan of *c.* 1800 of the waterfront properties from Billingsgate to the Tower (Fig. 3) shows a lane giving access to the Thames between 'Wiggin's Key' and 'Sab's Key'.[79]

Asselyne's Wharf lay to the west of this watergate. The terms of Richard Willysdon's lease of 1384, discussed below, suggest the plot had a minimum length north–south of 160 ft (48.77 m).[80] The survey of wharves in 1559 that resulted in the designation of the legal quays listed it as 'One other Kay in

London aforesaid called Gybsons Kaye conteyninge est and west in length liij footes and from the water of Thames south and north in breadeth lx footes'. The north–south 'breadeth' of 60 ft (18.29 m) indicates that only part of the plot was designated as a legal quay, the rest being presumably occupied by other buildings. The full north–south length of the property is not given, but was probably about 160 ft (48.77 m), similar to the nearby Haddock's Key and Dyce Key.[81]

The width of 53 ft (16.15 m) for Gibson's Key stated in 1559 matches closely with the 52 ft 5 in. (15.97 m) width of 'Wiggons key' given in a 1667 written survey of the waterfront prior to rebuilding.[82] Leake's plan immediately after the Fire locates Wiggins' Key between Young's Key west and Sabb's Dock east, with an overall length north–south of about 160 ft (48.77 m), with only slightly greater lengths for Young's and Ralph's Keys.[83] Ogilby and Morgan's map of 1676 appears to have reversed the names of Wiggins' and Young's Keys, but also suggests a depth of *c.* 160 ft (48.77 m), including the 40 ft (12.19 m) left open by order.[84] A plan drawn *c.* 1800 of all the quays from Billingsgate to the Tower (Fig. 3) indicates that the dimensions of the plots had changed little since the seventeenth century.[85]

Reconstructing the Buildings

As the preceding discussion shows, in the sixteenth and seventeenth centuries the footprint of Gibson's or Wiggins' Key was 52–53 ft (*c.* 16 m) wide east–west and some 160 ft (48.77 m) in length north–south. Any reconstruction of the premises on Browne's Key scheduled in 1384 and 1463 therefore needs to fit into a much smaller plot than that envisaged by Kingsford, who supposed that the property had a frontage of 130 ft (39.62 m) to Thames Street.

Thirteenth- and early fourteenth-century deeds only describe the property as a *tenementum* (property or holding) or as a messuage (dwelling) and wharf; a chamber, stable and cart access are mentioned in 1366.[86] The first of the documents giving significant detail of the buildings on the property is a memorandum of lease by John Cherteseye to Richard Willysdon, chandler, in 1384, for a hundred years. It bound Willysdon to rebuild the whole property within ten years, in new timber, and to extend the wharf towards the Thames, facing it with Maidstone stone. The street range was to measure 40 ft (12.19 m) deep, the wharf 80 ft (24.38 m), with enough space between the two to accommodate a 'chef Dwellyngplace' comprising a hall measuring 40 ft long by 24 ft broad (12.19 m by 7.32 m), a parlour, kitchen and buttery 'as to such a hall schulde long', and other chambers and houses for merchandise, all built over cellars, together with a cartway to the wharf. If the hall was oriented north–south, this would indicate a property at least 160 ft (48.77 m) north–south.[87]

While it cannot be known whether Willysdon did rebuild exactly as the lease specified, there was certainly a substantial complex of domestic and commercial buildings on the property by 1463, when Stephen Browne's executors made an agreement with his son's widow Agnes Pekham over her share in the property. Under the custom of London, a citizen's widow was entitled to live in the marital home for life, and to a one-third life interest in all other personal estate, including leasehold property. The agreement therefore lists all the rooms considered to be part of Browne's dwelling house, to which Agnes was entitled, and acknowledges her one-third interest in all the other rooms and buildings on the property, non-domestic or tenanted. As in the Willysdon lease, there is a hall, parlour, kitchen and buttery, and also a number of other chambers, cellars and garrets, and a chapel. Buildings towards the street ('tenauntries'), garners and the wharf with a crane are mentioned, but not as part of Agnes's dwelling. The text specifying the widow's entitlement in 1463 was repeated verbatim in the will of Thomas Bledlowe in 1478, who assigned the same parcels of the premises to his own wife Anneys.[88]

The description of the rooms and their connections in 1463 and 1478 is detailed but not always easy to follow, and some information is missing. Kingsford's and Godfrey's reconstruction of the layout of 'Browne's Place', while beautifully executed and drawing on considerable knowledge of medieval London houses, cannot be accepted as an accurate depiction of this property.[89] The plot was much smaller than they thought, and must have been a good deal more crowded. In his *Medieval London Houses*, John Schofield offers a plausible reconstruction of the medieval buildings, on a plot just over 50 ft wide.[90] It seems likely that the hall — assuming it had been built to the specifications of 1384 — was oriented north–south, and entered by steps on the east side. The agreement specifies an entry leading south out of the hall to a great parlour, with chambers on one side and a chapel on the other, and another parlour and a counting-house off an entry leading eastwards from the south end of the hall to a cloth-house. There was a kitchen range with a bolting-house and a pastry house (both presumably to do with food preparation), and the kitchen was connected with the hall by way of an entry. But it is hard to fit in a street range of 40 ft deep, a yard and garners or warehouses to the east of the hall, and a parlour, chambers and chapel to the south, especially if there was also a cartway through to the wharf. The parlour and chambers must have encroached on the 80 ft of the wharf space, as in Schofield's reconstruction, and the yard must have been quite narrow. It certainly appears that the domestic premises now included some of the street range — garrets and chambers above or beside the great gate. Schofield's reconstruction, reproduced here (Fig. 4) suggests how the buildings might have ben arranged, given the constraints of the site.

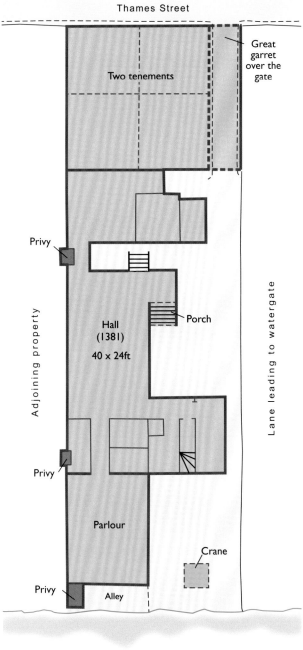

Thames Street

Two tenements

Great garret over the gate

Privy

Adjoining property

Hall (1381)

40 x 24ft

Porch

Lane leading to watergate

Privy

Parlour

Crane

Privy

Alley

Fig. 4. Reconstruction of the layout of Browne's Place, *c.* 1463, based on John Schofield, *Medieval London Houses* (London, 1994), no. 175, pp. 221–23. Redrawn by Giles Darkes, 2020. Reproduced by kind permission of John Schofield.

River Thames

How long these impressive buildings lasted in this form is not clear. The cellaring under the hall, parlour, kitchen, buttery and chambers specified in 1384 was presumably stone vaulting, as in numerous other examples in the city, and might well have endured to the Fire of 1666 or beyond.[91] The hall, too, could well have survived for some time, at least as long as it was required for domestic use.[92] When Sir Christopher Draper lived in the property it was presumably still a suitable dwelling for a prosperous merchant in his time, though he certainly engaged in some building works. The 1463 description seems to place the kitchen on the west side of the property, but Draper's kitchen must have been on the east side; he obtained permission to build a kitchen chimney in 1566 encroaching slightly onto the City's ground and sewer (the common lane leading to the watergate) lying between Draper's premises and the house of William Bulley, Fishmonger, occupant of Sabb's Key or Dock.[93] It is possible that more extensive rebuilding or rearrangement was undertaken at this time. But Draper was the last person of wealth and high status to live there. In 1582, 'that part of the key next to the Thames and certain other warehouses under the dwelling house of the said Sir Christopher Draper' were held on lease by William Wyggens at £50 rent; the dwelling house was said to be worth £30 a year. The property had one 'jebet' (gibbet) or crane.[94]

All the subsequent transactions concerning the freehold indicate that it was occupied by several tenants ranging from the head lessee to temporary lodgers.[95] A survey of divided houses in 1637 noted under 'Raphes Key precinct' in Tower ward that Widow Chidderley was an inmate (lodger) in Mr Ridgley's house on 'Wiggens key', and that Anthony Leaminges, his wife and child were inmates in Mr Chapman's house there.[96] Five householders or tithe-payers were listed at Wiggins' Key in 1638: Thomas Matthew, for a property valued at £40 per annum; Mr Bell, for one valued at £10; William Rolfe, £8; John Herne, £8; and James Bodwin, £30. Yearly values of £8–£10 suggest quite modest properties, though James Bodwin's £30 rent indicates a more substantial one, especially if Matthew's tenement included the commercial wharf. Interestingly, the values assigned to some other quays were significantly higher than Wiggins' Key. Porter's Key was valued at £300 per annum, plus three smaller units totalling £24; Bare (Great Bear) Key, also held by Thomas Matthew, was valued at £100, plus four lesser tenancies totalling £48; Raphes Key and Dyce Key were each valued at £150, plus several smaller units. Only Sabb's Dock, at £40 (£60 in all), and Mason's (alias Young's) Key, at £30 (£51 in all), were lower.[97] This was partly a function of size, since both Porter's and Dyce Keys were more than twice as wide as Wiggins' Key, but may also have indicated differences in facilities, equipment or state of repair.[98]

In March 1666 John Matthew occupied a house with three hearths on 'Wigonses Key'. The Hearth Tax does not capture the extent of commercial premises, but it looks as if there were by now three fairly substantial dwelling units (houses of six to eight hearths, probably over three or more floors) and three smaller ones with two to four hearths, one of them occupied by Matthew. This suggests there had been some fairly radical remodelling of the domestic accommodation, perhaps with a heightened or rebuilt street range. Three of the units were marked as empty, perhaps reflecting deaths or absences due to the recent plague.[99]

The Fire of September 1666, though mostly spreading westward from its starting-point in Pudding Lane, also burned fiercely eastward along Thames Street and the waterfront wharves, stacked with merchandise and marine stores. While the landlords and leaseholders of Porter's Key, Bear Key, Page's Key, Sabb's Dock and Young's Key resorted to the Fire Court to resolve their differences over rebuilding,[100] Humphrey Hyde and his tenants got on with rebuilding Wiggins' Key without litigation. John Matthew and Mark Mortimer together paid for four post-Fire foundation surveys in Thames Street in August 1667 and February 1668; Humphry Hyde paid for one in Thames Street near St Dunstan's Hill in April 1668.[101] Wiggins' Key had been rebuilt by July 1672, and Hyde appears to have accepted a reduced rent of £30, down from £80 before the Fire, which implies that the rebuilding costs had been borne by the tenants.[102]

Agreements in the Fire Court cast some light on the nature of the wharves and waterfront buildings before the Fire. Page's Key in 1646 comprised a wharf, a ruinous messuage (subsequently rebuilt) and a crane. (Great) Bear Key in 1647 included houses, buildings, warehouses, a crane, engines, waste grounds and yards. A lease of Young's Key in 1651 noted four messuages and other buildings, with cranewheel and gibbet; at the time of the Fire some upper rooms were occupied by tenants. Sabb's Key in 1662 comprised the quay itself, a way leading from Thames Street to the river, a crane, gibbet, bridge and stairs, a great warehouse under the old kitchen and another warehouse with a counting-house; there were also 'lodges', with rooms including a kitchen, on three floors over the warehouse, and several other chambers let separately.[103]

One stipulation for the rebuilding of the wharves was that a 40 ft open quay be left along the waterfront. As Reddaway has shown, this was achieved without compulsory purchase, though all the wharves were required to be levelled up to Somers Key, and the bounds of private properties marked by stones.[104] This was probably as much in the interests of the wharfingers as the Crown, and certainly it must have facilitated the operation of Wiggins', Young's and Ralph's Keys as a single unit by the Matthew–Mortimer partnership. They appear to have acquired their interests in Young's and Ralph's Keys after 1668, from the lessees in possession at the time of the

Fire.[105] By 1680 the partnership held the leases of 'three keys called Wiggins Key Ralphs Key & Youngs key', John Matthew's late dwelling house and another house, with the warehouses and cranes belonging thereto, valued together at £1,000 per annum; nine houses let at rents totalling £285 a year; and 'the back house vault and seller standing empty' valued at £30 a year.[106] The nine houses may have been along the Thames Street frontage of the three properties. John Matthew's dwelling house was on three floors with a cellar, and comprised four garrets, all with beds, three chambers all with beds and fireplaces, a 'dyneing room', a passage and yard, a kitchen and a counting-house. The rooms were well furnished: there was some modern furniture including a chest of drawers and cane chairs, a picture and a couple of looking-glasses, tapestry hangings in the main bedroom and gilt leather hangings in the dining room.[107]

A lease of 1687 indicates that there was still some domestic accommodation on the three quays — six or eight houses in all — but overshadowed by seventy-six warehouses, vaults and cellars.[108] By the end of the eighteenth century, and possibly much earlier, all trace of domestic buildings on Wiggins' Key had gone, at least at ground level. A plan of c. 1800 (Fig. 3) depicts it as a single large warehouse building divided in two, the roof supported by pillars, and with an arcaded front to the wharf. An open way to the wharf lay to the west. Young's was similarly simple, though without pillars and arcading, and with a covered way to the wharf. The plan of Ralph's Key was more complex, with several smaller rooms, though it is not clear if they were warehouses, offices, other commercial buildings or residential.[109]

Many elements of this story will be familiar to historians of London's topography and built environment, including the feasibility of reconstructing property histories over centuries, and the insights this can give into the changing character of the city; the profuse documentation generated by the vigour of the property market; the changing balance of citizen, institutional and non-London landholders; the divergence over time of ownership and occupation, and of residential and commercial uses. An unusual feature in this particular story is the survival of a wealth of detail for the domestic buildings on the plot in the later fifteenth century, and for the business being operated there in the later seventeenth, a sidelight on the economic and social transformation over that period. An equally dramatic transformation is encapsulated in the history of the huge new Custom House built across the site of Wiggins' Key between 1813 and 1817, as London's role as a centre of global trade reached new heights and dock facilities moved downriver. With repairs and partial rebuildings, it served as the headquarters of HM Revenue and Customs to 2019, though it is apparently due to be closed and sold in 2020.[110]

1. C. L. Kingsford, 'A London Merchant's House and its Owners, 1360–1614', *Archaeologia*, 74 (1924), pp. 137–58.

2. John Schofield offered a plausible reconstruction in *Medieval London Houses* (London, 1994), no. 175, pp. 221–23.

3. Vanessa Harding, 'The Port of London in the Fourteenth Century: Its Topography, Administration, and Trade' (unpublished PhD thesis, University of St Andrews, 1983), pp. 536–39, https://ethos.bl.uk/OrderDetails.do?did=2&uin=uk.bl.ethos.382535 [accessed on 1 March 2021]; 'Custom House Quay and the Old Custom House', in *Survey of London: Volume 15, All Hallows, Barking-By-The-Tower, Pt II*, ed. by G. H. Gater and Walter H. Godfrey (London, 1934), pp. 31–43, though some property identifications there are doubtful. See also *The Cartulary of Holy Trinity Aldgate*, ed. G. Hodgett, London Record Society, 7 (1971), nos 223, 226, 1051, 1054.

4. The fourteenth-century descents of all the waterfront properties are traced in Harding, 'Port of London'.

5. *A descriptive catalogue of Ancient Deeds*, I (HMSO, 1890), A 1778.

6. Harding, 'Port of London', pp. 558–66.

7. Harding, 'Port of London', pp. 539–40; Kingsford, 'A London Merchant's House', pp. 138–39.

8. Kingsford, 'A London Merchant's House', pp. 139–43.

9. Kingsford, 'A London Merchant's House', p. 144. 'Christchurch' was an alternative designation for Holy Trinity Priory. The 98-year term may represent the 18 years yet to come of the 80-year lease granted in 1444 plus a new lease of 80 years from 1524.

10. A. B. Beaven, *The Aldermen of the City of London temp. Henry III–1912*, 2 vols (London, 1908), II, p. 28. Gibson was elected alderman for Castle Baynard Ward in 1534 but discharged for 'insufficiency', as not worth the required 2,000 marks (£1,333 6s. 8d.): ibid., I, p. 91.

11. (Sir) William Foster, 'Nicholas Gibson and his Free School at Ratcliffe', *London Topographical Record*, 17 (1936), pp. 1–18.

12. Kingsford, 'A London Merchant's House', p. 144.

13. Kingsford, 'A London Merchant's House', p. 145.

14. *The Register of St Dunstan in the East, 1558–1654*, ed. A. W. Hughes Clarke, Harleian Society, vol. 69 part 1 (1939), pp. 92, 127, 134, 147, 148; John Strype, *A survey of the cities of London and Westminster … written at first in the year MDXCVIII by John Stow … now lately corrected, improved and very much Enlarged … by John Strype* (London: A. Churchill, J. Knapton, R. Knaplock, J. Walthoe, E. Horne, B. Tooke, D. Midwinter, B. Cowse, R. Robinson, and T. Ward, 1720), bk 2, ch. 3, pp. 43–44, https://www.dhi.ac.uk/strype/.

15. TNA, PROB 11/63/312 (will of Sir Christopher Draper); Inquisition Post Mortem Christopher Draper, 'Inquisitions: 1581', in *Abstracts of Inquisitiones Post Mortem For the City of London: Part 3*, ed. E. A. Fry (London, 1908), pp. 32–43; *British History Online*, http://www.british-history.ac.uk/inquis-post-mortem/abstract/no3/pp32-43 [accessed on 2 July 2018].

16. Beaven, *Aldermen*, II, p. 172, though Beaven is incorrect in stating that Bridget Draper married Nicholas Woodroffe, Alderman.

17. LMA, Husting Roll 269(78), now LMA, CLA/023/DW/01/268.

18. Kingsford, 'A London Merchant's House', pp. 145–46; TNA, PROB 11/59/32 (will of Stephan Woodroof); TNA, PROB 11/94/142 (will of Sir William Webbe); LMA, Husting Roll 269(78), now CLA/023/DW/01/268; Inquisition Post Mortem Bridget Billingesley, 'Inquisitions: 1590', in *Abstracts of Inquisitiones*, pp. 143–51; *British History Online*, http://www.british-history.ac.uk/inquis-post-mortem/abstract/no3/pp143-151 [accessed on 2 July 2018].

19. Inquisition Post Mortem Agnes Hickman, 'Inquisitions: 1600', in *Abstracts of Inquisitiones*, pp. 268–79; *British History Online*, http://www.british-history.ac.uk/inquis-post-mortem/abstract/no3/pp268-279 [accessed on 2 July 2018]. Cf. Ian W. Archer, 'Dixie, Sir Wolstan

(1524/5–1594), Merchant and Administrator, Mayor of London', *ODNB*, http://www.oxforddnb.com

20. TNA, PROB 11/94/142 (will of Sir William Webbe); Inquisition Post Mortem Christopher Webbe, 'Inquisitions: 1593–4', *Abstracts of Inquisitiones*, pp. 171–219; *British History Online*, http://www.british-history.ac.uk/inquis-post-mortem/abstract/no3/pp171-219 [accessed on 16 July 2018]; TNA, PROB 11/104/289 (will of Dame Benette Webbe).

21. Kingsford, 'A London Merchant's House', p. 146; LMA, Husting Roll 291(34), now CLA/023/DW/01/290.

22. TNA, C 2/Jas1/D11/33.

23. LMA, Husting Roll 291(35), now CLA/023/DW/01/290.

24. Kingsford, 'A London Merchant's House', pp. 146–47.

25. Beaven, *Aldermen*, I, p. 193; 'Queen Elizabeth — Volume 264: September 1597', in *Calendar of State Papers Domestic: Elizabeth, 1595–97*, ed. by Mary Anne Everett Green (London, 1869), pp. 496–507; *British History Online*, http://www.british-history.ac.uk/cal-state-papers/domestic/edw-eliz/1595-7/pp496-507 [accessed on 13 November 2020]; 'Cecil Papers: Miscellaneous 1608', in *Calendar of the Cecil Papers in Hatfield House: Volume 20, 1608*, ed. by M. S. Giuseppi and G. Dyfnallt Owen (London, 1968), pp. 287–315, *British History Online*, http://www.british-history.ac.uk/cal-cecil-papers/vol20/pp287-315 [accessed on 13 November 2020]; TNA, E 214/1351; 'Little Ilford', in *A History of the County of Essex: Volume 6*, ed. by W. R. Powell (London, 1973), pp. 163–74; *British History Online*, http://www.british-history.ac.uk/vch/essex/vol6/pp163-174 [accessed on 13 November 2020]; TNA, PROB 11/160/290 (will of Barnard Hyde of London); Strype, *A survey of the cities of London and Westminster*, bk 2, ch. 3, p. 46; City of London Livery Companies Commission, 'Reports on the Charities of the Salters' Company', in *City of London Livery Companies Commission. Report; Volume 4* (London, 1884), pp. 502–10; *British History Online*, http://www.british-history.ac.uk/livery-companies-commission/vol4/pp502-510 [accessed on 25 July 2018].

26. TNA, PROB 11/252/338 (will of Bernard or Barnard Hyde of Chiddingstone, Kent).

27. BL, Add. MS 5099. 35, fols 366–72.

28. TNA, PROB 11/569/59 (will of Humphry Hyde, gentleman, of St Anne, Westminster); W. G. D. Fletcher, 'The Family of Hyde, of Bore Place and Sundridge', *Archaeologia Cantiana*, 22 (1897), pp. 112–22 (there are some errors in this account); Centre for Buckinghamshire Studies, Aylesbury, MSS D–D/3/52, D–D/16/12, D–D/16/12A, D–D/8/67–68, D–D/3/55 (identified from TNA, Discovery catalogue; not inspected); TNA, PROB 11/917/77 (will of William Paine King); PROB 11/608/132 (will of Edward Hyde, gentleman, of New Inn, Middlesex); PROB 11/936/349 (will of Bernard Hyde, gentleman, of Southwark).

29. See below, nn. 51–53.

30. Purchase of London Quays Act, 1812, c. 49: 'Custom House Quay', pp. 31–43; *British History Online*, http://www.british-history.ac.uk/survey-london/vol15/pt2/pp31-43 [accessed on 13 November 2020].

31. Brian Dietz, 'Overseas Trade and Metropolitan Growth', in *London 1500–1700: The Making of the Metropolis*, ed. by A. L. Beier and Roger Finlay (Harlow, 1986), pp. 115–40; Brian Dietz, *The Port and Trade of Elizabethan London: Documents*, London Record Society, 8 (London, 1972).

32. Dietz, *Port and Trade*, pp. 161–64; BL, MS Lansdowne 35.38, fols 127–28.

33. P. E. Jones, *The Fire Court: Calendar to the Judgments and Decrees of the Court of Judicature Appointed to Determine Differences Between Landlords and Tenants as to Rebuilding After the Great Fire*, 2 vols (London, 1966–70), I, pp. 25–26, 123–24, 280–81; ibid., II, pp. 180–81, 268–69. The freehold of Bear Key was held by descendants of Sir William Roche, owner before 1549: ibid., I, pp. 280–81; cf. Dietz, *Port and Trade*, p. 162.

34. See above, n. 28.

35. Jones, *Fire Court*, passim; see below.

36. Dietz, *Port and Trade*, p. 162; BL, MS Lansdowne. 35.38, fol. 127v; TNA, SP 46/30, fol. 153; TNA, PROB 11/63/312 (will of Sir Christopher Draper); *Two Tudor Subsidy Assessment Rolls for the City of London, 1541 and 1582*, ed. by R. G. Lang, London Record Society, 29 (London, 1993), no. 378.

37. BL, MS Lansdowne 35.35, fol. 116.

38. *Register of St Dunstan in the East, 1558–1654*, p. 162. Four children of William Wiggins were baptized in the parish between 1566 and 1592: ibid., pp. 7–28.

39. TNA, PROB 11/124/50 (administration of the estate of William Wiggins); TNA, C 3/364/46; TNA, C 2/JasI/L6/3.

40. T. C. Dale, *The Inhabitants of London in 1638, ed. from MS. 272 in Lambeth Palace Library*, Society of Genealogists (London, 1931), p. 51; LMA, Husting Roll 294(40), now CLA/023/ DW/01/293.

41. TNA, PROB 11/177/462 (will of Thomas Matthew).

42. *Register of St Dunstan in the East, 1558–1654*, passim; *The Registers of St Dunstan in the East, London, 1653–1691*, ed. by R. H. D'Elboux, Harleian Society vols 74 and 75 (1954–55), passim.

43. Matthew Davies, Catherine Ferguson, Vanessa Harding, Elizabeth Parkinson and Andrew Wareham, *London and Middlesex 1666 Hearth Tax*, 2 vols, British Record Society (London, 2014), II, p. 895.

44. TNA, PROB 11/365/139 (will of John Matthew).

45. Ibid.; LMA, CLA/002/02/01/0155 (Orphans' Court inventory of John Mathew, citizen and grocer, 1680).

46. TNA, PROB 11/383/35 (will of Mark Mortimer).

47. LMA, CLC/B/137/MS10944/001-3.

48. LMA, CLC/B/137/MS10944/001-3.

49. TNA, PROB 11/699/424 (will of James Butlin, 1739); PROB 11/811/417 (will of Sarah, widow of James, 1754).

50. Patrick Colquhoun, *A treatise on the commerce and police of the river Thames: containing an historical view of the trade of the port of London . . . With an account of the functions of the various magistrates and corporations exercising jurisdiction on the river ...* (London, 1800), p. 29; Fig. 3.

51. James and Edward Ogle, shipbrokers, 7 Billiter Square: *London Directory* (1790); James and Edward Ogle, lightermen, Ralph's key, Lower Thames Street, also merchants and brokers, 25 New City Chambers: *Holden's Directory* (1802); Anthony Edmonds, *Jane Austen's Worthing: The Real Sanditon* (ebook, Stroud, 2013), ch. 2. Edmonds identifies Edward Ogle as the inspiration for Austen's 'Mr Parker'.

52. Edmonds, *Jane Austen's Worthing*, ch. 2.

53. *Old Bailey Proceedings Online* (www.oldbaileyonline.org, version 8.0), accessed 13 November 2020, April 1801, trial of JOHN-HENRY WACKERBARTH (t18010415-74).

54. Dietz, *Port and Trade* , pp. 156–60.

55. BL, MS Lansdowne 35.35–37, fols 111–25.

56. TNA, E 178/7075.

57. Brian Dietz, 'Overseas Trade and Metropolitan Growth', in *London 1500–1700: The Making of the Metropolis*, ed. by A. L. Beier and Roger Finlay (Harlow, 1986), pp. 115–40.

58. Dietz, *Port and Trade*, nos 702, 710.

59. Dietz, *Port and Trade*, p. 161.

60. 'Queen Elizabeth — Volume 264: September 1597', in *Calendar of State Papers Domestic: Elizabeth, 1595–97*, ed. by Mary Anne Everett Green (London, 1869), pp. 496–507; *British History Online*, http://www.british-history.ac.uk/cal-state-papers/domestic/edw-eliz/1595-7/ pp496-507 [accessed on 25 July 2018]; 'Cecil Papers: July 1603, 1–15', in *Calendar of the*

Cecil Papers in Hatfield House: Volume 15, 1603, ed. by M. S. Giuseppi (London, 1930), pp. 163–93; *British History Online*, http://www.british-history.ac.uk/cal-cecil-papers/vol15/pp163-193 [accessed on 25 July 2018]; TNA, SP 46/68/f011; E 214/1351; PROB 11/160/290 (will of Barnard Hide of London).

61. *Oxford English Dictionary*: 'wharfinger', 1552–53; BL, MS Lansdowne 35.35–37, fols 111–25.

62. TNA, E 215/1043; Dale, *Inhabitants*, p. 51.

63. LMA, CLA/002/02/01/0155 (Orphans' Court inventory of John Mathew, citizen and grocer, 1680); TNA, C113/13–14 (Chancery Masters' Exhibits, re. Phillips); John Chartres, 'Trade and Shipping in the Port of London: Wiggins Key in the Later Seventeenth Century', *Journal of Transport History*, 1.1 (1980), pp. 29–47; Henry Roseveare, 'Wiggins' Key Revisited: Trade and Shipping in the Seventeenth-Century Port of London', *Journal of Transport History*, 16.1 (1995), pp. 1–20.

64. *Old Bailey Proceedings Online*, February 1747, trial of Lucy Walker (t17470225-31); ibid., September 1790, trial of CHARLES EMBERY (t17900915-91); ibid., October 1799, trial of JAMES ROBERTS (t17991030-77).

65. *Old Bailey Proceedings Online*, April 1801, trial of JOHN-HENRY WACKERBARTH (t18010415-74).

66. *Monthly magazine or British Register*, vol. XXVII, part 1 for 1809, p. 510. For the prevalence of fires after 1666, and the significance of marine stores and warehouses, see David Garrioch, '1666 and London's Fire History: A Re-evaluation', *The Historical Journal*, 59.2 (2016), pp. 319–38.

67. 'Custom House Quay and the Old Custom House', in *Survey of London: Volume 15*, pp. 31–43; *British History Online*, http://www.british-history.ac.uk/survey-london/vol15/pt2/pp31-43 [accessed on 13 November 2020].

68. Harding, 'Port of London', pp. 539–41.

69. Ibid., pp. 531–51; Kingsford, 'A London Merchant's House', pp. 146–47.

70. Tony Dyson, *The Medieval London Waterfront* (London, 1989), p. 23.

71. Harding, 'Port of London', p. 541; *Catalogue of Ancient Deeds*, I, A 1778; LMA, Husting Roll 16(113), now CLA/023/DW/01/016.

72. *Munimenta Gildhallae Londiniensis. Liber Albus, Liber Custumarum et Liber Horn*, II, part 2, *Liber Custumarum*, ed. by H. T. Riley (London, 1860), pp. 446–47.

73. *London Viewers and their Certificates, 1508–1558: Certificates of the Sworn Viewers of the City of London*, ed. by Janet S. Loengard, London Record Society, 26 (London, 1989), nos 68, 71.

74. Kingsford, 'A London Merchant's House', pp. 144–45, citing Corporation of London Repertory 16, fol. 15. The sloping lanes down to the river drained the city's streets, and at least one other lane to the river was referred to as a sewer: Wolsies Lane, near Dowgate, is named 'the common sewer' in a plan of *c.* 1612: John Schofield, *The London Surveys of Ralph Treswell*, London Topographical Society publication No. 135 (1987), pp. 120–21.

75. Leake's plan, engraved by George Vertue 1723: COLLAGE: The London Picture Archive, ref. 30633. For the advance of the waterfront, see Gustav Milne, 'Medieval Waterfront Reclamation in London', in *Waterfront Archaeology in Britain and Northern Europe (Papers of the First International Congress on Waterfront Archaeology, London, April 1979)*, ed. by Gustav Milne and Brian Hobley, CBA research report no. 41 (London, 1981), pp. 32–36.

76. Peter Mills and John Oliver, *Survey of Building Sites in the City of London after the Great Fire of 1666*, Guildhall Library, MS 84, reproduced as London Topographical Society publications Nos 79 and 89 (1946 and 1956, with an introduction by Walter Godfrey) and 97–99 (1962, edited by Cyprian Blagden); the first two volumes were reissued in one volume as London Topographical Society publication No. 101 in 1964, and a further volume with

an introduction by P. E. Jones and T. F. Reddaway and indexes by P. E. Jones appeared as London Topographical Society publication No. 103 in 1967, vol. 4, p. 50v.

77. Strype, *A Survey of the Cities of London and Westminster*, bk 5, ch. 18, pp. 281–84.

78. TNA, PROB 11/365/139 (will of John Matthew).

79. London Picture Archive, no. 28206.

80. Kingsford, 'A London Merchant's House', pp. 155–57.

81. Dietz, *Port and Trade*, p. 157. The adjacent 'Younges Kaye' was said to extend 210 ft ('twoo hundreth and tenne footes') north–south and 46 ft east–west (64 m by 14.02 m), though as Dietz's map (p. 166) shows, this length is significantly greater than the seventeenth-century length of that property. This remains a puzzle, unless it projected much further into the river than its neighbours, something for which there is no other evidence.

82. Strype, *A Survey of the Cities of London and Westminster*, bk 5, ch. 18 pp. 281–84.

83. Leake's plan, engraved by George Vertue 1723: London Picture Archive, no. 30633.

84. Ralph Hyde, John Fisher and Roger Cline, *The A to Z of Restoration London*, London Topographical Society publication No. 145 (1992), p. 77. Harben notes this confusion: *A Dictionary of London* (1918), p. 632, 'Wiggin's Quay'.

85. London Picture Archive, no. 28206.

86. Harding, 'Port of London', p. 539.

87. Kingsford, 'A London Merchant's House', p. 155; also printed in L. F. Salzman, *Building in England down to 1540* (Oxford, 1952; rev. edn. 1967), p. 464.

88. TNA, PROB 11/6/413 (will of Thomas Bledlowe).

89. Kingsford, 'A London Merchant's House', pp. 156–57, and *English Historical Documents 4, 1327–1485*, ed. by A. R. Myers (London, 1969), pp. 1160–61.

90. Schofield, *Medieval London Houses*, no. 175, pp. 221–23.

91. Kingsford, 'A London Merchant's House', p. 155.

92. A similar hall building in Pancras Lane was in use in *c*. 1611: Schofield, *London Surveys of Ralph Treswell*, pp. 106–07.

93. Kingsford, 'A London Merchant's House', p. 145, citing Rep. 16, fol. 15. In 1541 Bulley was assessed at £40 in Tower Ward, and listed next to Jasper Sabe; in 1561, Jasper Sabbe's widow and son granted him Sabbes Key. William's widow (Mary) Bulley occupied 'Sabbes Key' in 1582: Lang, *Two Tudor Subsidy Rolls*, nos 150, 379; *Register of St Dunstan in the East, 1558–1654*, p. 142; LMA, HR 251(110), now CLA/023/DW/01/250; Dietz, *Port and Trade*, p. 162.

94. BL, Lansdowne MS 35.38, fol. 127v.

95. Inquisition Post Mortem Christopher Webbe, 'Inquisitions: 1593–4', *Abstracts of Inquisitiones*, pp. 171–219; *British History Online*, http://www.british-history.ac.uk/inquis-post-mortem/abstract/no3/pp171-219 [accessed on 16 July 2018].

96. TNA, SP16/359, fol. 103v.

97. Dale, *Inhabitants*, p. 51.

98. For measurements in 1667, see Strype, *A Survey of the Cities of London and Westminster*, bk 5, ch. 18, pp. 281–84.

99. Davies et al., *London and Middlesex 1666 Hearth Tax*, II, p. 895; *Registers of St Dunstan in the East, London, 1653–1691*, pp. 83–87; TNA, PROB 11/317/92, 11/325/27 (will and sentence of William Startute); TNA, PROB 11/227/468 (will of Joan Matthew); PROB 11/365/139 (will of John Matthew).

100. Jones, *Fire Court*, I, pp. 25–26, 123–24, 280–81; ibid., II, pp. 180–81, 268–69; BL, Add. MS 5103.64, fols 54–70.

101. Mills and Oliver, *Survey of Building Sites*, vol. 1, pp. 73, 74.

102. BL, Add. MS 5099, no. 35, fols 366–72. Hyde did have recourse to the Fire Court to seek abatement of a rent charge of £8 on the property, granted by William and Agnes Hickman to Emmanuel College, Cambridge: ibid., and see n. 19, above.

103. See above, n. 100; LMA, CLA/039/01/005 (Fire Court Decrees vol. E), fol. 235; Mills and Oliver, *Survey of Building Sites*, vol. 1, p. 59.

104. T. F. Reddaway, *The Rebuilding of London after the Great Fire* (London, 1940), pp. 223–43; Strype, *A Survey of the Cities of London and Westminster*, bk 5, ch. 18, pp. 282–83.

105. Jones, *Fire Court*, II, pp. 180–81; BL, Add. MS 5067.8, fols 50–65; Mills and Oliver, *Survey of Building Sites*, vol. 1, pp. 74, 63. Mark Mortimer had acquired the freehold of Young's Key by the time of his death in 1686: TNA, PROB 11/383/35 (will of Mark Mortimer).

106. LMA, CLA/002/02/01/0155.

107. Ibid.

108. LMA, CLC/B/137/MS10944/00-3.

109. London Picture Archive, no. 28206. An architect's design for a warehouse on Wiggins' Quay in 1804 is in Sir John Soane's Museum: http://collections.soane.org/THES73275. [accessed on 13 November 2020].

110. Harben, *Dictionary of London*, 'Custom House'; 'Custom House Quay and the Old Custom House', in *Survey of London: Volume 15*, pp. 31-43; *British History Online*, http://www.british-history.ac.uk/survey-london/vol15/pt2/pp31-43 [accessed on 13 November 2020]; Wikipedia, (https://en. wikipedia. org/wiki/Custom_House,_City_of_London) citing CoStar, 'City in Talks for North Bank Regeneration', 2018.

III. A SCHOOL ESTATE IN SOUTHWARK OVER FOUR CENTURIES

By DAVID ELIS-WILLIAMS

A BOUT a quarter hectare near the church of St George the Martyr in Southwark (Fig. 1) was, between 1557 and 1899, owned by Friars School in Bangor, North Wales. From information in the School's archives,[1] supported by other sources, it has been possible to trace a near-continuous history of this plot, from a few years before it was left to the School in the sixteenth century to the beginning of the twentieth century.

The story as it affects the history of the School has been outlined elsewhere[2] and an article in the London Topographical Society's *Newsletter* has dealt with the victualling houses;[3] this article outlines the story of the estate, its buildings and some occupants, as a contribution to the history and topography of this part of London.

Chronology

The foundation of Friars School is dated to 1557, the date of Geoffrey Glyn's will. Glyn was a native of Anglesey who had succeeded as an ecclesiastical lawyer in London. He had bought the former friary in Bangor itself, which he left to become the School building, and the land in Southwark, which was to form part of the School's endowment. Glyn's executors, his brother William Glyn, Bishop of Bangor, and Maurice Griffin (or Griffith), Bishop of Rochester, themselves died in the following year without completing Glyn's intentions, so the property transferred to Griffin's executors, all former parishioners of his at St Magnus the Martyr. These executors were distinguished Londoners: Sir William Garrard, a former Lord Mayor and MP, Sir William Petre, Secretary of State and a substantial benefactor to Exeter College, Oxford, and Simon Lowe, Master of the Merchant Taylors.[4] They were well placed to look after the Southwark land, which they administered directly until 1571, when it was handed over to the Dean and Chapter of Bangor Cathedral who became the School's trustees.

Garrard maintained accounts for this period, which have survived in the School archives.[5] These indicate three tenancies. One was for tenements at the White Hind, with rent of £2 a year payable by Walter Bexley; possibly the same Walter Bexley who from 1569 took another lease from the Dean and Chapter of Westminster.[6] The second related to the Boar's Head in Long Lane at £3 10s. 4d. a year, and a third whose tenant, Mistress Maws, paid £3 18s. The estate as a whole was further subdivided into sixteen tenements, originally eight cottages and eight gardens (Fig. 2).

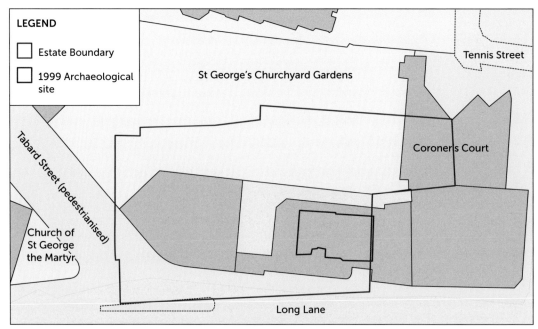

Fig. 1.   Position of former Friars School estate in relation to present day map.

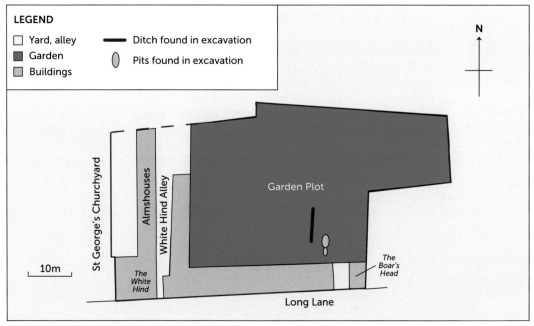

Fig. 2.   Estate Plan sixteenth century. Conjectured from descriptions in
text and later plans.

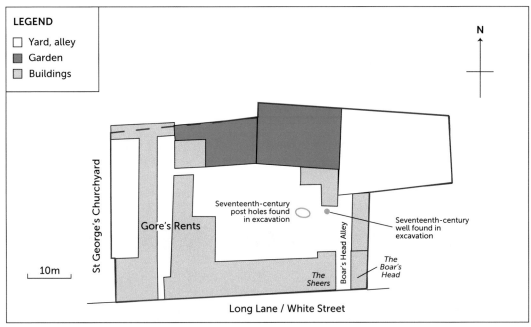

Fig. 3.   Estate Plan 1680s. Based on William Morgan map (see Fig. 19).

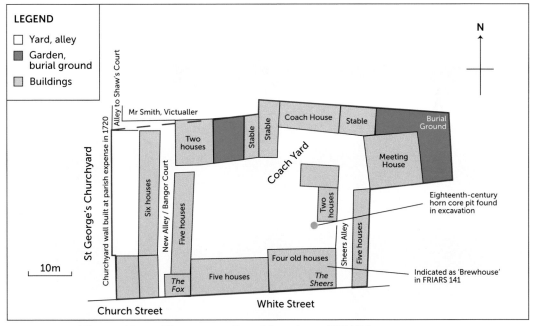

Fig. 4.   Estate Plan *c.* 1732. Based largely on FRIARS 140,141,142,
NLW G Richards 1 and Rocque (see Fig. 18).

The trustees, through Thomas Bates, paid for repairs to the estate, increasing its rental value. On transferring the land to the Dean and Chapter in 1571, they also leased the entire estate to Bates at a ground rent of £13 6s. 8d., with the intention that he, based in London, would look after the local subletting. Bates would have been known to the executors: he was a freeman of the Worshipful Company of Haberdashers,[7] where Garrard had been its Master, and one of the wardens of London Bridge,[8] on which Lowe had property.[9]

Thomas Bates's lease was renewed in 1583,[10] but he was to die in 1586, his property transferring to wife Martha,[11] and later to Edward Bates. Edward was another Haberdasher, Thomas Bates's executor and quite probably his son, who then renewed the lease in 1610.[12] He renewed again in 1617 at a rental of £20,[13] and that year was listed in a survey of landlords and tenants in Southwark, when he had seventeen tenants, the largest number in the manor.[14]

After Bates's death in 1627, the lease may have been given up or came to its term and was let in 1629 to John Gibberd. Unlike earlier or later leaseholders, Gibberd was not based in London, local to the estate,[15] and he soon disposed of it. We hear no more of the land until 1647, when arrears of ground rent were due, stretching back to 1642. Much has been made of this in the School's histories, for it seemed that, following the Civil War, Parliament had voided the corporation of the Dean and Chapter, still trustees of the School, thereby preventing them from recovering the debt. The School sent its Master, Thomas Meredith, all the way to London to see what could be done, supported by a letter from Caernarfonshire gentry.[16] Rather than the expected voided-corporation response,[17] Thomas Meredith encountered buck-passing between two other Thomases — Thomas Dyer, chandler, who had held the lease but who claimed that Thomas Webster, blacksmith, should have been paying the ground rent since 1643.[18] Ultimately, it was resolved that Dyer should hold the lease[19] and it was renewed with him, although even in 1653 the School was pursuing both Dyer and Webster for arrears.[20]

The lease was let again in 1661, this time to William Dixon (or Dickson), a freeman of the Worshipful Company of Clothworkers but in business as a distiller, and a wealthy man, passing on his death to his wife Mary.[21] The ground rent was still £20 a year, frequently paid several years in arrears.[22]

As Dixon's lease term was coming to an end, the estate had not changed a great deal since Geoffrey Glyn (Fig. 3). The terms of leases granted to date had typically been too short to allow leaseholders to undertake long-term development. It was on the fringes of the built-up area, with fields and gardens beyond.[23] Now, however, Southwark was growing, with infill developments along alleys spreading outwards to the parish of St George the Martyr.[24] If the School were to increase the value of the estate and earn higher rents, they needed to secure a leaseholder that would develop it, and on terms that gave him an incentive to do so. Somebody on the spot was needed to negotiate this. The School entrusted the job to Randle Wynne, a member of a Caernarfonshire family, possibly a former pupil, by now at Gray's Inn, in 1680 giving him power of attorney to deal with the School's land.[25]

Wynne was already acquainted with Walter Gore,[26] and this probably led to the latter's introduction as the new lessee. The outcome was a series of leases to Gore, in which he undertook to spend money on development and with the ground rent, although starting at £20, to increase in steps to reflect growing worth. The first surviving lease is dated 1688 and was for forty-one years, in which Gore was to lay out £700 within ten years, with the ground rent rising to £45.[27] Gore must have been pressing to extend his lease term, and the School pressing to increase his outlay and their rent, as, in a series of renegotiations, all these were extended.[28] At one point, Gore was slow with his rebuilding, because a separate agreement said that while 'it was always intended […] that Walter Gore should be obliged to build', he now agreed with the School that 'as often as he shall pull down one of ye houses, edifices, buildings, rebuild the same within six months after the same be pulled down'.[29] The last lease renewal was in 1697. By this time, Gore had laid out £800 in developing the land, and was to spend a further £400, the rent now rising to £50. This lease now incorporated the stipulation for rebuilding within six months, which was to become significant much later.[30]

Walter Gore died in 1712[31] with fifty-six years of the lease yet to run. In relation to the lease, his will specified,

> to John Chapman, Broom-man, in Trust only, the Lease of the ground I hold of the free Grammar School of Bangor in the County of Carnarvon situate in the parish of St. George the Martyr aforesaid for the use of my nephews William Gore and Walter Gore during the termination of the lease as hereafter […] and if either of my two nephews William Gore or Walter Gore shall depart this life and leave no issue of their respective bodies lawfully begotten, then to the daughter of my loving brother William Gore and the children of my sister Libby Price.[32]

Walter Gore the nephew was to die in 1716 and his brother William in 1718.[33] This led to a dispute over the meaning of Walter Gore (the uncle)'s will, and the Chancery case of *Forth v. Chapman*. Samuel Forth, a brewer, had come to an agreement with Elizabeth Gore, the younger William Gore's widow, who had inherited the lease,[34] and her new husband James Clifford, the couple now in occupation.[35] Francis Chapman, a victualler of St Saviour's parish, who held a mortgage on the property, was in collusion with Elizabeth Webb, the daughter of the elder William Gore, and Catherine Price, the daughter of Libby Price. As both the nephews William and Walter had died without issue, Chapman's case was that the lease should have transferred to Elizabeth Webb and Catherine Price, according to the 1712 will. Forth argued that this condition was too remote: it would have applied, had William and Walter died without issue by the time their uncle's will was proved — but once the property had transferred to them under the terms of the will, he argued, the conditions could not continue indefinitely. Forth won the case in 1719, but Chapman succeeded in having the decision reversed.

The case of *Forth v. Chapman* is referenced in legal texts because the appeal decision held that the same words could have a different meaning in law depending on whether they referred to freehold or leasehold property. In the case of the School estate, the interest was leasehold, the limitation not too remote, and Chapman's case prevailed. By 1720 he had bought out the entire lease from the cousins Elizabeth and Catherine.[36] After wresting control of the property from the Gore family, Chapman invested more in its development: by 1723 it included a coach-house and stables (Fig. 4).[37] The lease passed to his wife, then to his son George.[38]

George Chapman was a wastrel, who squandered his inheritance, probably on gambling. He died bankrupt in 1747, having mortgaged the School land for £400 to William Belchier, who now took it over.[39] Belchier was a banker and goldsmith, MP for Southwark, a dubious character involved in privateering, and later bankrupted twice (Fig. 5).[40] He was evidently a financier, not a landlord, and he quickly sublet to Moses Waite for the remainder of the term.

Meanwhile, in the long period since Gore first took the lease, place names had changed. This part of Long Lane was now called Church Street or Church Lane to the west of the junction with Kent Street, then to the east, White Street, this name appearing in a lease of 1647[41] but more common by 1700. By the turn of the eighteenth century, the White Hind had gone, the buildings sometimes called 'Gore's Rents', then was renamed Bangor Court.[42] The Boar's Head now gave its name to an alley behind it, and there was another victuallers' called the Sheers on the opposite corner of Boar's Head Alley; in time the alley became known as Sheers Alley.

One of the earliest recorded new buildings was the Anabaptist Meeting House, in the north-eastern corner of the land. This was a timber-built building, approximately 40 foot square,[43] with an associated burial ground. According to histories of the denomination, it was established in 1695, with Richard Robbins as minister, followed later by Richard Parks. From 1742 John Russell took charge, but there seems to have been a general falling-out between him and the remainder of the Baptists. Russell died in 1758, then a Mr Davies took over before the Baptist congregation came to an end in 1765.[44] The School rentals show continuing use as a meeting house after 1765, tenanted by a Mr Thwaite in 1768.[45] This was James Thwaite, a former glazier, and a Methodist; he published, and sold from 'Mr Thwaite's Chapel in White-street', a collection of psalms and hymns.[46] A later edition

Fig. 5.   *The Sequel or the Banker a Bankrupt*, anonymous satirical print showing
creditors demanding payment from William Belchier, *c.* 1760. © Trustees of the
British Museum *1855,0414.310.*

of the hymnal suggests that Thwaite had moved elsewhere by 1778. The
meeting house then became a brewer's warehouse.

Occasional burials at the burial ground around the meeting house
were recorded in the parish register, with a peak of seven burials in 1701.
Archaeological evidence was found on observation at a nearby site in 2002,
when disarticulated human bones were found, thought to have been moved
during Second World War bomb damage clearance.[47]

The lease given to Gore in 1697 and now held by Belchier, sublet to Waite,
was due to expire in November 1768 and the School sought advice from
a surveyor in anticipation of its reletting. However, before that could be
done, fire broke out on 14 July 1768. This started in Edmund Pickering's
tallow chandlery on the corner of Church Street and Bangor Court, and
spread to take down nearly all the buildings on that side of the Court.
The Fox, a victuallers' now occupying the corner site opposite, was partly
affected (Fig. 6). By now, the alley at the eastern end was better developed,
but no longer called Sheers Alley, as the victuallers' sign was now 'The
Bull'. The alley itself, together with the area behind the street frontage, was
known as the Coachyard.

At this point, the School commissioned the services of Anthony Gell as a London agent, the beginning of a long and productive relationship. Then a young man, Gell was to rise to become Receiver-General of Westminster Abbey and Westminster Coroner. He quickly found that neither Belchier nor Waite, with their leases about to end, would cooperate.[48] Rebuilding the fire-damaged properties would cost £400; Belchier had received £200 from his insurers but was not prepared to rebuild. Here he pointed to the clause in Gore's lease — although he was obliged to rebuild within six months when he had pulled down properties, the lease said nothing about fire, so he would not do it. The School sought a legal opinion,[49] but there was little it could do when the lease terminated, and Belchier walked away.

For a while, Gell conducted all the business of collecting rents from subtenants and paying local taxes, usually the leaseholder's job, also commissioning John Gorham to survey the estate and advise on reletting it.[50] One option was to lease it all out on a building lease — for a new developer to take it, demolishing and rebuilding *all* the buildings, in which case a rent of £75 per annum for a sixty-one-year term would be the best available. The other option was to let only the damaged area on a building lease, and the remainder on a repairing lease for twenty-one or thirty-one years. In this case, the surveyor advised, a rental of £110 could be expected on the repairing lease.[51] Either option would have represented a considerable increase on the former rental of £50. The School, not surprisingly, was to go for the latter option, but split the land into four areas, each separately leased. Three of the four new leases were repairing leases, for a term of thirty years, and all started on the same day, 12 June 1769.[52] Each was concluded with a local Southwark businessman.

James Bues was already established as the landlord of the Fox victualling house in 1768. While the Fox had been damaged by the fire, Bues quickly came to an arrangement with Gell for a temporary reduction in the rent,[53] then took on a new lease covering the Fox, the house adjacent to it on White Street, and the whole of the east side of Bangor Court.[54] John Atkinson took the second repairing lease. He already held a substantial part of the coachyard, and was subletting some other houses in the area, so the new repairing lease may have just been an extension of that arrangement. This lease took in the area occupied by coach-house and stables, the meeting house and its burial ground, the alley towards White Street, and houses on either side of that alley. On White Street, the Fox (No. 1, White Street) and No. 2 were in the Bues lease, and the Bull (No. 10) and No. 11 on the other side of the alley were in the Atkinson lease. Between these, Nos 3 to 9, each with a yard and shed behind, formed the third repairing lease, let to John Griffith, described as a broker. The area damaged by fire, comprising the west side of Bangor Court, took a little longer to let. Eventually, Charles Cole took it from Michaelmas 1769, on a building lease of sixty-one years.

With these four leases let, the School's annual income from Southwark had increased from £50 to £154 2s. 6d., rather better than the surveyor had anticipated.

The three repairing leases terminated in 1798, the estate now as in Figure 7. Two leases were renewed at their termination with the same family. William and Hannah Allen, Hannah being the daughter of James Bues, stayed on at the Fox, where her husband also had a line- and twine-spinning workshop. On the White Street frontage, John and Thomas Griffith continued the lease their father had taken out.[55]

What had been Atkinson's lease, now including a brewery run by James Hogg (with his warehouse in the former meeting house) and what had been Chapman's coach-house and stables, but now described as ruinated, were let to William Willmott from 1798. He, a carpenter and joiner, was to redevelop the area completely, to become 'Willmott's Buildings'. The lease required him to repair five houses along the alley and to build six new ones — but he went much further. By 1807 he was renting out two properties on the alley corners and a further twenty properties in Willmott's Buildings, grouped around a T-shaped alley. By 1815, he had thirty-one properties on the site,[56] including his own: he and his family lived in the largest building, at the intersection of the T. Willmott was behind the opening of the Antigallican, a victuallers' on the corner of the alley, which later became the Royal Standard. He renewed the lease in 1837 at a higher ground rent, and in due course it passed to daughter Emily Garrett, who added five more properties.[57]

Meanwhile, a widowed Hannah Allen had continued at the Fox until 1804, when she sold the lease, still comprising the Fox and the east of Bangor Court behind. She was followed by a succession of publicans who also took on the Court. It was Crown Dansie who renewed in 1831, then it was transferred again, culminating in William Paget holding the lease in 1857.

Anthony Gell, who had done so much for the School following the fire in 1768, had continued as the School's agent for many years, operating out of Westminster Abbey cloisters, his many roles later transferring to his son John Henry Gell. The latter was succeeded as Receiver-General by Robert Marsh, who seamlessly took on the School agency — so, nearly a hundred years after the fire, the line of succession of the Receiver-Generalship also determined who was acting for Friars School.[58] In 1858, Marsh wrote to the School about Paget's lease,

> The houses [in Bangor Court] have been condemned by the Police authorities under the Act, and have been taken down by Mr Paget. The public house (which he occupies) is shored up, and appears in a dangerous state. Mr Paget informs me he expects notice to pull down both the side walls in the Court at the back of the public house. He says he has already paid for the contract for

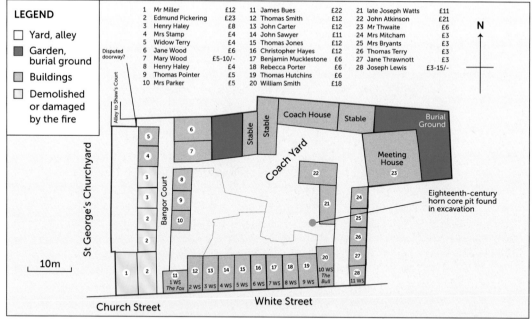

LEGEND

- ☐ Yard, alley
- ■ Garden, burial ground
- ▨ Buildings
- ☐ Demolished or damaged by the fire

1	Mr Miller	£12	11	James Bues	£22	21	late Joseph Watts	£11
2	Edmund Pickering	£23	12	Thomas Smith	£12	22	John Atkinson	£21
3	Henry Haley	£8	13	John Carter	£12	23	Mr Thwaite	£6
4	Mrs Stamp	£4	14	John Sawyer	£11	24	Mrs Mitcham	£3
5	Widow Terry	£4	15	Thomas Jones	£12	25	Mrs Bryants	£3
6	Jane Wood	£6	16	Christopher Hayes	£12	26	Thomas Terry	£3
7	Mary Wood	£5-10/-	17	Benjamin Mucklestone	£6	27	Jane Thrawnott	£3
8	Henry Haley	£4	18	Rebecca Porter	£6	28	Joseph Lewis	£3-15/-
9	Thomas Pointer	£5	19	Thomas Hutchins	£6			
10	Mrs Parker	£5	20	William Smith	£18			

Fig. 6. Estate Plan after the Fire of 14 July 1768 with rents and tenancies. Based largely on narrative in FRIARS 85, and other plans.

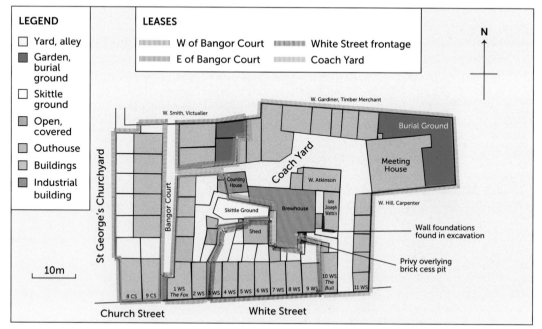

LEGEND

- ☐ Yard, alley
- ■ Garden, burial ground
- ☐ Skittle ground
- ▨ Open, covered
- ▨ Outhouse
- ▨ Buildings
- ■ Industrial building

LEASES

- ▦ W of Bangor Court
- ▦ E of Bangor Court
- ▦ White Street frontage
- ▦ Coach Yard

Fig. 7. Estate Plan c. 1798. Based largely on plans in FRIARS 121.

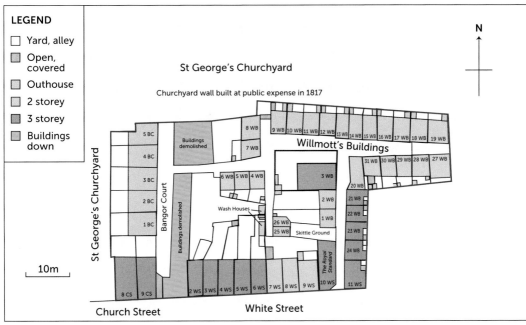

Fig. 8.   Estate Plan *c.* 1860. Based largely on TNA ED/6355 and later plans.

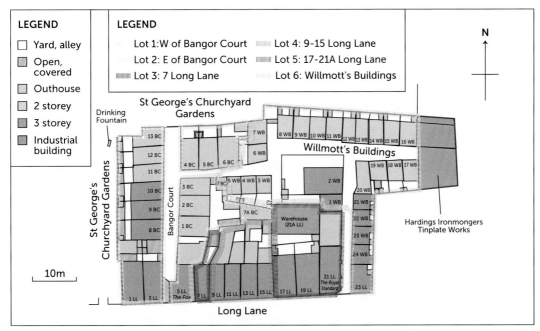

Fig. 9.   Estate Plan *c.* 1895. Based largely on property title plans in
LMA P92/GEO/334 and OS maps with Lot numbers for 1895 sale.

pulling down the houses and shoring up his own home £34. And he informs me he has laid out £191 in general repairs. This property is in a deplorable condition, and something must be done about it without delay. It may be advisable to take down the public house also, considering the state in which it is.[59]

It seemed clear that, with the buildings falling down, Paget was in great difficulty. He planned to travel to Bangor to plead directly with the School governors, although it is not clear what good this would have done. This trip probably did not happen, for by September Paget was in gaol. He was insolvent, having mortgaged the near-worthless property to the Meux Brewery, and imprisoned as a debtor at Horsemonger Lane Gaol.[60]

Inevitably, perhaps, the Fox also had to be demolished. It was pulled down in January 1859, when, according to Marsh, 'the thieves of the neighbourhood are helping themselves to what they can steal in the night'.[61] The estate plan of around 1860 (Fig. 8) shows an area of open ground where these dangerous buildings had once stood, and the School found itself again faced with problems. It took them until 1864 to recover full possession of the plot, now empty and boarded up, and they seriously contemplated selling off all the land.[62] However, having been advised that the interest they could earn on sale proceeds was well below a likely rent, they asked the Charity Commissioners if they could relet the property, and this was agreed.[63]

The School was once again looking for somebody to redevelop part of the estate on a long tenancy, and this went to William Humphries, who took the east side of Bangor Court on a 99-year lease. No. 2 White Street had also been part of the plot previously leased with the Fox, but this building was, just about, still standing, and formed a separate shorter lease, also taken by Humphries to become his wife's millinery and the family home. The buildings put up on the west side of the Court after the earlier fire were also in a poor condition, and there are suggestions that the long lease on that side had been neglected both by the School and its occupants, so when they were leased to Charles How in 1869 he, too, was required to rebuild. How went on to sublet the Court buildings (but not the part of the lease which fronted on to Church Street) to Humphries — so it seems that it was Humphries, the builder, who rebuilt both sides of this Court from 1869: buildings later photographed around 1900 (Fig. 10).

Up to the middle of the nineteenth century, sanitation at the estate was basic, with a small number of outdoor privies and cesspits, and wells for water supply. A public system of sewerage was introduced by the Metropolitan Commission of Sewers Act of 1848, the function later absorbed into the Metropolitan Board of Works. At Willmott's Buildings in 1856 the School reimbursed Emily Garrett £25 towards the costs of drains to the sewers, and later it was reported that she needed also to lay a water supply to each of the water closets, and to provide each house with a 'copper' for washing.[64]

Fig. 10.   Bangor Court,
looking northwards,
photograph, *c.* 1890.
© London Metropolitan
Archives, City of London
SC/PHL/01/365/991
(COLLAGE: The London
Picture Archive,
ref. 116050).

Although she appears only reluctantly compliant in this correspondence, an article in the *Lancet* in 1865 holds her up as one of the more enlightened landlords in this respect,

> Wilmott's-buildings [...] is the best-ordered series of houses visited [...] They possess an advantage, however, not enjoyed, we understand, by any other cottage property in St. George's, Southwark — viz. a constant water-supply. The proprietress, to her great honour be it known, has fixed two water-taps in the court, from which water may be obtained at all times. The use of these taps is not limited to the occupiers of Wilmott's Buildings.[65]

Humphries' rebuilding of the east side of Bangor Court from 1868 included from the outset the latest in sanitation. A plan sent to the School shows separate external WCs for each house, all connected to a nine-inch drain coming from within Willmott's Buildings and running the length of Bangor Court towards the road, and shows communal wash-houses.[66]

By the 1870s, Bangor Court had all been rebuilt and Willmott's Buildings was a single development from then on. The buildings of Nos 3–9 White Street, the remaining lease, had not had any comprehensive work done, and the School commissioned a survey of these properties in 1872 before considering what next to do. The results suggest a lot of work to be done on the three-storey buildings of Nos 3–6, but even more work required on Nos 7–9, where just about every part of the buildings required renewal.[67] After some weighing up of competing proposals, the School decided to split the lease area in two: Nos 3–6 were leased to Andrew Nelson, a haberdasher, already a subtenant at No. 3, who covenanted to spend £500 on repairs and took the properties for forty years. The older properties were leased for just three years to Nathaniel Kelly, a butcher who occupied one of the properties and who probably just wanted to stay where he was.

While the lease to Kelly may seem just to have deferred a problem for all, in fact it was cleverly timed to coincide with the end date of Garrett's lease on Willmott's Buildings. Preparing for that renewal, J. William Hughes, clerk to the governors, advised at some length on 9 October 1877.[68]

Hughes reported that the pub at No. 10 White Street, now the Royal Standard, leased to Robert Angel Freeman, was 'deficient', with a sitting room only 7 foot square, no urinal and no WC. Freeman had to use the former skittle ground outside as both scullery and stable, and had nowhere to store casks. Meanwhile, 1 Willmott's Buildings, just behind the pub, was a 'most wretched tenement' and it would be an improvement to pull it down. Nos 25 and 26 Willmott's Buildings, lying behind Nos 7–9 White Street, were small and also deserved demolition. Hughes recommended that Nos 1, 25 and 26 should be demolished and the land combined with Nos 7–10 White Street in a new lease, thereby giving the Royal Standard room to expand and provide a means of dealing with the dilapidations at Nos 7–9. Hughes had explored these recommendations with neighbouring occupiers, having had several proposals from them. He concluded that the best offer was from Freeman, to take a new lease covering Nos 7–10 White Street and the area of the properties to be demolished behind, paying a premium of £700 and an annual rent of £120.

These recommendations were accepted. A new lease from the School to Freeman covered the area of all these buildings. He was required to rebuild this block as envisaged by Hughes, with the School retaining a say in approving what would be built.[69] This led to three sets of architects' proposal drawings.[70] The choice made was of a design by Thomas Arnold, building three new properties on White Street where previously there had been four, allowing expansion of the Royal Standard. The buildings as they appear in Figure 11 are substantially as in Arnold's drawings. Despite the successful completion of the development, Freeman — beset by health and money problems — killed himself soon afterwards.[71]

While these redevelopments were taking place, what had been Church Street, White Street and Long Lane were consolidated into a single street name along the length: Long Lane, as it had been in the sixteenth century,

Fig. 11. White Street, looking westwards, photograph, *c.* 1890. © London Metropolitan Archives, City of London *SC/PHL/01/371/81/13102.* (COLLAGE: The London Picture Archive, ref. 114447).

and is today. This was to be numbered with odd numbers along the north side, so what had been Nos 8 and 9 Church Street became Nos 1 and 3 Long Lane. Nos 1–10 White Street, ten properties which after Freeman's rebuilding became nine, numbered 5 to 21 Long Lane, with No. 11 White Street on the eastern corner becoming No. 23 Long Lane.

Emily Garrett indicated that she was no longer interested in renewing the Willmott's Buildings lease now that the public house and three of the alley properties had been taken away. She retired to Penge, where she was to live to the age of 106, having been widowed for seventy-five years.[72]

The School invited tenders for the remainder of Willmott's Buildings, won by William Godbolt, but before the paperwork was completed Godbolt complained that the property was not what he expected, he would need to do it up and evict bad tenants, and he was not prepared to carry on with the lease unless the rent was reduced or the term extended.[73] This culminated in a temporary arrangement, in which Godbolt would act as the School's agent in return for a commission of 10 per cent of the rents collected, with the School reimbursing all his outlay on taxes and maintenance. Acting as agent only worsened Godbolt's opinion. He found that tenants would get into arrears, and traditionally relied on earnings from hop-picking each summer to pay their debts — but then the crop failed in 1879. Godbolt pulled out altogether. The School negotiated with William Walter Johnson, the second tenderer in the earlier exercise, and eventually agreed a lease with him but at a lower rent.[74]

G. Harding & Sons, the ironmongers to the east, was an expanding business, and had earlier expressed an interest in the School land. Negotiations between 1877 and 1880 led to Johnson subletting Nos 18, 19, 27 and 28 Willmotts' Buildings, the eastern corner, contiguous with Hardings. The School concurred, amending the covenants in the lease so that the trade of 'tinman' was no longer prohibited.[75] Hardings went on to pull down the tenements, and built glass-roofed offices here, connected to their larger site.[76] Consequent on the demolition of some of Willmott's Buildings, these properties too were renumbered. Figure 9 shows the land, with renumbered properties, as it was at the end of the nineteenth century.

Following the Welsh Intermediate Education Act of 1889, the School, which had been an independent foundation with its own endowment, was, despite resistance from its governors, transferred into the public sector with its endowment now vested in Caernarfonshire County Council as the education authority. The Council had no need of the Southwark estate but needed money for building, at Friars School itself and other schools. Accordingly, they arranged for Horne, Son and Eversfield to sell the estate at auction on 25 November 1895, in six lots corresponding to the leases then running. Five out of the six were sold that day, but the Willmott's Buildings site was still proving a problem in relation to its difficult tenants and did not attract sufficient interest. Before Caernarfonshire needed to decide what to do, it turned out that the London County Council (LCC) intended to take this land for street improvements and a sale was negotiated directly, the last piece of land disposed of in 1899.[77] The LCC went on to acquire all the freeholds recently sold by Caernarfonshire and the corresponding leases, the only exception being the sublease, now part of Hardings' works. The LCC also took the neighbouring churchyard. The resulting works widened Long Lane, so that what had been the street frontage of White Street is roughly in the middle of the present road. They built a short length of Tabard Street to the north-east of the church (pedestrianized today) and laid out the St George's Churchyard Gardens on the residual land. Building plots off the road were then sold off.

Although the buildings that stand today have been rebuilt since the LCC road works, the shape of the plots, the line of the road and the adjoining gardens are the same now as were created then. The story of the School estate ends here.

Residents

The School owned the freehold of the land, and the archives detail a succession of leaseholders, but who actually lived and worked here? A few leaseholders were also residents, but generally all of these sublet to many tenants, and these ordinary people are frequently missing from the archives. Just now and then do we get some glimpses.

At the very beginning of the period, we learn from legal action concerning the School's title to the land the names of a few of the tenants — Thomas Marler,[78] Alice Hannell[79] and Maryon Huntington.[80] The last testified to paying a penny a week for her tenement behind the White Hind, having been there for some forty years. No more is known about them.

In 1617, we learn something about the tenants. When Edward Bates was renegotiating his lease that year, his special pleading describes them as 'poor labouringe people [...] without any trade either of shopkepinge or of handycrafts men, but only daie labourers, chimneyswepers and brome men or such like', often leaving without paying their rents, to his loss.[81]

Registers of baptisms, marriages and burials, when first introduced, recorded only bare details. However, from 1698 up to his death in 1713, John Hopkins, clerk to the Rector of St George the Martyr, took it upon himself to record more than he needed in the christening and burial registers. At baptism, he got into the habit of recording a rudimentary address and occupation of the father (but nothing of the mother); at burial, he recorded similar details of the household head. Over the period, after eliminating duplicate mentions of the same persons, 132 men can be identified as residents within the School estate.[82]

There were seven soldiers, and twenty-three described as seamen or mariners: it is not always clear if these were naval or merchant seamen. Adam Bassett junior was the son of another Adam Bassett, a weaver, who had lived in Boar's Head Alley and was sexton of the church. The son initially followed his father's trade but then went to sea, joining Their Majesties' Ship *Ossory* in 1692.[83] Bassett junior's family continued to live in the alley, where it seems he was usually home for Christmas — as the baptism of all four of his children in August to October would suggest. TMS *Ossory* was a ninety-gun second-rate ship of the line of the Royal Navy, where Bassett served initially as an ordinary seaman. His naval career developed; he was described as a Trumpeter in 1700 and specifically a Sea Trumpeter after that. A Trumpeter was an important position on board a warship at this time, with some ceremonial functions, but also used just to make a lot of noise as ships went into battle.[84] Sadly, his naval career did not last long: Adam Bassett junior was buried at St George the Martyr in December 1702.

As well as the soldiers and sailors, there were a few unskilled workers (the labourers and broom-men earlier mentioned by Edward Bates, but no chimney-sweeper), but more with manufacturing and construction skills. Thirty of what Bates would have called handicrafts men — weavers, spinners, basket-makers and shoemakers — point to one group of local industries, and there were also glass polishers and a spectacle-maker. Six men were described as victuallers. There was also one Chelsea pensioner, four more described as pensioners and six people described as 'poor' or 'beggar'. This disparate picture suggests that the improvement in the properties following Gore's investment was now attracting a slightly better class of tenant.

By the mid-eighteenth century a survey of tenants undertaken for the School in 1755, Anthony Gell's detailed accounts in 1768 and the Poor Rate Records for the same period draw a broad picture. John Wood ran a tallow chandlery at the corner of Church Street and Bangor Court, later to be succeeded by Edmund Pickering, the proprietor at the time of the fire. Wood also rented a house at the north end of Bangor Court, where his widow Jane remained, reduced to a 'dealer in old clothes' by her burial in 1769. Next door to them was Mary Wood, maybe a sister-in-law, she a sextoness at the church. These two houses occupied by the Woods were a better class of house than the others in the alleys: they alone had gardens at this time and the houses themselves were bigger. Apart from these two, the properties in the alleys were of lower quality than the street frontage, commanding lower rents. Only the properties fronting the street and the two better houses in Bangor Court were liable to pay the Poor Tax, with Window Tax charged only on the larger properties, even on the street. In the smaller properties, we learn from Gell's accounts that Thomas Pointer and Mrs Terry were both very poor and already much in arrears; Jane Thrawnott was not only poor but had three children down with smallpox.[85]

From 1780, the availability of land tax records[86] gives names of some occupants. Some of the names recorded in 1768 were still there in 1780, and other names continue year after year after that, suggesting some stability of tenure both along the street frontage and behind. From various sources, we learn the trades of some of them: Alexander Curry in Bangor Court, a cordwainer;[87] in White Street, Elizabeth Stedman, a nurse, her husband John a carpenter,[88] William Secker, a dealer in coals and potatoes,[89] William Wiseman, a turner, his wife Sarah, a seamstress,[90] and John Child, a tinplate worker.[91] One of the longest-residing families was the Mucklestones. Benjamin Mucklestone and his wife Elizabeth christened three children and buried three stillbirths here between 1764 and 1774. He continued in the land tax records until 1798, but died that year, aged sixty-six.

After the turn of the nineteenth century, William Willmott's development of the former coachyard area created denser housing: many more, and smaller, properties. This drove it downmarket. Something similar happened once Hannah Allen sold on her lease to successors who did not have the same familial tie to the locality. In contrast, the properties fronting Church Street and White Street were now developing into a respectable row of shops, generally family businesses with the proprietors and family living above the shop. With the aid of Censuses, street directories and sundry other records, it is possible to sketch the development of the trades represented along the street over the course of the nineteenth century (Fig. 12).

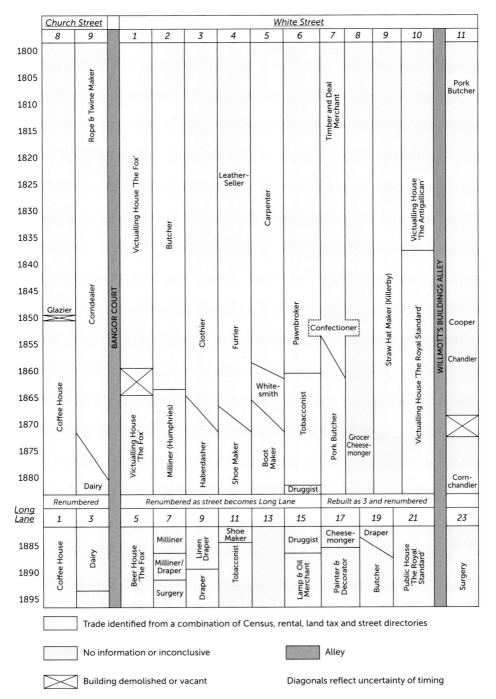

Fig. 12.   Trades of nineteenth-century street frontage shop occupiers.

One such family were the Killerbys. John Killerby and Charlotte Honeywood were married in 1821 in the parish of St Mary, Newington. After an intervening period at St Peter Paul's Wharf, by 1827 they had moved to No. 9 White Street, one of the three smaller cottages. John Killerby was recorded a maker of straw hats, but was made bankrupt, with Charlotte continuing the hat-making after that, carrying on the business long after being widowed in 1846.

On 18 May 1845, their eldest son John, then aged nineteen, was working for Craster Humble, a hop-merchant at No. 82 High Street, Borough, when a letter was received, threatening,

> I merely send you this to put you on your guard, and if you do keep John Killerby in your service, out of revenge I will take and murder one of your children; and at all events I will make the attempt to set your house on fire [...][92]

John's brother Henry, aged seventeen, whose handwriting matched the letter, was tried but acquitted of sending it. This was not the end of the trouble. In August of the same year, Henry Killerby was accused of attempting to poison ten-year-old Elizabeth Clouter. The poison was oxalic acid, as used in his mother's hat business. There was a continuing vendetta against the brother John, with one letter forged in John's name, claiming he had sent the poison. This time, Henry was convicted, and sentenced to twelve months' imprisonment.[93] Then, soon after his release, he threatened to murder Elizabeth Spriggs, another young neighbour, this time having made the threat in his own name, and was sent down for another twelve months.[94] In 1849 he was once more on the trail of Elizabeth Spriggs. He had threatened murder by poisoning, and was again convicted.[95] Clearly a serial offender, he was sentenced this time to fifteen years' transportation to Australia, where he died in 1852.

Charlotte Killerby remained at No. 9 White Street, with daughter Harriett now joining her in the trade. She had given birth to eight children, six of them here; three had died young, and one had now been transported. Charlotte's sister, also widowed, had moved in and the extended family was still there in the 1871 Census. Charlotte Killerby was the longest established of all the estate residents, having lived there nearly half a century, and with an attachment to the area that may explain why 'untenantable' properties were nevertheless still occupied. She was to die in 1876, shortly before the old cottages of Nos 7–9 White Street, including her home, were finally demolished.

The 1841 Census gives the first complete picture of residents: 314 in total. In the alleys, the most common occupation is simply 'Labourer', and just over half the adult population were born in Ireland. There was not the same stability of tenure as on the street: just four out of eighty households recorded in the alleys in 1841 were still there in 1851. However, the birthplace of children showed a much larger proportion had been born in the parish or neighbouring parishes, suggesting they were settled in the area, if not the particular property.

Some trends are evident over the course of the nineteenth century. The working-class occupiers of the alleys in 1841 and 1851 were generally migrants into London, the majority from Ireland. As time passed, the Irish migrants were joined by movers from the west country, other parts of England, and a handful from Wales, Scotland and overseas. The greater trend, however, was the consolidation of the London-born working class. By the end of the century, the alleys were predominantly London-born. Occupations of alley residents by 1891 were mainly manual labour, often at dockside, and other unskilled or semi-skilled trades. More than in earlier years, there are a number of occupations that suggest working in manufacturing, including tin workers, presumably at Hardings' neighbouring works. Figure 13 shows a few residents at the end of the century.

The alleys (but not the street) had reverted to the tenancy of the unskilled, as in Edward Bates's day — but, still, these were not the lowest class. In Charles Booth's poverty maps, they belong to the category 'Very

Fig. 13. Willmott's Buildings, looking eastwards, photograph, c. 1890. © London Metropolitan Archives, City of London *SC/PHL/02/0953/997* (COLLAGE: The London Picture Archive, ref. 281853).

poor, casual', which was his lowest-but-one category[96] and it was clear that Collier's Rents to the east was considered worse.[97] In contrast, the street-front properties housed what Edward Bates would have recognized as shopkeepers and craftsmen, and Booth called 'Fairly comfortable. Good ordinary earnings'.

Mapping the Topography from the Archives

How has it been possible to trace the estate back to the sixteenth century, and to relate this to the present-day layout? How reliable are the records and how accurately can the land be mapped? This cannot be deduced from the School archives alone. The evidence assembled here comes from plans and narrative descriptions, both in the School archives and elsewhere, combining in some cases with maps of the wider area around the site. Some corroboration has been possible from archaeological excavation in 1999–2000 described by Douglas,[98] even though the excavation was limited to part of the area and was principally concerned with Roman remains lower down.

The explanation is best given in reverse chronological order, starting with Figure 9 and working backwards.

Figure 9: 1895

Figure 9 shows the estate as it was when the School's ownership ended. It is derived from the 'Abstract of Title' from 1903 in the London Metropolitan Archives, of which Figure 14 is one part,[99] Ordnance Survey (OS) maps published in 1895[100] and the Goad Fire Insurance map of 1887.[101] There is a fair measure of agreement between these sources, even as far as yards and outhouses. The OS maps show the Church of St George the Martyr to the west and the former wall of the Marshalsea prison to the north, both features still standing, which allows the School estate buildings to be plotted in the same relative positions on modern maps. After overlaying the earlier plans of the buildings to the later plans, this was validated by reference to a similar overlay in a Land Tax redemption plan of 23 June 1908.[102]

The buildings are shaded as one-, two- or three-storey, derived from the Goad plans, photographic evidence of Figures 10, 11 and 13, elevation drawings and some narrative descriptions in the School archives.[103] The boundaries of the lots in the 1895 sale are shown. The land sublet to Hardings is shown in the Goad plan as brick-built with large glass rooflights over, shown in a little more detail in a Land Tax redemption plan of 1900 and in a later article about Hardings.[104] Building numbers have been taken from

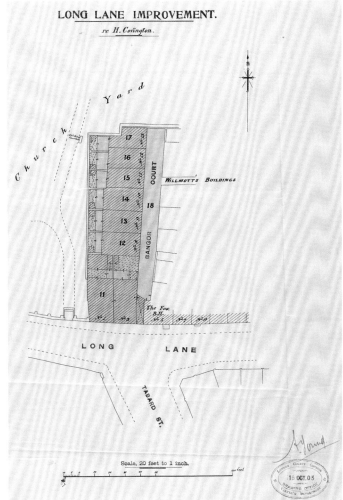

Fig. 14. Plan of Bangor Court and part of Long Lane from the Abstract of Title of the London County Council to Freehold Land, 1903. London Metropolitan Archives, City of London *P92/ GEO/334*, reproduced by permission of the parish of St George the Martyr, Southwark.

the 1903 plans, the same numbers also shown on a Land Tax redemption plan. The building labelled Warehouse (Emery Paper Works at the time of the Goad plan) was a later development by the successors to the Freeman lease, numbered 21A Long Lane.

Figure 8: 1860s

Figure 8 goes back further, to pre-date Hardings' acquisition of the corner and the redevelopment around the Royal Standard. The OS maps of 1878/9[105] show the boundary of the estate around the area later let to Hardings. Having been surveyed in 1872, the OS maps pre-date Freeman's redevelopment of the area around the Royal Standard, so they show the outline of the earlier buildings along what was then White Street; this also pre-dates the combination of Church Street and White Street into Long Lane. Willmott's Buildings is shown at its maximum extent, after Emily Garrett's additions and before the demolition of Nos 1, 24 and 25, and with the older numbering scheme.[106]

The area to the east of Bangor Court is shown as it was between 1859 and 1865, after the demolition of the Fox and the eastern side of Bangor Court, based on a plan in the National Archives.[107] This also shows five buildings on the west side of Bangor Court, when the later rebuilding created six on that side. In other respects, yards and outhouses are generally assumed to be the same as in Figure 9, except that the wash-houses opposite Nos 24 and 25 Willmott's Buildings and the skittle ground behind the Royal Standard are taken from a plan from just before the 1878 redevelopment.[108]

The northern boundary of the School land in Figure 8 was the wall of St George's Churchyard, built in 1816–17. Before that, the churchyard had been confined to a very small area around the church. Plans for an extension were drawn up that threatened to take parts of Shaw's Court, Bangor Court and Willmott's Buildings, and a Parliamentary Bill was introduced to authorize it. The School commissioned a surveyor to value its land and argue a case for compensation, but in the event the scheme as agreed took Shaw's Court and land right up to, but not extending into, the School land.[109] A tall wall was built as the boundary between the new churchyard and the School land. It bore the legend 'This Wall was built at the Expence of the Parifhoners of St. George, Southwark, in the Year of our Lord, 1817'.[110] The wall is clear in the background of Figure 10, and a trace of its foundations is hinted at by a faint ridge in the gardens today.

Figure 7: c. 1798

The source for the earlier plan of Figure 7 requires some explanation. Early in the nineteenth century, Parliament instituted commissioners to enquire into the affairs of charities, which elicited detailed responses from each charity and documented them in lengthy reports. To prepare for their enquiry, the School drew up 'THE BOOK OF THE BANGOR FREE GRAMMAR SCHOOL',[111] which collated in one place copies of all the fundamental documents concerning the governance and property of the School, for ready reference. This rich source to some extent duplicates material found in primary sources, but also provides a handy collation, even now. It seems that the School governors found it so useful that they continued to update the book with later records, after the original enquiries were complete. The Commissioners' report of 1834 when they dealt with Friars School is another snapshot of the School's situation. Despite the careful preparation, the commissioners' report is a little muddled, listing the land east of Bangor Court twice — once as a lease to Allen, then again as a lease to Dansie, although these were successive leases of the same piece of property.[112]

The School's 'BOOK' contains the next piece of evidence for the reconstruction, namely copies of plans attached to the three repairing leases entered into in 1768 and renewed thirty years later. It appears that plans were originally attached to the 1768 leases, which were then used again for the renewal: the plans as copied contain details relevant to both dates. Despite being only copies, the three separate plans, appropriately resized and rotated, fit into each other well. Moreover, because the lot numbers of the 1895 sale corresponded to leases, which continued, or were subdivisions of, earlier leases, it is possible, again after suitable resizing and rotation, to fit the 1768/98 plans directly on to the later reconstructions. Buildings such as the Brewhouse and Counting House are taken from the lease plans (Figure 15 is the example of Willmott's lease).

However, the 'BOOK' contained only three leases, with no equivalent detail for the longer-term building lease which had been let for the area west of Bangor Court. Details for this area have been derived from 1860 plans[113] showing the layout before the rebuilding undertaken by Humphries, with less detail as regards outbuildings.

The property described as 'late Joseph Watts's' is identified as such on the plan in the 'BOOK', Anthony Gell's accounts showing him as an ex-tenant in 1768.[114] The name of Joseph Watts has not been traced elsewhere, but the significance of this building is that its south-western corner was found in the archaeological excavation (Figure 16). This excavation found external walls and an internal floor, both of unfrogged orange brick, with buttresses of an internal fireplace. It originally had a doorway opening on to its south side. In a later phase dated to the mid-nineteenth century, a red brick floor was laid over the earlier one, and the original entrance on the south side was blocked up: a conversion that corresponds to William Willmott's development of the area: evidently he adapted the older building, with a new doorway opening on to the alley, and it became No. 1 Willmott's Buildings. A later phase included another layer of brick, interpreted in the archaeology as a later floor, corresponding to the outhouse behind the rebuilt Royal Standard.

Figure 7 also shows a four-seat privy straddling the boundary between the Coachyard lease and the White Street lease, with two seats facing the Watts building and one seat associated with each of Nos 8 and 9 White Street. This small building stood over a cesspit, found in the excavation, built of English-bonded orange and purple bricks. With a shard of pottery dated to c. 1810, the archaeological interpretation was an early nineteenth-century construction, but the plan evidence takes it back to an earlier date.

The degree to which the plans of 1768 and 1798 could be assembled and then correspond closely with the late nineteenth-century OS maps, which themselves can be overlain on modern maps, suggests that the lease boundaries, as shown in Figure 7, are accurate within a margin of error of less than a metre. Although only a faint feature, the ridge observable in the present-day gardens also helps to confirm the northern boundary. Then,

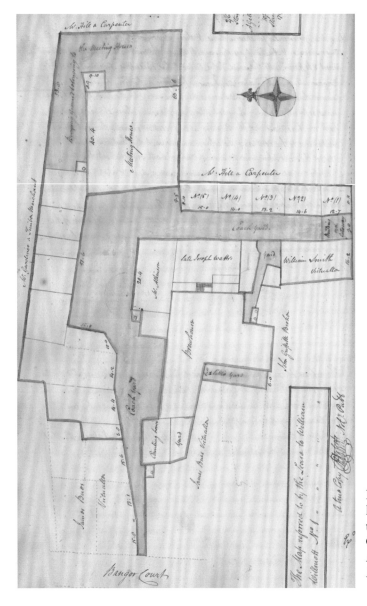

Fig. 15.   Copy of lease plan relating to Coachyard area. © Gwynedd Archives *FRIARS* 121.

Fig. 16.   Foundations of former Joseph Watts building, viewed from the south, 1999–2000 excavations, photograph. © Museum of London Archaeological Archive and Research Centre *File LGK99, Film 1.*

after drawing in the buildings from the eighteenth-century plans, the fact that both the Watts house and the cesspit under the privy were found in the archaeology in substantially the positions indicated also helps to confirm the accuracy of the drawing.

Figure 7 also shows a Brewhouse in 1798. Occupied by James Hogg from 1780, this had previously been run by William Atkinson, the tenant of the house on the northern corner of the L-shaped block, who had inherited from his father John on his death in 1777, the father having been the tenant in 1768. There is no mention of a brewhouse in the rental of 1768, simply 'house and lands', so it must be concluded that the Atkinsons developed a brewhouse on this site in the course of the 1768–98 lease.

The 1798 plan can be compared with the detail for this area in Horwood's 1799 map (detail in Figure 17). Horwood has the right number of properties along the street, but has no detail for the yard behind, with its meeting house, brewhouse and so on. Horwood has two through connections between Bangor Court and New Court (which had been Shaw's Court): there had been such a connection, but it would have been closed off by this date. Horwood's label for 'Bangor Court' is misplaced, and has a label

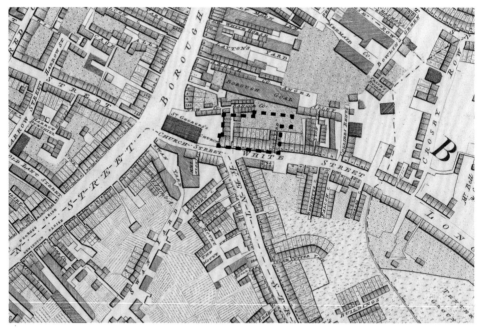

Fig. 17.   Richard Horwood, *Plan of the Cities of London and Westminster, the Borough of Southwark, and Parts adjoining*, 1799, detail. From the New York Public Library (*Carl H. Pforzheimer Collection of Shelley and His Circle, "E3"*).

'Goat Yard' for the eastern alley of White Street into the coachyard; this name has not been found in any other source, but may simply represent a mis-hearing of 'Coachyard'. This all suggests that a grand map such as Horwood's did not concern itself with the detail of outbuildings and back alleys; by the time of William Faden's 1819 revision of Horwood, the alleys had been more faithfully added, and it also showed the newly extended churchyard.

Figure 6: 1768

Figure 6 aims to show the estate in the immediate aftermath of the 1768 fire, largely based on Anthony Gell's reports to the School. An undated plan in the School archives, showing the west side of Bangor Court, has dotted lines indicating plot boundaries of what had been sites of burnt-down buildings; this is probably Gell's sketch plan of the fire damage. Two buildings at the back of Bangor Court still stood, and the connecting alley to New Court was open.[115] The coachyard buildings are shown as in the earlier plan described in the next section, but which were known to be still there in 1768 from narrative descriptions in leases. Buildings on White Street and on the east of Bangor Court are assumed to be much the same as in 1798. Dotted lines in the area between buildings show what were to become lease boundaries later in the year; given their irregular shapes, these must have corresponded to some features on the ground existing in 1768: in particular the area shown in 1798 as a skittle ground belonging to the Fox may have been established as such before 1768.

At this time, because Belchier and Waite had abdicated their leaseholding responsibilities, Gell was dealing directly with the tenants. Although he did not explicitly list who lived where, his logical documentation, corroborated by a few details from the 1755 survey,[116] has enabled tenants, and their rents, to be associated with each building, and these are labelled in Figure 6.

Figure 4: c. 1730

The plan of Figure 4 is derived principally from a plan of around 1732. In the 1901 History of Friars School, Barber and Lewis refer to a 1732 survey,[117] and their description of it matches a plan, now undated, in the School archives. This did not show individual houses, just numbering how many were in each block, yet it was drawn to a scale.[118] If this plan belongs to 1732, it is nearly contemporaneous with another important document. During what had been Gore's long lease, eventually taken over by Chapman, the Bishop of Bangor commissioned John Willit to enquire, covertly, about what changes had been made to the estate. Willit reported back in 1729,

> Ye estate here with its tenements has varied its names; so what in the Lease is Called ye Alms house is now Called Bangor Court; containing several messuages & now let to twelve undertenants the whole amounting to £64.10s p/annum; & brick buildings & is a thoroughfare from Whitestreet through Bangor Court into Shaws Court & so into the Borough which passage into Shaws Court & a house of £6 p/annum, what was added to the Premises by Walter Gore. The Garden Plott then so called is now built into several Coach houses, & stable with a large old tenement (but in good repair) with a meeting house let at £25 p/annum. Brick buildings the premises one time in the Possession of Edward Bates abutting south on the King's highway; & of Thos. Bates lying in Long Lane is now called White Street & all from houses from St. George's wall on the street side & one house beyond the sheers att Sheers ally end; containing 19 houses now let at £140 p/annum; all but two of them are brick buildings & all in good repair & 5 of them new & I believe are generally well tenanted. The totall of the Rack Rent is £265.10s p/annum.[119]

After redevelopment begun by Gore and continued by Chapman had transformed the site, Willit's letter is a key document that enables the lay of the land to be reconciled with narrative descriptions in earlier leases, and the 1732 plan supports this. What had once been White Hind Alley was now Bangor Court (although was more frequently referred to as New Alley in official documents). The Sheers gave its name to the alley behind, when earlier it had been named after the Boar's Head. As to the western boundary of the School land, Willit referred to 'St George's wall'; this would have been a fairly new wall at that time, as, in a later plan,[120] it is annotated 'St George's Church Yard Wall built at Parish Expence in 1720 as appears by a Stone in the s^d wall': a wording echoed in the 1817 wall.

The 1732 plan shows '4 old houses' at what would later be called Nos 7–10 White Street. These and the site of the Fox were the only buildings identified as 'old', so probably therefore included the two non-brick buildings mentioned by Willit, suggesting that they had not been included in the redevelopment by Gore or Chapman. No. 10 was later rebuilt to become the Antigallican, then the Royal Standard, but the shabby two-storey cottages of Nos 7–9 White Street, lived in by Benjamin Mucklestone, Charlotte Killerby and others, and still standing in 1873, were possibly still the early buildings. Although in that year there was some brick in their construction, a proposal then that brickwork could be taken down and rebuilt[121] suggests this was infill in a building that was essentially timber-framed. This evidence together suggests that the buildings which survived until 1873 could have been those which stood in Geoffrey Glyn's time.

Figure 4 also includes the L-shaped block in the coachyard to the same dimensions as the block occupied by Atkinson and formerly by Watts in 1768, therefore including the corner of the building identified in the archaeology. The 1732 plan having been drawn to scale, it indicates that this is indeed the same size and shape as in 1768, requiring a little reinterpretation of the archaeology, which had concluded the building was no older than 1760.

The archaeological excavation also identified a substantial feature of a refuse pit, lined with cattle horn cores, just to the south-west of the Watts house, and dated to the period 1710–60 by artefacts found in its fill. The archaeological assessment suggested this was a waste pit for industrial and, later, domestic waste. As the Atkinsons developed brewing here, this may have been theirs.

The plans of Figure 4 (c. 1732) and Figure 6 (1768) can be compared with the detail of Rocque's London map of 1746 (detail in Figure 18). Rocque has more, and better, detail of the alleys than Horwood, showing the Coach Yard and Meeting House (A.M. for Anabaptist Meeting). Here, Bangor Court is shown as New Court, although New Alley occurs more commonly around this time, and the connection through to Shaws Court is clearly there. The alley connection is also shown in Homann Heirs map of 1736, which otherwise is more sketchy on the alleys.

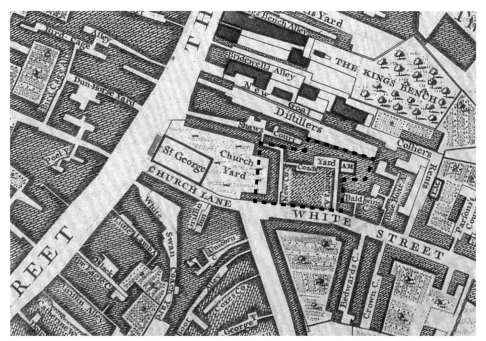

Fig. 18.   Jean Rocque, *A Plan of the Cities of London and Westminster, and Borough of Southwark*, 1747, detail. Private collection.

Figure 3: c. *1680*

Figure 3 reconstructs the site at the beginning of Gore's lease and draws on Morgan's 1682 map of London (detail in Figure 19) as the only plan source for this time. As a documentary source, the records of births and burials made by John Hopkins in 1698–1713 tell a little about the topography as well as about the people. Residence does not comprise full address and is not always consistent, but there are several mentions of, for example, Gore's Rents, Boar's Head Alley, by the Meeting House, against the Sheers, sometimes in combination. During this period, too, the usage of 'White Street' for this stretch of Long Lane had become more prevalent. These records indicate that both the Sheers and the Boar's Head were operating at the same time, on each corner of the alley with White Street;[122] there was also a victuallers' called the Anchor (or Blue Anchor) inside Boar's Head Alley. All of this suggests that this alley at the eastern end of the land was by then well developed.

The connection between Shaw's Court and Bangor Court, which Willit said Gore had opened up, is not yet there in Morgan's map, and neither is the meeting house, opened in 1695. The alley at the western end (Hopkins did not mention either the name of White Hind Alley, or Bangor Court) is

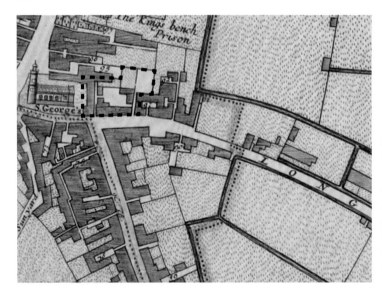

Fig. 19. William Morgan, *London & c. Actually Survey'd*, 1682, detail. © British Library Board *Maps Crace Port. 2.58.*

built up. Morgan's map legend has '94 Bores head Court', but the number 94 is missing from the map itself. The placement of Nos 95 ('Shawes Court') and 93 ('Baldwins Court') either side clarifies that it ought to label the alley in the School estate.

Morgan also shows an L-shaped building in the coachyard, near the later Atkinson/Watts block. These are probably not the same buildings, as the arms of the L are about equal in Morgan's map, whereas measurements in the later scale plans show the southward wing to have been longer in 1732 and 1768. Also, the archaeology found a possible seventeenth-century well within the footprint of the Watts building. Accordingly, it is concluded that the earlier L-shaped block shown in Figure 3 was a little smaller than its successor and stood just to the north of the area excavated by the archaeologists. In the archaeology, this phase was characterized by horticultural soils sealing earlier features, which could represent Gore re-laying gardens after his redevelopment.

Before the 1680s, the wider area that later became the coachyard was generally described as the 'Garden Plot'. It was once subdivided — Geoffrey Glyn's purchase said there were eight messuages and eight gardens,[123] later described as sixteen tenements. This may have had its origin in each tenant of the almshouses (see Fig. 2) having had an associated garden to grow food. The archaeology here identified a sixteenth-century ditch, interpreted as a property division, running approximately north–south within the area. Pits from this period, towards the southern boundary of the excavated area, were interpreted as tanning pits or cesspits. Faithorne and Newcourt's map

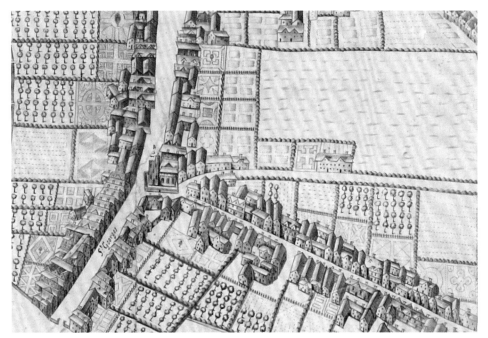

Fig. 20.   Richard Newcourt and William Faithorne Senior, *London*, 1661 edition, detail. © British Library Board *Maps R.17.a.3.*

of 1658 (detail in Figure 20) probably does not reproduce the exact buildings, but gives the general impression of gardens behind this and other properties being regularly divided into rectangular plots. All this is consistent with the narrative description of a subdivided garden.

Figure 2: Mid-Sixteenth Century

Figure 2 reconstructs the land as it would have been in the sixteenth century, the land left by Geoffrey Glyn and transferred to the School by Garrard, Petre and Lowe. This is necessarily less precise than the later reconstructions, its principal source now simply the narrative descriptions of early papers. These refer to the Almshouses, White Hind Alley, the Garden Plot and properties along Long Lane, whose relative positions can be inferred from Willit's letter and later plans. Maryon Huntington's witness statement of 1577 locates the White Hind as a house on the east side of the churchyard, with other tenements 'under the same roof'.[124] The Boar's Head is mentioned in Garrard's accounts[125] so it was already there, probably not yet with an alley behind. As in Figure 3, a ditch found in the archaeology would represent one of the boundaries between eight gardens within the garden plot.

Fig. 21.   Anthonis van den Wijngaerde, Panorama of London, *c.* 1543–44, pen and
ink, detail. © Ashmolean Museum Oxford *WA1950.206.6.*

Can this sixteenth-century reconstruction be compared with Anthonis
van den Wijngaerde's panorama of *c.* 1544, where this area is shown in the
foreground of drawings VI and VIII? At the time of Wijngaerde's drawing the
land would not yet have been acquired by Geoffrey Glyn, but the drawing is
still relevant. Wijngaerde shows Rochester House along the river. This was
the London residence of the Bishop of Rochester; when Glyn chose Maurice
Griffin as one of his executors, he may have considered him to have a nearby
base here, convenient to keep an eye on the land. Figure 21 is a detail of
drawing VI, including what is now Borough High Street and the Church
of St George the Martyr, as it then was, opposite Suffolk Place. Figure 22,
as a detail of drawing VIII, continues the scene eastwards, so some of these
buildings should be those on the School land. However, the panorama is
'often unreliable in detail'.[126] Wijngaerde did not reproduce every single
building — he would have drawn principal buildings such as churches and
mansions, filling in the gaps with an approximation to ordinary buildings.
Although the church is shown, he does not have Long Lane immediately next
to it as it should be, and there does not appear to be enough intervening detail
northwards between the church and the river. The layout of the buildings
in drawing VIII does not match the land considered here. All that can be
concluded is that the one- and two-storey buildings in the foreground, some

Fig. 22.   Anthonis van den Wijngaerde, Panorama of London, *c*. 1543–44, pen and ink, detail. © Ashmolean Museum Oxford *WA1950.206.8*.

with a hint of an arch leading to an alley behind, may be typical of buildings such as the White Hind and the Boar's Head. If Nos 7–9 White Street were survivors to 1873, they may have looked something like these buildings.

Some Conclusions

The School archives in Caernarfon have been the principal source for this tale, but they are not complete. Because the Dean and Chapter of Bangor Cathedral were its trustees for much of its history, some Chapter papers had references to School business, and, after disestablishment of the Church in Wales, found their way to the National Library of Wales. John Willit's letter, the key document linking old and new names of properties in 1729, was a personal deposit at the National Library by the Very Revd Gwynfryn Richards, a former Dean of Bangor. The survival of the Gell ledgers as muniments at Westminster Abbey has provided another source, often duplicating or amplifying School records. Together with the National Archives and London-based records, it has been possible to piece together the history of the estate, with a high degree of corroboration from different sources.

To give a few examples: the William Dickson mentioned cursorily in the School archives as a leaseholder can be conjectured to be William Dixon, the freeman of the Honourable Company of Clothworkers who died in 1669, Although his will referred to leases only in general terms,[127] in his widow's will she referred to the lease specifically from the 'Lord Bishop of Bangor',[128] which confirms this is the right Dixon. The case of *Forth v. Chapman* is not referred to at all in the School papers, but can be pieced together from two boxes in the National Archives and the Peere-Williams legal text, which then explains the context of a Counsel's opinion in Caernarfon which refers only to 'W. B.'.[129] The various sources put together allow a near-complete reconstruction of the School's rental income over the entire period.[130]

Nothing in the School archives suggests that its freehold holding was added to, or affected by any disposals, in the course of the School's dealings. Before plans were attached, leases generally described the land but, crucially, clarified that they referred to the same land as was included in a previous lease, thus providing continuity. With one possible exception discussed below, the boundaries of the land owned by the School in 1895 (shown in red on the plans here) would have been those of the land as it was acquired by Geoffrey Glyn. Glyn had bought the property from Robert Andrews, who had the land from Robert Curson, who in turn had bought from the Guild of Our Lady and St George the Martyr.[131] This can be compared with Martha Carlin's findings: because her sources generally referred to land holdings in relation to their boundaries with each other, her gazetteers identify relative positions on a map; this land is her gazetteer number 87,[132] but it is also possible now to delineate its boundaries on the ground and determine its shape and size.

The possible exception concerns Walter Gore's lease on land in Shaw's alley, said by Willit to have been taken from George Shaw. Subsequent litigation between Gore and the Shaw family[133] suggests that Gore had advanced £50 to George Shaw, who had died around 1689. The land was held on a 99-year lease according to the *Forth v. Chapman* papers. Gore also had a freehold house in Shaw's Court,[134] and he opened up the access that joined Shaw's Court to what was to become Bangor Court, perhaps to allow himself access to his tenants, or vice versa. The extent of this extra piece of land is not known, but around 1788, Shaw's successors in title to the freehold would have been entitled to take it back from the successors to Gore. Some light is thrown on this by a dispute concerning a doorway in 1791, when the School took legal action against a victualler called Crease because he had opened up a doorway into Bangor Court without the School's consent.[135] No more details are given as to where this doorway might have been, but the most obvious explanation would be that the way through to Shaw's Court had been shut off by a closed doorway. The disputant could have been Richard Creese, recorded in the licensed victuallers' lists (either the younger or the elder; there were two in the parish),[136] and who land tax records place nearby. The matter appears to have been resolved by 1795, when the perpetrator was reported to be in prison. In relation to the passage opened up by Gore, when the 99-year lease came to an end, the pragmatic solution for the freeholders may have been for each to take a part of their freehold land on their respective sides of the doorway: even if this entailed some adjustment to what had been the boundaries beforehand. This would have created the kink in the boundary at the position of the doorway, not shown in the 1732 plan. When the churchyard came to be extended in 1817, it respected this kink in the boundary line; later, what had been the passage was built over. If there was a mutually agreed adjustment to the boundary between the estate that had been Shaw's, then, at this corner, it must be accepted that Geoffrey's Glyn's title may have been slightly different to the red lines shown in plans here (and therefore shown dotted in Figures 2–4).

Rendle, an early historian of Southwark, refers to the Guild of Our Lady and St George the Martyr. This Guild, or fraternity, was a religious body that raised money — by begging, or otherwise — for the maintenance of the clergy; Rendle speculates that it may have had a guildhall, which was normally close to the church.[137] According to Carlin, 'by December 1541, however, the fraternity was maintaining only one priest, and by 1548 the incumbency was void, although its endowment was worth £6.2s.8d a year'.[138] Documents that have survived from the early disputes concerning the School's title to the land establish that the land had originally been acquired from the Guild by Curson.[139] Gore's leases referred specifically to there having been a Guildhall on the land.[140] A hall would probably have been used to accommodate members of the Guild, and given that their main function was to solicit alms to support the clergy, it is plausible that the building would have been known as 'almshouses'. The almshouses described by Alice Hannell in 1577 and in successive leases are shown in Figure 2, their position within the land as described in Willit's letter and the early leases. This pre-Reformation Guildhall may not have survived, but, if future archaeologists should seek it, the evidence presented here suggests part of it would be under what is now open land, to the right of the entrance gateway from Tabard Street to St George's Churchyard Gardens.

Acknowledgements

This article is dedicated to the memory of my late father, Myrvin Elis-Williams, sometime headmaster of Friars School.

I am most grateful for the help of staff at archives consulted, the encouragement and support of the late Stephen Humphrey, and the perceptive input of the editor. Errors remain my responsibility alone.

1. Caernarfon, Gwynedd Archives, XES/5/FRIARS (hereafter FRIARS).
2. David Elis-Williams, 'Elsewhere Within the Realm of England: Friars School's Southwark Endowment', *Transactions of the Caernarfonshire Historical Society*, 77 (2016/17), pp. 60–96.

3. David Elis-Williams, 'Victuallers of White Street, Southwark', *London Topographical Society Newsletter*, no. 82 (2016), pp. 10–12.

4. The three were recorded as the principal mourners at Griffin's funeral in *A London Provisioner's Chronicle, 1550–1563, by Henry Machyn: Manuscript, Transcription, and Modernization*, ed. by Richard W. Bailey, Marilyn Miller and Colette Moore. http://quod. lib.umich.edu/m/machyn [accessed on 9 October 2020].

5. FRIARS 88.

6. *Acts of the Dean and Chapter of Westminster, 1543–1609, Part Two*, ed. by C. S. Knighton, Westminster Abbey Record Series, II (London, 1999), p. 43.

7. London, Guildhall Library, MS 15857/1, f. 59v.

8. FRIARS 5; LMA, CLA/007/EM/03/167.

9. Dorian Gerhold, *London Bridge and its Houses, c. 1209–1761*, London Topographical Society publication No. 182 (2019), p. 67.

10. FRIARS 16, 35.

11. TNA, PROB 11/69/186, f. 128.

12. FRIARS 16.

13. Bangor University MS 22808.

14. LMA, CLA/043/01/008, p. 2.

15. Gibberd was an associate of the Bishop of Bangor and does not appear in any of the London-based records consulted.

16. FRIARS 60.

17. The voided-corporation argument was not valid, as Parliament clarified that it did not apply to chapters in their capacity as charity trustees, an argument which Meredith had advanced. See C. H. Firth and R. S. Raits (eds), *Acts and Ordinances of the Interregnum, 1642–1660* (London, 1911), pp. 81–104.

18. FRIARS 50; TNA, C2/CHASI/B40/1.

19. FRIARS 16.

20. FRIARS 17.

21. FRIARS 16; TNA, PROB 11/266/321.

22. FRIARS 90.

23. An impression of the area can be gained in the distance of Jan Griffier, *View of the River Thames and Lambeth Palace in London*, c. 1700, Turin, Galleria Sabauda.

24. Jeremy Boulton, *Neighbourhood and Society: A London Suburb in the Seventeenth Century* (Cambridge, 2005), p. 173.

25. Aberystwyth, National Library of Wales (hereafter NLW), GB 0210 NLWDEEDS 119.

26. TNA, C 7/144/74, a Chancery case on an unrelated property matter in 1686 is signed by Wynne as Gore's barrister.

27. FRIARS 11.

28. FRIARS 12, 13, 14.

29. FRIARS 18.

30. TNA, C113/25.

31. LMA, P92/GEO/143, 30 May 1712.

32. LMA, DW/PC/05/1712/009; TNA C113/25.

33. LMA, P92/GEO/143, 30 December 1716 and 29 April 1718.

34. LMA, DW/PA/05/1718/043.

35. London, Southwark Local History Library (hereafter SLHL), Poor Rate books for St George's parish.

36. Most case details of *Forth v. Chapman*, and associated documents, are at TNA C 113/25, with Samuel Forth's oration at C 11/2365/49. The judgment is at *Reports of cases argued and determined in the High Court of Chancery, and of some special cases adjudged in the Court*

of King's Bench: collected by William Peere Williams, In two volumes, 1 (London, 1740), pp. 663–68.

37. SLHL, Poor Rate books.
38. TNA, PROB 11/660/310, PROB 11/710/166.
39. TNA, C113/25, PROB 31/286/739; FRIARS 51.
40. *The History of Parliament: the House of Commons 1754–1790*, ed. by L. Namier and J. Brooke (London, 1964), pp. 80–81.
41. NLW, GB 0210 DIOCBANGOR, Diocese of Bangor Records, 1408–2009 B/DL/171.
42. But referred to in many official documents as New Alley for many years.
43. FRIARS 121.
44. Joseph Ivimey, *A History of the English Baptists: Comprising the Principal Events of the History of Protestant Dissenters, from the revolution in 1668 till 1760, and of the London Baptist Churches During that Period, Volume, III* (London, 1823), pp. 490–92; W. T. Whitley, *The Baptists of London, 1612–1928* (London, 1928), pp. 124–25; Walter Wilson, *The History and Antiquities of Dissenting Churches and Meeting Houses in London, Westminster and Southwark including the lives of their ministers from the beginning of Nonconformity to the Present Time*, IV (London, 1808), pp. 329–30.
45. FRIARS 85.
46. James Thwaite, *A collection of psalms and hymns, Extracted from Various Authors, For the Use of the children of God* (London, 1770).
47. Museum of London Archaeological Services, Site Summaries: 29–35 Long Lane SE1 reference LLE02 (2002).
48. FRIARS 81, 86, 92, 93.
49. FRIARS 51.
50. FRIARS 91, 92, 93, 94.
51. FRIARS 61.
52. These leases have not survived but the successor leases in FRIARS 121 refer to the surrender of previous leases, all of this date.
53. FRIARS 85.
54. FRIARS 86, 93, 121 p. 40.
55. The family all commemorated by plaques in the Church of St George the Martyr.
56. LMA, CLC/B/192/F/001/MS11936/467/911093.
57. FRIARS 63, 26 July 1858.
58. Their ledgers of transactions with the school survive in the very same building, now Westminster Abbey Muniments Room (Muniment 35519).
59. FRIARS 63, 26 July 1858.
60. *London Gazette* 22182, 14 September 1858, p. 4155; FRIARS 63, 14 September 1858.
61. FRIARS 63, 19 January 1859.
62. TNA, ED 27/6354, 16 July 1860.
63. TNA, ED 27/6355, 8 June 1864.
64. FRIARS 63, 26 July 1858.
65. 'Reports on the Old Cholera Haunts and Modern Fever Nests of London', *The Lancet, II*, Volume 86, Issue 2204, 25 November 1865, pp. 602–04.
66. FRIARS 148.
67. FRIARS 122, 123.
68. TNA, ED27/6369.
69. FRIARS 25.
70. FRIARS 136, 145, 146.
71. See Elis-Williams, 'Victuallers'.
72. Plaque in the church of St George the Martyr; *The Times*, 5 July 1923.
73. FRIARS 23, 66; TNA, ED27/6369.

74. FRIARS 24; TNA, ED27/6369.

75. NLW, GB 0210 DIOCBANGOR, Diocese of Bangor Records, 1408–2009 B/MISC/253.

76. LMA, LT/92/01.

77. Caernarfon, Gwynedd Archives, EM 3/2; LMA, P92/GEO/334.

78. FRIARS 40, 41.

79. FRIARS 39, 42.

80. FRIARS 47.

81. FRIARS 58.

82. LMA, Church of England Baptisms, Marriages and Burials, 1538–1812 (accessed via ancestry. co.uk).

83. TNA, PROB 11/469/308.

84. Ian Woodfield, *English Musicians in the Age of Exploration*, Sociology of Music No. 8 (Stuyvesant, NY, 1995), pp. 33–37.

85. FRIARS 85.

86. Woking, Surrey History Centre, Surrey Land Tax (accessed via ancestry.co.uk).

87. LMA, CLC/B/192/F/001/MS11936/400/634420.

88. *Coroners' Inquests into Suspicious Deaths, 2 Jan 1790–30 Dec 1790*, London Lives https:// www.londonlives.org/browse.jsp?div=LMCLIC65003IC650030208 [accessed on 9 October 2020].

89. LMA, CLC/B/192/F/001/MS11936/400/642614.

90. LMA, CLC/B/192/F/001/MS11936/377/583403.

91. LMA, CLC/B/192/F/001/MS11936/387/601156.

92. Henry Joseph Killerby. Breaking Peace: threatening behaviour, 5 January 1846, Proceedings of the Old Bailey https://www.oldbaileyonline.org/browse.jsp?id=t18460105-451&div=t18460105-451 [accessed on 9 October 2020].

93. Henry Joseph Killerby. Breaking Peace: wounding, 23 February 1846, Proceedings of the Old Bailey   https://www.oldbaileyonline.org/browse.jsp?id=t18460223-782&div=t18460223-782 [accessed on 9 October 2020].

94. Henry Joseph Killerby. Breaking Peace: threatening behaviour, 16 August 1847, Proceedings of the Old Bailey https://www.oldbaileyonline.org/browse.jsp?id=t18470816-1992&div=t18470816-1992 [accessed on 9 October 2020].

95. Henry Joseph Killerby. Breaking Peace: threatening behaviour, 29 January 1849, Proceedings of the Old Bailey https://www.oldbaileyonline.org/browse.jsp?id=t18490129-604&div=t18490129-604 [accessed on 9 October 2020].

96. Charles Booth's London, maps https://booth.lse.ac.uk/map/18/-0.0907/51.5009/100/0 [accessed on 9 October 2020].

97. Charles Booth's London, Ernest Aves' Notebook: Police District 32 [Trinity Newington and St Mary Bermondsey], 1899, BOOTH/B/364, p. 35 https://booth.lse.ac.uk/notebooks/b364# ?cv=20&c=0&m=0&s=0&z=291.3732%2C223.5952%2C1878.8529%2C1117.5045 [accessed on 9 October 2020].

98. London, London Archaeological Archive and Research Centre, LGK99, Alistair Douglas, Phased Summary and Assessment Document of Excavation at 5–27 Long Lane London Borough of Southwark, SE1 (2008); Alistair Douglas, 'An Excavation at 5–27 Long Lane, London Borough of Southwark, London SE1', *Transactions of the London and Middlesex Archaeological Society*, 58 (London, 2007), pp. 15–51.

99. LMA, P92/GEO/334.

100. Ordnance Survey, London 1:1,056 — Sheet VII.85 and Sheet VII.86 (1895), National Library of Scotland.

101. BL Maps 145.b.22.(.4), Insurance Plan of City of London Vol. IV: sheet 94-1.

102. LMA, LT92/01/086, pp. 15–16 (accessed via ancestry.co.uk).

103. FRIARS 143, 147.

104. 'A Century and a Quarter of Hardware Factoring', *Hardware Trade Journal*, 26 February 1960.
105. Ordnance Survey, London (1st edns *c.* 1850s), XLIV (Lambeth St Mary; Southwark) (1879); London (1st edns *c.* 1850s), XLV (Bermondsey; London; Stepney) (1878) National Library of Scotland.
106. Derived from TNA, ED/6355, ED/6369 and the Goad map, all consistent in their numbering.
107. TNA, ED/6355.
108. FRIARS 136.
109. LMA, P92/GEO/326–333; FRIARS 121; London, Westminster Abbey, Muniment 35519, p. 266.
110. *The Survey of London, Volume 25: St George's Fields (The Parishes of St George the Martyr and St Mary Newington)*, ed. by Ida Darlington (London, 1955), p. 38.
111. FRIARS 121.
112. House of Commons, 'Further Report of the Commissioners appointed in pursuance of an Act of Parliament made and passed in the 1st and 2nd Years of His present Majesty. C.34, intituled "An Act for appointing COMMISSIONERS to continue the Inquiries concerning CHARITIES in ENGLAND and WALES for Two Years, and from thence to the End of the next Session of Parliament"' (10 January 1834), printed 13 August 1834. House of Commons Parliamentary Papers Online 1834 (606) 28 https://parlipapers.proquest.com/parlipapers/docview/t70.d75.1834-014974?accountid=12799 [accessed on 9 October 2020].
113. TNA, ED/6355.
114. FRIARS 85.
115. FRIARS 142.
116. FRIARS 119.
117. Henry Barber and Henry Lewis, *The History of Friars School, Bangor* (Bangor, 1901), p. 38.
118. FRIARS 140.
119. NLW, Gwynfryn Richards papers 1973 deposit/1.
120. FRIARS 142.
121. FRIARS 123.
122. Although shown in Figure 3 with the Sheers on the western corner, they could have been the other way round.
123. FRIARS 35.
124. FRIARS 47.
125. FRIARS 88.
126. *The Panorama of London circa 1544, by Anthonis van den Wyngaerde*, ed. by H. Colvin and S. Foister, London Topographical Society publication No. 151 (1996), p. 5. A similar approach was followed in other drawn panoramas: the 'Rhinebeck' panorama of 1807–11 has this estate but the ordinary buildings drawn are not correctly.
127. TNA, PROB 11/331/175, PROB 4/16365.
128. TNA, PROB 11/335/227.
129. FRIARS 51.
130. See Elis-Williams, 'Elsewhere Within the Realm of England'.
131. W. P. Griffith, 'Some Passing Thoughts on the Early History of Friars School, Bangor', *Transactions of Caernarfonshire Historical Society*, 49 (1988), pp. 117–50, deals in more detail with the sixteenth-century history and the associated legal challenges to the title of the land.
132. Martha Carlin, 'Urban Development of Southwark, c. 1200 to 1550' (doctoral thesis, University of Toronto, 1983); Martha Carlin, *Medieval Southwark* (London, 1966); Carlin has Robert Andrews as Robert Sanders.
133. TNA, C 7/134/39.

134. LMA, DW/PC/05/1712/009.
135. FRIARS 121.
136. Woking, Surrey History Centre, Licensed Victuallers, 1785–1903 (accessed via ancestry. co.uk).
137. William Rendle, *Old Southwark and its People* (London, 1878), pp. 70–74.
138. Carlin, *Medieval Southwark*, p. 94.
139. Griffith, 'Passing Thoughts'.
140. FRIARS 11,12.

IV. WILLIAM HOLE'S MAP OF THE FINSBURY FIELDS ARCHERY MARKS AND THEIR NAMES

By MALCOLM JONES

A HAND-COLOURED printed map of *Finsbury Fields* signed by William Hole preserved at the Bodleian Library, Oxford, shows a part of north London roughly a square mile in area that was set aside for the practice of archery in the sixteenth and seventeenth centuries. It stretches northwards from the present site of Finsbury Square crossing what was already known as Old Street with 'Perelous pond', remembered now in Peerless Street, in the centre and, at the east, the well of 'Dame Annis [Agnes] a Cleere' at the present junction with Pitfield Street and Great Eastern Street (Fig. 1). The map measures about 23 × 14 cm and is pasted to oak boards hinged in the middle, enabling it to be folded in half, making it both durable and portable; indeed, there are the remains of hook-and-eye clasps which would have secured the boards together. Later in its life, it was given a black roan cover and wallet-style case to protect it.[1] There are engraved close copies of the map in the London Metropolitan Archives (formerly referred to as the Guildhall map)[2] and the Bethlem Royal Hospital.[3]

The Fields were studded with targets — known as 'marks' — set at varying distances apart from each other. The marks themselves were wooden posts standing three to four feet high (a metre or a little more), usually bearing a crest or emblem for identification, and frequently named after the persons who created them and were perhaps also responsible for their upkeep. Though many wooden posts or 'stakes' remained permanently in place, stone pillars were later established by the Honourable Artillery Company (HAC) to replace the decaying wooden markers. Many marks were surmounted by a carved or painted device or picture. In his *Whimzies* (1631) Richard Brathwaite includes a character-sketch of 'A Painter [who] Now and then ... turnes Rover, and bestowes the height of his Art on Archers stakes'. Some marks may have been painted a distinctive colour such as that named *Maidens Blush* in 1601, denoting a delicate pink hue.

The earliest depiction of such marks known to me is to be seen in the foreground of the panoramic *View of the Cittye of London from the North towards the Sowth* where men are shown practising archery in open fields on the edge of Elizabethan London; at the moment the view cannot be dated more precisely than 1577–98 (Fig. 2).[4] Though tiny, the five marks represented have the appearance of stout wooden posts about the height of a man, four of which are surmounted by a vaguely spherical object. In only slightly closer focus, two marks are visible in the background of the frontispiece woodcut to Gervase Markham's *The Art of Archerie* (1634)

Fig. 1.   William Hole, *Map of Finsbury Fields*, dated here to *c.* 1618. The Bodleian
Libraries, The University of Oxford *Arch.A.d.1.*

Fig. 2.   *The View of the City of London from the North*, engraving, 1577–78 (detail looking towards Gray's Inn). The Burden Collection.

(Fig. 3). The mark on the right of the cut is surmounted by a large bird of some kind — see the names *Puttock* (1601), *Poores Partridge* (1628), or even *Red Dragon* (1628) below. On Hole's map some effort has been made to delineate individual marks. They are not represented by a uniform symbol but are mostly depicted as columns of wood or stone with stylized but non-figural tops; the few exceptions include the mark named *Sea-Griphon* (sea-griffin), which features what looks like a very large bird, and *Spindle*, which is perhaps topped by an outsize spindle full of yarn. Two animals' heads are recognizable — though in neither case is the appropriateness evident: *Rogers stake*, which is surmounted by an unmistakable unicorn head, and *Guiowar:nls*, topped by a bull's head. Use was also made of naturally occurring marks, such as the tree labelled *Target tree*, and the smaller tree next to the mark named *Lion*, which is labelled *Sapling by Lion*. John Williams discussed the marks in the 1850s, comparing Hole's map with a manuscript list of marks compiled by Henry Dickman in 1601, which he helpfully transcribed:

> Some again are from well-known places or objects, such as Bunhill, Beech-lane, London-stone, Honey-lane, and Kingston-bridge [though I note that 'Beech' and 'Honey' lanes do not appear in his printed transcript of the 1601 list].

Fig. 3. Frontispiece to Gervase Markham,
The Art of Archerie (London, 1634), woodcut.
© British Library Board, *1040.a.10*.

There also occur Robinson and Robinson's Leg; Box arm and Box leg, and other similar … Some are ascertained by their position, as Tree John, Stone by Style, Tree Gate, Two Tree Camel, Target Tree; and the occurrence of Beadle Gate and of Stocks as marks seem to shew that not only was there an officer whose duty it was to see that order was preserved, but that there were also the means of punishing in a summary manner any refractory person who might not feel inclined to submit to his authority.[5]

In this type of 'roving' archery, it was the prerogative of the bowman whose arrow landed closest to or 'hit the mark' to choose the next target. From 1594 at the latest, a guidebook updated every few years, entitled *Ayme for Finsburie archers*, recorded the distances in scores and yards for every mark to assist archers in their practice. As long ago as 1832, A. J. Kempe reproduced a copy of Hole's map and suggested, I believe correctly, that it was

> originally drawn to illustrate one of those little guides for Archers, which were arranged in the manner of the modern books of hackney-coach fares, and were printed and reprinted in several editions, varying as the marks were changed.[6]

Eighteenth- and nineteenth-century bibliographers record a 1594 edition of *Ayme*, no longer known, printed by Arnold Hatfield (active 1581–1612) for E. B. and I. I., who may be identified as two of his fellow Eliot's Court Press partners, Edmund Bollifant (active 1583–1602), and John Jackson (active

1584–1596).[7] Frederick W. Foster's 'Bibliography of Archery'[8] lists what is apparently another 1594 edition for the same publishers and sold from the same bookseller's shop, but 'printed at London by R. F.'.[9] Although no source is given, as the extant 1601 edition[10] was also printed by R[ichard]. F[ield]. (1589–1624),[11] this seems plausible enough. Both editions were sold by F. Sergeant whose shop was in Grub Street, trading at the sign of the *Swan* in 1594, but by the time of the 1601 edition, at the sign of the *Frier* in the same street, not far from Finsbury Fields, and as noted by Stow, a street in which archery-related craftsmen also plied their various trades:

> In the east end of Forestreete is More lane, then next is Grubstreete, of late yeares inhabited for the most part by Bowyers, Fletchers, Bowstring makers, and such like occupations, now little occupied, Archerie giuing place to a number of Bowling Allies and dycing houses [which] in all places are increased, and too much frequented.[12]

The preface to the 1601 edition is signed by I. N., who also signed the preface of the lost 1604[13] and 1626[14] editions, as well as the extant 1628 edition.[15] The identity of I. N. is unknown, though he was presumably an enthusiastic archer and so almost certainly a member of the Honourable Artillery Company. The earliest records of the Company date from its 're-founding' in 1611, and before 1615 only two men are listed with suitable initials, a Jonas Newton, admitted 21 September 1612, and a John Norman, admitted 23 October 1614.[16] The former may be our I. N., perhaps related to the Ninian Newton who was another of the Eliot's Court Press partners who printed and published the 1594 *Ayme*, and it is probably the same Jonas Newton who is recorded as the father of an apprentice of the Goldsmiths' Company in 1624. James Partridge, whose name appears on the title page of the 1626 and 1628 editions, was admitted to the HAC on 16 March 1618.

We shall see that there are reasons to believe the Goldsmiths' Company was particularly interested in the encouragement of archery — as the prominent display of the Company's arms on Hole's map suggests.

In 1840 George Agar Hansard, apparently following a pamphlet privately printed by Kempe, lists the names of only twenty-two marks (and three butts) from the now lost 1594 edition.[17] The 1601 edition stresses on its title page that it is 'Corrected and amended of diuerse errours with addition of those Markes which wanted in the former printed Bookes'. Note that 'Bookes' implies more than one antecedent edition, in addition to that of 1594 — which is likely enough for this sort of handy pocket-size (16mo) guide. Earlier writers suggest an edition of 1590, for which I have seen no evidence, and I believe they may rather have been referring to *The Tectonicon of Ffinsbury feildes* licensed to John Pyrrin on 19 November of that year in the Stationers' Registers, of which no copy survives.[18]

From W. M.'s account of a major City pageant which took place in 1583 (see below), we learn that the Goldsmiths' Company had its own stake so named in Hoxton Fields, and from the 1601 *Ayme* that there was another 'Goldsmiths' stake' in Finsbury Fields. Indeed, the absence of the name from Hole's map — which so prominently displays the Company's arms — must surely have implications for its date.

As we have noticed above, the 1601 *Ayme* states on its title page that it is 'Corrected and amended of diuerse errours with addition of those Markes which wanted in the former printed Bookes', and earlier bibliographers[19] supply us with the full title of the lost 1594 edition *By I.I. and E.B.*, which also includes the phrase, *both by the map and dimensuration of the line* in its title. The lost 1626 and extant 1628 editions of *Ayme*, however, have dropped any mention of a map from their titles. It thus seems not unreasonable to suppose that a map was bound in with the (lost) 1594 and extant 1601 editions (though no map is present in the only surviving copy of the latter), but for reasons given below that map cannot have been the print signed 'Will. Hole' and entitled 'FINSBURY-FIELDS' reproduced here.

William Hole (fl. 1599–1624)

Hole's earliest known work is usually said to be the twenty-one maps he engraved for the second, 1607, edition of Camden's *Britannia*, but he also signed a set of playing cards designed by William Bowes which include miniature county maps perhaps as early as 1605.[20] The *Britannia* maps are far more sophisticated than the present plan, which is sketchy in comparison, though that does not therefore imply that it is some juvenile effort, its function being rather different from that of a county map.

Little was known of Hole's biography until recently, but now, with publications by Laurence Worms and Ashley Baynton-Williams[21] and David Mitchell,[22] we are considerably better informed. The key fact is that — like many other early print-engravers — he was a member of the Goldsmiths' Company. The Company's records show that he was made a freeman in 1607, having submitted 'A sylver bolle with the Companies armes engraven thereon by him which is allowed to be his masterpiece'. Mitchell notes that he had apparently been apprenticed to Richard Martin the younger about 1599, the year Martin was appointed as joint Master-Worker of the Mint with his father, Sir Richard Martin, who was sixty-five at the time.

> At the beginning of his career, William Hole seems to have worked both as an engraver and as a specialist spoonmaker. He had a number of spoons broken by the Wardens: twenty in November 1607, thirteen in February 1608, 'certain spoons' in December 1609, eight in May 1611 and sixteen in August of the same year. Some had their heads worse than standard but their bodies standard, while others, presumably slip spoons (made in one piece), were

simply recorded as being worse than standard. Nevertheless, his offences were not grave and he either had his fine remitted or was fined 12*d*.

Unaware of the existence of our map, Mitchell goes on to speculate that rather than using his initials as his mark, as was usually the case, Hole may have used a device and — as a Company member who already specialized in engraving — may well have used the appropriate device of that tool essential to engravers, a pair of compasses.

Silver spoons with the pair of compasses mark and hallmarks for 1607, 1609, 1611 (seal-top finials) and 1612 (maidenhead finial) have been recorded at auction,[23] and the prominence of just such a pair of compasses behind the cartouche on the map of Finsbury Fields bearing Hole's signature must surely strengthen this probability. Reviewing in this light the entire corpus of Hole's printed work, which appears to come to an end in 1618, the year he was appointed 'Head sculptor of the Iron for money in the Tower' — that is, chief engraver to the Mint — one cannot but be struck by the title page he engraved for William Browne's *Britannia's Pastorals* in 1613: a shepherd

and shepherdess hold aloft their crooks so that the tops meet and form an inverted V, looking very like a pair of giant compasses (Fig. 4)!

Hole was employed at the Mint from 1618 until his death in 1624 and was responsible for James I's Third Coinage. Writing in the *Numismatic Chronicle* for 1913, H. Symonds noted, 'In the twelve months ending March 31, 1620, Hole was paid £120 for making twenty-six patterns, stamps, and irons for the coining of the newly made gold moneyers; this occupied him for half a year'.[24]

Fig. 4.   William Hole, frontispiece to William Browne, *Britannia's Pastorals* (London, 1613), engraving. The Huntington Library, San Marino, California *RB* 83042.

Another prolific maker of silver spoons, Edward Hole, son of William Hole, yeoman of Castle Cary, Somerset, was evidently a relation, probably a younger brother, and it would be perfectly normal for our William to have been named after his father. Hole's Somerset origins are further suggested by what is known about his apprentices. Edward Hole was apprenticed to John Saunders, Senr. of Castle Cary in 1614 for eight years, but Saunders's son, John Saunders, Jnr., though originally apprenticed to Daniel Cary in 1605 (whose mother was *née* Alice Hole), was subsequently turned over to William Hole, perhaps on account of Cary's death. Cary is last heard of in 1608, which would be the earliest date at which Hole could take on an apprentice according to the Company's rules, one year after achieving his freedom. As late as 9 August 1622 William Hole took on another apprentice, one Francis Baker, son of Robert Baker, Carpenter of London.

The present plan of Finsbury Fields is dedicated to 'his affect[ionate] frends Mr R Baker & Mr R Sharpe'. Worms has suggested that 'Mr R Baker' may have been the City carpenter who was the father of Hole's apprentice, Francis Baker, and in 1832 Kempe suggested that the 'Mr R Sharpe' may have been the R. S. who wrote *A briefe treatise to prove the necessitie of archery*, published in 1596. Former Company Librarian, Susan Hare, noted that a Robert Sharpe was made free of the Goldsmiths' Company in 1570 and that from 1569 he worked at the Sign of the Basket, a shop on Goldsmiths' Row, Cheapside, and that he had a son, also named Robert Sharpe, born in 1560.[25] The Company records also list a Robert Sharpe as Master of a man made free in 1604.

1583 Pageant

As noticed above, there is reason to believe that the Goldsmiths' Company took a special interest in the promotion of archery well before the date of Hole's map.

A lost Elizabethan account by one W. M. of a major City pageant which took place in 1583 was fortunately republished by William Wood in a collection of documents relating to the history of archery: *A remembrance of the worthy show and shooting by the Duke of Shoreditch* describes in great detail the pageant as it progressed through the streets of the City, and the following archery contest in Hoxton Fields. The 1583 *show and shooting* was a major public event, featuring no fewer than 3,000 archers marching through the streets of London with a climactic assault 'at the end of Houndsditch on the Image of a monstrous Giant, which in times past dwelt in that place'.[26]

Though other livery companies evidently took part in the pageant — there is mention of the Merchant Taylors, the Haberdashers and the

'Feryers' (presumably Farriers) — the Goldsmiths' Company was clearly paramount, and their part of the pageant by far the most elaborate.

In the entourage of 'the Duke of Shoreditch' were several other facetiously titled personages, including 'the Marquess of Shacklewell', 'the Baron Stirrop' and 'the Marques Barlo chief of the Goldsmiths'[27] (see the Finsbury marks, *Stirrops stake* 1601; *Stirrupe* Dickman (but not marked on Hole map), and *Barlow*, Hole, 1601, 1628, Dickman). When 'Prince Arthur' and his knights arrived at Hoxton Fields to greet 'the Duke of Shoreditch', 'Forthwith the Goldsmiths made forth to meet them, staying at their own Stake against their coming'.[28] Not only does this suggest the pre-eminence of the Goldsmiths on this occasion, it also incidentally testifies to the fact that archery stakes might be sponsored by livery companies (see below).

The Goldsmiths' contribution included a pageant float in the shape of a treasure-ship laden with gold and silver from the Indies, followed by 'pages' — played by Company apprentices, presumably — carrying pick-axes, spades and hammers. The author of the account, W. M. — perhaps a Goldsmith himself? — points the moral: 'Thus every one had his Page bearing these Tools, like Workmen by whose Labor many things are made out of Gold and Silver to the use of all men, and to the avoidance of Idleness'. Other pages carried ingots of gold and silver, some of which were later given as presents to the visiting 'Prince Arthur' and his knights. Also part of the Goldsmiths' pageant was a Coronet borne aloft on a staff, 'whereat hung three Arrows of Silver, very workmanly made'. At the end of the proceedings it is again 'the Marquis Barlo with all the Goldsmiths and his convoy of men at Arms [who] safe conduct the Duke home'.[29]

'Marquess Barlo', chief of the Goldsmiths and 'the chief in the Forefront of the skooters [*sic*]' is twice described as 'alias Covell' — 'the Train being now marching along, and the Duke ["of Shoreditch"] passing by, the Marquess Barlo, alias Covell, presented to his Nobleness a Wedge of Gold, in sign of good will, which the Duke very thankfully accepted'.[30]

He must accordingly be the Goldsmith Thomas Covell apprenticed to John Mabbe in 1569 and recorded as having an apprentice himself in 1579, which would put his own freedom from the Goldsmiths' Company a year or two earlier. According to the Company's Rent Book he leased a shop in Cheapside from 1599 to 1620,[31] and according to their 'Ancient Vellum Book', a Thomas Covell was admitted to the Honourable Artillery Company on 26 September 1614, and served as Captain — on the same day, incidentally, as the stationer, Adam Islip (for whom, see below).

Prizes

A series of royal proclamations issued during the latter half of the sixteenth century sought to encourage the practice of archery by means of open competitions — probably held annually — at which prizes of considerable value were awarded.[32] G. A. Raikes conveniently reproduces the proclamation of 1557 from the Minutes of the Proceedings of the Court of Common Council of the City of London. It advertises 'a severall game of showtinge in the felde called ffynessburie feld', to take place on 29 August of that year.[33]

Three types of contest are specified, to be shot with three different types of arrow: the *standard*, the *bearing* and the *flight*.[34] To judge from the monetary value of the prizes offered, 'the game of the flight' would appear to be the poor relation -- first prize, 10s. — whereas the first prize for the *standard* and *bearing* arrow competitions was 13s. 4d. (i.e. a mark — was this a merely fortuitous coincidence — a mark to him who hit the mark?).[35] That the contest with the *standard* arrow was regarded as the supreme competition, however, is suggested both by the fact that it appears first, and by the alternative to the monetary sum awarded to the winner of the first prize, viz. a 'Crowne of golde' — clearly a kingly coronet, not the contemporary coin so named, the monetary value of which was a mere 5s. — whereas the alternative physical prize for the *bearing* arrow competition was 'an arrowe of golde'. The winner of the *flight* arrow competition might similarly choose, in preference to the 10s., 'a flight of golde of the value of x s'.

We may imagine the *victor ludorum*, the king of the games, being carried off the field of play in triumph, his golden crown glistening on his brow. The archer described as both 'the first' and 'the best' in the 1583 pageant, wore 'a Cap of Velvet, and a golden Band about the same' — which sounds not unlike 'the Crowne of golde' of the 1557 proclamation, but also featuring suggestively in the Goldsmiths' part of the 1583 pageant was 'a Coronet borne aloft on a staff, whereat hung three Arrows of Silver, very workmanly made'.

It is these prizes, I suggest, which provide the link between the Goldsmiths' Company and the Finsbury and other archery fields, and explain the Company's particular (vested) interest in the promotion of the sport. The 1557 games in Finsbury Fields required three gold crowns and six gold arrows to be available as prizes — amounting to the value of £4 3s. — artefacts that only members of the Goldsmiths' Company could supply.

In similar vein, both the lost Elizabethan tracts reprinted by William Wood refer to the prize of a 'gilded gun',[36] described in the 1583 account as 'a Gunn worth three pound, made of Gold, to be given unto him that best deserved it by shooting in a Peece at the Mark which was set up on purpose at Saint Iame's Wall'.[37] A miniature silver gun perhaps once gilt, dated 1587, awarded as a shooting prize, survives in Kircudbright — and is still shot for.

While I know of no such gold arrow archery prizes extant, there are seventeenth-century silver arrow prizes still surviving at Scorton in Yorkshire from *c.* 1673,[38] and at Musselburgh in Scotland, where the arrow is associated with a commemorative medal dating from 1603.[39] The tradition of awarding silver arrows as prizes seems best attested in Scotland; Hugh Soar states that 'circumstantial evidence suggests an earlier [namely pre-1676] gathering of Edinburgh archers to shoot for silver arrows at Kelso, Stirling, and other places',[40] and I note the mention under the year 1666 in the Peebles Burgh Records of 'The silver arrow which wants the ridge or fether and ane hanging pendicle'.[41] The Society of Finsbury Archers is recorded as having purchased a silver arrow, presumably as a prize, in 1670,[42] and in 1684 Sir Gilbert Talbot presented a silver arrow prize to Harrow School, which is still shot for annually on 4 August.[43]

History of Finsbury Fields as Archery Range

Finsbury Fields already had a long history of use as an archery range by the time of Hole's map. Stow records how

> In the yeare 1498 all the Gardens which had continued time out of minde, without Mooregate, to wit, about, and beyond the Lordship of *Fensberry*, were destroyed. And of them was made a plaine field for Archers to shoote in.[44]

In 1520 the Court of Aldermen of the City ordered that the Bowmen should muster in Finsbury Fields,[45] and the following year we have the first mention of the frequent, probably annual, open competitions for archers held there.[46]

But as Stow notes, citing *Hall's Chronicle* for the earlier part of the century, and as he himself confirms for the Elizabethan era, the sixteenth century was a period of repeated encroachment on what was popularly regarded as the common land of the shooting fields. A typical complaint against a citizen who had planted hedges preventing free access to 'Stebbynhyth [Stepney] feyldes' also usefully enumerates eight of the traditional practice grounds for archers at the beginning of Elizabeth's reign:

> 20 January, 1561—True Bill that, (whereas the citizens and other inhabitants of London have been accustomed from time beyond the memory of man to shoot with bows in all the open fields in the parish of Stebbynhith co. Midd. and elsewhere near the said city, viz. in the common lands called Stebbynhyth feyldes, Ratclyff feyldes, Mylende feyldes, Blethnall grene, Spyttlefeildes, Morefeldes, Fynnesbury feyldes, Hoggesdon feyldes, co. Midd. without hindrance from any person, so that all archers have been able to go out in the same open fields to shoot with the bow and come out from them at pleasure, in such manner nevertheless that the said archers do no harm to growing corn nor to grass reserved for seed) John Draney citizen and clothier of the city of London has notwithstanding, on the aforesaid day, trenched in with deep ditches a certain open field called Stebbynhithe Close and against custom has planted it with green hedges, in order that the said archers may no longer be

able to enter, pass through and leave freely and at their pleasure the said field of Stebbynhithe Close.

A memorandum at the foot of the bill notes that, at the Session of the Peace held at Westminster on 21 May next following, John Draney was fined 12*d*.[47]

Here is Stow's summary of the state of affairs in his day:

Officers of the Citie: namely the Shiriffes, Serieantes and Yeomen, the Portars of the kinges beame, or weigh house, and other of the Citie were challengers of all men, in the suburbes... in *Fensbery fielde*, to shoote the Standarde, broade arrow, and flight, for games: but now of late yeares the [shooting] is onely practised ... some three or foure dayes after [*Bartilmew day*] ... in one after noone and no more. What shoulde I speake of the auncient dayly exercises in the long bow by Citizens of this cittie, now almost cleane left of and forsaken. I ouer passe it: for by the meane of closing in the common groundes, our Archers for want of roome to shoote abroade, creepe into bowling Allies, and ordinary dicing houses, nearer home, where they haue roome enough to hazard their money at vnlawfull games: where I leaue them to take their pleasures.[48]

According to Stow's continuator, Edmund Howes, the practice of

armes & martiall discipline in the Artillerie Garden without Bishops gate ... hauing beene discontinued euer since the yeere, one thousand fiue hundred eightie eight, was this present yeere, one thousand six hundred and ten ... newly erected, exercised, and set on foote, again

or as the side-note succinctly summarizes, 'The practize in the artillery Garden reuiued'.[49]

In addition to their practice ground in the Artillery Garden, in 1614 the Honourable Artillery Company was granted the use of the uppermost field in Finsbury by the Corporation of the City of London. The founding members of this 'renewal' of the HAC are recorded in the Company's 'Ancient Vellum Book'.

The Names of the Finsbury Marks

Exceptionally, we have no fewer than four witnesses to the roster of names in the earliest period to 1628. The earliest sources, both dated 1601, are the *Ayme for Finsburie archers* referred to above, and a manuscript list belonging to the Society of Antiquaries written by one Henry Dickman,[50] then there is the fourth, 1628, edition of *Ayme for Finsburie archers. Or An alphabeticall table of the names of euery marke within the same fields* compiled by James Partridge, and the present undated printed map engraved and signed by William Hole. A useful comparandum is afforded by the corpus of names published in *Aime for the archers of St.Georges Fields containing the names of all the marks ... by Richard Hannis, issued in 1664.

The table below gives the names of all the archery marks as spelled on the Bodleian map. Names on the map that are not the names of marks are not included here. Trivial spelling variants — especially presence or absence of *e* — have mostly been ignored; 'long s' has been silently modernized as *s*.

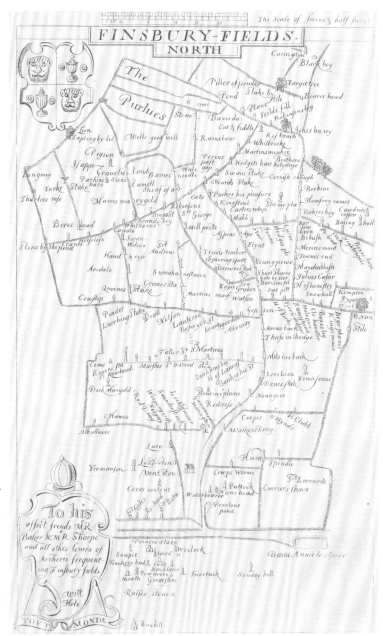

Fig. 5. After William Hole, *Map of Finsbury Fields*, engraving. London Metropolitan Archives, City of London *SC/GL/PR/F1/FIN/FIE/p5372611*.

The first form given is as found on the Bodleian map. The following columns give the names as found on the close copy formerly held in the Guildhall but now at LMA (Fig. 5), the names in the two earliest extant editions of *Ayme* (1601 and 1628), in the lost 1594 edition of *Ayme* from which some twenty names are preserved in Hansard (see note 17), and in Henry Dickman's manuscript list of the Finsbury Fields marks compiled in 1601 and preserved in the Library of the Society of Antiquaries of London. The final column includes comments on individual names.

It is clear that the map at the Bodleian is an original version of Hole's *Finsbury Fields*. The LMA map is a close copy but lacks the leaf border and thus the names of three of the cardinal points, only NORTH surviving, because inside the border — which has led the archery historian Hugh Soar to believe the map is actually entitled *Finsbury Fields North*.[51] More glaringly on the LMA map, Hole's motto, TOVT LE MONDE — punning perhaps on his surname if we translate the motto as '*whole* world' — is lacking the LE, and the names of several marks have been misread, and where the mistakes are not obvious, the Bodleian versions can be shown to be original from the forms given in the 1601 and 1628 *Ayme* editions. The abbreviated form *Qui:pill* appears thus on the Bodleian map, for example, but as *Out:pill* on that in the LMA; the correctness of the Bodleian version is confirmed both by Dickman's 1601 manuscript list which gives *Quins Piller*, and by *Ayme* (1628), which reads *Quinies Pillar*. The stake named after a certain *Norington* appears wildly misread on the LMA copy as the meaningless *Nonngere*. (*Norringtonne* Dickman; *Norington* 1601). The Bodleian *Lambeartsgoodwill* appears as *I heartygoodwill* on the LMA map (*Lamberts goodwill* 1628), and *Vper Gardiner*, that is *Upper Gardiner*, appears as *Vyer Gardiner* on the LMA map (*Vpper Gardiner* 1601; *Vpper Gardner* Dickman). The LMA map lacks the definite article in the mark named *Theefe in the hedge*, and numerous other, mostly slight, spelling differences show that it is secondary, though it is always this version which has been reproduced hitherto, for example in J. P. Malcolm's *Londinium Redivivum* (1802–07), facing p. 26, where the map is described as traced from 'an old print in the Bodleian Library, inserted in a work on Archery by William Hole'. If we supply a comma after 'Archery', we dispose of Hole's authorship of a book on archery, but may be left with another copy of Hole's map in its later, LMA, version seemingly somewhere else in the Bodleian Library.

Commentary on the Names of the Marks

The colourful nature of the names prompted one of the very few earlier commentators to describe them as 'of course arbitrary, and frequently very fanciful'[52] — in my typological analysis of the names below, I consider how just this estimate is.

Hole map, Bodleian	Guildhall/ LMA	1601 Ayme	1628 Ayme	1594 Ayme	Dickman	Notes
			Adam Bell			Not marked on Hole map
Allhallowes		Allhallowes			Allhollows	Probably named after one of the several parish churches dedicated thus, see the saints' names below.
Alloway		Allowayes house of the George			Allowaies George	The surname here may be that more usually spelled *Halloway*. A John Halloway is one of the gentlemen addressed in James I's 1605 patent.
Amias back		Amias back			Amis back	For back, see *Mils his back* below. *Amias* is a rare enough name to suggest some connexion perhaps with Sir Amias Paulet, d. 1588.
Archdale	Arcdale	Archdale	Archdale		Archdalle	
Aspin[als] Ape	Aspine Ape	Aspinals Ape sometimes blacke Prince			Aspinalls Ape	The *Black Prince* appeared as one of the entourage of the *Duke of Shoreditch* in the elaborate pageant of 1583 (Wood, *Bow-man's Glory*, p. 52).
B[lacke] Nan		Blacke Nan	Blacke Nan		Blacke Nanne	
Baines needle	Baines noodle		Baines his needle			
Bakers boy		Bakers boy, or Grey-hound			Baikers Boye	
Bankes his st[ake]		Bankes his stake			Banckes	
B bush		Bush under bush	Bush under bush		Bush under bush	

Hole map, Bodleian	Guildhall/LMA	1601 Ayme	1628 Ayme	1594 Ayme	Dickman	Notes
Barlow		Barlow	Barlow		Barlow	The 1583 *show and shooting by the Duke of Shoreditch* (p. 41) reprinted by Wood is the earliest authority for the story that Henry VIII awarded the facetious title *Duke of Shoreditch* to a member of his bodyguard named *Barlo* who outshot the best archers in the country: 'This noble King at another time keeping a Princely Court at Windsor, caused sundry Matches to be made concerning shooting in the Long-Bow: and to which came many principal Archers, who being in Game and the upshoot given, as all men thought, there was one Barlo yet remaining to shoot, being one of the Kings Guard; to whom the King very graciously said, Win them all and thou shalt be Duke over all Archers. This Barlo drew his Bow, and shooting won the best. Whereat the King greatly rejoiced, commending him for his good Archery; and for that this Barlo did dwell in Shoreditch, the King named him Duke of Shoreditch.' It is odd that in the 1583 pageant the principal, the *Duke of Shoreditch*, is evidently not identical with Barlo, who is here a mere *Marquess*.
Bassings hall	Basing hall		Basings hall			The building so named was demolished in Stow's lifetime and Blackwell Hall built on the site, but its name is commemorated in that of the ward, which was perhaps in some way responsible for the upkeep of the mark.
Beares head		Beares head	Beares head		Beares head	

Hole map, Bodleian	Guildhall/ LMA	1601 Ayme	1628 Ayme	1594 Ayme	Dickman	Notes
Beehiue		Bee-hive, sometime Portingale crosse			Beehive	
Begr-phoenix			Begraves phoenix			This rare surname seems to be restricted to Cheshire — there seem to be no suitable early bearers of the name.
					Bell Clapper	Not marked on Hole map
Beswyck st		Beswikes stone	Beswicks stake		Beswick	Stow, *London*, p. 176, mentions an alderman William Beswicke, d. 1567.
Bings st[ake]		Bings st[ake]			Bingge	
Black boy					Cox Boye [Williams's conjecture]	
Bores head		Bores head	Bores head		Boores head	
Boxes Arme		Boxes Arme			Box Arme	
Boxes leg		Boxes leg			Box Legg	
Brands boy		Brands boy			Brands boy	
		Brewers Aperne				Not marked on Hole map
Bricklaier		Bricklayers stake	Bricklayer		Bricklaire	
		Bricklayers finial	Bricklayers mold		Finiall	Not marked on Hole map

Hole map, Bodleian	Guildhall/LMA	1601 Ayme	1628 Ayme	1594 Ayme	Dickman	Notes
Brothers holydaye			Brothers holiday			
Brownestak		Brownes stake	Brownes stake		Browne	The 1601 form shows this was understood to be the stake of a man named Brown(e) and not a stake that was brown in colour. A suitable candidate would be the John Browne listed amongst the gentlemen addressed in James's *Letters Patent* of 1605. It is perhaps the same John Browne who was admitted to the HAC on 15 August 1611.
Bunhill		Bunhill	Bunhill		Bunhill	
Camell		Camell	Camell		Camell	
Candle		Candle			Candle	
Carington		Carington			Carington	
Carters whip		Carters whip	Carters whip		Whipp	
Cat & fiddle		Cat & fiddle	Cat & fiddle		Catt Fidle	I suggest it is in fact the name of an inn (above); it is also found as the name of a mark in St George's Fields (Hannis, *St Georges Fields*).
Cato						Hole's map appears to be the sole source for this name which seems unlikely to commemorate the ancient Roman orator. The contraction mark over the final letter suggests the name is to be expanded to give the English surname Caton.
Cawdries coffer		Cawdries coffer			Cawdries coffer	

Hole map, Bodleian	Guildhall/ LMA	1601 Ayme	1628 Ayme	1594 Ayme	Dickman	Notes
Clo handle	Clo handler		Clarks delight			Not marked on Hole map
Cock		Cloth-workers handle			Cloth-workers Hand	
Coleb:		Cock			Cock	
Conie		Colbrand	Colbrand		Collebrande	
Cooper		Cony			Connyes	
Cornish chough		Coopers stake			Coopers Chevall	
Cowp[er]s Worme		Cornish chough			Cornish choufe	
Cowslip			Cowpers worme			
Coxes content		Couslip			Cowslipe Antlope	
Cucoe			Coxes content			A William Cox was admitted to the HAC on 29 September 1614 (Raikes, *Ancient Vellum Book*, p. 22).
Curriers shaue		Cuckow, sometime Momford	Cuckoe		Cockkowe	
D: Deed		Curriers shaue				
		Dayes Deed	Dayes deed	Daysdeed	Daies Deede	

Hole map, Bodleian	Guildhall/ LMA	1601 *Ayme*	1628 *Ayme*	1594 *Ayme*	Dickman	Notes
Dains de=	Davis da=	Daines delight	Daines delight		Daimes delight	
Diall		Diall		Diall or Monument	Dyall	
Dick:Marigold		Dickmans marigold	Dickmans marigold			It is noticeable that this name does not appear in Dickman's manuscript list, though Marygoulde does — is this a rare instance of authorial modesty?
Diogenes, sometimes Candle-sticke					Candle-sticke	Not marked on Hole map
Doues stake	Deues stak:	Doues stake:			Dove	
		Doues Redbrest				Not marked on Hole map
			Dudleis darling	Dunstan's darling		Not marked on Hole map
Durhams boy		Durhams boy			Derhams Boye	A John Durham was admitted to the HAC on 10 October 1614 (Raikes, *Ancient Vellum Book*, p. 22).
Egpie		Egg Pye	Egg Pye	Egg Pye		
Faul						
Feilds fell[owship]			Fields fellowship			
		Flying Horse			Flying Horse	Not marked on Hole map
Flynt		Flynt			Flynt	

Hole map, Bodleian	Guildhall/ LMA	1601 Ayme	1628 Ayme	1594 Ayme	Dickman	Notes
Foun=sonne	Fown sonne	Founders sonne	Founders sonne		Founders sonne	
Friertuck		Frier Tucke			Frier Tucke	
Fuller st[ake]		Fullers stake			Fullers	
Gate by Har[ison]		Gate by Harison	Gate by Harison			
					Gate Little John	Not marked on Hole map
			Golden cup		Gouldene Cup	Not marked on Hole map
		Goldsmiths stake			Goldsmiths stake	Not marked on Hole map
Gos-son	Gose son	Gosson	Gosson		Gossonne	A Henrie Gosson was admitted to the HAC on 21 April 1612 (Raikes, *Ancient Vellum Book*, p. 18).
Grauelis lamb & Stone	Grauelie lamb	Gravelesse lambe	Graveleys lambe		Gravells Lambe	
Greatstone		Great stone by the Bricklayer	Great stone			
Greenes sta[ke]		Greenes sta[ke]			Greens	
[Gu]iowar: nls	Guiowarsels		Guy of Warwicke			

Hole map, Bodleian	Guildhall/LMA	1601 *Ayme*	1628 *Ayme*	1594 *Ayme*	Dickman	Notes
Hand & rose		Hand & rose	Hand & rose		Hand ros	
Harisons fel[lowship]	Harisons sol	Harisons fellowship	Harisons fellowship		Harrisons Fello	An Arthur Harrison was admitted to the HAC on 10 October 1614 (Raikes, *Ancient Vellum Book*, p. 22).
Hawes		Hawes	Hawes		Hawes	An Andrew Hawes was admitted to the HAC on 16 October 1611 (Raikes, *Ancient Vellum Book*, p. 17).
H[ercules] Clubb		H[ercules] Clubb	H[ercules] Clubb		H[ercules] Clubb	
Hodges ple[asure]		Hodges pleasure, sometimes Sheepes stake	Hodges pleasure		Hoges pleasure	
Hodgets hart		Hodges hart	Hodgets heart			
		Horne-booke				Not marked on Hole map
Horselofe	Horselose	Horselofe			Horse Loafe	
H[ouse] of honestey		H[ouse] of honestey	H[ouse] of honestey		H[ouse] of honestey	
H[ouse] of Lancas[ter]		H[ouse] of Lancas[ter]	H[ouse] of Lancas[ter]		H[ouse] of Lancas[ter]	
H[ouse] of York		H[ouse] of York	H[ouse] of York		H[ouse] of York	

Hole map, Bodleian	Guildhall/LMA	1601 *Ayme*	1628 *Ayme*	1594 *Ayme*	Dickman	Notes
Huls pump		Huls pumpe			Hulls Pumpe	
Humfrey iames		Humfrey Iames, or Crosses stake	Humfrey James		Humphrei Jeams	
Hurst		Hurst			Herst	
Islippe	Isappe		Islips			Isappe looks like a misreading and the 1628 form is likely to be correct. Islip is a relatively uncommon surname, and one of the gentlemen addressed in James I's 1605 *Letters Patent* is named Adam Islipp, perhaps the same Adam Islip who was admitted to the HAC on the same day as Thomas Covell, 26 September 1614.
Jonas						
Jones his joy						The name is clearly written on the map but appears to be unique to Hole. Though of the fanciful type, surname plus abstract noun, it does better evidenced by the 1628 listing, it does not appear in the edition of Ayme published in that year — testimony perhaps to the often ephemeral nature of the mark names. It is not possible to suggest which particular Jones this mark commemorates: a John Jones was admitted to the HAC on 21 April 1612 and several other men of the surname during the course of 1614. Inigo, the only famous Jones of this era (1573–1652), architect and theatre designer, is not known to have had any interest in archery.

Hole map, Bodleian	Guildhall/ LMA	1601 Ayme	1628 Ayme	1594 Ayme	Dickman	Notes
Julius caesar			Julius caesar			Sir Julius Caesar is one of the knights addressed in James I's *Letters Patent* of 1605 —and in that of Elizabeth of 1596. He was admitted to the Worshipful Company of Goldsmiths in 1583 and was MP for Westminster in 1607, and Middlesex in 1614.
Kempton		Kempton	Kempton		Kempton	Not marked on Hole map
			Kings kindnesse			
Kings mace		Kings mace	Kings mace		Kinges Maise	
Kingston-bridg	Kingstonb	Kingstone bridge			Kingston Brige	
Lambearts-goodwill	I hearty-goodwill		Lamberts-goodwill			
Lanterne		Lanterne			Lanthorne Den	
Lees Lion			Lees Lion			A Rowland Lee was admitted to the HAC on 15 August 1611; he was both Lieutenant of the Company and Company Treasurer in 1612 (Raikes, *Ancient Vellum Book*, p. 16).
			Lees lurching			Not marked on Hole map
Lion		Lion			Lion	
Locklis mout	Locklis mour	Lockleys mouth	Lockleies Mouth		Lockleies Mouth	

Hole map, Bodleian	Guildhall/ LMA	1601 Ayme	1628 Ayme	1594 Ayme	Dickman	Notes
Lond: ston		London stone	London stone		London stone	'London Stone' is the name given to a piece of Roman stonework now preserved within a niche in the wall at 111 Cannon Street — it is mentioned by both Camden and Stow and was regarded as one of the 'sights' of London at the date of our map. In Samuel Rowland's *Humors Looking Glasse* (1608), amongst the attractions the country bumpkin visiting the City must see are 'The Bosse at Billingsgate, and London stone, / And at White-Hall the monstrous great Whales bone'. See several articles by John Clark, most recently *London Stone: History and Myth*, January 2017, Academia, https://www. academia.edu/1190846/London_Stone_History_ and_Myth [accessed on 31 October 2020].
Longmeg					Long Mege	Long Meg [of Westminster] was a fictional late Elizabethan folk-heroine, a 'roaring girl' whose jest biography first appeared in 1590, see Patricia Gartenberg, 'An Elizabethan Wonder Woman: The Life and Fortunes of Long Meg of Westminster', in *The Journal of Popular Culture*, 17 (1983), pp. 49–58.
			Loues increase			Not marked on Hole map
Lurching stake		Lurching stake	Lees lurching		Lurching	
Lure					Lewer	
Lyon					Lyon	
Mabb		Mab	Mab		Mabb	

Hole map, Bodleian	Guildhall/ LMA	1601 Ayme	1628 Ayme	1594 Ayme	Dickman	Notes
Maiors marygold		Maiors marygold			Marygoulde	
Marshes st[ake]		Marshes st[ake]	Marshes st[ake]			
Martins maif:		Martins May-floure			Martins May-floure	
Martins monkie		Martins Munkie				The West Country family of Martyn/Martin had as crest to their arms 'on the stump of a tree couped and erased, *argent*, a monkey, sejant, proper, collared and lined, *or*, looking in a mirror, framed, *or*.' It can be seen, for example, on the memorial brass of Adam Martyn (d. 1597) in the church at Crewkerne, Somerset. The motto of the family is given as 'He who looks at Martin's ape, Martin's ape shall look at him'. Sir William Martyn's alabaster tomb of c. 1503 in the church at Puddletown, Dorset, includes the effigy of a chained ape. Sir William had been Lord Mayor of London in 1493 and it is perhaps this connection that familiarized the citizens of London with 'Martins munkie'.
Mayden-blush		Maidens Blush			Mades Blush	
Mercers maid		Mercers maid			Mercers Made	The badge of the Mercers' Company.
Mill poste		Mill				
Mils his back		Mils his back			Mills Back	A Thomas Milles was admitted to the HAC on 23 October 1614 (Raikes, *Ancient Vellum Book*, p. 24).

Hole map, Bodleian	Guildhall/ LMA	1601 *Ayme*	1628 *Ayme*	1594 *Ayme*	Dickman	Notes
Morington		Morington				
Mouth		Mouth			Mouth Stone	
N: Hynde		Nortriges hinde			Nortage Hind	Nortrige is attested as a rare contemporary surname.
Nelson		Nelson				
			Neues delight			Not marked on Hole map
			Neues tissick			Not marked on Hole map
Nightingale		Nightingale				
Norington	Nonngere	Norington			Norring-tonne	Looks like the surname.
Nosgay						
Nuns head		Nuns head				
				Old Gawthorn or Jehu		Not marked on Hole map
					Oxx Yoake	Not marked on Hole map
Parkes his pleasure		Parkes his pleasure	Parkes his pleasure			Perhaps Nicholas Parks, one of the gentlemen to whom James I's *Letters Patent* of 1605 was addressed.
Parkins hare		Parkins hare				

Hole map, Bodleian	Guildhall/LMA	1601 Ayme	1628 Ayme	1594 Ayme	Dickman	Notes
Perins past		Perins past-brush	Perins past-brush		Perins Pas	See Arber, *Stationers*, II, p. 568: 19 November 1590. 'John Pyrryn—Entrcd for his copie under Master Cawoodes hand, *The Tectonicon of Ffinsbury feildes*. Vjd.' The printed forms seem to suggest that the second word is 'paste-brush', a compound that the *OED* does not record before 1764.
Pew doore		Pew doore			Pew doore	Not marked on Hole map
Pigion		Pigion	Piggins loue		Pigeon	
Piller of powles		Pillar of Paules			Poulles Stone [*?recte* Poulles Stake]	The 1601 form seems to suggest this is 'pillar of [St] Paul's [church]'.
Pinder		Pinder			Pinder	As a common noun, 'pinder' means an official who rounds up and impounds stray animals, but it thus became a fairly common 'occupational' surname: a Thomas Pinder was admitted to the HAC on 19 April 1614 (Raikes, *Ancient Vellum Book*, p. 20).
Plaice					Place	
Pond						
			Poore's Partridge			Not marked on Hole map

Hole map, Bodleian	Guildhall/ LMA	1601 *Ayme*	1628 *Ayme*	1594 *Ayme*	Dickman	Notes
Pol[pes] head		Popeshead			Popes Heade	This might be thought a surprising name to find in early seventeenth-century London. The inn of this name in Southwark had changed its name to *King's Head* by 1542, and an establishment of the same name in Cornhill to *Bishop's Head* at the same date — yet it is on record as *Pope's Head* again from the 1590s until its destruction in the Great Fire, so might perhaps be an instance of a mark sponsored by an inn. See Bryant Lillywhite, *London Signs* (London, 1972).
			Prichard's hope			Not marked on Hole map
Princes stake		Princes stake	Princes stake		?=Princes of America	The spelling of Princes in 1601 and on Hole's map is unfortunately ambiguous — it could represent modern 'Prince's', 'Princes'', 'Princess' or 'Princess's'.
Puttock		Puttock	Puttock		Puttock	A now obsolete term for a bird of prey, especially the red kite.
Pyper		Pyper			Pyper	
Queenes stake		Queenes stake	Queenes		Queenes stake	See discussion on p. 141 on the names of the marks.
Qui: pill	Out pill		Quinies Pillar		Quins Piller	See 'Pakes his Pillar' cited by Knight, *London*, p. 177, as one of the alliterative names to be found in the now lost 1594 edition of *Ayme*.
		Quin's Fauchon			Quin's Fauchon	Not marked on Hole map

Hole map, Bodleian	Guildhall/ LMA	1601 Ayme	1628 Ayme	1594 Ayme	Dickman	Notes
Rainebow		Rainebow, sometimes New-foundland	Rainebow			
Ralfes stone		Rolfes stone			Rolfe Stone	
Rameshead		Rameshead			Rameshead	
Redcross		Redcross			Red Crosse	
Red Drag[on]			Red Dragon			A Welsh badge?
Ro: hood		Robinhood	Robinhood		Robin Hoode	
Robinsons		Robinson				Perhaps William Robinson, one of the gentlemen to whom James's *Letters Patent* of 1605 was addressed.
Robinsons leg		Robinsons leg			Robinsons leg	
Rogers sta[ke]		Rogers stake			Rogers	A Briant Rogers was admitted to the HAC on 16 October 1611 (Raikes, *Ancient Vellum Book*, p. 17). It is this mark which is surmounted by a unicorn's head.

Hole map, Bodleian	Guildhall/ LMA	1601 Ayme	1628 Ayme	1594 Ayme	Dickman	Notes
Ros[emary] bra[n]ch				Rosemary branch		A mark named *Ros:brach* which could feasibly be located close to the Rosemary Branch inn, the only building known to have existed in the area at this period. Allegedly it was a meeting place for Levellers a few years later, each identifying themselves with bunches of rosemary in their hats. It was rebuilt a little further to the north in 1783, and survives as a thriving pub and theatre in a Victorian building.
Sapling by lio[n]					Saplin Lyon	
Saunders back		Saunders back	Saunders back		Saunders back	
Sawpit		Sawpit	Sawpit		Sawpit	
Sct Andrew			Sct Andrew			
Sct Botu=		Saint Botulphe	Saint Butolphes		St. Buttalls	
Sct George			Sct George			
Sct Gyles		Sct Gyles			Sct Gyles	
Sct Leonards					Sct Leonards	
Sct Martines		Sct Martines	Sct Martines		Sct Martines	
Sea-Griphon		Sea Griphon	Sea-griffin			
Sheaf of arr[ows]		Sheffe of arrows	Sheffe of arrowes		? = Sheather	
Short starre						i.e., Short's star?

Hole map, Bodleian	Guildhall/ LMA	1601 Ayme	1628 Ayme	1594 Ayme	Dickman	Notes
Snowball		Snowball	Snowball		Snoballe	
Sonday hill		Sonday Hill			Sounday hill	Hole's map shows this mark a little to the north east of the one named 'Bunhill' and a little south west of the well of 'Dame Annis [Agnes] le cleere' in Old Street. It may well represent a slight local eminence.
Speed st[ake]		Speedes stake			Speedes	
Speering-sport			Speerings sport	Old Speering		A prime candidate for this mark must be the Nicholas Speering listed as one of the 'founder' members of the revived Honourable Artillery Company in 1611; he became one of its Captains in 1612 when he also held the office of Treasurer and left the Company a legacy of £10 in 1618 (Raikes, *Ancient Vellum Book*, pp. 4, 16, 115). Perhaps 'Old Speering', the name of a mark recorded in the lost 1594 *Ayme*, commemorated his father?
Spindle		Spindle			Spindle	
Sr Rowland		Sir Rowland	Sir Rowland			Probably named after Sir Rowland Hayward, see below.
Stake by stile		Stake at the stile			Style Poast	
Sta.mye.pla [sta.in ye.pla]		Stake in the plaine				
Star		Star	Star	Star or Dial	Starr	
Stile		Stake at the stile			Style Poast	

Hole map, Bodleian	Guildhall/LMA	1601 Ayme	1628 Ayme	1594 Ayme	Dickman	Notes
Ston[e]		Stirrops stake			Stirrupe	Not marked on Hole map
Stone by the pond					Stone Martin	On the map 'Stone' is next to 'Sct Martines'.
Stone in ye plaine			Stone in ye plaine			
		Sudlowes swan			Sudlos Swanne	Not marked on Hole map
Swan-harnestman		Swan harnest man	Swan harnesman		Swan Har.	See below.
Swan= Wilcox		Swan Wilcox	Swan wilcox		Swan Will	It is difficult to know quite how to construe this name. Was it formerly called Swan, but is now more usually known as Wilcox? A Richard Wilcocks was admitted to the HAC on 25 October 1614 (Raikes, *Ancient Vellum Book*, p. 24).
Swans stake		Swans stake	Swans stake		Swan Ould	
Target tree		Target tree			Target tree	
Teuels timber			Teuels timber			This seems to be the surname more usually spelled Tewell in contemporary records.
Theefe in the hedge	Theefe in hedge	Theefe in the hedge	Theefe in the hedge			
3 Cranes	Cranes	Three Cranes	Three cranes		Three Craines	

Hole map, Bodleian	Guildhall/LMA	1601 Ayme	1628 Ayme	1594 Ayme	Dickman	Notes
Thurloes rose		Thurloes rose			Thurloes rose	
Tinckers bud[get]		Tinkers budget	Tinkers budget		Tinckers Buget	An obsolete sense of 'budget' is defined by the *OED* as 'A pouch, bag, wallet, usually of leather'.
Townes end			Townes end			
Turkes stake	Turke stake	Turkes-whale	Turks whale	Turkes-whale	Turke	
Vent ston		Vent stone			Vent stone	
Vper Gardiner	Vyer Gardiner	Vpper Gardiner			Vpper Gardiner	
Walkers Drag[on]			Walkers dragon			
Wards stake		Wards stake			Wards stake	
Waterbearer		Waterbearer			Waterbearer	
Watergap	Wale gap	Watergap			Water Gappe	
Watson		Watson			Watson	
Weeping cross		Weeping cross	Weeping cross		Weeping cross	See below.
			Welds friendship			Not marked on Hole map
Wells good will			Wilies good-will			
			Wells his phissick			Not marked on Hole map

Hole map, Bodleian	Guildhall/ LMA	1601 Ayme	1628 Ayme	1594 Ayme	Dickman	Notes
Whitbrooke		Whitbrooke			Whitbrooke	
Whithorne		Whithorne			Whithorne	
Wrilock		Wridocke			Wrydocke	There is a rare surname Wrydock (e.g. a Norfolk man so named in a lawcase of 1589), suggesting that Hole's form is mistaken and that those of 1601 are correct.
Yeomanson		Yeomanson			Yeomanson	
Young powel	Youngpewe	Yong Powell	Yong Powell		Yonge Powell	

The longevity of mark names evidently varied considerably — within
the space of a generation, to judge from the earliest extant editions of the
Ayme, there could be considerable attrition and replacement — only eighty
names recorded in the 1601 guide are still found in that of 1628, which
contains 163, so that a generation later half the names have disappeared.
This attrition may also be inferred from the fact that a number of marks
have alternative names given to them in the (lost) 1594 and 1601 editions of
Ayme: *Aspinals Ape, somtimes blacke Prince* 1601 (*Aspinalls Ape* Dickman);
Bakers boy, or Greyhound 1601 (*Baikers Boye* Dickman); *Bee-hive,
sometime Portingale crosse* 1601 (*Beehive* Dickman); *Cuckow, sometime
Momford* 1601 (*Cockkowe* Dickman); *Dial or Monument* 1594 (*Dial* 1601;
Dyall Dickman); *Diogenes, sometimes Candlesticke* 1601 (*Candlesticke*
Dickman);[53] *Hodges pleasure, sometimes Sheepes stake* 1601 (*Hoges
pleasure* Dickman); *Humfrey Iames, or Crosses stake* 1601 (*Humphrei
Jeams* Dickman); *Old Gawthorn or Jehu* 1594; *Rainebow, sometimes New-
foundland* 1601 (*Rainebow* Hole; 1628); *Star or Dial* 1594.

While the Goldsmiths' Company is not represented amongst the stakes
on Hole's map, several other livery companies are — by association, at least:
the Tilers and Bricklayers[54] (*Bricklaier*), the Clothworkers (*Clo[thworkers]
Handle*), Coopers (*Cooper*), Curriers (*Curriers shave*), Fullers (*Fuller St[ake]*)
and Mercers (*Mercers maid*). We have noticed above that it is possible to
make out representations of two animal heads, a bird and a spindle topping
four of the marks. In the case of the livery companies, it would appear that
a representation of or even an *actual* tool characteristic of the trade carried
out by the Company in question topped the mark. *Curriers* used a *shave*
to scrape hair from the skins they curried, and Dickman's 1601 manuscript
listing of the marks gives a fuller version of Hole's *Cooper* in the form
Coopers Chevall. This sense of *cheval* is not registered in *OED*, but note the
Dictionary's definition of 'horse', sense 8d — 'a cooper's tool used in driving
the staves of a cask closely together', or, as Cotgrave defined the term in
1611, 'the Coopers horse; an yron toole which he vseth in the hooping of
Caske'. The map's *Clo[thworkers] Handle* is not immediately meaningful,
the 1601 documents have *Clothworkers handle* (1601) and *Clothworkers
Hand* (Dickman). The arms of the Clothworkers' Company are blasoned,
'sable a chevron ermine between in chief two havettes *argent* and in base
a teasel cob *or*'. The *havette* — also known as a *habick/habeck* — was a
flexible double-ended hook used to attach cloths to the shearing bench and
is shaped like a handle, as still depicted on the Company's arms.[55] I suggest,
therefore, that *Clothworkers Handle* is the correct form of the name of this
particular mark, again showing the LMA map's *Handler* to be a secondary
and unreliable form. *Mercers maid* also alludes to the arms of the company,
the head of a young woman with flowing locks.

A sub-group of trade-related names exemplify almost proverbial compounds: *Brewers Aperne* (not in Hole or 1628; 1601; Dickman), *Bricklayers Finial* (not in Hole; 1601; just *Finiall* in Dickman; *Bricklayers mold* 1628), *Carters whip* (Hole; 1601; just *Whipp* in Dickman; 1628), *Tinckers Buget*[56] (Hole; 1601; Dickman; 1628).

In his contemporary *Survay of London*, Stow enumerates 123 parish churches, and at least seven of the names of the marks given on Hole's map can be construed as those of churches,[57] and it may be that some churches were happy to sponsor a mark in recognition both of the utility of archery as a martial exercise that could be put to good use in defence of the nation, and as a healthy alternative — as both official proclamations and contemporary promoters of archery never fail to point out — to more dubious pastimes such as drinking and gambling.

It is therefore possibly ironic that several marks bear names also found as those of contemporary taverns: *Bear's Head*,[58] *Boar's Head*, *Cat & Fiddle*, *Flying Horse*,[59] *Mouth*, *Ram's Head*, *Red Cross*, *Three Cranes*. It is possible that the upkeep of these stakes was the responsibility of the establishment so named — and, of course, a useful advertisement, too — though we know nothing of the practicalities of such arrangements. A small clutch of names reflects the resurgence of interest in Robin Hood and his company in late Elizabethan England as attested by Anthony Munday's two-part *Downfall* and *Death of Robert, Earl of Huntington*, written in 1598,[60] and the contemporary manuscript *Memoir of Robin Hood*.[61] *Ro: hood* appears on Hole's map (*Robinhood* 1601; *Robin Hoode* Dickman) and is still listed in the 1628 *Ayme*, while his *Friertuck* (*Frier Tucke* 1601; Dickman) has disappeared by 1628. Only Dickman's 1601 manuscript list records the name *Gate Little John*, but the rather later listing of the marks in St George's Fields (1664) includes both *Robin Hood* and *Little John*.[62] The 1628 *Ayme* opens its alphabetical listing with the mark named *Adam Bell*, another legendary archer.

As at Finsbury, there was doubtless a mark named *Queenes stake* on every archery field, and another of the Elizabethan documents reprinted by Wood — also otherwise unknown — is entitled *A Brief description of the Show made at S. Martins in the Fields, in setting up Her Majesties Stake* (n.d.),[63] but less exalted contemporaries are also commemorated in the names of the marks. In the account of the 1583 pageant there is mention of one of the Duke's facetiously named Captains, *Baron Stirrop* 'whose costly Stake will be in memory after he is dead, now standing at Mile-end'.[64]

Williams suggested — reasonably enough — that the names of some marks 'appear to be the names of eminent archers', citing *Banckes*, *Browne*, *Carrington* and *Humphry James*,[65] to which A. R. Kench adds *Baines his Needle*, *Hodge's Pleasure* and *Pritchard's Hope* (1628)[66] — but in neither case is any evidence offered to support the alleged eminence, or, indeed, the very existence of these archers. Where the names of marks on Hole's map could well be surnames I have annotated them accordingly, but only where the name is sufficiently uncommon and can be found in either James I's *Letters Patent for the Encouragement of Archery in the City of London* of 1605, or in the earliest records of HAC members, that is, 1611–20.

Of course, it is inherently likely that several marks should commemorate contemporary worthies not necessarily famed for their prowess with the bow, but nevertheless keenly interested in the sport. The mark named *Sir Rowland* (1601, 1628), for example, was surely named after Sir Rowland Hayward/Heyward (d. 1593). A major figure in the politics as well as the business of the City of London, Hayward was MP for the City from 1572 to 1583 (and participated in the 1583 *show and shooting*), and naturally served on House of Commons committees concerning London's trade and industry. He was Lord Mayor in 1570–71 — when he was knighted — and again in 1591. As 'Father of the City' (senior alderman) from 1586, he was involved in matters as various as military preparations in case of Spanish attack, the management of the City's property and the furtherance of its interests in parliament. He was a mainstay of City government in the crisis caused by plague in 1593, when he was in his seventies, just as he had been thirty years before, in the devastating epidemic of 1563.[67]

Julius Caesar is unlikely to allude to the Roman Emperor, but rather to Sir Julius Caesar (1558–1636) who is one of the knights addressed in James I's *Letters Patent* of 1605 — and in that of Elizabeth of 1596. He was also a member of the Goldsmiths' Company admitted in 1583, and was MP for Westminster in 1607 and for Middlesex in 1614.[68] Similarly, *Mabb* is unlikely to refer to Shakespeare's queen of the fairies, but rather to a contemporary mortal of that name, such as the John Mabbe (*c.* 1515–82) who served as chamberlain of London in 1577 and was also a well-known member of the Goldsmiths' Company — it is less likely to commemorate his son of the same name who was also a goldsmith, but was outlawed for debt some time before March 1589.[69]

It is tempting to associate the Perrin of *Perins past[-brush]* with the *John Pyrryn* who paid 6d. to license *The Tectonicon of Ffinsbury feildes* (see above) and to link the Speering of *Speeringsport* (*Speerings sport* 1628) with the Nicholas Speering listed as one of the 'founder' members of the revived Honourable Artillery Company in 1611. The Dickman of *Dick[man's] Marigold* is surely the Henry Dickman who in 1601 listed the marks in Finsbury Fields in the manuscript now in the collection of the Society of Antiquaries.

How are we to construe names of the *Aspinall's Ape* type, that is, surname followed by name of object? I suggest that names of this type record marks maintained at the expense of the archer named, and presumably surmounted with a two- or three-dimensional representation of the object.

Presumably even the poorest archers from time to time managed to 'hit the mark', damaging or even destroying it totally, so that fairly regular maintenance of the device was needed, and this would have been done at the expense of the individual commemorated in the mark's name. A name such as *Swan harnest man* (1601; Hole; 1628), therefore, would denote an image of a man in armour (*harnessed* — *OED*, sense 2) surmounting and identifying the mark maintained by a man named Swan. Other names in this category are: *Cawdries Coffer*, *Doves Red-breast*, *Gravells Lambbe*, *Kings Mace*, *Lockleies Mouth*, *Martins May-floure* (1601), *Majors Marigold* (1601), *Quins Fauchon* [i.e. falchion, broadsword] (Dickman; 1601), *Sudlos Swanne*, *Thurlos Rose*, and so on.

A number of legendary heroes (though not necessarily archers) are to be found in the corpus: *Long Meg* presumably alludes to the folk-heroine, a sort of female Robin Hood, whose 'biography' was entered in the Stationers' Register in 1590 as the 'Life of Long Meg of Westminster'. *Guy of Warwick* appears in the 1628 listing and is probably disguised behind the perhaps somewhat garbled form on Hole's map which I transcribe *[Gu]iowar: nls*. Guy's giant adversary *Colbrand* also appears in 1628 and in Dickman's manuscript list [*Collebrande*]; the name is abbreviated on Hole's map as Coleb.

The HAC's regulations required its members to be 'soundly and religiously affected to the King and State' (1614),[70] that is, Protestant, and in this context one can imagine a degree of unholy glee afforded by shooting at the marks named *Nuns Heade* and *Popes Heade*. In Reformation London two inns known as *The Popes Head*, in Cornhill and Southwark, had prudently changed their names to *The Bishop's Head* and *The King's Head* as long ago as 1542.[71] Details of the 1583 pageant shed an interesting sidelight on such late Elizabethan burlesquing of Catholic dignitaries, 'causing great laughing and sport':

> the most part were Haberdashers of London; who very orderly marched through the City of London, being sumptuously apparelled in Velvet Jerkins, and Hats agreeable, with Chains of Gold about their Bodies, and Pages bearing their Shields of fine workmanship, and a worthy Train of good Archers wearing green Scarves and Ribbons of the same colour. The show of Feryers proceeded, which was One hundred handsome Fellowes with Calivers [light muskets] on their Necks, all trimly decked with white Feathers in their Hats; so had all their Company of Archers throughout: Then their Ensign and two Cardinals, wearing broad Hats of Tawny colour, with two silk strings buttoned under their Chins; the ends hanging down to their feet, apparelled in red Velvet and Satten; next followed two Friers clothed in black Robes, with bald Crowns and Beads in their hands, seeming to pray very devoutly, and blessing them that passed by, causing great laughing and sport.[72]

Williams, comparing Hole's map with Dickman's list, omits to mention a domestic category, those marks apparently named after household items, everyday objects such as *Beehive, Bell Clapper, Candle, Candlestick, Dyall, Gouldene Cup, Horne Booke, Horse Loafe* [loaf made from beans, bran, etc. to feed horses], *Lanterne, Oxx Yoake, Pew Dore, Sheffe of arrowes, Spindle.* In some such cases the object itself rather than a representation of it probably topped the mark.

The 1628 *Ayme*'s listing shows a considerable increase in a type of more fanciful abstract name that is found only occasionally in the earlier lists,[73] consisting of a surname followed by an abstract noun: *Clarks delight, Coxes content, Dudleis darling,*[74] *Kings kindnesse, Lamberts goodwill, Lees lurching, Neues delight, Piggins loue, Prichards hope, Welds friendship* — and alliteration plays a part in less than half of these. More difficult to categorize are *Neues tissick* [i.e. phthisic], *Wells his phissick* [physic?] and *Loues increase.*

I close with a few miscellaneous names that are intriguing or puzzling. Dickman records a *Princes of America* in which the first word is more likely to represent modern English 'princess' than 'princes' (the other sources have what appears to be a shortened form of the name, *Princes stake*). In this era the American 'princess' who springs to mind is Pocahontas, of course, but her arrival in England post-dates Dickman's 1601 manuscript list.

All the sources — and the St George's Fields listing of 1664 — give the name of one of the archery marks as *House of Honesty.* This sounds to me like one of those facetious names denoting a brothel, with 'honesty' being synonymous in this period with 'chastity' — there are plenty of parallels in Gordon Williams's *Dictionary of Sexual Language and Imagery in Shakespearean and Stuart Literature* (London, 1994), at 'house' — for example, 'house of accommodation', 'house of hospitality', 'house of entertainment', 'house of ease' — though admittedly not this particular one.

Weeping Cross is another interesting name. At least three places of this name are recorded, none of them in London, and whatever the name originally denoted — a monumental cross, or a crossroads, perhaps — by 1564 at the latest, to 'come home by weeping cross' had become a proverbial phrase meaning to 'suffer grievous disappointment or failure' (*OED*). The tiny outline of the mark so labelled on the map does appear to have short arms not unlike a monumental cross and a perhaps floriate head.

Dating the Map

The map is undated and unfortunately — in so far as they can be plausibly identified — the dates of the dedicatees (above) offer no help. Nineteen of the names of the marks on the map are not found in the 1601 listings, but are found in the 1628 edition of *Ayme*, which at least suggests the map was executed between these two dates. Hole's dated maps, title pages and single-sheet prints fall between 1607 and 1618, but he continued to engrave for the Mint thereafter, and died in 1624. Strictly speaking, there seems to be no evidence to help us narrow down the date of the map between 1601 and 1624 and the names of the marks themselves offer no unequivocal help — *King's Mace*, for example, is already found in the 1601 listings, so does not even provide a *terminus post quem* of 1603 (but see further below).

One decidedly puzzling fact is that the map prominently bears the arms of the Goldsmith's Company — of which Hole himself was a member from 1599 onwards (freed in 1607) — and we have seen above how interested in the exercise of archery the Company was. We know that according to the 1601 *Ayme* (and Dickman's contemporary manuscript list) one of the marks at Finsbury was named *Goldsmiths stake*, and yet there is no mark so named on Hole's map — but neither was there according to the 1628 edition of *Ayme*. We have noticed above the considerable degree of attrition amongst the names of the marks and, even though we might expect a mark sponsored by a City livery company to endure, it seems that it had at least disappeared by 1628. As it is not marked on the present map it had surely disappeared by 1624, the date of Hole's death — but we have noticed the considerable degree of 'turnover' amongst the marks above. Despite its relative simplicity, then, it seems likely that the map dates from the end of Hole's career.

The editions of *Ayme for Finsburie Archers* we know of were published in 1594 (lost), 1601, 1604 (lost), 1626 (lost) and 1628. That as little as two years separates two of the editions suggests a comparative frequency of publication for these cheap little guidebooks during the early seventeenth century, and doubtless several other editions have escaped notice altogether. A lost edition issued at some point in Hole's engraving career (1605–18), especially towards the latter part, would provide a suitable home for his map to be folded and bound into. If we look for a suitable occasion, the granting to the recently revived[75] Honourable Artillery Company of the use of the uppermost field in Finsbury by the Corporation of the City of London in May 1614 may well provide it. Such an occasion might well call for a new, special edition of the map.

The 'founder-members' of this 'renewal' of the Honourable Artillery Company are recorded in the Company's 'Ancient Vellum Book' under the date 15 August 1611. They include Nicholas Speering and Rowland Lee. Islip is a relatively rare surname, so there seems a good chance that the mark labelled *Islippe* on Hole's map commemorates Adam Islip, admitted to the HAC on 26 September 1614.

Speerings sport, *Lees Lion* and *Islippe* are names found only on Hole's map and in the 1628 *Ayme*, and I suggest that all three marks were named after these prominent officers of the HAC at some point between the 'renewal' of the Company in 1611 and 1614 when it was officially granted the use of Finsbury Fields.[76] For these reasons, it seems to me that Hole's map is unlikely to be any earlier than 1614.

According to Bagford, the lost 1626 quarto edition of *Ayme* was 'Printed for J[ohn]. Partridge at ye sign of ye Sun in St Pauls Church Yard, 1626', but the names of the marks were *gathered and amended, ye 2nd impression*, 'by James Partridge and by him dedicated to ye Archery of Finsbury'.[77] The extant 1628 24mo. edition claims also that its names are 'Newly gathered, and amended by Iames Partridge' who was doubtless some relation of the bookseller. The lost 1626 edition of *Ayme* amended by James Partridge evidently declared itself 'ye 2nd impression', implying an earlier *ante* 1626 impression. If we can assume that the James Partridge who was admitted to the HAC on 16 March 1618 is the same man, then given his interest in the marks and his stationer relation, John, 1618 or a little later might be considered a plausible date for Hole's map to appear in an edition of *Ayme*.

1. The Bodleian Library, The University of Oxford, Arch. A d.1. The map was discussed in a post on the Bodleian Library's Map Room blog, *History*, on 20 February 2018 by 'Tessa', blogs.bodleian.ox.ac.uk/maps/2018/02 [accessed on 7 March 2021]. There may be another impression in the Bodleian Library: according to J. P. Malcolm (*Londinium Redivivum* (1802–07), IV, p. 26) the map was described as 'an old print in the Bodleian Library, inserted in a work on Archery'; A. R. Kench (see note 66) assumed it to have been bound in the now lost 1594 edition of *Ayme for Finsburie Archers*.

2. London Metropolitan Archives (LMA), SC/GL/PR/F1/FIN/FIE/p5372611. The LMA online catalogue suggests 'c.1650?' as the date of the impression with William Hole as the 'artist' and attributes the work to an 'anonymous' engraver.

3. London, Bethlem Royal Hospital, Museum of the Mind, EO-026 Series Box no. A07/3. Here the online catalogue https://archives.museumofthemind.org.uk/EO.htm [accessed on 19 October 2020] gives the date of the Hospital's impression as '1735?–1765?'.

4. Reproduced and discussed in *Tudor London: A Map and a View*, ed. by Ann Saunders and John Schofield, London Topographical Society publication No. 159 in association with the Museum of London (2001).

5. John Williams, 'Comparison of a MS. in the Possession of the Society of Antiquaries, Containing a List of the Archers' Marks in Finsbury Fields, with William Hole's Map of the Same Fields Laid Out as Archery Grounds', in *Proceedings of the Society of Antiquaries*, 1st ser., 4 (1856–59), pp. 50–60.

6. A. J. Kempe, 'Archery in Finsbury Fields', in the *Gentleman's Magazine* (March 1832), pp. 209–213.

7. These printers are identified in the searchable *British Book Trade Index* (BBTI), http://bbti.bodleian.ox.ac.uk/ [accessed on 20 October 2020].

8. Foster's 'Bibliography of Archery', in *Notes and Queries*, ser. 5, vol. IX, no. 226, 27 April 1878, p. 325.

9. Kempe, 'Archery', p. 210 — 'republished by R.F. in 1604, the title not so full'.

10. Pepys Library, Magdalene College, Cambridge.

11. BBTI, see n. 7.

12. John Stow, *A Survay of London* (1598), p. 354.

13. Kempe, 'Archery', p. 210.

14. The record derives from a note by John Bagford in BL, MS Sloane 5900, fol. 35, as quoted

by Foster, 'Bibliography', p. 325.

15. BL, 1041.b.31. It seems likely that several other editions appeared between 1604 and 1626.

16. G. A. Raikes, *The Ancient Vellum Book of the Honourable Artillery Company* (London, 1890), pp. 20, 23.

17. G. A. Hansard, *The Book of Archery* (London, 1840), p. 417. In his *London* (London, 1841), p. 177, Charles Knight stated that the 1594 edition listed 164 marks, but he misunderstood Kempe ('Archery'), who listed the 164 marks in the extant 1628 edition of *Ayme*.

18. Edward Arber, *A Transcript of the Registers of the Company of Stationers of London 1554–1640*, 5 vols (London, 1875–94), II, p. 568.

19. Foster, 'Bibliography', p. 325.

20. British Museum, 1878,0808.15–73.

21. Laurence Worms and Ashley Baynton-Williams, *British Map Engravers* (London, 2011), pp. 324–45.

22. David Mitchell, *Silversmiths in Elizabethan and Stuart London: Their Marks and Their Lives* (Woodbridge, 2017).

23. Christie's London auctions of March 1933, 1941 and 1920, respectively. I am most grateful to Mr Jeffrey Lassaline of Christie's for this information. Mr Lassaline also adds that a maidenhead spoon bearing the compasses mark was sold at Christie's in 1903 but that, despite the fact that it was 'engraved with the date 1612', because it also bore the date letter P, was mistakenly described as made in 1572.

24. H. Symonds, 'Engravers of the Tudor and Stuart Periods', *The Numismatic Chronicle and Journal of the Royal Numismatic Society*, 13 (1913), p. 361.

25. Laurence Worms (personal communication).

26. William Wood, *The Bow-man's Glory, or, Archery revived* (London, 1682), p. 55; the volume was reprinted in 1691, and again in 1801.

27. The last-named appears thus in ibid., p. 60.

28. Ibid., p. 57.

29. Ibid., p. 63.

30. Ibid., p. 43.

31. Goldsmiths' Company Rent Book, MS 1913, B393.

32. G. A. Raikes, *The History of the Honourable Artillery Company, volume 1* (London, 1878), p. 27, gives references for the years 1557, 1564, 1583, 1589 and 1596.

33. Ibid., pp. 26–27.

34. Stow, *London*, p. 77, refers to what is here termed the *bearing* arrow as the *broad* arrow.

35. *Oxford English Dictionary* (*OED*): mark, sense n.2 2. a. 'In England: a monetary unit equivalent in value to two-thirds of a troy pound of pure silver or two-thirds of a pound sterling'.
    1573 *Record's Ground of Arts* (rev. ed.) I. I. sig. N.iiijv Poundes, Markes, and shillinges, whiche though they haue no coynes, yet is there no name more in vse then they.
    1607 J. NORDEN *Surueyors Dialogue* IV. 173 Thirteene shillings and foure pence, or a Marke of money.

36. Wood, *Bow-man's Glory*, p. 49.

37. Ibid., p. 48.

38. Hugh D. H. Soar, *The Romance of Archery, a Social History of the Longbow* (Yardley, PA, 2008), pp. 47ff.

39. Ibid., p. 56.

40. Ibid., p. 54.

41. R. Renwick, *Extracts from the Records of the Burgh of Peebles*, II (Glasgow, 1910), p. 73.

42. Soar, *Archery*, p. 48.

43. Ibid., pp. 66–67 (where misdated 1664). Gilbert Talbot, like William Wood, another gentleman archery-revivalist, features in Wood's *Bow-mans Glory*.

On March the 21st. Anno Domini 1661. Four hundred Archers, with their Bows and Arrows, made a splendid and glorious Show in Hide-Park, with flying Colours, and Cross-bows to guard them. Sir Gilbert Talbot Baronet, was their Colonel ...

Upon the 26th of May [1676] following, the Archers marched to Tuttle-feilds to Shoot their Whistling-Arrowes. They Randezvouz'd in the Military-Ground near Bloomsbury, and march't from thence through part of Holbourn, through Chancery. Lane, through Temple-barr, and so through the Strand to Whitehall ... Sir Gilbert Talbot being the Colonel.

44. Stow, *London*, p. 351.

45. Raikes, *History*, p. 24.

46. Ibid., p. 25.

47. 'Middlesex Sessions Rolls: 1561', in *Middlesex County Records: Volume 1, 1550–1603*, ed. by John Cordy Jeaffreson (London, 1886), p. 37.

48. Stow, *London*, p. 77.

49. *The annales, or a generall chronicle of England, begun first by maister Iohn Stow* (1615), pp. 906–07.

50. Described in Foster's 'Bibliography' as 'MS. Archers' Marks in Finsbury Fields. — *Per me Henricus Dickmanus nomine: scribebam hunc librum et scriptus erat in anno Domini 1601, quarto die Mayij.* — London, 1601. 24mo. ff. 93, paper — The Marks are listed in alphabetical order. Lib. Soc Ants.'. The names are transcribed in Williams, 'Comparison'.

51. Soar, *Archery*, p. 37.

52. Williams, 'Comparison', p. 53.

53. Unless we suggest that *Candlestick* was a 'popular' nickname for *Diogenes* — perhaps the philosopher's famous candle-lit lantern once topped the mark?

54. Charter obtained in 1568.

55. See Geoff Egan, 'A Shearman's Hook from London', in *Transactions of the London and Middlesex Archaeological Society*, 30 (1979), pp. 190–92.

56. Also found on St George's Fields (Richard Hannis, *Aime for the archers of St. Georges Fields containing the names of all the marks* (London, 1664).

57. I.e. *Allhallowes, Sct Andrew, Sct Botu[lphes], Sct George, Sct Gyles, Sct Leonards, Sct Martines.*

58. It is perhaps a mere accident of survival that there is no record of a tavern so named in Bryant Lillywhite, *London Signs* (London, 1972), before the 1650s.

59. 1601; D only — not found on Hole's map.

60. R. B. Dobson and J. Taylor, *Rymes of Robyn Hood* (London, 1976), pp. 220–30.

61. BL, Sloane MS 780, fols 46–48, see Dobson and Taylor, *Rymes*, pp. 286–87.

62. Hannis, *St Georges Fields*.

63. I suspect it too is to be dated 1583 and may, indeed, be part of the previous document, as it bears the same running title as it. While no date as such is given, the stake in question is said to have been set up on 'Wednesday being the Second day of October last past'. 2 October fell on a Wednesday in six years during Elizabeth's reign: 1560, 1566, 1577, 1583, 1588, 1594. On p. 48 of the 1583 *Remembrance of the worthy show and shooting* reference is made to 'setting up the Queens Majesties Stake in Holborn fields, which Stakemaster Knevit,* one of the Gentlemen of her Majesties Chamber, gave unto [St Clement's parish] at his costs and Charges'. The setting up of the Queen's stake in Holborn fields is dated just ten days before the *Duke of Shoreditch*'s pageant, i.e. 7 September 1583. Despite the title of *A Brief description of the Show made at S. Martins in the Fields, in setting up Her Majesties Stake*, the text itself informs us that 'they went to set up [the stake] in S. Iames Field'. Where the Holborn fields pageant had included St Clement (being in St Clement's parish), the present pageant which served as prelude to the setting up of this 'very sumptuous stake', included 'Pan, with Fame and Honour attending on Vertue, then Saint Martin, and Eliza, as superior, accompanied with the four Vertues [see below], the Muses attending very seemly'. The

stake itself is described thus: 'upon this Stake stood a golden Lion holding a Shield with her Majesties Arms, the supporters whereof were Fortitude, Justice, Temperance, and Prudence, the Lion having a whole Crown on his head'.

* Thomas Knyvett (1545/6–1622) had been admitted to the Privy Chamber by 1572 and remained a gentleman of the bedchamber throughout Elizabeth's reign. The year after the pageant he was MP for Westminster, and in 1597 married the eldest of Sir Rowland Hayward's daughters (*ODNB*); in 1605 he is one of the knights addressed in James I's *Letters Patent*.

64. Wood, *Bow-man's Glory*, p. 52.
65. Williams, 'Comparison', p. 53.
66. A. R. Kench, *The Finsbury Marks*, website of the Worshipful Company of Bowyers (November 2007), https://www.bowyers.com/bowyery_finsburyMarks.php [accessed on 20 October 2020].
67. Information summarized from *ODNB*.
68. Information summarized from *ODNB*.
69. Information summarized from *ODNB*.
70. Petition dated 16 November 1614 (Raikes, *History*, p. 43).
71. Lillywhite, *London Signs*, p. 416, items 1870 and 11581, respectively.
72. Wood, *Bow-man's Glory*, pp. 46–7.
73. E.g. *Harrisons fellowship* D, *Hoges Pleasure*, *Jones his Joy*.
74. Knight, *London*, p. 177, quotes a *Dunstan's darling* from the lost 1594 *Ayme*.
75. *The practize in the artillery Garden reuiued* — as the side-note to the continuation of Stow succinctly summarizes the paragraph for the year 1610 (*The annales, or a generall chronicle of England, begun first by maister Iohn Stow* (1615), pp. 906–07).
76. To these three might be added *Coxes Content* also named only on Hole's map and in the 1628 *Ayme* — see p. 123 above.
77. See n. 14.

V. WHO HID THE CHEAPSIDE HOARD?
A GOLDSMITHS' ROW MYSTERY RESOLVED

By ROSEMARY WEINSTEIN

A SPECTACULAR find of early seventeenth-century jewellery was unearthed in 1912 at the time of the demolition of the whole block on the western corner of Cheapside and Friday Street (Fig. 1). The discovery was not the result of a controlled excavation, but a chance find by workmen who came across what was to become known as the 'Cheapside Hoard' (Fig. 2) in a

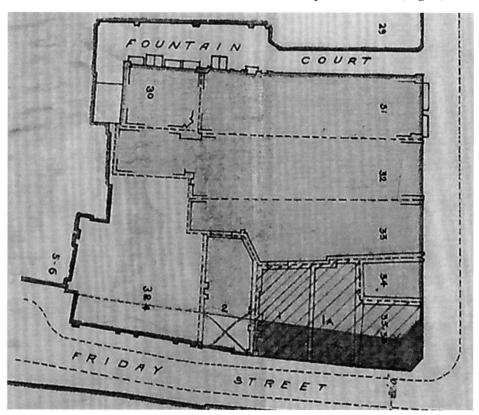

Fig. 1.   The City Engineer's plan of the demolished area between St Matthew's Alley/ Fountain Court and Friday Street, June 1911, showing the site of Wakefield House, 30–32 Cheapside, developed by 1916 (detail). [Key] "Hatched Red shews property to be acquired   Blue colour shews Freehold Property of Goldsmiths Company Green colour shews Freehold Property of Ecclesiastical Commissioners to be Sold to Goldsmiths Co.   Red colour shews Land to be thrown into the Public Way" © London Metropolitan Archives *COL/PHD/PL/01/003*.

Fig. 2.   The Cheapside Hoard: early seventeenth-century jewellery said to have been
found on the site of 30–32 Cheapside. © Museum of London.

wooden casket that had survived under a cellar floor. It was buried in chalky soil, which indicates proximity to a wall or other standing structure which probably helped it to survive deep basementing in the nineteenth century.[1] Sir Mortimer Wheeler, Keeper of the London Museum from 1926 onwards, described the find as having been made on the site that was developed as Wakefield House, 30–32 Cheapside.[2]

The jewellery was subsequently acquired by the former London Museum, together with selections of chains and rings gifted to the British Museum, Victoria and Albert Museum and Guildhall Museum. It has been on public display since at least 1928, when the first (and only) catalogue was published.[3] The jewellery dates to the first three decades of the seventeenth century and is much studied and published. The Hoard is important for knowledge of Jacobean jewellery and is very wide ranging — from exquisite engraved gems and cameos, a large hexagonal emerald watch, to thirty-five gold enamelled chains set with tiny stones and forty-eight finger rings. The large number of unmounted gemstones reveal trade routes across the known globe. The recent (2013) welcome redisplay and exhibition at the Museum of London reunited those portions held by the British Museum and V&A[4] and we look forward to its future display at the new Museum of London in Smithfield in due course.

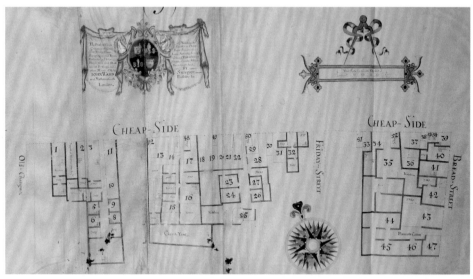

Fig. 3.   John Ward's Survey of Goldsmiths' Company property in Cheapside (detail of sheet 9), 1692. Properties with Lease numbers 26–29 and 50 were on the site developed in the twentieth century as Wakefield House, 30–32 Cheapside.
© Archive: The Worshipful Company of Goldsmiths.

The focus of this article is to see which of the documented goldsmiths on the site could have been responsible for burying the jewellery. Why was it hidden so securely under a cellar floor and 16 feet (4.9 metres) below present-day street level? The question will be answered by examining early seventeenth-century leases and other sources from the period, based largely on the records

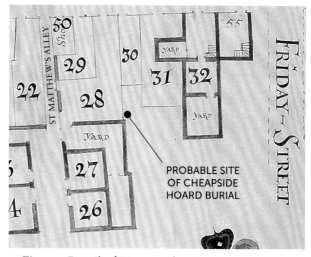

Fig. 4.   Detail of Figure 3 showing property west of Friday Street. Brick walls are marked in red.
© Archive: The Worshipful Company of Goldsmiths.

of the Goldsmiths' Company which owned many of the properties in that part of Cheapside then known as the western extension of Goldsmiths' Row, the site of today's One New Change. Several leases survive from the first half of the seventeenth century, but there is no detailed plan of the Goldsmiths' properties until John Ward's Survey of 1692 (Figs 3 and 4); lease numbers on Ward's survey — 26–32 and 50 — are used here to identify the properties concerned. It is unfortunate that when street numbering was introduced in the 1760s the buildings in that part of Cheapside were numbered 30–36 (Fig. 5): the coincidence of some of these street numbers

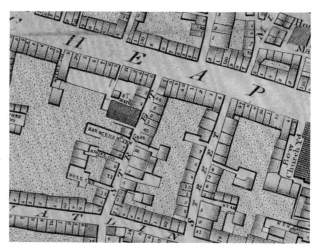

Fig. 5.   Richard Horwood, *Plan of the Cities of London and Westminster* (detail), 1799, showing 31–32 Cheapside. Private Collection.

with the earlier lease numbers has previously caused some confusion in attempts to identify the site of the Hoard.

The Black Moor's Head/Leases 26–28/32 Cheapside

The starting point of this article is the identification of a seventeenth-century property on the site that was to become part of 30–32 Cheapside, where the Hoard was found. This allows an investigation of the goldsmiths who worked there and in neighbouring buildings.

On 12 May 1769 the jeweller and working goldsmith William Smith announced in the *Daily Advertiser* that he was moving from 32 Cheapside. This was only a few years after the introduction of street numbering; Smith had traded from the premises since at least 1760, when his address was given as the Black Moor's Head, opposite Gutter Lane, Cheapside (Fig. 6). The name Black Moor's Head was indicative of exotica and luxury. The researches of F. G. Hilton Price and Ambrose Heal have revealed a sequence of goldsmiths at that address from the 1650s to the 1760s: Thomas Smith or Smithes, William Gibbon, Robert Cuthbert, Thomas Beach, Thomas Wildman, William Smith.[5] Further research (see below) takes the sequence back to the beginning of the century. One of these goldsmiths, or a near neighbour, would have been responsible for the Cheapside Hoard. Evidence is to be found in the Goldsmiths' Company records.

John Ward's Survey of 1692 shows Company property in various London locations, each numbered in a bold contemporary hand; sheet '9' shows several Cheapside properties between Old Change and Bread Street (Fig. 3).[6] Of particular interest in this study are Company properties due west of Friday Street, Leases 26–32 and shop number 50 (Fig. 4). This shop

Fig. 6. Trade card of William Smith at the Black Moor's Head, Opposite Gutter Lane, Cheapside. © Trustees of the British Museum *Heal, 67.131.*

is on the eastern corner of Cheapside and St Matthew's Alley (short and very narrow — some 4 feet (1.2 metres) wide at the Cheapside end) that cut through to Friday Street past St Matthew's Church. The Alley is a useful boundary in identifying Company leases (as is the parish designation of St Matthew's Friday Street); it had been re-named Fountain Court by 1911 when it marked the westward extension of the area demolished, then stretching eastward to Friday Street. The Goldsmiths' Company had no property along the western side of Friday Street, as Ward shows. From now on we will be identifying properties by the lease numbers given in the Survey.

The Survey is indexed in the Goldsmiths' Company Rental of 1692 (MS 2839), which cites lessees, landlords and tenants. This evidence leads to another important discovery, first published in this article: the Black Moor's Head corresponds with Leases 26, 27 and 28, which were held by Robert Cuthbert. Cuthbert was recorded there from before the Great Fire. So the discovery of the Cheapside Hoard at 32 Cheapside can now be placed at or near the Black Moor's Head, Leases 26–28. The site can be seen on Ward's Survey to the east of St Matthew's Alley. Cuthbert and, indeed, the holders of Leases 29–32 and the shop 50 are also recorded in Peter Mills and John Oliver's record of rebuilding after the Fire,[7] confirming the contemporary date for the Rental.

Robert Cuthbert

Who was Robert Cuthbert and how was he associated with these leases? He was the son of Nathaniel Cuthbert, Clerk, of Warmington, Northamptonshire, apprenticed to Cardinal Orme (also from Warmington) in 1634 and made free as a member of the Goldsmiths' Company in 1646. He pursued a career as a smallworker and jeweller, like his master, producing snuff boxes, rattles, brooches, buttons, buckles and so on. He also sold engraved seals and hilts for the newly fashionable small sword after the Restoration, some of which fell below the required standards.[8] It is uncertain how much was made in-house by retailing goldsmiths by this date.

By the time of the Restoration Cuthbert had been elected to the Livery and already had two apprentices: Robert Woolley in 1655 and Thomas Wicks in 1658 (free 1665). He built up sufficient business by 1664 to be able to afford the lease of the nine-hearth property in Cheapside.[9] His apprentices would have lived in the property, probably in a garret room, and received daily meals and maintenance as well as goldsmith instruction. There is no record of Woolley achieving his freedom but Wicks became a successful smallworker like his master, set up shop in the Strand and is remembered by his surviving business ledger, recording particularly plate and jewellery transactions between 1673 and 1684, although probably not of his manufacture. Business documents rarely survive, so this makes a particularly important contribution to our understanding of goldsmithing networks which extended even to the King. The Strand and its goldsmiths escaped the devastation of the Fire in 1666, not so Robert Cuthbert at the Black Moor's Head, destroyed on Thursday 4 September when flames engulfed the street. He presumably had time to remove his valuables, and he had enough capital to start rebuilding after permission was granted in 1668, having paid the 6s. 8d. fee for the surveys and laying out of the foundations.[10] Properties were rebuilt on the previous boundaries to avoid disputes and foster the City's recovery, but many people were ruined as rents were lost for years.

Robert Cuthbert was granted his new lease by the Goldsmiths' Company on 3 July 1672 for 95 years at £6 p.a. rent in consideration of rebuilding.[11] His lease was granted him:

> in consideration of the surrender of a lease to William Gibbon demised to Robert Cuthbert, a messuage and shop [Lease 28] on the South Side of West Cheap [i.e. Cheapside] in St Matthew Friday Street and two other tenements in St Matthew Alley [Leases 26 and 27], all which tenements lie together between the tenement of Bonner late Wheeler … And now Davenport on the east Mr Farr and the Alley on the west and between St Matthew's Church on the south and Cheapside on the north and contain the dimensions following:

> in the tenement on Cheapside one cellar lying under the fore shop containing from the outside of the wall north to the diversion south fifteen feet and in breadth from the party wall east to ditto west nine feet and a half and south west thereof another cellar containing in length from north to south fifteen feet seven inches from the middle of the party wall west twelve feet; on the first storey [ground floor] one shop containing in length from the outside of the front wall next the street to the Door case leading to the Back Shop south twenty one feet and from the middle of the timber partition east nine feet eight inches west.

John Davenport's back shop yard (Leases 31/32) was connected by a tunnel. His rebuilding to the east encroached upon Gibbon's land (see below).[12] Above the shop were four floors of chambers and over them 'a flat of lead' (i.e. a roof) on both the north and south sides. The yard to the south of the tenement of Purbeck stone measured 23¾ feet east–west and 8 feet 9 inches north–south with a further yard to the south. A funnel from Cuthbert's shop fireplace (furnace) was visible outside to people in the neighbouring property (Lease 29). *The London Gazette* had advised people rebuilding after the Fire to build strong cellars arched with brick and stone which had proved so useful in protecting goods during the Fire.[13]

Included in Cuthbert's lease were the two tenements in St Matthew's Alley adjoining (Lease nos 26 and 27) each measuring 29 feet 5 inches north–south by 20¼ feet east–west with a cellar, 'three rooms upright' and a garret each. Mills and Oliver record the laying out of one of these foundations for Cuthbert and with corresponding measurements and plan.[14] These Alley properties represent the one-room plan house found in narrow thoroughfares in post-Fire London, but in fact had more rooms, though smaller ones, before the Fire as mentioned below. Building regulations allowed the post-Fire shops timber frontages; no brick walls are recorded along Cheapside on Ward's survey for Leases 28–31 and shop 50, nor any internal walls.[15]

We know nothing of any furnishings but would expect coffers and chests in Cuthbert's shop for his banking business (see below) together with 'glasses' or display cabinets for his wares. The contemporary illustration of a goldsmith's shop by William Badcock in 1677 (Fig. 7) shows a spacious

Fig. 7. William Badcock's shop and workshop with jewellers working near the windows; frontispiece to *A Touch-stone for Gold and Silver Wares, or, A Manual for Goldsmiths and all other Persons, whether Buyers, Sellers, or Wearers of any manner of Goldsmiths Work how to know Adulterated Wares*, 1677. © Archive: The Worshipful Company of Goldsmiths.

and, no doubt, idealized shop interior with jewellers working on a bench near the very large window. Silversmiths with their anvils and other equipment hammer plate in the back shop. Cuthbert himself was to have a brush with Badcock concerning 'an Issue plate and hook' for a sword as being substandard,[16] Badcock having taken on the role of informer for the Goldsmiths' Company, and with an especial interest in the newly fashionable silver-inlaid sword hilts that Cuthbert was selling. Badcock was also a member of the Cutlers' Company.

An advertisement in the *London Gazette* in January 1675 offering a reward for a stolen parcel of plate saw the first recorded post-Fire use of the name Black Moor's Head for Cuthbert's re-opened premises.[17] He established a banking, or 'running cash', business there for which he is listed in Samuel Lee's *Little London Directory* of 1677, the earliest such directory in the City.[18] Promissory notes (early cheques) would be issued to third parties, based on the value of the deposit. Several high-profile goldsmith bankers such as Edward Backwell and Sir Robert Dyer had loaned large sums of money to the Crown, only for Charles II to stop payments from the Exchequer in 1672, crippling these and other lenders. Cuthbert was not so entangled, it appears.

This must have been a busy time for Cuthbert at the Black Moor's Head, with the developing business and several apprentices including his sons, Robert junior and Haviland, to train. In addition, he acted as a Common Councillor for Farringdon Ward Within from 1669–71, 1674–81 and 1689–90 — challenging and time-consuming roles.[19] He also served as a Governor of Bethlem Hospital in the 1670s at the time of the move from the old premises near Bishopsgate to a new building at London Wall west of Moorgate. The Court of the Hospital, to show their appreciation of their Treasurer, Benjamin Ducane, awarded him a pair of silver flagons for his work in achieving the new building. They turned to their Goldsmith member, Robert Cuthbert, for advice, and even state in the court minutes that he supplied the flagons. The touchmark reveals the actual maker — a widow, initials IR in a lozenge (the usual heraldic device of widowhood). She has been identified as Jane, widow of Daniel Rutty (d.1674).[20] As a Warden, Cuthbert's duties would include testifying the work of an apprentice. Daniel Rutty had three apprentices still completing their service at the time of his death in 1674, one of whom, James Tendring, was made free in 1676 with his 'service testified by his Mistress and Mr Warden Cuthbert'. Perhaps Tendring even helped Jane Rutty with the flagons. Did they come into the shop at the Black Moor's Head prior to collection? Cuthbert was elected Prime Warden in 1689; he died ten years later and was buried in the chancel of St Matthew, a fitting end for a wealthy parishioner.[21] He was succeeded by Robert junior (d.1705) by which time the Black Moor's Head was one of the most significant businesses in the Row, a centre for 'running cashes', local banking and goldsmith's work. As a jeweller and 'small worker' in his early career, could Robert senior have owned, or even made, part of the Hoard? This seems unlikely — if so, presumably he would have removed them with other valuables at the time of the Fire as it approached down Cheapside, and efficiently recycled them afterwards.

Who lived in the Alley property attached to the Black Moor's Head (Lease 26)? Thomas Marriott, 'taylor', was the long-term tenant here from 1622 to the Fire. According to the Hearth Tax of 1664 it was a three-hearth property. Cuthbert rebuilt it on the old foundations.[22] Marriott had no goldsmith links although the post-Fire tenant, one Pulford resident by 1669, may have been a goldsmith: George Pulford became free of the Company in 1691 and was living there by 1692, as recorded in the Rental of that year. As noted above this property, later with the street number 30 Cheapside, as shown on the City Engineer's Plan (Fig. 1), was attached to the Black Moor's Head and on the site of the twentieth-century Wakefield House, but it does not appear significant for our search for the Jacobean goldsmith-jeweller of the Hoard as Marriott had no metal-working links. His long-term residence is useful in eliminating this property from our search.

The Gibbon-Smithes Partnership

Cuthbert's lease of 3 July 1672 shows that the previous lessee and tenant of the Black Moor's Head was William Gibbon. Gibbon's lease expired in 1667, having been granted to his father Simon in 1637. The pre-Fire property was described in the Goldsmiths' Company Lease book of 1651/2 (MS 1731, fol. 28v) when it was held by Jane Gibbon, widow of Simon, and tenanted by their son William and his partner Thomas Smithes:

> Jane Gibbon
>
> A tenement in possession of Thomas Smithes and William Gibbon containing a cellar under the shop, part of the parlour and kitchen. A shop, a parlor, a yard, a kitchen, a buttery (two chambers and two garrets over the kitchen taken out of the house in St Matthews Alley.) A compting housing over part of the parlor, a hall, three chambers, three closets and leads upright over the accounting house worth £55 p/a.

This was Cuthbert's nine-hearth building recorded in the Hearth Tax of 1664.[23] It had a hall as the main living area, 'closets' for keeping valuables, one of which, a 'cockloft' — variously described as a 'gilding room' or garret — was perhaps a garret used for such work. The more general term 'chamber' is usually applied to rooms in the post-Fire building. The cellar ran south from Cheapside but was only 5 feet at that end, widening to 8 feet at the southern end — perhaps a coal chute? A 'divided staircase' shared with next door (Lease 29) gave access at this southern end. The cellars appeared less extensive than in the post-Fire property but ran under the big shop parlour and kitchen. The shop measured 10 feet 8 inches wide along Cheapside by 23½ feet long and had an 'entry' from the street, and a staircase in its south-west corner leading up to the first floor. The staircase measured 9 feet long north–south by 3 feet 6 inches wide. The entry to the west of the staircase led through to the kitchen, backyard and parlour at the back of the shop, which was itself divided into a front and back shop by a wooden partition. Upstairs were the hall and counting house, up a vized (spiral) staircase. The hall measured 11 feet 6 inches along the Cheapside frontage, of which 3 feet 4 inches extended over the property next door westwards (of Richard Taylor, later William Farr). Above were two chambers and a lobby and three more chambers over these with the garret and leads to the street (Cheapside) front and to the south of the building, described as a 'flat frame covered with lead', on which the occupants could sit outside or walk about.

The smaller tenements in the Alley were the one next the church, which had 'one shop, a buttery behind it laid back unto the next tenement northwards', two chambers over the said shop and buttery and two other chambers over these with a 'garrett divided' at the top of the property (Lease 26). Thomas Marriott, 'taylor', was the long-term tenant here until the Fire, as noted above.

The third tenement in the Alley (Lease 27) had a yard running 28 feet east–west and 36 feet north–south, with a well which would have served the kitchen and the buttery, now attached from the property next door southwards, that is, Marriott's. There were two chambers, one above the other, and a garret divided and a cockloft over it. The Gibbons' lease emphasized that the premises (Leases 26, 27 and 28) comprised 'one entire lease'. They sublet part to Marriott (see above) and cannibalized part of 27 for their own use with the capital messuage 28; this was regularized in the post-Fire building, but the layout of the yards appears unchanged on Ward's Survey.

Goldsmiths normally worked alone, so the Gibbon-Smithes partnership was unusual, and we have little evidence of how partnerships worked in practice. The Commonwealth period (1650s) when William Gibbon and Thomas Smithes were running their business at the Black Moor's Head (named as such by 1656) was a time of reduced trade, so they no doubt benefited from their combined input. Both had been apprenticed to Gibbon's father Simon, a successful shop-keeping goldsmith of some repute. Smithes was free in 1620 and William Gibbon in 1627. As a partnership they would have shared the profit or loss, but Gibbon was seemingly more active in the craft with apprentices and purchases from specialist goldsmiths such as Robert Juggs, spoon-maker, in September 1631.[24] There followed a dispute because some of the touched ('marked') spoons were 'standard' silver, others said to be made of the same silver were not (i.e. were substandard). Unfortunately, there is no evidence of how this was resolved.

Smithes was very active within the Company (Livery 1628, Assistant 1638, Upper Warden 1654) appearing on committees preparing petitions to the House of Commons, and other Company business. Of a philanthropic nature, he re-mortgaged a property to provide funds for the Company poor box. Only one of a partnership was required to undertake Company duties so Smithes's election as Touchwarden in 1648 enabled Gibbon to decline this duty in 1649 (though with a £30 fine).[25] Gibbon had joined the Livery in 1632, became Assistant in 1648 and Upper Warden in 1658 and 1662.

Like Robert Cuthbert, Gibbon was called upon to perform civic duties and was elected Common Councillor for Bread Street Ward in 1658–59 and 1663–67.[26] In 1662 he took on a new role as Treasurer of Christ's Hospital, the City's charity for orphaned children. As Treasurer his role would have required raising money as well as spending it, so he must have been noted for his business acumen. To commemorate his new position as Treasurer, his portrait was painted, as is still the tradition, and it hangs in the Court Room

Fig. 8. Anonymous, Portrait of William Gibbon, Goldsmith, Treasurer of Christ's Hospital, 1662, oil on canvas. © Courtesy Christ's Hospital.

Treasurer
An.° 1662

to the present day (Fig. 8). He helped to evacuate the children to Islington during the Plague (1665) and Fire (1666), then helped to rebuild the Hospital and to defend its properties in lawsuits that came in quick succession. The Hospital *Annals* records that Gibbon was in a bad way and wanted to resign. It had 'pleased Almighty God very much to impare his estate by the late Fire' but what he seems to have felt still more was the 'lameness in one of his legs.' He was, it would seem of a nervous temperament, for the moment they told him to go on in his office and 'cheerfully execute the same,' he took courage, and did as he was told.[27]

He was fortunate in that he received a pension of £52 p.a. and had his rent paid after the Fire (presumably because the Treasurer's House had been destroyed). He continued as Treasurer until 1679, 'dying in harness', and was buried in the Hospital cloister as he had requested. A photograph of his memorial tablet and his beautifully scripted account books for Christ's Hospital survive at LMA and a child's eulogy dedicated to him at the BL.[28] The discovery of a mid-seventeenth-century goldsmith's portrait and the account books are welcome additions to the small number of tradesmen's artefacts of this period.

Gibbon appears to have been a plate-worker, like his father Simon, and a shop-keeping goldsmith, and there is no evidence of any jewellery specialism. Smithes's training was similar but, apart from being Touchwarden (responsible for striking the leopard's head following assay), there is little evidence of goldsmithing activities in the surviving documentation, or how long the partnership with Gibbon continued. Both men would have presumably taken their valuables (including shop stock) with them when they left the Black Moor's Head by 1664 or sold them either to the incoming trader Robert Cuthbert or elsewhere. Neither do they refer to jewels in their wills.[29] It does not appear that they had any connection with the Cheapside Hoard.

Simon Gibbon, Shop-Keeping Goldsmith

If William Gibbon is commemorated by his portrait, his father Simon is remembered by the spectacular silver-gilt and crystal salt of 1576/79 (Fig. 9) which he donated to the Company in 1632. There is speculation as to why he presented this salt shortly after a Company search of Cheapside. Did he have something to hide? It was given with his 'free love', so perhaps simply a generous gift at the time the Company was building up its collection of plate? Simon had already served as Upper Warden in 1629, but his son William was now in line to be elected to the Livery. Was this gift a sweetener? Three months later William was duly elected.

Heal notes that Simon Gibbon started his career in the parish of St Peter Cheap on the north side of Cheapside in 1598. Apprenticed to James

Nuthead, he was free in 1593 and renewed his lease there in 1622. He appears to have made his home, however, in St Matthew Friday Street parish where he served as a churchwarden and where his children were baptized. He is listed as a 'householder' (i.e. housekeeper in the modern sense) here in the tax assessments for 1621 and 1624 and subsidy of 1628 when he paid £6 16s. — the highest amount (in goods) of any of the parish inhabitants.[30]

In 1634 we have more precise information of where he is living as he is listed in a tax assessment[31] compiled by himself as Common Councillor for the Ward of Farringdon Within that shows him with neighbours William Wheeler (east) and Richard Taylor (west) in Cheapside, as in the other tax lists, all with 'a house and shop'. Also in St Matthew's Alley a reference in the 1634 list to the 'Two rooms with a garret up one pair of stairs over the kitchen of Simon Gibbon in the Alley'

Fig. 9.   The Gibbon Salt. Silver-gilt and crystal, London, 1576/79. © The Worshipful Company of Goldsmiths.

shows that it was the property described in William Gibbon's lease, and that already by 1634 Thomas Marriott was Simon Gibbon's tenant with a house and shop in the Alley next to the church. Records show that Simon Gibbon acquired the lease of the property only in 1637,[32] so he was probably renting it prior to that date.

Simon sold plate and possibly some jewellery, as there is a reference to gold buttons of his being stolen, and by 1624 he was evidently regarded as a leading goldsmith when he was commissioned by the Prerogative Court of Canterbury to inventory the jewellery collection of the Queen's Jeweller George Heriot, who had died in 1623. Also commissioned were the lapidary, Jacob Hardret of Blackfriars, and David Papillon, merchant.[33] Their splendidly detailed inventory listed both worked jewellery and large numbers of unmounted stones — mainly diamonds. These loose stones have been estimated as one third of the total value of the inventory. Any jeweller would need a large source of gem material to draw upon for commissions and such material has been interpreted as a 'liquid reserve' by historians, which could be sold or traded to gain credit, a necessity for a working jeweller or goldsmith.[34] The various sections of the inventory are signed off by the three men (Fig. 10) and the whole was overseen by Sir Peter Van Lore, merchant jeweller. The inventory is of interest also in that it shows how gems were stored — in leather bags, boxes with contents and prices, small items in cabinets and frequently just 'in a paper'.

Gibbon would have been paying particular attention to the gold settings as 'fashion' and the workmanship of the jewels. At the subsequent sale of Heriot's belongings, gems were purchased by several local goldsmiths, aristocrats including the Earl of Arundel, the royal physician Gideon Delaune, and even the East India Company which availed itself of a crystal cup, garnished with gold and set with emeralds, rubies and sapphires. Sir Peter Van Lore paid £1,400 for '6 great rings and 6 pairs of brasletts', but Gibbon did not buy anything.

Adding to his stock of plate, however, was important for Gibbon. He bought from working goldsmiths such as Peter Guy whose shop was at the

Fig. 10. George Heriot's inventory (detail), 1624, signed by Simon Gibbon, David Papillon and Jacob Hardret. National Records of Scotland GD421/1/1/7. © George Heriot's Trust.

north-west corner of Friday Street with Cheapside. There was a problem with the scroll salt bought from Guy in that the three scrolls (for supporting a plate or napkin) had been added after the salt had been marked, contrary to Company regulation.[35] Salts seem to have been a speciality of Cheapside.

It would have been a busy workshop with apprentices including Gibbon's own son William, Thomas Smithes, Alphonsus Fowle (free 1614) who became a wire drawer, John Marlow, and Peter Preswick who later had the shop on the corner of Cheapside and St Matthew's Alley (Lease 50) as tenant of William Wheeler, Goldsmith, who lived next door to the east of the Black Moor's Head. Preswick also had a 'dwelling house' further along the Row on the corner of Friday Street, as shown in the 1638 parish tithe list.[36] His will indicated that he was prosperous;[37] judging by his goods (including work in Oxford) he was, or had been, a plate-worker like his Master. In 1648 he was fined £30 to avoid the office of Touchwarden. There is no evidence of any connection with the jewellery trade.

Simon Gibbon was Upper Warden in 1629. He also served as Common Councilman for the period 1630-34.[38] His will of 1645 makes no mention of the tumultuous years of Civil War and destruction. He divided his goods between his wife Jane and his son William, his particular concern being that William had a large — 'competent' — sum of money 'for his advancement in marriage'. There were bequests to the poor of his hometown, Stowmarket, Suffolk, and to the children of Christ's Hospital, as well as family including Aunt Cobb.[39]

A respected and successful shop-keeping goldsmith in Cheapside, his priority was to see his son successful in business. It is unlikely that Simon Gibbon would have hidden valuables without William's knowledge, even in the difficult years of the Civil War. There is no evidence of his selling gems, so we can exclude him from any connection with the Hoard.

Hugh Myddelton

It was noted above that Simon Gibbon had taken over the lease of the property later known as the Black Moor's Head only in 1637, but that he had been living there since at least 1634, presumably renting from the previous lessee. This lessee was none other than Sir Hugh Myddelton of New River fame who had been granted the lease in 1607, as the 1610 Lease Book informs:[40]

Hugh Midleton Tenement 1607–1637 Hugh Midelton [occupant]

Simon Gibbon this tenement with 2 in St Matthew's Ally all in one lease for 30 years from Michas 1637 Simon Gibbon [occupant].

The property was probably then known as the Golden Tun (perhaps a pun on Myddelton's name); it was an address to which his Welsh tenants wrote.[41] Myddelton celebrated becoming Upper Warden in 1610. By 1613 the New River work was completed or at least open for some supplies of water, and he put on a pipe to his Wood Street property, moving there by that year when his youngest son Simon was born.[42] He did, however, keep on the Cheapside shop at least until 1617, as we know from the testimony of one of his apprentices, Richard Clay, who had been taken on in 1610. Richard states that he was 'minding the shop' of his Master when a client entered wishing to see Myddelton concerning the purchase of a manor in East Anglia. Myddelton kept out of sight and the client became vexed.[43] It was in 1616 that Myddelton gave Oswestry, Ruthin and Denbigh, the North Wales towns of his home neighbourhood, silver-gilt cups (maker IS, date letter for 1616), which they still retain.[44] Myddelton's biographer suggests all three were made in his shop on Cheapside and emphasizes Myddelton's early career as a goldsmith and merchant jeweller — he helped in the valuation of the jeweller Nicholas Herrick's stock in 1592,[45] supplied silver-gilt bowls for important overseas customers at the request of his brother Sir Thomas Myddelton, and provided beautiful diamond jewellery for the Crown and courtiers: 'a carcanet of pearle' costing £120 for Queen Elizabeth and a diamond pendant at £250 for Queen Ann.[46] Myddelton had learned how to appraise jewellery during his apprenticeship with Thomas Hartop, merchant jeweller, who had supplies of gems, particularly pearls, 'both orient and Scottish' at his death, and had spent time in Antwerp, a specialist gem-cutting centre.

Like his brother Thomas, and many another wealthy merchant, Myddelton loaned money on securities (pawns), especially jewels. Recent research by the present author reveals one such pawn of particular interest as it involved Gunpowder Plotter Robert Catesby acting as an intermediary for his friend Grey Bridges, Lord Chandos. Myddelton loaned £200 on a jewel only referred to as a 'commodity' by Chandos, who had difficulty paying off the debt.[47] Catesby had been shot dead on 8 November 1605, and Chandos died at Spa, Belgium, in 1619 without retrieving it from Myddelton. Frustratingly, we will never discover what this 'commodity' was exactly or what became of it.

But Myddelton the entrepreneur had already moved on to other projects — leasing Welsh lead mines, draining Brading Harbour, Isle of Wight, and setting up the Adventurers for the New River. This latter, in 1619, appointed twenty-nine Adventurers who included members of the Myddelton family, wealthy City men, grandees like Sir Peter Van Lore (see above), but also past apprentices like a former neighbour Gabriel Newman, Goldsmith and merchant.[48] Myddelton was able to show the practical uses of the New River by quenching a large fire in Broad Street in the City in 1623, and for which the Court of Alderman did 'bestowe upon him a Chayne of Gould of the value of two hundred markes, as a token of their love and kinde remembrance'. The pendant was enamelled with the City arms and the chain set with diamonds, and Myddelton oversaw the making of it 'as a Goldsmith himself'. He is seen wearing it in his portrait by Cornelius Johnson. The following year, 1624, he was elected Upper Warden for the second time.

Myddelton and family lived in various properties, including Bassinghall Street and Bush Hill, Enfield, his country home, but his spiritual home was St Matthew Friday Street, and it was here he was buried in 1631. His lengthy and precise will refers to the gold chain given to him by the City, and all the jewels his wife had in her keeping: 'all the chaines, rings, jewells, pearles, bracelettes and gold buttons which she had in her custodie and useth to wear at festivals'.[49] It seems very unlikely he would have forgotten any such items at the Golden Tun/Black Moor's Head. Neither is there any reference to a business deal with any goldsmith-jeweller. Some of the Cheapside Hoard jewels have been dated to c. 1630, so rather too late for Myddelton's involvement.

There is thus no evidence of an important goldsmith-jeweller working on the site of the Black Moor's Head in the period 1607–66, so we need to investigate the other leases that made up the site of the later Wakefield House — that is Lease 29 and the shop 50 as seen on Ward's Survey (Figs 3 and 4).

Lease 29

For forty years (1652–92) William Farr, Grocer, brother of Ralph Farr, Goldsmith, who initially leased the property, held this tenement next door westwards from the Black Moor's Head. Having rebuilt after the Fire, Farr received a new lease from the Goldsmiths of ninety-eight years from 1671 at £5 p.a. rent. In 1692 he sublet the post-Fire property to one Tilyard, and we can trace his occupancy of the premises back from there.[50]

The post-Fire property was of four storeys with cellars and garrets, it had a frontage of 15 feet 2¾ inches and a first-floor dining room, which replaced the older style hall, but which still lay over John Chauncey's shop to the west (Lease 50) at first-floor level. There were leads (lead-covered flat roofs) for walking or sitting, although the lead funnel chimney from Robert Cuthbert's shop may have been obtrusive. William Farr, like Cuthbert and William Gibbon his earlier neighbour, were all serving as Common Councillors during this difficult period, so were very busy men, knowledgeable about many aspects of ward activity.[51]

The previous lessee, Richard Taylor, had died by November 1649 and his widow finally came to terms with William Farr about buying out the remainder of her lease in 1652, when it is described in the Lease Book of that year:

[Mrs] Taylor or the assignee of Richard Taylor

A tenement in the possession of John Kerwyn and Roger Layton containing a cellar, a shop, a Hall, a kitchen, three chambers upright over the Kitchen, two garrets and a turret worth p.a. £45.[52]

This was a smaller property than the Black Moor's Head (valued at £55 p.a.) and presumably with fewer hearths. William Farr is not listed as occupant in the 1664 Hearth Tax and neither are Kerwyn or Layton, so it is difficult to identify the property amongst the list of names (see Table, pp. 177–79). Neither of the latter was a Goldsmith.[53]

Particular features of interest are the hall on the first floor as the main living space, in the older tradition. It was narrower than the post-Fire chamber which replaced it (10½ feet where 6¾ feet extended over Chauncey's shop on the west). The kitchen was next to the hall and lay over the back shop, parlour and entry to the Gibbon/Smithes property. Presumably water came from a pipe in the yard and had to be carried upstairs. The kitchen was larger than the hall at 21 feet north–south by 12½ feet east–west, but gave on to the Alley, so may have been darkened by the close proximity of other buildings, the Alley being only 4 feet wide at its northern, Cheapside, end though it did broaden out into a court further south. The Goldsmiths leased the 'right of light' from part of the kitchen window (actually an area of 3 feet by three 3½ feet in the window) in the south-west corner of the kitchen to one Bawe, probably John Baugh, Goldsmith. This was 'light into the last-mentioned entry', that is into the yard of Thomas Smithes and William Gibbon. John Baugh was indeed living on the west side of the Alley in 1650 and, having become free in 1604, was then in his seventies.

The Goldsmiths' Company reserved their right of access through Gibbon's yard:

to one piece of ground whereon part of several chymneys belonging unto the parlor of the aforesaid Robert Hodges [lessee from 1643] or his assignees now stand and also the ground where an old brick wall is set splayed and from the aforesaid chymneys to the northwest corner post of the aforesaid Richard [sic] Hodges citizen. And also except one part of a staircase as now it is sloped of lying on the north side of the entry leading into the aforesaid yard which said part of the staircase is belonging to the messuage or tenement of the aforesaid Richard Taylor deceased.[54]

The significance of this is that here we have evidence of another property — that of Hodges, abutting west on the Black Moor's Head yard, south on the church of St Matthew, east on houses in Friday Street, north on the row of houses in Cheapside. The men who lived in this property (Lease 32) before the Civil War are of particular importance to our investigation.

The cellars of Farr's property (Lease 29) were substantially built of brick and stone 'now separated and divided' and running beneath the Gibbon/

Smithes cellar, including a small one (7 feet wide by 5 feet north–south) at the Cheapside frontage — perhaps a coal drop.

Did Farr, Grocer, keep more than spices and pepper here by the 1650s? No doubt he would have made the most of the prime Cheapside location. Cheapside shops owned by the Goldsmiths' Company were to be run only by Goldsmiths, although non-Goldsmiths might lease other parts of the buildings,[55] so perhaps brother Ralph was also using the building. For all the substantial cellars, we have no evidence that William Farr had any transactions in the jewellery trade or would have hidden any in the cellar here.

This property (Lease 29) appears to have been an addition to William Farr's portfolio of City properties as revealed in his will of 1692, presumably as an 'investment'. He made his own home in the parish of St Margaret Moses further south down Friday Street in Bread Street Ward for which he was Common Councillor, 1666–73.[56]

Farr's predecessor was Richard Taylor, Goldsmith, already referred to, from whose widow Farr had bought out nineteen years of her lease.[57] Taylor had become free of the Company in 1603. As a young goldsmith-jeweller he fell foul of the Company in 1607 owing to his large quantity of substandard jewellery:

> a greate quantity of small gold and silver wares as lovers knotts seale ringes hoope rings jeualls chaynes beade ringes deathes heads enameled ringes enamelled buttons of gold currall [coral] chaynes. A paire of Snuffers, bodkyns forkes sylver and guilte ringes graters buttons thymbles and curralls all of sylver with … at the assies thereof were formed very fowle and course … [a] fowle offence.

Some he might have made himself — such as bodkins, which were broken and returned to him. Their standard was so low he was sent to prison in the Compter. All were confiscated and broken by the Company. It was a 'very fowle offence to the honest reputation of members of the Company, dwellers and Shopkeepers in Cheapside'.[58]

The exciting thing for us is that these items appear similar to the jewellery in the Cheapside Hoard, even more so since the gold in the Hoard had been found to be 19.2 carats — the Paris Touch — far below 22 carats expected since 1576 in England.[59] But it is interesting that so much ready-made jewellery was in circulation, as opposed to high-status bespoke 'heirloom' pieces. There were many confiscations during Company searches of similar pieces as in the Hoard.

Taylor had married Elianor Stanley, daughter of the respected goldsmith Leonard Stanley, and assisted his father-in-law in the distribution of his wares. Stanley was a plate-worker, making personal drinking cups called Magdalen ('Maudlin') cups in 1599. Three bowls he gave to his son-in-law Richard Taylor to sell at 'West Chester' (Chester Fair presumably) were found to be untouched (unmarked), contrary to the Ordinances, so Stanley was fined 5s. in 1607.[60] He died in 1611.[61] It appears that Taylor continued something of a peripatetic way of life after Leonard Stanley's death, as seen by his remarks to the Company wardens trying to pressure him into undertaking the role of Touchwarden in 1630, that he 'lives in the country in summer and is troubled with gout in the winter'.[62] He paid £10 to avoid the office.

Taylor had been a Liveryman since 1614 and was elected Assistant in 1630. For the Poll Tax of 1641 he is a 'commissioner for raising tax' and had been fined £6 13s. 4d. 'for Warden' (i.e. to avoid being Warden). The last reference we have for him alive is 1643 when he donated to the Irish subscription to develop the Plantations there. The Court Minutes of the Company in November 1649 provide evidence of his death, referring to the garden in Jewen Street (Barbican) formerly leased by the Company to Mr Richard Taylor deceased.[63] The gardens were something of a status symbol and much in demand. There are various references in the surrounding parishes' burial records to 'Richard Taylor' during the 1640s but no identification as Goldsmith so we cannot trace him, neither is there a will clearly attributed. Did he die in the country while on one of his business trips, or due to some conflict during the Civil Wars?

Given his absences during the summer months his shop must have been run by his family, as he had few apprentices; similarly, the shop he tenanted from Walter Chauncey in the Alley prior to Peter Preswick (up to 1638). It seems likely Widow Taylor and family would have known of any valuable stock hidden on the premises while he was away. Neither does Richard Taylor appear to have the status required as the owner of valuable pieces such as those in the Hoard, nor is there evidence of further jewellery transactions after the early misdemeanours.

Richard Taylor was granted the lease in 1633; John Harris had held it from 1610.[64] Harris was free of the Clothworkers, but sworn to the Ordinances of the Goldsmiths in 1594. He supplied some outstanding diamond jewellery to the Jacobean court, including 'one great jewel of gold set with diamonds value to £530', 'one fair rose diamond set in a ring of gold at £400', 'a tablet of gold with pictures'[65] and also a broader range of vessels, such as silver-mounted stoneware and New Year's gifts, to a wider clientele, but there is no evidence that he was a working jeweller. John Harris died in 1618,[66] long before those jewels in the Hoard dated to the 1630s were made. He was evidently a merchant jeweller, and shop-keeping goldsmith, and had connections in the Court, but is not relevant to our inquiry.

Leases 30 and 31

Leases 30 and 31 were to Goldsmiths William Wheeler and James Gosson, who in turn sublet to other Goldsmiths.

William Wheeler, at Lease 30 next door (eastwards) to the Black Moor's Head, was a shop-keeping goldsmith, there since 1622 on a thirty-year lease. He also leased the shop, Lease 50, as noted above. Wheeler died in 1639 having had no known jewellery transactions.[67] Joan, his widow, renewed her lease and in 1652 sublet to Francis White, Goldsmith, who involved her in some conflict with the Company as he had in turn sublet to a 'ribbon man' who was about to 'open up shop there'.[68] The Wheeler property is described as having a Mr Hodges to the south, let previously to John and Francis Simpson (this was Robert Hodges whose chimneys had been accessible to the Company through the Gibbon/Smithes yard off St Matthew's Alley (Leases 26–28) as noted above). That is significant for our investigation as the Simpsons were Royal Jewellers. Joan Wheeler does not appear to have used the shop at her property, but had her own stall in Aldersgate Street 'under St Botolph's church' where she was apprehended selling sub-standard silver medals — perhaps of parliamentary campaigns — on 24 August 1648.[69]

In 1652 the property was described as her leasehold:

Joane Wheeler

A tenement in possession of Francis White containing a cellar, A shop, A hall, a kitchen, four rooms over them and a garret worth £33.[70]

Francis White had been apprenticed to the plate-worker James Fearne in 1636, becoming free in 1643. He had two apprentices, John Wheldale in 1646 and William Shuter in 1648, so both were presumably still working with him in 1652, assuming eight-year apprenticeships. Having trained as a plate-worker it is unlikely that he was associated with the jewellery trade. There is no record of him in the Hearth Tax of 1664 for St Matthew Friday Street precinct.

Joan remarried one John Bonner, who was a jeweller with a shop in the Royal Exchange, and who was fined on occasion for substandard wares. He is described as 'of the Poultry', and they made their home in the parish of St Mary Woolnoth, where they are recorded in the Hearth tax of 1666 with four hearths in Exchange Alley.[71] The Bonners rebuilt their Cheapside property after the Fire and sublet to a 'Mr Allum', who was not a Goldsmith and who obtained the lease himself in 1705.[72] Presumably they would have removed any of their valuables from the premises ahead of the Fire, as would Francis White if he was still in occupation.

Neighbour James Gosson (Lease 31), son of Richard Gosson, was free of the Company by patrimony, and was described as 'of the University of Cambridge, gent.' when he renewed his lease in 1652. He was an absentee landlord with a series of four goldsmith tenants as follows:

1. Gaius Newman (d.1614), shop-keeping goldsmith, his lease from 1610 to 1637 inherited by his son, Gabriel, merchant, former apprentice of Hugh

Myddelton and an Adventurer of the New River, who moved to Addle Street by 1642 as recorded in the Company Poll Tax of that year.

2. Hester Rogers, shop-keeping goldsmith, lease from 1634 to 1638, the widow of William Rogers who supplied diplomatic and other jewels to the Crown. She had to pursue the payments of £4,000 due to her husband at his death in 1631. Rogers had also bought valuable stones such as 'balas rubies' and topaz in partnership with jewellers like Thomas Simpson, which led to conflict.[73] There is no record of his living in Cheapside. William Rogers was master to Cardinal Orme, himself Robert Cuthbert's master. Hester Rogers subsequently signed a Company bond for Thomas Frith to open shop there.[74]

3. Thomas Frith, former apprentice of William Rogers, held the lease from 1638 to 1643 when he was instructed to repair the 'sink' (watercourse or drain) running near Mr. Simpson's entry in Cheapside next door and paid 15s. towards this. He took an apprentice in 1637 and paid the poll tax in 1641.

4. Andrew Parker, Goldsmith, Gosson's tenant by 1652 when the property was described as 'A tenement in possession of Andrew Parker containing a cellar under the shop, A shop, A hall over the shop, A chamber, a kitchen, two chambers and a garret over the back part, worth £36'.[75] It was thus a similar size property to Lease 30 next door. Little is known about Parker and he had left by 1664 when the local Hearth Tax return was compiled.

James Gosson, the lessee, died in 1659 in Stepney where he appears to have lived as a gentleman, according to the possessions in his will, including viols and other musical instruments.[76]

An important newcomer, John Davenport, Mercer, of St Vedast Foster Lane parish then acquired Lease 31. After the Fire he rebuilt it as one property along with Lease 32 next door eastwards. In 1670 he was granted a new lease of this combined property which had frontage of 15 feet 9 inches and stretched south to St Matthew's church, east to abut William Rawlins's property in Friday Street and west to the Gibbon and Bonner properties (Leases 26–28 and 30).[77] There were yards of Purbeck stone and two interior buildings with a kitchen and various chambers and garrets above. Cellars lay under all parts of the property, and also extended under the Bonners' to the west. Ward's survey shows it to be a prominent building with brick walls and of particular interest to us as are details of the pre-Fire lease, as this, and the Wheatsheaf next door eastwards (marked '55' on Ward's survey), are the remaining properties likely to have been the location for the Hoard. The full extent of the property is seen on Ogilby and Morgan's map of 1677 (Fig. 11).

By the 1790s (see Fig. 5) Leases 31 and 32 are numbered 34 Cheapside, and Leases 29 and 28 are 31 and 32 Cheapside. There is no number 33. That property (Wheeler's, Lease 30) had been absorbed by either or both neighbours. By the early twentieth century street number 34 had been changed to 33 with the site of the Wheatsheaf as 34 — as shown on the City Engineer's plan of 1911 (Fig. 1). In short, the future site of Wakefield House appears to have absorbed on its eastward side parts of both the Hodges/ Simpson and Wheeler/ Bonner properties.

A Goldsmiths' Company Survey of 1778 shows the outlines of the properties clearly. This is by Kenton Couse, who gives the same eighteenth-century

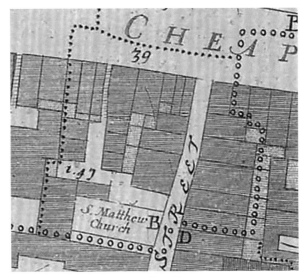

Fig. 11.   John Ogilby and William Morgan, *A Large and Accurate Map of the City of London* (detail), 1677, showing Leases 26–32 rebuilt and the extent of Davenport's property (Leases 31/32), previously Simpson's. Private Collection.

numbering as Horwood — that is, number 34 for Simpson/Hodges (Lease 32) and 35 for the Wheatsheaf. It shows the vicinity of Fountain Court and the Church clearly.[78]

Lease 32: *The Pre-Fire Property*

The larger property John Davenport acquired (Lease 32) had been let by 1644 to Robert Hodges, citizen, for £350, of which the fine (deposit) was £200, together with three payments of £50 each for which he had to provide sureties, that is, they had to be underwritten by a third party, and which Hodges had difficulty in obtaining, though finally agreed by acquaintances of his, Mr Child and Mr Fenton (the former possibly of future banking fame). Like so many other lessees, Hodges used the property as an investment in the form of short-term lets to George Courthope, Goldsmith; the Girdlers' Company; Mr Yeomans, Dyer, of Thames Street; and lastly Edward Potts, Haberdasher.[79]

By 1650 Potts had died and Hodges was sorting out the lease with his executrix, Widow Potts. Potts had been a wealthy Haberdasher from Islington and his will provides interesting details of his extensive estates in Cheshire and particulars of tenants at his Cheapside property. He had hoped, he says, that this property could have been let to an 'Uncle Lane', but that one 'William Taylor Body seller' had already moved in.[80] Not as grim as it sounds, for this occupation was selling bodies (bodices — stays or corsets), then in vogue (with or without whalebones) for women's dresses. There were other 'body sellers' in Cheapside near Bow Church.[81] They were probably Merchant Taylors, like William Taylor himself.

At that date (1652) the property comprised

> A tenement containing a shop, and an entry, a little yard, another yard, a kitchen, a little room behind, two cellars under them and the yard, a parlor, two rooms over the kitchen and little room, a workshop, little garret, two rooms upright over the parlor and two rooms over the entry and a garret over them; worth pa £45.

The valuation of £45 is a substantial increase from 1638 (£25, see table below) and reflects Simpson's rebuilding before 1642 when he stated that he wanted a reduction in a new 'fine' because of his work in rebuilding his hall; he also built a tall chimney, annoying his neighbours. The neighbouring properties of Wheeler and Gosson (Leases 30 and 31) stayed at £35, not increasing.

Hodges's parlour chimneys had to be accessible to the Company wardens from St Matthew's Alley, as noted in the Gibbon/Smithes lease above.[82] This would indicate the parlour was on the west side of the building near the Gibbon/Smithes' yards (Leases 27, 28). In William Taylor's lease of 1654 (see below), following Hodges, the boundaries of the property extended from Friday Street in the east, St Matthew's Church south, the Bonners' and Gosson's north, and Gibbon/Smithes west. Neighbours to the east were, on Cheapside, Fabian Browne (at the Wheatsheaf) and Mr Whaplet, Citizen and Vinter, and, on Friday Street, Edward Parks, tenant of William Rawlins, citizen and Blacksmith, and John Strange, citizen and Merchant Taylor, living at the Rose and Pomegranate. Strange was termed an 'Ancient'. Of particular concern to the Goldsmiths' Company were the 'right of lights' from some of William Taylor's windows to Whaplet and Strange, leased separately to them by the Company. Some were long, thin windows, others casement and sash. Whaplet and Rawlins rebuilt their properties after the Fire, apparently with two foundations each, but it is Strange who is the long-term occupant, from 1628 to 1650, when he is recorded in the subsidy of 1628 and the parish tithe assessments of 1638 and 1650[83] as set out in the table below.

By 1650 Strange also had two properties abutting St Matthew's Church. Other long-term residents are Mr Preswick (probably Peter Preswick, d.1662, Simon Gibbon's apprentice, and now apparently one of Whaplet's tenants in Cheapside), occupant in 1638 and 1650; in 1664 the occupant was Thomas Preswick. The Preswicks, John Staughton (1638 tithe) and Peter Guy in his shop (1638 tithe) are the only known goldsmiths east of

Inhabitants in the parish of St Matthew Friday Street in 1638, 1650 and 1664, being the Friday Street, Cheapside and St Matthew's Court sections of tithe and hearth tax assessments, that is, from the Church to St Matthew's Court/Alley; showing tenants resident at those dates.

The author's starting point is T. C. Dale, *The Inhabitants of London in 1638* (London, 1931).

1638 tithe	1638 Rents	1650 tithe	Hearth Tax 1664 St Matthew Friday Street. Probable locations of identified inhabitants and Goldsmiths	Number of hearths
Lambeth Palace Archives MS272, p.238a		LMA P69/ MTW/B/005/ MS01016/1 Churchwardens' Accounts St Matthew Friday Street	TNA E179/ 252/27 rot 21	
Friday Street (west)		**Friday Street (west)**		
A girdler's shed at the chancel end of St Matthew Friday Street	1/10 of its value (i.e., the tithe)	The shed under the chancel	Richard Aunsham Cheapside (east side of Friday Street)	7
Mr Dent	30	Mr Strange		
Mr Strange	36	Mr Strange	Giles Rawlins Friday Street (west side)	5
Mr Parks	30	Mr Plampin		
Mr [Peter] Guy's shop **G**	10	A shop	Mr -- Guy Friday Street (west side)	
Cheapside		**[Cheapside]**	**[Cheapside]**	
Mr Staughton	30	Mr Dixly (not known)		

Mr Preswick **G**	20	Mr Preswicke **G**	Thomas Preswicke? **G**	6
John(?) Wallis [Wheatsheaf] **?J** tenant Walter Chauncy **G** lessee	25	Mr Horne, possibly Edward Horne, d.1685 **G** (Mitchell, 79) [Wheatsheaf] Walter Chauncy **G** lessee	John Chauncy **G** lessee Fabian Browne tenant Allanson Clarke sub-tenant [Wheatsheaf]	3
Mr Simpson **J**	25	Mr Taylor **MT**		
Mr Frith **G**	25	Mr Aunsham		
Location uncertain				
Mr Wheeler **G**	25	Mr Wheeler **G**	Edward Hanson **G**	4
Mr Gibbon **G**	40	Mr Gibbon **G**	Robert Cuthbert **G**	9
Mr Taylor **G**	25	Mr Taylor **G** [deceased] Mr Kerwyn tenant		
Mr Preswick's shop **G**	8		John Chauncy (shop) **G** (previously Walter)	
Cheapside on west side of St Matthew's Alley				
Mr Acton **G**	35	Mr Acton **G**	John and Andrew Rothwell	8
Mr Elton's shop **G**	8	shop		
St Matthew's Court [East]		**St Matthew's Alley [East]**		
Mr Gibbon **G**	5	Mr Gibbon **G**		
Mr Marrett **MT**	8	Mr Marriott **MT**	Thomas Marriott **MT**	3

G = Goldsmith. It is unclear how much, and what, in-house work was undertaken by retailing goldsmiths by the early seventeenth century.

J = Jeweller. Goldsmiths might do a variety of work, or none; but jewellers and goldsmiths were largely separate by this time.

MT = Merchant Taylor

William Taylor's lease (1654) cites neighbours eastwards as Whaplet (lessee), Rawlins (lessee and tenant) and Strange (tenant).

the Wheatsheaf or on Friday Street (west). Preswick and Guy were plate-workers and shop-keeping goldsmiths; John Staughton was apprenticed to Robert Gardner in 1615 but never became free of the Goldsmiths so must have been pursuing some other career. The Merchant Taylor Plampin (1650) and his Master Edward Parks (1638) both became Aldermen.[84] From at least 1638, before the Civil War, to the Fire in 1666, there were no known jewellers east of the Wheatsheaf or on the west side of Friday Street.

William Taylor's Lease of 1654 is of considerable interest and is quoted here in full.[85]

Cheapside, 6 August 1654

A demise to Wm Taylor, cit & Merchant Taylor of London. All that their messuage or tenement with shops, cellars, sollars & other the appurt[enance]s sett lying & being in West Cheap of London on the south side of the same street within the parish of St Mathews in Friday St Butting east part upon the tenement in Cheap now or late in the occpn of Fabian Browne as under tenant to Walt Chauncy Goldsmith part upon the back part of several tenements in Friday St. West part upon the tenement in the occpn of James Gosson or his undertenant and north, part upon Cheapside and part upon the several tenements of John Bonner and Joanne his wife, lately called Wheeler widow and on the tenement formerly demised to Simon Gibbon Goldsmith, deceased and now in the occupation of Thomas Smythes and William Gibbon Goldsmiths or their undertenants and south upon St Mathews Church and in front along Cheapside from the outside of the post next the street to the middle of the post supporting the superstructure towards the west 9 ft. 3 ins. of assize little more or less and in depth from the outside of the post next the street to the outside of the post next to the first yard 23 ft and a half a foot of assize.

Also one piece of ground southward of the last mentioned measure containing in length from E to W 22 ft & ½ a ft of assize & in depth from north to sth 17' & 1 quarter a ft of assize.

Also one other piece of ground southward of the last mentioned measure conteyning in length from E to W about the middle thereof 18' & ½ a ft of assize & in depth for N to S 4 ft & ½ ft of assize.

Also one other piece of ground southward of the last mentioned measure conteyning in length E – W 13 ft & ½ ft of assize & in depth from N to S 23 ft of assize.

Within the compass of which several measures are conteyned these rooms following. That is to say In the front next to street one shop and an entry 4 cellars whereof 2 are arched with brick, 2 yards paved with purbeck stone, one parlor, one kitchen

In the second story 3 chambers & 2 closetts one over part of the fore yard & one over part of the backyard. In the third story backward one workshop divided one chamber and one flat frame covered with lead.

Also one room in the second story on the east side of the staircase leading up into the demised premises lying over the back part of the shop in Friday St now or late in the occpn of William Rawlins his tenant or assign containing in length from N to S 14 ½ ft & in breadth E & W 7 ½'.

Also one chamber over the same room cont. in length N & S 15 ½' or in breadth E & W 7 ½ & one garret over the same chamber.

All which demised premises were sometime in the holding of Francis Sympson & John Sympson & afterwards in the occupation of Robert Hodges or his assigns & now in the possn of the aforesaid Wm Taylor. Except & always reserved unto the said Wardens & Commonality their successors tenants & assigns & every of them all that skylight which is now enjoyed by Thomas Whaplut citizen & Vintner of London his tenants or assigns destending [sic] with two tenements of the said Thomas Whaplet by & through one window or light as now it is used being barred & glazed conteyning 15 ft of assize little more or less upright in height & in breadth at the top & middle 3 ft or there unto and at the bottom three foot which window or light is formerly demised by the said Wardens & Commonality unto the said Thomas Whaplett for a certain term of years which are not yet expired. And also excepted that sky light destending out of the north into a little yard & back part of a shop in Friday St late in the occpn of Edward Parker as tenant of Mr Wm Rawlins citizen & Blacksmith of London & the same was enjoyed by the said Edward Parker through a glass window & an open casement framed over the said little yard cont in length & breadth 5 ½' square little more or less which said light is formerly demised to the said Wm Rawlins for a certain term of years which are not yet expired. And also except all those 4 lights destending through 4 windows as they are now used & enjoyed by John Strange citizen & Wax Chandler of London unto his tenement or dwelling house & shop commonly called or known by the name or sign of the Rose & Pomegranate in Friday St out of & from the yard or backside of the demised premises being on the west side of the tenement & shop of the said John Strange which said window or lights conteyne in length from N to S being measured all together with the post between them 19 ft & ½' little less or more being part glass & part with wooden windows to be drawn up with cords & pulleys some part of the said windows or lights being shadowed by a chimney lately built by Francis Simpson & John Simpson or one of them when they inhabited the demised premises which said 4 lights are severally demised by the said Wardens & Commonality unto the aforesaid John Strange use & made a term of years which are not yet expired.

Lease 80 years from Lady Day 1664,[86]

Yielding & paying £5 yearly rent.

Immediately next-door eastwards was the Goldsmiths' property called the Wheatsheaf leased since at least 1622 to Walter Chauncey and inherited by his son John.[87] The Chaunceys also leased the shop (Lease 50) at the head of St Matthew's Alley recorded by Mills and Oliver with a frontage of 7 feet 6 inches by 13 feet 6 inches.[88] They were goldsmiths but lived and worked elsewhere. In 1652 the Wheatsheaf is described as 'A tenement containing A cellar, A shop, a hall, a kitchen, four chambers and a garret divided, a little leads, Worth £36'. It was comparable to the Bonners' and Gossons' tenements in size. The name is typical of beer-selling establishments and it is likely to have had this function at some stage of its existence. Such names survived, whilst shop names changed according to their owners. Tenants at the Wheatsheaf included 'Mr Wallis' in 1638, possibly the goldsmith/jeweller who informed on the Simpsons (see below), but the tenant particularly associated with the Wheatsheaf was Fabian Browne, who issued the token 'FAB'. He challenged the lessee John Chauncey to the right to rebuild the property after the Fire and won his case against his landlord in the Fire Court. As leaseholder in 1692 he sublet to a Goldsmith, John Partridge, who supplied plate to the City Corporation.[89] Working goldsmiths had regained one foothold at least in Cheapside, and the property remained the 'Wheatsheaf'.

Lease 32: The History Prior to the Civil War; the Simpsons in Cheapside and Oxford

We left our investigation of the tenants and leaseholders of this property with Robert Hodges, who had obtained his lease by 1644, the year in which Rent Warden Tutt recorded that no rents had been received that year from the Simpsons, then lessees and tenants. The accounts returned by Warden Death for his year in office — 1642–43 — show that the property had been sequestered (confiscated) by parliament, with the purpose of taking its rent for parliamentary purposes.[90] With no rent having been obtained the Company were put in a difficult position. The reason given for the sequestration was that the Simpsons were regarded as 'delinquents', that is supporters of Charles I. Indeed, the Simpsons had abruptly left London in January 1642 to follow the Court, which went, ultimately, to Oxford where it set up its new base and 'Oxford Parliament' for the duration of the Civil War until the surrender of its garrison in 1646. What was the Simpsons' role which motivated them to risk their established business in Cheapside?

Francis and John Simpson lived in Cheapside from at least 1634; the lease taken up by their father Thomas (d.1631) in 1624 was due to expire at Midsummer 1641.[91] In 1638 at a Court meeting of the Company on 14 February, Francis Simpson was called to renew his lease of the house in Goldsmiths' Row as it was nearing termination. The Court pressed him to declare what fine (deposit) he would give for renewing it. He said the Company would need to take his 'new ordering' of the hall into consideration but would give a £20 fine. The Court said this would be referred to the Viewers who were going to see Mr Acton's house (west of the Black Moor's Head and St Matthew's Alley). Consideration had also to be given to Mr Strange's 'lights' (in Friday Street), the lease for which was continuing. At the Court of 22 June 1642 they were no further forward as Simpson thought the money he had spent on the property was a sufficient amount to offset the fine, but offered an additional £30. The Company responded by offering a lease with a fine of £300, with certain conditions, and asked how long he would take to give an answer. His reply was 'till Doomsday'. The Court Minutes record that 'though this answer is considered scornful and affronting he is given 20 days'. The lease having lapsed, the Simpsons were now renting the premises, presumably with family and employees running the business since they were by then in Oxford with the Court where, no doubt to their great satisfaction, they were made working jewellers to the Crown.[92]

On 27 August 1642 (the day the Civil War broke out) Sir John Wollaston, Warden, produced a letter from Francis Simpson enclosing a warrant under the Queen's hand for a buck (for a dinner) for the Company's service. It was agreed that the Company would not accept the present. There followed another long discussion with Simpson about his Cheapside property. He was to pay the fine and sureties or he would be out by Michaelmas (29 September). In fact, he was still a 'suitor' for the lease on 19 October 1642 as nothing had been agreed.

The Company was being pressed to make loans to parliament and said it needed to proceed as it saw fit.[93] Events of the Civil War were now moving rapidly – the battle of Edgehill was fought on 23 October, the Battle of Brentford on 12 November and the stand-off at Turnham Green on the following day.

At the Court meeting on 24 February 1642/43 Francis Simpson's letter was read, stating that he could not come to London before Lady Day (25 March) next. On 16 April 1643, the Court of the Company received another letter from him. It was:

> sealed up in a paper … but the letter had neither date nor place set down from whence it came. The bringer thereof was George Smith at Sir Maurice Abbotts [Governor of the East India Company] house in Cornhill … it was now read and being of a high nature in treating the Company about granting of a lease … to one other of the tenements in Cheape which he usually withholds from the Company without lease.[94]

The Court decided to put the letter aside for further consideration. The Company had already set out the terms for any new lease for him. A 'fine' was set at £350 for a lease of twenty-one years. It was to be broken down into £200 at sealing with 'good security' for the remaining £150: £50 at Michaelmas 1643, £50 on Lady Day (25 March) and £50 Michaelmas 1644. In addition, an annual rent of £4 13s. 4d. was to be paid from the expiration of the lease in 1641. Rent Warden Tutt complained in 1645 that no rent on Simpson's property had been paid during his year of office (1644–45). The Company was being as accommodating as it could be. The Sequestration Committee had been set up in March 1643 and in London sat uncomfortably close — at Armourers' Hall, and the Committee for Compounding at Goldsmiths' Hall. The Company had little option in the circumstances but to offer the lease to another tenant, and it was duly let to Robert Hodges, citizen, for the same fine (see above).

What of the Simpsons, now at the court of Charles I in Oxford? Promotions came in rapid succession — they were appointed Royal Jewellers in 1642, presumably in the absence of Jacques Duarté the previous Royal Jeweller, and then in October 1643 they became 'Jeweller and Workman Jeweller to the King and to his royal son Prince Charles … for making of Badges of Honor in as ample manner as Alexander Herriot [Royal Goldsmith] or any other had'. Experts debate whether they would have made the three-dimensional enamelled 'Garter' badges or others similar. No new Royal Goldsmith would be appointed until the Restoration.[95]

On 24 June 1646 Oxford surrendered. Francis Simpson returned to London. Had he come to try and deal with the sequestration of his property, and to try to gain access to the premises and retrieve hidden jewels?

Whatever his designs, he was arrested and sent to Wood Street Comptor. The Sequestrators had caught up with him. He had 'taken up arms' for the King so consequently would have lost all his estate. On 2 December 1646, the two Sheriffs of London, Thomas Cullom and Simon Edwards, were summoned to bring Francis Simpson, their prisoner, from the Wood Street Comptor to the Bar of the House of Commons. He was charged with failure to pay the charges of his sequestration including rents for his Cheapside property. He was not released at that time.

However, it would seem that Francis and John Simpson paid off their fine, possibly even swearing an oath not to take up arms against the Parliament, because in 1650 we find them living in Drury Lane, where they are described as jewellers and delinquents. David Searle, merchant, had informed on them that Richard, Lord Newport owed them money for a jewel they sold him in Oxford whilst it was the King's garrison city. Of the £120 purchase price, £80 had already been paid but Searle urged the authorities not to allow them the remainder of the money.[96]

It was an accepted ploy to impoverish 'Papists' and 'Delinquents' and drive them out of the country. A twenty-mile ban was also passed by Parliament to prevent possible royalist plotters from entering London. From 17 November 1653 John Simpson's garden in Jewen Street in the City by the Barbican was sequestered and let out to John Clarke, the rent being paid to Parliament for the war effort.[97]

It is not clear what happened to the Simpsons during the 1650s, whether they were able to stay in the Drury Lane area and supply wealthy clients, or retire to the country, or indeed go into exile with their new master Charles Stuart (Charles II), who had fled following his defeat at the Battle of Worcester on 3 September 1651. Under the 'Articles of Oxford' they held passes allowing them to go abroad unmolested. Did they use them? Evidence has recently emerged that they received bounty payments out of Secret Service funds,[98] so perhaps they were agents at some time.

Within a few months of the Restoration, Francis and John Simpson sent a letter to the Goldsmiths' Company on 2 July 1660, 'The contents thereof very tedious and many impertinencies therein'. The matter was deferred for a further discussion, which took place on 27 July 1660; one of those on the committee was Thomas Smithes — William Gibbon's partner of the Black Moor's Head. The subject was again the Simpson's former Goldsmiths' Row lease. It seemed to the Company that their own dealings had been 'so fair and just', and that the 'particular proceedings are so many and large entries thereof in several books belonging to the Company that they are too tedious to insert a report … That a verbal answer would suffice. They had done only what was good and just and that there could be no complaint'. On 9 November 1660 Francis Simpson came in person to the Court of the Company demanding an answer to their letter. He was given a verbal reply that 'the Company had done nothing wrong with its leases and there were no grounds for complaint … After which Mr Simpson departed the Court'.[99]

Was that the end of the matter? Oh, no — the Simpsons knew that sequestered property had to be returned to its former owners at the Restoration, so they petitioned Parliament for £20,000 to cover loss of estate 'through sequestration and plunder'.[100] The Jewen Garden property was returned, but not that in Goldsmiths' Row. Their lease on that had expired in 1641, and subsequently they had paid no rent. This was probably the Simpsons' biggest mistake.

They were, however, reappointed as Royal Jewellers. They then made their homes in Axe Yard, Westminster, near the Abbey and Royal Court.[101] Francis was buried in St Margaret Westminster on 22 December 1666, just three months after the Fire of London.

The Simpsons as Jewellers

The careers of Thomas Simpson and his sons, Francis and John, span nearly ninety years, from about 1584 when it is thought Thomas became free of the Goldsmiths' Company, until 1667 after the death of his sons. Thomas was known as a belligerent but innovative member of the Company, interested in the manufacture of 'counterfeit' gems (pastes), as were many of his contemporaries. Sons Francis and John were known as Royal Jewellers to Charles II, providing fashionable diamond jewellery. This much we know about them.[102] Here we look at the main pre-Restoration career of the brothers and provide additional details for Thomas their father. We can establish precisely where they lived and show that it was located near the site of the Hoard's discovery.

Thomas was elected to the Livery in 1604, as Assistant in 1611, and Upper Warden in 1631, the year of his death aged about seventy. His career was not, however, smooth. He was put out of the Goldsmiths' Company on 13 October 1608; restored on 26 August 1612; put out on 19 November 1624; restored on 29 November 1627.

The first dismissal was a result of his involvement with 'imitation or counterfeit' gems, culminating when he tried to export them to the Grand Turk via the Levant Company, which was not deceived.[103] For some years merchants had complained of London jewellers exporting counterfeit gems (pastes) to the 'King of Barbary', who after 'he had discovered the fraud was inclined to deal hardly with the merchants in their goods'.[104] There were various recipes for their manufacture, for which Thomas Simpson had his own and on the development of which he spent £1,000. There was competition from elsewhere, however, and Paris particularly had a vigorous export trade. Pastes were to be set in base metal to avoid deceiving the customer. One jeweller was imprisoned for setting his in gold 'contrary to the Company's ordinances and the oaths of its members'.[105] A paste in the Cheapside Hoard is set in gold, intended to deceive the customer.[106]

Thomas had particular interest in copying 'balas rubies', that is, spinels, and he took casts of original ones, sometimes bought in partnership with William Rogers (see above), a well-known jeweller who supplied the Crown.[107] The crystal substitutes were heated up, then plunged in a cold dye solution; the resulting fissures opening up allowed the dye to penetrate, turning the crystal a pinkish colour. These were mounted in gold. The motive appeared to be pure profit, not just scientific investigation.

The resulting scandal at this behaviour made the Company confiscate all Thomas Simpson's counterfeit gems, and there followed a discussion of his employment of Strangers, noting 'and it be remembered that there yet remaineth in the Companies treasure a great leather bag where is conteyneth Simpson's counterfeit stones, which bag is sealed up and a label there unto with this inscription "Sympson's counterfeit stones"'.[108] He had to agree that his fake 'balas rubies' were destroyed. Were they all? There are two such 'balas rubies' in the Hoard.

By 1624 Simpson had served as Rent Warden, collecting Company rents and monitoring properties for his year of office. But there were problems with his accounts, money was owing to the Company and he was dismissed from the Company again. In 1626 he brought forward new pleas to screen his accounts from further investigations, saying that he was the Queen's jeweller and therefore one of the Royal domestics, and that 'as such he appeals to the Earl of Montgomery Lord Chamberlain'. He also wrote to supplicate the Lord Mayor, stating that he was old and full of years, and that 'his earnest suit and prayer to God is that he may bless all of the Company at his death'.[109] In 1627 he was brought back into the Company following a request from the Queen.

Simpson had supplied Henrietta Maria with 'rings and other things' in 1627 at a cost of £98 6s., although his sons had to chase up payment for this after his death.[110] He had taken on an apprentice, Edward Lynckhorne (perhaps Blynckhorne, a 'smallworker'), in 1624 and is reported to have worked with Stranger jewellers, so probably these were newly manufactured rings, and not supplied as a merchant jeweller.

On 4 July 1628 Simpson, William Terry, Goldsmith, James Heriot, nephew of George, the former Royal Jeweller, and Philip Jacobsen, Royal Goldsmith, valued some old Crown jewels but Simpson does not appear to have bought any, unlike Terry.

At his death in 1631 he left a considerable estate of over £5,000.[111] After bequests to family members, his goods and chattels went to his sons, Francis and John, and they in turn gave the Company a little Italian work cup garnished with gold and set with precious stones in his memory. Thomas would have been about seventy years of age and Francis and John about forty and royal jewellers themselves. This probably enabled them to work in the City, as it is not clear whether they belonged to any City Company. They were supplying the Crown by warrant, as their father had done, and many other merchant jewellers and goldsmiths beside. This was distinct from being appointed Royal Jeweller, who, at that time, was Jacques Duarté. Thomas Simpson had never been appointed in this way; Francis and John were appointed only in 1642 as discussed above.

The Work of Francis and John Simpson, Suppliers of Jewellery to the Crown

The brothers were working in partnership, but it is Francis's name that is usually recorded as the active partner. We learn more about the family from the *Visitation of London* of 1633. This shows that the family came originally from York and had married into the Fairfax family there. James was an elder brother, but Francis and John were their father's executors.[112]

Francis and John Simpson's work as jewellers seems to have overlapped with that of their father, and it is likely they were working from the same large premises (Lease 32). In 1629 Francis petitioned the Queen's Council that, according to ancient custom he, as 'Jeweller to the Queen' was enabled to 'elect strangers for Her Majesty's workmen, and by virtue of his place had made choice of Daniel Eughstler and three others to practice the art of jewellery, but by information of Samuel Wallis and others they were disturbed and impeached'. The three others were Cornelius More, John Larme and Michael van Winterbanck; all four were imprisoned at Guildhall.

Francis Simpson made the case of the need for workmen due to the pressure of work to complete royal orders. The Wallis brothers cast doubt on this 'pretended' pressure, and in so doing revealed the real problems — that they themselves had not been commissioned to undertake the work, and their concern about alien (Stranger) competition.[113]

Competition from Strangers was a real issue for London jewellers during the first half of the seventeenth century. After the Restoration, by comparison, silversmiths suffered competition from incoming makers of highly fashionable plate, particularly Huguenot plate-workers. The last Stranger jeweller to be sworn into the Company Ordinances had been Giles Bishop, a Dutchman and pearl specialist in 1623.[114] No more Stranger jewellers were admitted to the Company after this time, with the result that they 'went underground' and it was difficult to find and trace them, especially in the sanctuaries of St Anne Blackfriars and St Martin le Grand. Perhaps this is where three of Francis's 'Stranger' workmen went after their arrest. Michael van Winterbanck, however, had been granted denization and continued to work in St Matthew's Alley, a neighbour of Giles Bishop in 1634.[115] He was a member of the Dutch Church, married a girl from St Giles Cripplegate and had moved to the parish of St Martins in the Fields by 1639 where he is described as a 'jeweller'.[116] Unfortunately, we do not know the specialisms of these Stranger jewellers, or what work they had completed, if any, for the Queen.

Bishop was involved in setting gems taken from the East India Company ship *Discovery*, which had docked in November 1631. The sale of a chest of jewellery belonging to a Dutchman called Polman, who had died at sea, had caused much interest. Its story had already got out, but the chest and its contents were taken to the Customs House initially. Interested parties were Polman's family and lawyer, and the East India Company through its Treasurer Robert Bertie, 1st Earl of Lindsey. One of the first to hear about the cargo was James Simpson, jeweller, elder brother of Francis and John, who in turn told Lindsey about it. Some of the jewellery had already been dispersed among the crew, so both Polman's family and Lindsey were keen to track it down. This story has been told before[117] so we will just note additional details of interest that throw light on the Cheapside Hoard and the Simpsons. These were recorded in witness depositions filed ten years later in October 1641.[118] Lindsey involved the Simpsons in valuing the stones, helping track down certain items and cutting for him some cornelian seal rings. In the depositions Francis and John are described as 'gent' and aged about fifty, and James as 'jeweller' aged fifty-seven. Asked to name whom they knew among those involved in the case, James named Sir Abraham Dawes of the East India Company, Lindsey, and Dr Higenius, Polman's administrator. Francis and John knew only Lindsey. None of the Simpsons knew any of the other London jewellers who got involved, which rather set them apart, at least socially. The range of gems rivalled that of the Cheapside Hoard — turquoise, agate and cornelian beads, topaz and jasper beads and blue chalcedonies, jacinthe, rubies, garnets and emeralds. Some of these were in a rough state, others cut and polished in strings. The Earl was recorded with a small bag of diamonds.

About a year after seeing these gems in Lindsey's house, Francis and John said the Earl showed them a rough emerald 2 inches long by 1 inch thick, which was 'bought of a gentleman'.[119] There had been several sightings of large emeralds, but the work done on one for Lindsey and Lady Falkland provides insights into the cutting of these fabulous gems. Robert Russell, the emerald specialist and lapidary from Aldersgate Street, described cutting a ring from the core of this coarse stone, and then faceting it.[120] We would have been even more interested to learn what they did with the hollowed-out emerald afterwards! Would it have taken a small watch movement? The large emerald watch in the Hoard is usually described as having been cut and mounted in Geneva, a city renowned for skilled stone-cutting and watchmaking. But the Huguenot influx into London had brought people like Peter Williame, a watchmaker born in Geneva, who had lived in England since 1623 and was in St Botolph's Aldersgate in 1635.[121] He had probably got watch movements with him. Lapidaries skilled in cutting emeralds included Robert Evetts of St Anne's Aldersgate who worked for Lindsey's son, Lord Willoughby.[122] Was he skilled enough to cut the lid and case of the emerald watch, a jewel of world status? Robert Russell went on to work for the Crown after the Restoration, so was evidently well regarded.

Francis Simpson was employed by Lindsey in cutting some cornelian seal rings for him, and the brothers bought — 'turquoise with some drosse inured in them, as they were taken out of the earth' — rather like the condition in which the turquoise from the Hoard was found in 1912.[123] Turquoise then, as now, was regarded as an amulet and very popular. There are few pieces in the Hoard — perhaps all that the Simpsons had cut had been sold? Interestingly, there are several necklaces with imitation (ceramic) turquoise 'gems'. Perhaps there had been difficulty obtaining supplies from Persia (Iran). Apart from a pile of turquoise 'dross' from cutting, the Hoard also contains some cut and polished stones. We can imagine the dross as being on the workbench when the property was sequestered in 1643 and being hurriedly scooped up to hide any evidence of precious stones.

Lindsey asked Francis Simpson to acquire two bezoars' stones (stomach concretions of some ruminants) from one of the ship's company, Edward Charleton, Trumpeter, but he was not able to do so. The Earl thought 'bezoars stones were a fine thing'. They were believed to protect against jaundice and fevers.[124] There is no bezoar stone in the Hoard but there are a quantity of 'toadstones' — actually fossilized fish teeth from certain limestone areas such as Dorset, Surrey and Oxfordshire. Resembling the 'warts' on a toad's head, they were believed to be an antidote to poison if worn against the skin in a ring or bracelet.

Valuations are difficult to extract from the depositions because it is not clear what quantities of gems were being discussed, and some were rough, others cut and polished. Francis Simpson paid with a diamond ring worth £12 (approximately £2,750 today according to the Bank of England inflation calculator), for half a bushel or so (i.e. four gallons) of turquoise. Rubies were probably the most expensive stones at £5 (approximately £1,150 today) for '2 or 3 dozen', whilst '3 dozen' cornelian rings cost '40 or 50 shillings' (£450–£575 today).[125]

Giles Bishop, the Dutch jeweller from St Matthew's Alley, was given by Lindsey the job of setting many of the cut stones. He appears to have worked with a wider range of gems than just pearls. He probably did this at the Earl's house as was customary when working for the aristocracy. As he died in 1637 leaving all his jewels to his wife Lucy, there is no deposition in his name.[126] Could the Simpsons have bought up this stock?

We learn from the deposition of James Smith, aged thirty-seven, of St Bartholomew the Great, that he bought half a dozen agate hafts (knife handles) perhaps resembling those now broken in the Hoard?[127] It has been suggested that the Hoard contains some gems from Polman's chest, and that it was hidden from Polman's lawyers when they were hunting for missing items of his treasure during the 1630s.[128] But there was another reason for the hasty deposit just prior to the Civil War as discussed below.

In 1637 Francis and John Simpson were continuing with their main work — supplying the Court with fashionable jewellery. In that year they were paid £370 for a large diamond ring 'fair facetted'.[129] Multiplying by about 220 to get a modern equivalent, we can see that this must have been quite a gem, and made in their workshop in Cheapside very probably. Francis was also promoting his ideas for getting goldsmiths to return to Goldsmiths' Row and stimulate trade there, and had already been in contact with the King and his advisers about this.[130] The Company was seeking to get the

Simpsons to renew their Goldsmiths' Row lease; they were no further forward by late 1641.

Then came the attempted arrest of the five Members of Parliament by the King in 1642, and his pursuit of them into the City. The situation had become dangerous and the brothers left London with the Court to spend four apparently successful years as described above.

Following the Restoration Francis and John were reappointed 'Jewellers in Ordinary' to the Crown and petitioned to be paid £15,599 for jewels they sold after 1660. They were now facing 'inevitable ruin'. Occasional bills were paid, such as one 'for work made repaired and delivered at Oxford with diamonds sold and forwarded ... amounting to £35'.[131] This stressful situation continued for the remainder of their careers and afterward for their widows and ten children: the 'late King at Oxford' was still in arrears, according to Francis's will.[132] The brothers had supplied diamond jewellery in the form of pictures of the King set in diamonds with crystal mounts to ambassadors and envoys, but there is no extant evidence that they made or supplied any of the Coronation Regalia.[133]

The Simpsons and the Cheapside Hoard

The Simpsons' priority was providing bespoke fashionable diamond jewellery to the court. We would expect, then, to see some noteworthy jewels in the Hoard if it was part of their stock left in Goldsmiths' Row.[134] There are two diamond-only pieces in the Hoard — a beautiful pendant fragment with foiled table-cut stones, and an enamelled gold ring with a splendid solitaire table-cut diamond. Burmese rubies of good quality were expensive and highly valued and there are a few in the Hoard, including on the bow brooch to be worn in the centre of the bodice, a jewel increasingly popular towards the Restoration.

The Byzantine cameo of white sapphire showing the Incredulity of St Thomas probably came from a shrine and would have been re-mounted in the late sixteenth or early seventeenth century. It is one of the most important jewels of its type. The group of religious jewellery reflects contemporary piety and may have been collected for use at the court of the Catholic Queen Henrietta Maria. There are several crosses, a cross reliquary pendant, now lacking its relic, and a bloodstone diptych of Christ wearing the Crown of Thorns and the Virgin Mary. A group of unusual blue glass pilgrim souvenirs may have been set in a cabinet or mounted in gold as pendants like their Venetian counterparts, and there are several other gems with religious iconography.

Secular jewellery included an enamelled scent bottle with its three opal and one opaline chalcedony plaques engraved with a herringbone pattern and tiny table-cut and drop-cut rubies and diamonds. Its white enamelling is of superior workmanship to the rest of the rings, chains and pendants and shows French influence with its 'peascod' decoration. The watch set in a hexagonal emerald with a gold dial (Fig. 2) is one of the world's most remarkable jewels. No doubt regarded more as an accessory and jewel than a time-keeper, it may have been brought in as a pawn — like the alarm watch of copper alloy, made by Gaultier Ferlite, resident of Geneva 1599–1633. There were already specialist watch shops, like that of Francis Torrado in Gray's Inn who owned 'brass', crystal and silver watches along with various dials. A burglary in 1646 deprived him of over seventy-four watches and dials.[135]

The Simpsons were Jewellers in Ordinary, or working jewellers, not simply shop-keeping jewellers or gem merchants, and there is evidence in the Hoard of work being carried out. As stated above, they had bought half a bushel of rough turquoise, 'with some drosse mixed with them as they were taken out of the earth', the cutting of which was presumably ongoing work at the time of sequestration of the property. Would the ceramic turquoise jewellery have been regarded as 'counterfeits' as they were set in gold?

The turquoise cuttings 'drosse' included lumps of enamel, of which the Hoard reveals several types. It is not of the highest standard but is regarded as of English origin. What has previously been unrecorded is that there is some enamelling equipment in the Hoard: hardstone bowls for use as mortars, knife hafts of jade and agate as pestles (Figs 12 and 13), and agate spoon bowls.[136] Glass was crushed in the bowls, then added to the gold mounts for firing. Tin oxide

Fig. 13. Nephrite jade knife haft for use as a pestle, Cheapside Hoard. © Museum of London A14083.

Fig. 12. Hardstone bowl for use as a mortar, Cheapside Hoard. © Museum of London A14345.

opacified the white enamel 'ground' on which the enamel colours of green, blue, translucent orange, black and amber were applied. Enamelling was a specialist task but we know the name only of Peter Sage, goldsmith and possible enameller, from St Anne Blackfriars whose settings were enamelled in black and white designs for Thomas Simpson;[137] this colour scheme is not well represented in the Hoard.

The turquoise cuttings also include a variety of tiny stones, garnets, amethysts and others. Were the Simpsons repairing some items or recycling them? Jewellers required a variety of stones as raw material for their various commissions from wealthier clients or to make up stock for general retail. In its dazzling array of gems, the Hoard shows the extent of early seventeenth-century trade and sources for import. It was a lucrative market for many gem merchants, such as Sir Peter Van Lore, and senior members of the Levant and East India Companies who traded in emeralds and sapphires on their own accounts.[138] James Simpson, elder brother of Francis and John, is described as 'jeweller' and is noted 'in company' with mariners at Gravesend.[139] He, too, may have provided gems for the brothers.

There was another reason jewellers might have needed to have a good store of stones — it could be used as a 'liquid asset' — to be sold off in part when they needed to buy other (usually expensive) raw materials. This is still a pre-banking era, although it is interesting that Robert Hodges got a 'Mr Child' to offer 'surety' for his intended purchase of Lease 32 in 1644, as noted above. This was probably Francis Child who became a junior partner in Blanchard and Child. The Simpsons had a similar and urgent need — to raise £350 to secure the very same lease — £200 deposit and £50 in three instalments, but in their case the gems could have provided a major part of the amount. George Heriot's inventory at his death in 1623 reveals that loose stones (mainly diamonds) amounted to one third of its total value .[140]

The Gold

The Goldsmiths' Company Assay office revealed that most of the Hoard was of only 19.2 carat gold, known as 'Paris touch'; well below the required 22 carat standard required by London since 1576.[141] Had the Simpsons intended to upgrade the gold settings, or to recycle the stones? There is little gold to be salvaged from the settings, being so slight. It is unlikely the Simpsons would have bought rather obvious 'counterfeit' gems; these would have been seized by the Company Wardens on one of their regular searches. Was the extensive enamelling intended as a disguise? Counterfeit jewels and 'fowle' stones make their appearance in other jewellers' stock, such as that of Nicholas Herrick, showing this to be a familiar problem. For many stranger jewellers working unsupervised, perhaps in one of the sanctuaries of St Martin le Grand or St Anne Blackfriars, 19.2 carat gold would have been the usual standard to which they worked, following Continental practice. No wonder London jewellers complained. Perhaps working practices were rather less strict than expected?

Retailing and the Cheapside Hoard

As well as their workshop in the rear of the premises, the Simpsons had a shop fronting Cheapside as shown in the 1652 lease. It is commonly stated that the Hoard is the stock-in-trade of a jeweller, but did it actually have goods that customers were requiring, about 1640? The experience of a (fictional) Jacobean lady customer described in a contemporary text visiting a Royal Exchange goldsmith's shop in 1605 gives insight into what was sought by well-off London shoppers.[142] She asks to see his pearls 'the biggest, the most oriental and roundest that you have', but quibbles at the price of £3 each. To persuade her the goldsmith invites her into his inner shop to examine them more closely and offers to take her up into the upper chamber, 'For it is light sommer'. She is persuaded and decides to buy them all 'if you be reasonable'. He had enough to make a 'carcanet' or necklace. She offers £100 in gold for him to make it, and more is promised if that is not enough. By comparison, the pearls in the Hoard are mainly small and possibly of freshwater origin, probably Scottish. They include a chain of pearls with garnets, some wire-work pearl earrings as worn by Lady Bathurst[143] and a 'decayed pearl' hat aglet and chain. The two largest pearls to survive are the blister pearl ship bodkin and that attached to the Byzantine cameo noted above.

The valuations of pearl jewellery given following a theft in 1638 provide contemporary prices — much lower than those quoted above: 'a bracelet of round pearls worth £4 6s. ... a great pearl set in gold like an acorn worth fifteen shillings ... one hundred and six gems called pearls worth seven pounds'. All taken in a burglary from the house of Frances, Lady Vaughan, widow, in St Botolph Bishopsgate.[144]

Were other pearl carcanets decayed beyond trace, or had the Simpson brothers taken the best ones to use in Oxford? Pearls were all the rage at the Caroline court, especially pearl chokers or single strands seen in contemporary portraits. Since 1625 the fashion was for restrained pearl and diamond jewellery, not the 'bling' effect of the Jacobean period. The absence of the pearl choker and the presence of the many chains and much enamelling provide something of a dating guide to fashions around 1625, although there are a number of 'cluster' breast jewels and hair pendants that continued to be fashionable after 1630.

The lady customer in 1605 also asked to see rings: 'There is a fair diamond, what is it worth? Five hundred crownes?'.

The sale of rings was the mainstay of many jewellers and the Hoard has a great variety — from Roman intaglios, cameo rings, enamelled rings with cabochon emeralds or garnets round a flat circular bezel — a popular style — and two cornelian rings, one of a Roman intaglio showing Silenus (companion to Dionysus) and a satyr and a tiny fragment with the arms of a widow, possibly Baroness Stafford.

Cornelian was relatively easy to carve and so popular for seal rings. Lindsey had asked Francis Simpson to carve some for him, presumably with his arms. Indeed, the fashion for seal rings may have extended to those not entitled to wear them, as revealed by the letters of the Verney family: 'seals and stones for rings are much in request at home' worn 'twenty strung upon a ribbon, like the nuts boys play withal; the oddest and oldest are most prized'. The collecting and trade in such stones seems to have become popular amongst exiled Britons during the Civil Wars.[145]

By contrast was the work of Francis and John Simpson in diamonds: the large diamond faceted ring they sold to Queen Henrietta Maria in 1637 for £370 (noted above) must have been superb. The gentry and upper echelons of society might have been able to afford large, faceted stones, the middling classes could not, and chose only tiny stones to decorate their jewellery. Such was the judgement of David Gabay, a Jewish Portuguese diamond merchant living in St Katherine Cree parish in the City of London about the time of the Restoration.[146] He also stresses that stones had to be rose cut, the most sophisticated cutting then available, but that this must be properly undertaken. (There are several rose-cut stones in the Hoard, but also a lot of the earlier cabochon (domed) variety.) David Gabay's comments regarding small stones and the middle classes ring true of so many of the jewels in the Hoard, where stones are small and not of the highest quality but are used with enamelling to great decorative effect. Whilst valuable jewellery and large stones were more likely to have been inherited by successive generations, chains like those in the Hoard have not survived, and so it has become the most valuable source for studying Jacobean jewellery.

The Simpsons had tried hard to return to their workshop, even during the Civil Wars. The reason why they would have left behind the jewellery that was to become known as the Cheapside Hoard was that, as jewellers of bespoke diamond jewellery to the Crown, it was simply not relevant to their current work.

Conclusion

The goldsmiths of Goldsmiths' Row maintained the high profile of the craft throughout the seventeenth century despite competition from other developing areas of London. Contrary to the criticisms of King and Company, the portion of Goldsmiths' Row within the parish of St Matthew Friday Street was occupied by Company members until the 1650s, when a wealthy Grocer and Mercer obtained leases; they also rebuilt Company properties after the Fire, so consolidating their positions. As might be expected, the occupants were notable men: Sir Hugh Myddelton, Goldsmith and entrepreneur of the New River, Simon and William Gibbon, the former, donor of one of the most splendid Elizabethan salts extant, and his son William commemorated by a hitherto unknown portrait. Robert Cuthbert was one of the earliest bankers in Cheapside, offering 'running cashes' by 1677 and with an apprentice, Thomas Wicks, the survival of whose business journal makes a major contribution to our knowledge of goldsmithing links of the Restoration period.

The only working jewellers in this small group of properties were the Simpson family — father, Thomas, and sons, Francis and John — who had a workshop employing at least four Stranger jewellers by 1630, providing bespoke jewellery for the Court. Their property abutted the Black Moor's Head, later numbered 32 Cheapside and identified as the site where the Cheapside Hoard was retrieved in 1912. The casket of jewellery was buried beneath a cellar beside a substantial wall — such as the supporting wall that would have separated the Simpsons' property from the Black Moor's Head, as noted in the Gibbons' 1652 lease.

From our point of view, the Simpsons were in the right place at the right time, and also had a cast-iron 'alibi' as to why they quickly buried it and did not return. Their failure to renew their lease in 1641/42 deprived them of any grounds in arguing for its return at the Restoration when sequestered properties were returned to pre-Civil War owners. Instead they tried to claim £20,000 from the Crown 'for sequestration and plunder'. All to no avail. Come the Fire of 1666, they must have considered the jewels gone for good. Fortunately for posterity, that proved not to be the case.

Sources

CH   Christ's Hospital

GC   Goldsmiths' Company Lease Books, Court Minutes, Property Surveys and Rentals, Wicks Ledger. The Goldsmiths' Database compiled by Dr David Mitchell, with assistance from Mark Merry

GL   Guildhall Library, *London Gazette*

BM   The British Museum, Trade card collection of Sir Ambrose Heal.

BL   The British Library

NLW   The National Library of Wales, Chirk Papers

LMA   London Metropolitan Archives, Parish records, wills, City Lands, Christ's Hospital Archive.

TNA   The National Archives, State papers, wills, Chancery Returns

Acknowledgements

I am most grateful to David Beasley, Eleni Bide and Sophia Tobin of the Goldsmiths' Company for their assistance with the Company Archive and discussion over many years research; to the Society's Editor, Sheila O'Connell, for insights and advice; and to those who commented on drafts of the text, David Mitchell, Dorian Gerhold, John and Bridget Cherry and Hazel Forsyth.

1. According to contemporary newspapers and museum records, the Hoard was apparently contained in a variety of bags, 'a wooden box', a casket with trays and drawers, and a leather 'bucket', none of which survived.
2. The *London Directories* record Wakefield House as 30–32 Cheapside from 1916. It was named after its owner Sir Charles Wakefield, Lord Mayor, 1915–16, philanthropist and entrepreneur, who developed the lubricating oil *Castrol*.
3. *The Cheapside Hoard of Elizabethan and Jacobean Jewellery*, London Museum Catalogues, No. 2 (1928); Museum of London records.
4. In the accompanying book, Hazel Forsyth, *The Cheapside Hoard: London's Lost Jewels* (London, 2013) describes the discovery of the Hoard in detail. A summary appears on Wikipedia with links to other sites (https://en.wikipedia.org/wiki/Cheapside_Hoard [accessed on 17 January 2021]).
5. F. G. Hilton Price, 'Signs of Old London', *London Topographical Record*, 4, London Topographical Society publication No. 20 (1907), pp. 26–111, records shop-signs in Cheapside as part of a London-wide survey and provides us with a sequence of goldsmiths at the Black Moor's Head, Cheapside, distinguishing it from other properties of the same name in adjacent parishes; names include that of Robert Cuthbert whom we shall be following. Ambrose Heal, *The London Goldsmiths 1200–1800* (London, 1935), based on Heal's own trade card collection (bequeathed to the British Museum in 1959), provides a similar list of goldsmiths' names at the Black Moor's Head including those of William Smith and Robert Cuthbert, and including the information from Smith's newspaper advertisement.
6. Derek Keane and Vanessa Harding, 'A Survey of Documentary Sources for Property Holding in London before the Great Fire', *London Record Society*, 22 (1985), pp. 21, 22. I am grateful to Dorian Gerhold for his comments on John Ward's Survey of 1692, the accompanying Rental, MS 2839, and the eighteenth-century compilation of earlier Company deeds by Thomas Bankes, Clerk.
7. Mills and Oliver, *Survey of Building Sites*. For full details, see p. 60, n. 76 of this volume.
8. Goldsmiths' Company (hereafter GC), Court Book 7, 1673–76, fol. 246 regarding an Issue plate and hook in February 1677.
9. M. Davies et al. (eds), 'London and Middlesex 1666 Hearth Tax', *British Record Society*, Series 9, Nos 129–30, 2 vols (London, 2014), II, p. 1721: St Matthew Friday Street Precinct. The average size of a goldsmith's house was of four hearths (David M. Mitchell, *Silversmiths in Elizabethan and Stuart London: Their Lives and their Marks* (Woodbridge and London, 2017), p. 78).
10. Mills and Oliver, *Survey of Building Sites*, vol. 4, fol. 6 and vol. 1, fol. 27. Ledger of Thomas Wicks, Goldsmiths' Company Archive.
11. GC, Robert Cuthbert MS 1725 B393, Leases 26, 27 and 28.
12. GC Court Book 5, fol. 161v, 19 February 1668.
13. 'That no person erect any House or Building but of brick or stone, and that they be encouraged to practice the good husbandry of strongly arching the cellars by which divers

persons have received notable benefits in the late Fire.' *The London Gazette*, No. 88, September 1666, pp. 13–17.

14. Mills and Oliver, *Survey of Building Sites*, vol. 4, fol. 6, 16 March 1668.

15. T. F. Reddaway, *The Rebuilding of London after the Great Fire*, 2nd edn (London, 1951), p. 80, n. 3, 'modifications necessary for shops'.

16. GC, Court Book 7, fol. 246, 5 February 1676/77.

17. *The London Gazette*, 1059, 10 January 1675, p. 2: Stolen Jan. 7. at Salisbury, one Silver plain Cup, with two Ears and a Cover, one Silver emboss'd Cup with two Ears, one Silver Bowle, one deep old fashioned Tankard without a Lid, one Silver Tumbler, one Silver Chafing-dish Frame, two Silver Plates with two Coats of Arms on each Plate, viz. a Cheverne between three Lyons heads, and three Swans between three Balls, six new fashioned Silver Porrengers with two Ears each, marked in the bottom B. W. two old fashioned Silver Porringers with one handle, four new fashioned flat-handled Silver Spoons marked B. W. four old fashioned Silver Spoons marked W. 33 Silver Counters with several Kings Arms on one side, and their Effigies on the other, with a Silver Box to put them in. If any discover the said Plate, and give notice to Mr. Robert Cuthbert at the Blackamoors-head in Cheapside Goldsmith, or to the Lady Wyndham in Salisbury, they shall have Five pounds Reward.

18. Simon Davidson, 'Goldsmiths that Keep Running Cashes: Seventeenth-Century Agents for Obtaining and Retailing Plate', *Silver Studies: Journal of the Silver Society*, 27 (2011), pp. 97–100.

19. J. R. Woodhead, *The Rulers of London 1660–1689* (London, 1965).

20. R. Weinstein, 'A Goldsmith's Widow of the 1670s', *Silver Studies: The Journal of the Silver Society*, 10 (Autumn 1998), pp. 50–52.

21. 'Upper' Warden was replaced by 'Prime' Warden in the Goldsmiths' Company during the 1680s. A. M. Bruce Bannerman (ed.), 'The Registers of St Matthew Friday Street, London, 1538–1812 and the United Parishes of St Matthew and St Peter Cheap, Marriages, 1754–1812', *Harleian Society*, 63 (London, 1933): 'Robert Cuthbert, 21 April 1698 Chancel'.

22. Hearth Tax, Lady Day 1664 (M. Davies et al., 'Hearth Tax', p. 1721).

23. Ibid.

24. GC, Court Book R, Pt I, p. 32, September 1631.

25. Sir Walter Sherburne Prideaux, *Memorials of the Goldsmiths' Company being Gleanings from the Records between the Years 1335 and 1815*, 2 vols (London, 1896), I, p. 245.

26. Woodhead, *Rulers*, p. 76.

27. E. H. Pearce, *Annals of Christ's Hospital* (London, 1901), p. 211.

28. LMA, Christ's Hospital Treasurers' Account Books CLC/210/C/001/MS12819/009 and 010, and photograph, SC/PHL/02/0218/53/178/32 (COLLAGE: The London Picture Archive, ref. 179632); BL, Sloane MS 996: 'Dedication to William Gibbon from Jeremiah Mills Orphan 1662, March 15th'.

29. TNA, Will of William Gibbon, PROB 11/360/593, 16 September 1679, amongst other bequests were £5 to his 'Taylor', interestingly one Thomas Marriott, Taylor of Praed Street — possibly the tenant in the Alley or a relative; Will of Thomas Smythes [*sic*] of Great Carlton, Lincolnshire, PROB 11/367/86, 25 June 1681.

30. LMA, St Matthew Friday Street Vestry Minutes 1576–1743, MS 3579, p. 356, assessments, 1624; St Matthew Friday Street Ward assessments, Farringdon Within, 1628 subsidy, MS 9257; Church Wardens Accounts, St Matthew Friday Street, MS 1016/1, fol. 254r, householders, 1621.

31. LMA, St Matthew Friday Street Vestry Minutes 1576–1743, MS 3579, assessment 1634, fol. 348r.

32. GC, MS 1913 Lease Book 1610, unpaginated.

33. National Records of Scotland, Inventory of George Heriot, 1624: GD 421/1/1/7.

34. Bruce Lenman, 'Jacobean Goldsmith Jewellers as Credit-Creators: The Cases of James Mossman, James Cockie and George Heriot', *The Scottish Historical Review*, 74.2, No. 198 (October 1995), p. 197.
35. GC, Court Book 2, fol. 429, 17 January 1634.
36. T. C. Dale, *The Inhabitants of London in 1638* (London, 1931), p. 136, St Matthew Friday Street Precinct. As everybody paid the tithe (i.e., tax of one-tenth of a person's annual produce of land or labour to support the parish church and clergy) these are useful comprehensive listings of inhabitants. This particular listing prompted the present writer in the 1980s to investigate those people living in Goldsmiths' Row between St Matthew's Alley and Friday Street as a possible owner of the Cheapside Hoard. It was indeed one of these names listed, as shown in the table pp. 177–79.
37. TNA, Will of Peter Preswicke [*sic*], PROB 11/311/67, 2 May 1663.
38. LMA, Journal of the Court of Common Council, 1630–34, COL/CC/01/01/036 to 038.
39. TNA, Will of Simon Gibbon, PROB 11/192/524, 17 March 1645.
40. GC, MS 1913 Lease Book 1610, unpaginated.
41. J. W. Gough, *Sir Hugh Myddelton: Entrepreneur and Engineer* (Oxford, 1964), p. 13. Heal (*London Goldsmiths*) mis-transcribes the name of the sign as the 'Golden Inn'.
42. Ibid., p. 14. Simon, the youngest son, was baptized in St Alban Wood Street in 1613.
43. TNA, C24/446 Pt.1 [Hugh] *Middelton v.* [Sir Edward] *Fynes*, 29 October 1617.
44. L. F. W. Jewitt and W. H. St J. Hope, *The Corporation Plate and Insignia of Office of the Cities and Towns of England and Wales* (London, 1895); Gough, *Myddelton*, p. 10.
45. Leicestershire Record Office, Herrick Papers. Helen Clifford, 'The Inventory of Nicholas Herrick, Goldsmith: Life and Trade in Sixteenth-Century London', *Apollo*, 147 (January–June 1998), pp. 22, 23.
46. Gough, *Myddelton*, p. 6. F. Devon, *Issues of the Exchequer being payments made out of His Majesty's Revenue during the reign of King James I extracted from the original records belonging to the ancient Pell Office* (London, 1836), p. 19.
47. TNA, C2/James I/C3/92 *Chandos v. Middelton*.
48. Gough, *Myddelton*, pp. 70, 71.
49. TNA, Will of Sir Hugh Myddelton, PROB 11/160/808, 21 December 1631, cited in Gough, *Myddelton*, p. 131.
50. GC, MS 1725 B393, 10 April 1671, Lease to William Farr: property Lease 29 on John Ward's Survey, 1692. 1692 Rental, MS 2839.
51. Woodhead, *Rulers*, p. 67.
52. GC, MS 1731, fol. 28r.
53. M. Davies et al., 'Hearth Tax'.
54. GC, MS 1721, fols 74–77c: Lease to William Gibbon; fol. 135, ibid. William Gibbon abutting William Taylor.
55. Prideaux, *Memorials*, p. 271. Court of Assistants, 10 May 1650 regarding Joanne Wheeler's shop, let to a 'ribbon man'.
56. Woodhead, *Rulers*, p. 67. TNA, Will of William Farr, PROB 10/7363/6, 24 February 1692.
57. GC, MS 1731, fols 29r, 31, 35v: Taylor and Farr.
58. GC, Court Book 2, 24 January 1607.
59. See J. S. Forbes, *Hallmark: A History of the London Assay Office* (London, 1999), p. 73, for background to the Statute; Forsyth, *Cheapside Hoard*, pp. 60 and 62.
60. GC, Court Book O, Pt 3, 1604–11, p. 341.
61. TNA, Will of Leonard Stanley, PROB 11/117/367, 9 April 1611.
62. Prideaux, *Memorials*, p. 152.
63. Ibid., p. 265. Court of Assistants, 28 November 1649.
64. GC, MS 1913 Lease Book 1610, unpaginated.
65. Devon, *Issues of the Exchequer*, p. 19.

66. See also R. Ashton, *The City and the Court 1603–1643* (Cambridge, 1979), p. 19, for John Harris's ventures with Sir Peter Van Lore, royal gem merchant, the Merchant Adventurers, and others; Goldsmiths' Company Database.

67. GC, MS 1913 Lease Book 1610, unpaginated. The Goldsmiths' Company acted as guardian of his son William's inheritance until his twenty-first birthday; Commissary Court Act Books, MS 9168/19.

68. Prideaux, *Memorials*, p. 271, see note 55 above.

69. Prideaux, *Memorials*, p. 253.

70. GC, MS 1731, fol. 28r.

71. M. Davies et al., 'Hearth Tax'. John Bonner was employed by Thomas Fowle to set some jewellery, 18 February 1667. TNA, C114/179 Day book, 'Paid Mr Bonner for fashion[ing] 10/–'.

72. GC, MS 1914, Lease 1668 for thirty-eight years. Demised to Thomas Allum, 20 April 1705.

73. GC, Court Book P, 2, fols 360 and 366 (1605–25). Regarding a half-share in a topaz. Also a half-share in a 'balas ruby' sold on to John Williams, the King's goldsmith: TNA, C2/James I/S21/48, *Simpson v. Rogers*; also a reference to sapphires sold by Sir William Garraway, Levant Company.

74. GC, Court Book. Hester Rogers' bond for Frith to open shop in Cheapside, 13 January 1637.

75. GC, MS 1731, fol. 28r.

76. TNA, Will of James Gosson, PROB 11/294/567, 17 August 1659.

77. GC, MS 1725, Property Leases 31/32, 30 April 1670 to John Davenport, a messuage, formerly two. The combined property is still represented as two separate ones on the Ward Survey (Figs 3 and 4), however. Davenport was accused of encroachment on Gibbon's land in 1668.

78. The relevant detail of Kenton Couse's survey is reproduced in Hazel Forsyth, 'The Cheapside Hoard', *Goldsmiths' Review* (2002), p.16.

79. GC, Court Book H, fol. 212, 15 November 1644; fol. 283, 14 February 1645.

80. TNA, Will of Edward Potts, Haberdasher, PROB 11/212/25, 5 April 1650.

81. D. Keene, 'Well Court: Documentary Evidence', in J. Schofield, P. Allen and G. Taylor, 'Medieval Building and Property Development in the Area of Cheapside', *Transactions of the London and Middlesex Archaeological Society*, 41 (1990), p. 109.

82. See p. 170.

83. GC, MS 1915, fols 130–33. Lease to William Taylor, 6 August 1654; Dale, *Inhabitants*, 1638, tithe assessment; LMA, St Matthew Friday Street Churchwardens Accounts, 1547–1678, MS 1016/1, fols 204v–205r (1650 tithe assessment); Vestry Minutes, St Matthew Friday Street, MS 3579, 1624, 1634 assessments.

84. Woodhead, *Rulers*, p. 131.

85. GC, MS 1915, fol. 130. The Hoard was found on its western boundary with the Black Moor's Head (Leases 27 and 28).

86. It is not clear why the date '1664' is given here, but it may be that of a new lease granted to William Taylor, the former (1654) having been a sub-lease from Robert Hodges. Note the early reference to a sash window.

87. GC, MS 1913 Lease Book 1610, unpaginated. On Ward's Survey it is subsumed under Lease 32.

88. Mills and Oliver, *Survey of Building Sites*, vol. 4, fol. 151v.

89. *The Fire Court*, ed. by P. E. Jones, 2 vols (London, 1966–70), I, p. 105, A371 (John) *Chancy v.* (Fabian) *Browne and* (Allanson) *Clarke*. For Browne's token, see G. C. Williamson, *Trade Tokens issued in the Seventeenth Century … A new and revised edition of W. Boyne's work*, 2 vols (London, 1889), no. 574: O. Fabian Browne – a castle / or wheatsheaf; R. In Cheapside – FAB. For Partridge, see Hilton Price, 'Signs', p. 53, Cheapside, John Partridge, 1691–1706, and B. R. Masters, 'The History of the Civic Plate, 1567–1731', in *Collectanea Londiniensia: Studies in London Archaeology and History Presented to Ralph Merrifield*, ed. by J. Bird, H. Chapman and J. Clark, *London and Middlesex Archaeological Society, Special Paper*, No. 2 (1978), pp. 301–14.

90. GC, Court Book, fol. 295, 2 May 1645.

91. LMA, St Matthew Friday Street Vestry Minutes, assessments for 1624 and 1634, MS 3579; GC, Court Book, 1642–45, fol. 4.

92. TNA, LC3/2, 26 (1642); PSO5/7; Grant, May 1644.

93. GC, Court Book, fol. 4, June 1642.

94. GC, Court Book, fols 44 and 52, 24 February 1642/43.

95. TNA, LC3/1, fol. 4v (1642); LC3/2; LC5 – 135 Warrant, 5 October 1643, PSO5/7 Grant, May 1644; H. D. W. Sitwell, 'The Jewel House and the Royal Goldsmiths', *The Archaeological Journal*, 117 (London, 1960), pp. 131–51; C. Blair, *The Crown Jewels: The History of the Coronation Regalia in the Jewel House of the Tower of London*, 2 vols (London 1993), I, p. 391.

96. *Calendar of the Proceedings of the Committee for Advance of Money, 1642–1655*, ed. by M. A. E. Green (London, 1888), Pt 3, 1650–55, p. 714, 21 March 1650.

97. *Calendar of the Proceedings of the Committee for Compounding with Delinquents, 1643–1660*, ed. by M. A. E. Green (London, 1888–93), Pt 1, 1650–55, pp. 465 and 661. GC, Court Book 2, fol. 124v, Lease expired, 2 November 1658.

98. Blair, *Crown Jewels*, p. 391.

99. GC, Court Book, 1659–60, fol. 313r, 2 July 1660; Court Book, 1660–63, fol. 3r, 27 July 1660 and fol. 34v, 9 November 1660.

100. *Calendar of State Papers Domestic: Charles II, 1660-1*, ed. Mary Anne Everett Green (London, 1860), vol. I, p.77 (cited in D. Scarisbrick, *Jewellery in Britain, 1066–1837: A Documentary, Social, Literary and Artistic Survey* (Wilby, Norfolk, 1994), p. 171).

101. *Calendar of State Papers Domestic: Charles II, 1660-1*, vol. II, pp. 17–34. TNA, E403/2714 Letters Patent, 1660–63. LC9/388. LC7/1, fol. 57. M. Davies et al., 'Hearth Tax': St Margaret Westminster, 1664, eight hearths. *Register of St Margaret Westminster*, 22 December 1666.

102. Scarisbrick, *Jewellery in Britain, 1066–1837*, pp. 154 and 171; Blair, *Crown Jewels*, p. 391; Forsyth, *Cheapside Hoard*.

103. GC, Court Book O, fols 588–90, Friday 8 October 1608, and cited in Forsyth, *Cheapside Hoard*, pp. 68–72.

104. Prideaux, *Memorials*, pp. 110–11.

105. Prideaux, *Memorials*, p. 111.

106. Forsyth, *Cheapside Hoard*, p. 74.

107. Forsyth, *Cheapside Hoard*, pp. 68–72; TNA, C2/James I/S21/48: *Simpson v. Rogers*; see also note 73 above.

108. Forsyth, *Cheapside Hoard*, pp. 68–72; GC, Court Book P 2, fol. 360: 'Simpson's counterfeit stones', 16 November 1627.

109. Prideaux, *Memorials*, pp. 143 and 153.

110. TNA, LR5/64. Paid in 1633.

111. TNA, Will of Thomas Simpson, PROB 11/161/8, proved on 29 March 1632. Simpson died on 30 October 1631.

112. *The visitation of London anno domini 1633, 1634, and 1635 made by Sir Henry St. George, Richmond Herald, and Deputy and Marshal to Sir Richard St. George, Clarencieux King of Armes*, ed. by Joseph Jackson Howard and Joseph Lemuel Chester, 2 vols, Harleian Society, vols 15 and 17 (London, 1880–83), II, p. 274: Simpson.

113. *Acts of the Privy Council of England Volume 45, 1629–1630*, ed. by R. F. Monger and P. A. Penfold (London, 1960), pp. 156–57, *British History Online*, http://www.british-history.ac.uk/acts-privy-council/vol45 [accessed on 20 December 2020]; Mitchell, *Silversmiths*, p. 57. GC, Archive Paper J.V. 2, Jewellers Queries, c. 1641.

114. Mitchell, *Silversmiths*, pp. 55 and 65, n. 35: Giles Bishop 1623.

115. LMA, Vestry Minutes St Matthew Friday Street MS 3579, fol. 348r, 11 October 1634, tax assessment, signed by Simon Gibbon, Common Councillor.

116. I. Scouloudi, *Returns of Strangers in the Metropolis 1593, 1627, 1635, 1639: A Study of an Active Minority*, LVII (Quarto series of the Huguenot Society of London, 1985), p. 347.

117. K. Lane, *Colour of Paradise: The Emerald in the Age of Gunpowder* (New Haven, 2010); Forsyth, *Cheapside Hoard*, especially pp. 96–143 (p. 131 for Francis and John Simpson, pp. 108, 110, 123, 128 and 131 for James Simpson).

118. Parliamentary Archives, HL/PO/JO/10/1/199 and 71. James Simpson deposition 9, 7 August 1641; Francis Simpson deposition 66, 21 October 1641.

119. Ibid., deposition 66, 21 October 1641, emerald seen 1632.

120. Forsyth, *Cheapside Hoard*, p. 132.

121. Scouloudi, *Returns of Strangers*, p. 352.

122. Forsyth, *Cheapside Hoard*, pp. 132–33.

123. Forsyth, *Cheapside Hoard*, p. 131.

124. Parliamentary Archives HL/PO/JO/10/1/199, deposition 66. Gideon de Laune, Royal Physician bought one from George Heriot's collection.

125. Ibid.

126. TNA, Will of Giles Bishop, PROB 11/174/601, 7 August 1637.

127. Parliamentary Archives, HL/PO/JO/1/199, deposition 5, James Smith.

128. Lane, *Colour of Paradise*, pp. 120–24.

129. TNA, LR5/66, July 1637. Warrant to pay Francis Simpson £370.

130. Prideaux, *Memorials*, p. 175, 28 February 1637. GC, Court Book, 1637–39, ff. 59 and 107, indicates a close link with the Company, if not actual membership.

131. TNA, SP29/50, fol. 30, 26 February 1662.

132. TNA, Inventory of Francis Simpson, PROB 32/9/47, 4 June 1667.

133. TNA, LC5/137, p. 117. Blair, *Crown Jewels*, p. 391.

134. There are excellent photographs of the jewels in Forsyth, *Cheapside Hoard*, and on the Museum of London website, https://collections.museumoflondon.org.uk/online/search/#!/results?pageSize=35&page=1&terms=cheapside%20hoard [accessed on 10 December 2020].

135. *Middlesex County Records (Old Series)*, III, *Middlesex Sessions*, ed. by J. C. Jeaffreson (London, 1888), p. 95.

136. Hardstone mortars, still popular kitchen accessories today. I am indebted to Peter Page, designer-goldsmith, for this insight.

137. Scouloudi, *Returns of Strangers*, p. 205; Forsyth, *Cheapside Hoard*, p. 71. Alexander Heriot, Royal Goldsmith to Charles I, made bequests to enamellers from Blackfriars.

138. Lane, *Colour of Paradise*, p. 104. Sir Maurice Abbot, Governor of the East India Company had a private account importing emeralds (Lenman, 'Jacobean Goldsmith Jewellers') and Sir William Garraway imported packets of sapphires, see note 73 above (TNA, C2/James I/S21/48, Simpson v. Rogers).

139. Parliamentary Archives HL/PO/JO/1/199, deposition 9, item 15, 7 August 1641.

140. Lenman, 'Jacobean Goldsmith Jewellers', p. 177.

141. Forsyth, *Cheapside Hoard*, p. 59. Forbes, *Hallmark*, for discussion on standards, which were not as strictly adhered to as expected.

142. C. Hollyband and P. Erondell, *The Elizabethan Home Discovered in Two Dialogues: The French Garden*, ed. by M. St Clare Byrne (London, 1949), pp. 61–64.

143. See Scarisbrick, *Jewellery in Britain*.

144. Jeaffreson, *Middlesex County Records* (Old Series), III, p. 87, theft from Francis, Lady Vaughan, 18 March Charles I, 1643.

145. Sir Harry Verney, *The Verneys of Claydon* (London, 1968), p. 77.

146. Cited in E. Samuel, *At the End of the Earth: Essays on the History of the Jews in England and Portugal* (London, 2004), p. 235.

VI. MUDDY FIELDS, LITIGATION, DISPUTES AND DITCHES: THE STORY OF A SITE AT ROGER STREET, CAMDEN

By GUY THOMPSON and AMELIA FAIRMAN

Introduction

AN archaeological watching brief and excavation was carried out by Pre-Construct Archaeology on behalf of Chris Dyson Architects LLP prior to the redevelopment of 14 Roger Street, Camden, in 2014. The work entailed the excavation of new service trenches and a lightwell positioned between the property and the adjoining building (Figs 1, 3). It became apparent that the strip of land between the two buildings, despite being less than 2 m wide, was almost entirely of an archaeological nature. This 'island' of well-preserved deep stratigraphy beyond the construction cuts for both buildings

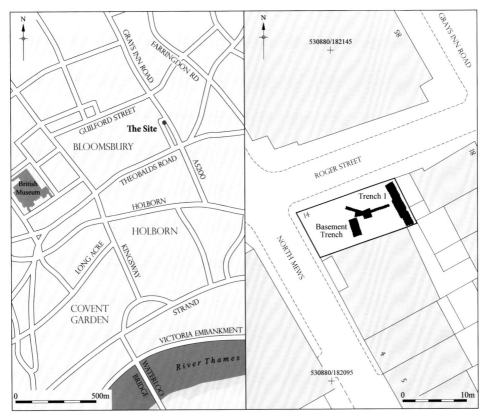

Fig. 1. Site and trench location.
© Crown copyright 2021 Ordnance Survey *100022432*.

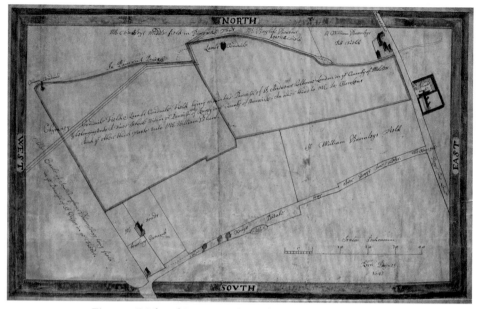

Fig. 2.   Richard Daynes, Plan of Conduit Close, 1643.
The National Archives *MPA 1/2*.

had undergone very little impact by modern development or services. What was revealed was an archaeological sequence, over 5 m thick, which was exclusively post-medieval in date.[1]

The main excavations involved the reduction of the entire area to a set project level, followed by a deeper excavation for a sump within the central section. Owing to waterlogging from a depth of approximately 3 m below ground level, a hand auger was used to identify the depth and nature of the underlying archaeology.

Additional works involved a watching brief on small service trenches within the extant basement. This highlighted that archaeological horizons extended here.[2] A total of six phases of activity were identified, including natural horizons. Natural ground was overlain by an initial phase attributed to flooding, followed by three further phases of ground consolidation and dumped debris.

In comparing the archaeology of the British Museum area[3] with that of Roger Street, there were similarities in the archaeological sequence both in the stratigraphy and in the types of material culture found, suggesting that both of these sites shared a common historical development illustrating the transformation of Holborn from late sixteenth- to early seventeenth-century open farmland to an eighteenth-century suburb. These are discussed further below.

Plotting the exact location of the excavated features associated with the English Civil War and the defences created between 1642–43 as the 'Lines of Communication' in the Holborn area has proven somewhat elusive. By projecting a line eastward from the known fortification at Southampton Fort (east of the British Museum) it seems conclusive that this defensive ditch ran within close proximity of Roger Street before continuing onto to the fort known as the Pindar of Wakefield on the east side of Gray's Inn Road. The section of deeply stratified archaeology found at 14 Roger Street was indicative of the infilling of such a feature with similarities noticed in the material culture present in the infill of the Civil War ditch excavated to the west of the British Museum.[4] However, on closer examination of Richard Daynes's 1643 map of Bloomsbury (Fig. 2), there is a clear indication that the line of the Civil War defence runs up to the north-western corner of Lamb's Conduit Field but then turns north-east on its route toward the Pindar of

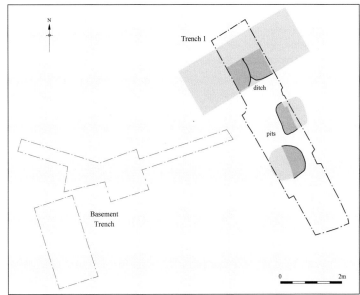

Fig. 3.   Phase 5, archaeological features dating 1680–1710. © Pre-Construct Archaeology.

Wakefield Fort, thus heading away from Lamb's Conduit Field and to the north of present-day Roger Street. Daynes's map also clearly marks the northern boundary of the Duke of Bedford's land which coincides with the line of a parish boundary ditch indicated on the St Andrew's Holborn Parish Map (1720; Fig. 6), Greenwood (1827; Fig. 8) and thereafter on Ordnance Survey mapping running on the same alignment as Roger Street. The later cartographic evidence clearly maps this feature as a parish boundary ditch and field boundary dating from at least 1643.

The Archaeological Sequence

Hackney gravels (Phase 1) were exposed in the deeper excavations for the sump and in augering works. The waterlogging led to frequent loss of cohesion within the deposits exposed in the boreholes, resulting in a loss of the affected material. This meant that underlying trends in the topography could not be mapped with any accuracy. The gravels were observed at a level of 12.68 m OD.[5]

A second phase of activity attributed to the late medieval/early post-medieval period comprised initial relatively clean alluvium, overlain by a distinctive burnt horizon (Phase 2a). This comprised compacted silty clay with crushed building material and daub with coal and charcoal flecks. The latter was identified within both the sump excavations and in the augering works, suggesting a widespread horizon across the entirety of the area, with a slightly undulating upper horizon. This may be related to brick-making activity, which is known to have occurred at the site and in its vicinity (see below). Similarly, in the British Museum excavations at the World Conservation and Exhibitions Centre the disturbed subsoil below the English Civil War ramparts was noted as containing crushed ceramic building material and charcoal.[6]

A 0.60 m thick horizon of dumped debris/ground consolidation deposits dated to the early seventeenth century (1610 to 1650) (Phase 3) was identified at 14.76 m OD. The animal bone assemblage from this phase was noteworthy for containing an abundance of cattle bone from young individuals, representing veal calves. The presence of the latter suggests that waste was probably being dumped in local ditches and watercourses during this period. The waterlogged conditions of some of the contexts resulted in the survival of numerous fragments of leather from shoes and cobbling waste. Fragments of seventeenth-century glass goblets and stamped clay tobacco pipe bowls were also recovered. The latter were stamped with the London maker's mark 'PC', probably of Peter Cornish, an individual documented from at least 1634. Other finds of note included a piece of iron pyrite or fool's gold, glazed Flemish floor tile and worked stone. This material is very similar in character and date to that associated with the ground consolidation material filling in the British Museum excavations, where it was interpreted as material lost during the construction of the Civil War ditch and rampart and associated with the levelling of these, which took place in c. 1647 by order of Parliament, or closely thereafter.[7]

A single refuse pit was identified between two episodes of dumping attributed to this phase at Roger Street. This pit contained a comparable assemblage to the underlying dump layers and was overlain by silty clay dumped deposits which exhibited indications of water scouring. This suggests periodic flooding continued to affect the area at this time.

A second phase of seventeenth-century dumping and ground consolidation (Phase 4) was present from a level of 15.60 m OD. This 0.90 m thick horizon, dated largely by the ceramic and clay tobacco pipe assemblage as between 1640/50 and 1680, contained a greater quantity of cultural material than earlier phased deposits. The animal bone suggested a wider selection of food species was being exploited than previously. In addition to the cattle and sheep/goat at least three major varieties of poultry were identified.

Also of note was a further large piece of iron pyrite. This was used during this period to ignite the charge in firearms, particularly the contemporary expensive wheellock-mechanism pistols and muskets. Wheellocks featured a cock, which held a piece of pyrite against a circular wheel. On firing, this rotated, striking sparks to ignite the powder in the barrel through a small hole and discharge the weapon. Interestingly, several fragments of medieval building material were also recovered, which suggests the demolition of earlier properties within the vicinity, the debris from which was perhaps brought in from nearby Holborn to use in ground consolidation.

The date of the deposits, and their proximity to the documented location of the 'Military House' in Conduit Close (discussed below), suggest that weapons were kept nearby. Several metal special finds were also recovered from these deposits, including a small, near-complete Jew's harp and a squared iron buckle, in addition to three non-locally sourced clay tobacco pipe bowls. Of the latter, two were dated c. 1650–80, and were stamped 'JOH/N HU/NT', a maker who worked in Bristol between 1651 and 1653. A third bowl was stamped with a gauntlet in relief and may have affinities to products from the West Country. It is interesting to note that features associated with and immediately post-dating the English Civil War ditch identified at the British Museum contained a comparable assemblage of at least eight bowls from Bristol or the West Country, five of which were stamped with the name of John Hunt. It is likely these finds came from waste that had been dumped on both sites. It has been suggested that these pipes had originated at the Middle Temple, which admitted students from the West Country.[8] A second parallel with the British Museum site is in the mid- to late seventeenth-century ceramic assemblages associated with the ground consolidation following the Civil War. Both sites contained large proportions of green-glazed Surrey-Hampshire border white ware (BORDG)[9] pottery and in particular the squat form of drinking jug previously identified as typical of material associated with the Inns of Court.[10]

The upper 1.70 m of the excavated sequence (Phase 5) comprised a series of levelling deposits and cut features dating from the later seventeenth to early eighteenth centuries (1680–1710) (Fig. 3). The earlier cut features were interpreted as refuse pits, whereas the later linear feature probably represented a ditch. The material culture included bone-working waste and metal-working slag. The animal bone comprised bone from relatively large cattle, reflecting the known increase in the size of British cattle during the early post-medieval period. The building material contained fragments of kiln furniture.

The greater thickness of ground consolidation material reflects gradual accretion, in comparison to the earlier phases. The upper metre of stratigraphy (Phase 6) was seen in section and comprised mid-eighteenth-century levelling. This phase reflects development of the urban layout and the consolidation of Roger Street (formerly Henry Street) during this latter period.

The History of Conduit Close, 1559–1642

The excavation took place in what was the north-east corner of Conduit Close, a 24-acre field which lay at the western edge of the parish of St Andrew Holborn, Middlesex. The field lay at the southern end of an area of pasture and rough grazing known as the Conduit Fields, whilst the eastern boundary of Conduit Close was defined by Gray's Inn Lane (Fig. 2). To the south were two areas of pasture on the north side of a road known in the seventeenth century as the King's Way, which subsequently became Theobalds Road. Adjoining the western boundary of the Close lay a substantial pasture of more than forty acres known as Long Field, the south-westernmost of the Bloomsbury, later Southampton, Fields.

Conduit Close itself contained two parcels of meadow or pasture respectively called Chimney Conduit Field and Lamb's Conduit Field. During the Middle Ages certain districts and institutions in the City of London obtained fresh water piped from springs in these fields.

By an indenture of sale dated 18 November 1559 Lawrence Sheriff, Citizen and Grocer of London, purchased Conduit Close from John Streete of Holborn for £320.[11] Subsequently, Sheriff bequeathed all of his freehold property in Middlesex to his widow Elizabeth, following whose death the estate was to be divided equally between his sister Bridget (who had married a certain John Howkins of Rugby, Warwickshire), his nephew Anthony Howkins (Bridget's eldest son) and Bridget's second son, Thomas Howkins. By means of a codicil to his will, Sheriff revoked the grant of a third share to Bridget Howkins, bequeathing it instead in trust to George Harrison and Barnard Field, for the profit and rents arising to be used to establish and maintain almshouses and a free grammar school in the parish of Rugby, for the boys of Rugby and Brownsover. No effort was made to partition Sheriff's property into separate allotments, which meant that the three holdings remained intermingled.

This arrangement with Rugby School continued satisfactorily up until the end of the 1590s when Nicholas Greenhill, the master of Rugby School, was forced to launch a suit in Chancery against a Barnard Daykin (descended from Barnard Field) who responded by selling his third share in Conduit Close to one John Vincent. From 1602 to 1642 the property descended to Vincent's widow Rose Wood who, despite not paying the annual rent due to the trustees of Rugby School and through a circuitous route, remained the tenant of their land in Conduit Field for life until her death in 1641. Following her death, John Howkins (a descendant of the original bequest) extended his one-third hold over the field by obtaining a lease on the trustees' share in Conduit Close, even though it was already sublet to one John Pytt. For the following eleven years Howkins collected the rent of the trustees' share originally tenanted to Rose Wood, as well as collecting the rental paid under Pytt's sublease, which he withheld from the trustees. Howkins assigned the lease on Pytt's share of the field over to William Blunt of Holborn in 1642.[12]

The Impact of the English Civil War on Conduit Close

The English Civil War of 1642–48 left a lasting mark on the fields of Holborn and its adjoining parishes, despite the fact that the fighting itself never came anywhere near. From the outbreak of hostilities in the summer of 1642, the parliamentarian government of the City of London feared that their royalist opponents would launch a lightning assault on the capital to bring the rebellion to a swift conclusion. During the autumn months efforts were made to fortify the western approaches to the capital through the construction of defensive earthworks, whilst guard posts and barricades were erected along the principal road routes into the Cities of London and Westminster.[13]

Although the initial royalist advance against London was checked at Turnham Green in November 1642, renewed fears of attack the following spring prompted the City authorities to approve proposals to construct an ambitious circuit of fortifications around the City and its suburbs. On 23 February 1643 the Common Council of London passed an Act 'for the better defence of the City, by fortifying the same with Out Works at certain Places', which stipulated the construction of fourteen fortifications at named sites north of the River Thames.[14] Eventually at least twenty-five fortifications were built along the defensive circuit when it was completed in June 1643.

As the forts were approaching completion, the attention of the City authorities turned to the construction of the interconnecting ditches and ramparts — known as the 'Lines of Communication'. At the end of April an order was read out in churches across London instructing heads of households to 'send their servants and children to assist the raysing of the Outworkes and Trenches for the defence of the City'.[15] In order to complete the works, a huge volunteer workforce was raised by the City livery companies and the parochial authorities of the City and suburbs, overseen by the Common Council of London. In his account of the defences, written shortly after he claimed to have walked the entire circuit in a single day in June 1643, the Scottish travel writer William Lithgow described the Lines of Communication as the 'circulatory line' and the rampart as the 'trench dyke'. According to Lithgow the latter was 'three yards thick and on the ditch side twice as high', which broadly corresponds with the dimensions recommended by contemporary military manuals.[16] The construction of defences on this scale inflicted considerable damage upon the fields through which they were built. Lithgow described how 'it grieved me to see so many rich grounds of grasse utterly spoyled with the erection of these works, insomuch that horse and cattell certaynels will come short of their food there for seven years and the owners thereof must fall pittyfully short of their yearly profits'.[17] The records of the Parliamentary Committee for the Advance of Money contain numerous complaints from aggrieved citizens who suffered financial loss as a result of their land being taken from them for the building of the defences.[18]

Amongst the landowners and tenants who claimed to have lost land and income was John Howkins of Conduit Close. For a period of four or five years after the construction of the Lines of Communication, Howkins made deductions from the £10 annual rent that he passed on to the trustees of Rugby School for 'damage sustained by Breastworks [...] drawn through the said Close and for taxes out of the said rent'.[19] It soon became apparent, however, that Howkins had greatly overstated the damage caused by the defences to the school's portion of Conduit Close. In 1652 Joan Pearce, the widow of the late master of Rugby School, alleged that 'whereas the [trustees' share of the] said Close containeth Ten acres or thereabouts [...] not the quantitie of one acre thereof was spoyled by the said Workes'.[20] Pearce alleged that, by these and other means, Howkins had deprived her husband of the moneys necessary to maintain the school, the stress and hardship of which had contributed to his early death and her impoverishment.

A contemporary plan of Conduit Close surveyed by the map-maker Richard Daynes (Fig. 2) confirmed that Howkins had indeed exaggerated the damage caused by the defensive works. The plan shows the trench and rampart heading diagonally north-eastward across the north-west corner of Chimney Conduit Field to a point on the northern boundary of the latter, which it then followed until it met the western edge of Lamb's Conduit Field, which it then followed as far as the north-western corner of the latter field. From this point the line resumed its former south-west–north-east alignment, heading north-east towards the Pindar of Wakefield fort, which stood on the east side of Gray's Inn Road. Lamb's Conduit Field itself appears to have been untouched by the earthworks, although it is possible that turf may have been stripped from the fields during the construction process to reinforce the rampart.[21]

Conduit Close During the Second Half of the Seventeenth Century

The extent to which the Howkins family had misused the profits rightfully belonging to Rugby School was revealed in 1653 by a Commission set up to resolve the proceedings in Chancery. Ironically, the case had been revived the previous year by John Howkins, who presumably expected the Commission to rule in his favour. By the terms of a decree of 16 May 1653, John Howkins was ordered to pay the trustees rent arrears on their share of Conduit Close amounting to £73 15s.[22] The trust itself was reconstituted and made responsible for the maintenance and repair of the school, which had previously been the responsibility of the schoolmaster.[23]

Both John Howkins and William Blunt died in 1678, the former at the age of ninety-nine. In his will of 16 November 1678, Howkins bequeathed all of his freehold property in Hertfordshire, London and St Andrew, Holborn to his cousin William Howkins.[24] At the time of his death William Blunt was also a wealthy man, his estate including the freehold possession of a one-sixth share in Conduit Close in addition to the leases he held on Howkins's and the trustees' shares in the field.[25] Blunt instructed that the major part of his estate be placed in trust for his granddaughter Mary Blunt, who subsequently married one Charles Newman.[26] In 1686 two-thirds of Conduit Close were still in the possession of the Howkins family and the trustees of Rugby School, whilst the remaining third was divided equally between the Newmans and a couple named Mary and Thomas Bonny, the latter of whom had also acquired the late William Blunt's lease of the entire field.[27]

By the time of Blunt and Howkins's deaths, Bloomsbury was beginning to acquire many of the characteristics of an affluent and expanding suburb. The development of the district began in earnest with the construction of Southampton (later Bedford) House, which was built for the 4th Earl of Southampton in the 1640s and 1650s. The rapid growth of the district brought with it the inevitable problem of sanitation. In 1676 the Governors of Christ's Hospital school complained to the Commissioners of Sewers for Middlesex and Westminster about the contamination of the springs that fed the Chimney Conduit, the school's principal source of drinking water, by a drain leading into a pond at the rear of Southampton House.[28] The pond in question was situated close to the eastern boundary of the Long Field, only a stone's throw away from the conduit head in Chimney Conduit Field. In response, the commissioners instructed that a dam be built in Long Field in order 'to prevent the dirty and filthy water from poysoning the heads of several springs' that supplied the Chimney Conduit.[29]

> The same year it was reported that an individual residing att the Military ground in or neere Southampton Buildings, had, notwithstanding a late order of the Comm[ttee] of Sewers for Midd[x], threatened to take up a damm [i.e. the aforementioned dam] that was made in p'suance of the said order, att the

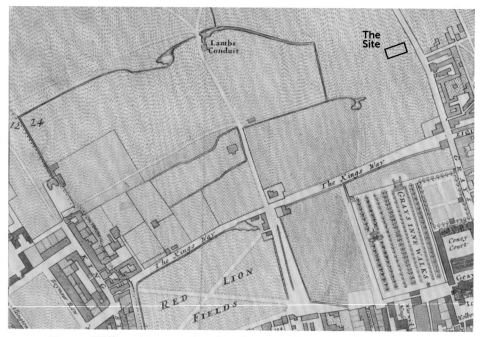

Fig. 4. William Morgan, *London &c. Actually Survey'd*, 1682 (detail).
© The British Library Board *Maps Crace Port. 2.58.*

south corner of a Ditch that comes downe to the Springs of the Chimney Conduite, which belongs to the Hospitall.[30]

Documents dating from the mid-1680s reveal that the 'military ground' was an enclosure which lay in the 'upper' (i.e. western) part of Chimney Conduit Field, in or adjacent to which stood a property known as the 'Military House'.[31] The Holborn Military Ground may have been depicted on William Morgan's map of 1682 as a rectangular enclosure in the south-west corner of Chimney Conduit Field (Fig. 4). This was almost certainly the same 'Military Ground near Bloomsbury' where the gentlemen archers of London assembled prior to a parade held in 1676.[32] An inverted L-shaped building shown in the north-west corner of the enclosure may have been the Military House.

*The Acquisition and Development of Conduit Close
by Dr Nicholas Barbon, 1686–98*

The rent charged by the trustees of Rugby School for their portion of Conduit Close remained the same for more than thirty years after the Commission in Chancery decree of 1653. It cannot have escaped the trustees' attention that the potential return from developing the school's eight-acre plot greatly exceeded the annual rent paid by Thomas Bonny, especially given that one of their number, Sir William Bromley, owned two of the neighbouring properties.[33] In the autumn of 1686 the trustees found in Dr Nicholas Barbon a partner whose unparalleled track record in property development promised to greatly increase the school's income from its Holborn estate.

Barbon was the son of the Puritan preacher and politician, Praisegod Barbon, who lent his name to the Barebones Parliament, the 140-strong assembly of nominated members which briefly governed the Commonwealth in 1653.[34] Nicholas Barbon was born in London and studied medicine at the Universities of Leiden and Utrecht in the early 1660s. Seizing the opportunities created by the Great Fire of London of 1666, he quickly established himself as one of the leading builders and property developers of the age. Barbon's commercial activities were informed by his radical economic theories, which he set out in his *Discourse of Trade* (1690) and *An Apology for the Builder* (1685). In these volumes Barbon challenged the dominant mercantilist ideology, arguing that consumer demand was not static but constantly increasing because of natural population growth.

In accordance with the terms of a lease dated 20 October 1686 the trustees agreed to lease 'all that their third parte [of Conduit Close] [...] together with all ditches mounds fences thereabouts waters watercourses paths passages profitts easements comodityes advantages and whatsoever' to Dr Barbon for a term of fifty years from the following Christmas at an annual rent of £50.[35] Barbon agreed to commence construction within five years and to lay out a further £1,000 in building upon the land.[36] Barbon also covenanted with the trustees to sue for a writ of partition against the owners of the remaining parts of Conduit Close in order that the field should be divided equally between the three owners.

Having secured the lease, Barbon exhibited a bill in Chancery against the Bonnys and the Newmans and William Howkins in order to divide the school's third part of the field from theirs.[37] Howkins promptly countered by means of a lawsuit in which he claimed that Barbon, the Bonnys and the trustees had jointly taken the best fourteen acres of the field

> and have without [Howkins's] consent [...] inclosed the said fourteen acres from the rest [...] and have digged and broken up the soyle and have made Bricks [...] and carried the same away and still go on to digg and make more brick [...] which [...] will stand to [Howkins's] great damage.[38]

Although Howkins initially demanded that he receive one-third of the profits of the ground by way of compensation for the alleged damages, he seems to have realized that there was little to be gained by standing in Barbon's way and promptly came to terms with his new neighbour.

Shortly afterwards, Barbon obtained a lease on Howkins's land, raised a mortgage on it and at the same time used the ground rent covenanted for in the lease as a means of raising money for other purposes.[39] Howkins's fellow freeholders the Bonnys and the Newmans evidently suspected that something was up when they complained to the court that, before the field could be divided, Barbon 'or some other person unknown' had purchased Howkins's share of the field and that Barbon had since threatened to dig the whole of it up.[40] In his answer to the Bonnys' and Newmans' complaint, Barbon denied knowing any member of the Howkins family and all knowledge of the transaction.

In fact, this was fairly typical of Barbon's business methods, whereby he raised substantial loans against the security of his estates out of all proportion to his original outlay.[41] Having obtained the lease on a piece of land, Barbon would divide up the ground and let it out on building leases to speculative builders, which would kick-start the building process and provide security against which further capital could be raised.[42] This is exactly what Barbon proceeded to do at Conduit Close.

On 28 April 1687, on the instruction of a Commission appointed by Chancery, Conduit Close was finally measured and divided into three equal parts prior to partition.[43] The Commission decreed that henceforth Dr Barbon and William and John Howkins (as the freeholders) 'doo hold and enjoy the Upper [westernmost] part of the said feild whereon standeth the Divells Conduit and the Military House', whilst the 'Middle part' was to be held by the trustees of Rugby School (and by extension, Nicholas Barbon, who held the lease). The easternmost or 'Lower part' was held by Thomas and Mary Bonny and Charles and Mary Newman. This included the future site of Roger Street.

The Continued Development of Conduit Close
by Sir William Milman, 1702–13

By the mid-1690s Barbon's plans to develop Conduit Close had stalled. Although the principal roadways including Red Lion Street and Great Ormond Street had been set out and much of the westernmost third of the field developed by speculative builders, the middle portion lay 'ruinous and unbuilt' at the end of the decade.[44] The easternmost part remained entirely undeveloped and continued to be used as pasture.

Following Barbon's death in 1698, the trustees of Rugby School sued his creditor William Milman for non-payment of rent arrears which had built up over several years. By an agreement of March 1699, Barbon's executors agreed to release the equity of redemption of the mortgaged premises to Milman.[45] Milman promptly applied to extend Barbon's lease so that he could continue developing the site. In March 1702 Milman was granted a new lease, with an extension until Christmas 1779 for £60 per annum.[46] Having obtained the lease extension, Milman began issuing building leases to interested parties. Their sale enabled Milman to pay off the rent arrears accrued by Barbon over the next three years.[47] A plan and schedule of the ground leased to Milman (Fig. 5) shows the new street layout and how the plots were apportioned.[48]

The development of Milman's estate did not proceed without objection. The principal obstacle was his neighbour Thomas Griffith, who held the field to the north of Conduit Close by a lease dated 5 December 1681.[49] Griffith's field, which was pasture, like most of the surrounding farmland, contained a pond, which was shown on Daynes's map of 1643 lying astride the boundary between his field and the trustees' ground (Fig. 2). A century later the cartographer John Rocque depicted the pond lying a short distance to the north of the field boundary (Fig. 7). The boundary between the fields was defined 'by an Antient Ditch or Fence', which according to the terms of Barbon's lease of 1686 belonged to the trustees of Rugby School.

In 1705 Milman claimed that the pond in Griffith's field had 'through length of time worne itself and gained upon the trustees' ditch and ground, depriving them of the use thereof'.[50] Several years earlier Nicholas Barbon had arranged to have the ground staked out in order that the boundaries of the respective properties could be defined. Milman maintained that Thomas Griffith had consented to this and approved the demarcated boundary. However, when Milman built the garden walls of a property at the northern edge of his estate 'downe into the said Ditch' between the two fields, Griffith instituted proceedings against him in Chancery. Griffith subsequently accused Milman of trespass, alleging that on 12 May 1704 Milman 'did break and enter into his [Griffith's] ground and dig up 100 feet south to north and 20½ feet east to west and enclose it with a wall'.[51]

Griffith's allegations led to a trial by jury. When the jury visited the site in November 1704, Milman accused Griffith of having 'from time to time by undue ways and means enlarged and overflowed his pond and thereby gained on [Milman's] ground by washing away the Banks of the sᵈ Ditch'. Milman produced witnesses who testified that Griffith had 'lately caused three or four hundred loads of Earth or soyle to be dug and carried out of his Pond and enlarged the same'.[52] Eventually the court found in favour of Milman, though this did not prevent Griffith from launching a further 'troublesome and vexatious' suit soon afterwards.

Rugby School's share of Conduit Close was still not fully built upon by the time of Sir William Milman's death in 1713; the houses east of Lamb's Conduit Street were only built on leases from Milman's heirs in 1719–20.[53] The easternmost one-sixth of Conduit Close remained in the possession of the Newmans until it was sold in 1705.[54] The descent of this portion thereafter is uncertain. A map published in 1720 shows little in the way of

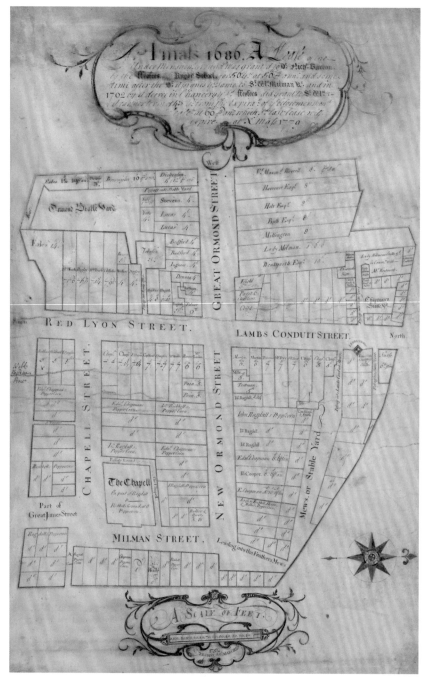

Fig. 5.   T. Robins, Plan of and Schedule of Conduit Close, 1752 (detail).
© The British Library Board *Maps Crace Port. 15.27.*

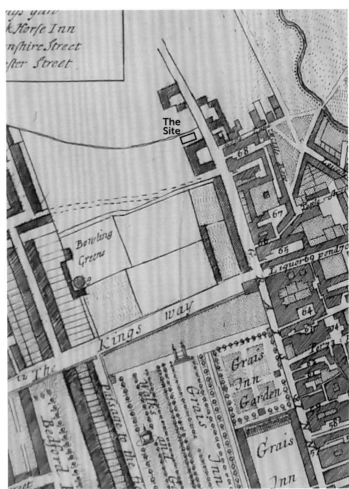

Fig. 6. Richard Blome, *A Mapp of St Andrews Holborn Parish* published in John Strype's edition of John Stow's *Survey of the Cities of London and Westminster*, 1720 (detail).

development, other than a footpath crossing the southern portion of the field from the eastern end of Chapel Street and a substantial winged building fronting Gray's Inn Lane (Fig. 6). By the mid-1740s the eastern third of the field had been developed, with the remainder laid out as a market garden (Fig. 7).

In 1748 the trustees of Rugby School obtained a private Act of Parliament in order to raise finances from their estates in Warwickshire and Middlesex.[55] The following year the trustees borrowed £1,800 on the security of their Holborn estate in order to fund the rebuilding of the school. In 1777 the school obtained additional Parliamentary powers to raise a further £10,000 through the sale of parts of the trust estate, including its interest in the former Conduit Close.[56] The school arranged to exchange its eight acres of ground

with the governors of Foundling Hospital, which had owned the fields to
the north of Conduit Close since 1741. In 1785 the governors of the Hospital
announced their intention to develop their estates under the supervision of
the architect and surveyor Samuel Pepys Cockerell.[57] The development of the
southern end of Doughty Street (originally called Upper John Street) began
in 1792, when Henry Doughty granted building leases to George Slaton
and Joseph Wigg. Although not shown on the earliest edition of Richard
Horwood's map of 1792–99, both Doughty Street and Henry (later Roger)
Street had been laid out and partially developed by the 1820s (Fig. 8).

By the mid-1820s the site of the archaeological investigation lay at the
junction of Henry Street and North Mews, part of a row of stables and
associated businesses that extended north from King's (later Theobalds)
Road behind the premises fronting the west side of Gray's Inn Road (Fig.
8). In 1862 the property was occupied by the Henry Street Baptist Chapel,
which was depicted on the First Edition Ordnance Survey map of 1871
(Fig. 9).[58] The chapel appears to have closed by the mid-1890s, by which

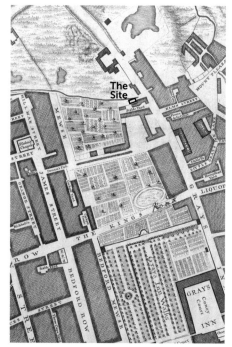

Fig. 7. John Rocque, *A Plan of the
Cities of London and Westminster and
Borough of Southwark*, 1747 (detail).
Private collection.

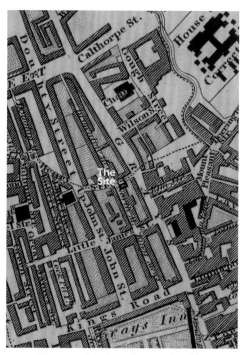

Fig. 8. Christopher and John
Greenwood, *Map of London*, 1827 (detail).
© MacLean Collection, Chicago.

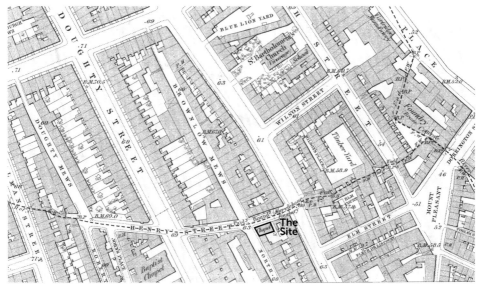

Fig. 9.   Ordnance Survey Map of London, 25-inch, first edition, 1877 (detail).
*Reproduced under a Creative Commons Attribution-NonCommercial-ShareAlike
4.0 International (CC-BY-NC-SA) licence with the permission of the
National Library of Scotland.*

date the premises were occupied by a printing firm. The former chapel was
destroyed by bombing during the Second World War, after which a new
building was erected on the site.[59]

Discussion and Conclusions

A small-scale excavation on an unprepossessing site in central London
provided an unexpected insight into the suburban development of the
capital in the late seventeenth and eighteenth centuries.

The archaeological record supports documentary evidence that indicates
that the site was located at the eastern end of a large pasture in the early
post-medieval period. Silty clay deposits dating to the first half of the
seventeenth century probably reflect periodic re-cutting of the boundary
ditch that separated Conduit Close from the field to the north, which
formed part of a separate property.

Whilst cartographic and documentary evidence proves that the site lay at
some distance to the south-east of the Civil War Lines of Communication,
the discovery of large pieces of iron pyrites, likely used in conjunction
with wheellock firearms, in the seventeenth-century deposits suggests
an association with the little-documented 'Military House' which stood

near the north-west corner of Conduit Close. The origins of the 'Military Ground' and the 'Military House' in Chimney Conduit Field are obscure. Their names suggest that they may have been connected with either the Holborn Trained Band or one of the other volunteer militias established during the first half of the seventeenth century. The latter bodies included the Military Company, which was founded during the reign of James I and modelled on the Artillery Company that exercised in Spitalfields.[60] The success of these 'two great Nurseries or Academies of Military Disciple' inspired the formation of other volunteer units, including the Martial Yard of Southwark, and the Cripplegate and Townditch militias.[61] These bodies instructed their members in battlefield drills and went on to provide a substantial number of the leading officers of the Trained Bands.

In 1616 the Military Company developed a 3½-acre plot of land in the vicinity of present-day Gerrard Street, Soho as an exercise ground, which became known as the 'Military Ground'.[62] The latter was subsequently developed by Dr Nicholas Barbon in the 1670s and 1680s. The Military Company also built a brick armoury and mess room adjacent to the latter site, which may be analogous with the 'Military House' in Chimney Conduit Field.

The documentary evidence for the development of Conduit Close by Dr Nicholas Barbon in the 1680s and 1690s reveals the tactics used by this larger-than-life and often unscrupulous figure to achieve his commercial goals. In contrast to his earlier schemes, the development of the Rugby School estate was something of a failure, which remained largely incomplete at the time of Barbon's death in 1698. Court papers show how his creditors Nathaniel Curzon and William Milman were left to pick up the pieces of the scheme, encountering opposition along the way from neighbours such as Thomas Griffith. Griffith's experience mirrors that of the lawyers of Gray's Inn, who in June 1684 fought a pitched 'battle' against workmen employed by Nicholas Barbon to develop the nearby Red Lion Fields. Whereas there is no documentary evidence to suggest that Griffith ever came to blows with Milman's builders, traces of the former's attempts to frustrate the development by flooding the ancient ditch that separated his land from Conduit Close may have been preserved in the archaeological record of the Roger Street site. This evidence represents a vivid illustration of how the development of the fringes of late seventeenth- and early eighteenth-century London came to disrupt long-established boundaries and patterns of land use and to threaten the social and behavioural bonds between neighbours.

Acknowledgements

The authors wish to thank Gary Brown and Helen Hawkins for project management and Frank Meddens for post-excavation management and editing. Further thanks are due to Alexis Haslam and Fergal O'Donoghue for their supervision of the works, and the field-staff for their assistance with the excavations. We are particularly grateful to Sheila O'Connell, the Hon. Editor of the London Topographical Society, for her help and guidance in getting this paper published.

1. Amelia Fairman, '14 Roger Street, London Borough of Camden, WC1N 2JR An Archaeological Watching Brief and Excavation' (unpublished report, Pre-Construct Archaeology Ltd, 2014).

2. The term 'horizon' is used as defined in the OED (sense 5c) as 'A level at which a particular group of remains is found, or which is taken as representing a particular culture or cultural period'.

3. Rebecca Haslam and Victoria Ridgeway, *Excavations at the British Museum: An Archaeological and Social History of Bloomsbury*, The British Museum Research Publications 210 (London, 2017); British Museum site code: MPB09.

4. Haslam and Ridgeway, *Excavations at the British Museum*; 14 Roger Street side code: ROG14.

5. OD = Ordnance Datum, the mean sea-level at Newlyn, Cornwall, to which heights are referred in the Ordnance Survey and in archaeological practice.

6. Haslam and Ridgeway, *Excavations at the British Museum*, p. 25.

7. Ibid., p. 32.

8. Ibid., p. 150.

9. BORDG is a fabric code for Surrey-Hampshire border white pottery ware with green glaze dating between 1550 and 1700.

10. Haslam and Ridgeway, *Excavations at the British Museum*, p. 44.

11. W. H. D. Rouse, *A History of Rugby School* (London, 1898), pp. 375–77.

12. Ibid., p. 404.

13. V. Smith and P. Kelsey, 'The Lines of Communication: The Civil War Defences of London', in *London and the Civil War*, ed. by Stephen Porter (London, 1996), p. 121.

14. R. R. Sharpe, *London and the Kingdom: A History in Three Volumes*, III (London, 1895), Appendix A, No. 62.

15. *A Perfect Diurnall*, 1 May 1643–8 May 1643 (BL Thomason Tracts E 249/2).

16. William Lithgow, *The present Surveigh of London and Englands state. Containing a topographicall description of all the […] forts […] and trenches newly erected round about the citie […] And a perfect relation of some fatall accidents, and other disasters which fell out in the city and countrey during the author's abode there* (London, 1643); Thomas Venn, *Military & Maritine [sic] Discipline in three Books. Book II: An Exact Method of Military Architecture, the Art of Fortifying Towns, with the Ways of Defending and Offending the Same. Rendered into English by John Lacey, out of the Works of the late Learned Mathematician Andrew Tacquet* (London, 1672), pp. 43–44.

17. Lithgow, *The present Surveigh of London*.

18. Norman G. Brett-James, 'The Fortifications of London in 1642/3', *London Topographical Record*, 14 (London Topographical Society publication No. 57, 1928), p. 23; David Flintham, *London in the Civil War: The Civil War Defences of London — A Social and Economic History* (Leigh-on-Sea, 2008), p. 23.

19. Rouse, *A History*, p. 384.

20. Ibid., p. 404.

21. Flintham, *London in the Civil War*, p. 23.

22. Rouse, *A History*, p. 386.

23. 17 Geo. III 1777 Cap. 71.

24. TNA, PROB 11/358/284.
25. TNA, PROB 11/357/294.
26. LMA, P69/ALH6/A/001/MS17824.
27. TNA, C 6/257/33; TNA, C 113/203; *Denbigh et al. v. Barbon*, 20 October 1686.
28. Philip Norman, 'On an Ancient Conduit-Head in Queen Square, Bloomsbury', in *Archaeologia*, 56.2 (1899), p. 263.
29. LMA, CLC/210/D/006/MS22535.
30. Norman, 'On an Ancient Conduit-Head', p. 263.
31. TNA, C113/203, Jackson, *Bland v. Milman et al.*, 25 October 1692; TNA, C22/489/22.
32. Thomas Roberts and Sir William Wood, *The English Bowman. Or, Tracts on Archery; to which is Added the Second Part of the Bowman's Glory* (London, 1801), p. 280 ; see pp. 147–48, n. 43, for a longer quotation.
33. TNA, MPA 1/2; TNA, PROB 11/373/301; *A History of the County of Warwick: vi, Knightlow Hundred*, ed. by Louis Francis Salzman (Victoria County History, 1951), pp. 22–26; <http://www.british-history.ac.uk/vch/warks/vol6> [accessed on 30 October 2020].
34. R. D. Sheldon, *Nicholas Barbon*, ODNB, <http://www.oxforddnb.com/view/article/1334> [accessed on 20 October 2015].
35. TNA, C 113/203, *Denbigh et al. v. Barbon*, 20 October 1686.
36. TNA, C 6/404/63; Rouse, *A History*, p. 88.
37. TNA, C 6/259/3.
38. TNA, C 6/257/33.
39. TNA, C 113/203, *Jackson, Bland v. Milman et al.*, 25 October 1692.
40. TNA, C 6/259/3.
41. Francis H. W. Sheppard (ed.), *Survey of London: xxxiii and xxxiv, St Anne Soho* (London, 1966), pp. 360–79, <http://www.british-history.ac.uk/survey-london/vols33-4> [accessed on 30 October 2020].
42. Elizabeth McKellar, *The Birth of Modern London: The Development and Design of the City, 1660–1720* (Manchester, 1999), p. 59.
43. TNA, C 22/489/22.
44. TNA, C 113/203, *Asgill v. Milman*, 4 March 1699.
45. TNA, C 113/203, *Asgill v. Milman*, 4 March 1699.
46. 17 Geo. III 1777 cap. 71.
47. Rouse, *A History*, p. 95.
48. BL Maps Crace Port. 15.27.
49. TNA, C 6/404/63.
50. TNA, C 6/404/63.
51. TNA, C 6/404/63.
52. TNA, C 6/404/63
53. McKellar, *The Birth of Modern London*, pp. 227–28.
54. Camden Archives and Local History Centre, M0663 (information from Frank Kelsall).
55. 21 Geo. II 1748 Cap. 23.
56. 17 Geo. III 1777 Cap. 71.
57. Walter Godfrey and William McB. Marcham (eds), *Survey of London: xxiv, the Parish of St Pancras, Part 4: King's Cross Neighbourhood* (London, 1952), pp. 25–55, <http://www.british-history.ac.uk/survey-london/vol24/pt4> [accessed on 30 October 2020].
58. Sarah Barrowman, '14 Roger Street, Bloomsbury, London Borough of Camden, WC1N 2JR An Archaeological Desk-Based Assessment' (unpublished report, Pre-Construct Archaeology Ltd, 2013), p. 22.
59. Laurence Ward, *The London County Council Bomb Damage Maps, 1939–1945* (London, 2015), p. 80.
60. Sheppard (ed.), *Survey of London*, pp. 380–84.

61. Lawson Chase Nagel, 'The Militia of London, 1641–1649' (doctoral thesis, University of London, 1982), p. 20; Richard Elton, *The Compleat Body of the Art Military, divided into three books* (London, 1650), p. 67.

62. Sheppard (ed.), *Survey of London*, p. 380.

VII. EDWARD JERMAN AND GREAT WINCHESTER STREET

By DORIAN GERHOLD

THE carpenter Edward Jerman is well known for his contribution to the rebuilding of London after the Great Fire of 1666. He designed the Royal Exchange, St Paul's School and at least six company halls.[1] However, this activity occurred at the end of his life, shortly before his death in October 1668. Much less has been known about his activities before the Fire. Now new evidence has been discovered which identifies one of his major pre-Fire projects, for which visual evidence survives. It also provides information about the break-up of one of the City's major aristocratic estates and the creation of new streets in the 1650s and 1660s.

Edward Jerman was born in about 1605. He belonged to the fourth generation of a family of carpenters active since the 1540s. He was apprenticed in 1623, and from 1633 he shared with his father Anthony the office of City Carpenter, continuing to perform that role after his father's death in 1650 until his resignation in 1657. He was also a City Viewer from 1650 to 1655 and one of the two City Surveyors from 1655 to 1657.[2] In 1645 he was engaged as surveyor to give advice about building new houses on London Bridge, and provided a plan. A different design was adopted for the ten new houses, drawn up by the Bridge House's master carpenter, but that was probably an adaptation of Jerman's plan, as he was later paid the substantial sum of £13 6s. 8d. for it.[3] The episode shows that Jerman was already designing buildings rather than just constructing them.

By the time Jerman resigned from his last City office in 1657 he was already working for several livery companies: as carpenter to the Goldsmiths from 1650 and the Haberdashers by 1663, and as surveyor to the Fishmongers from 1654 and manager of their woodlands from 1662. His work for the companies consisted of viewing and surveying rather than building, and there is no evidence of him carrying out any carpentry work after 1657. He was the designer of the Lord Mayor's Show from 1656 to 1664, and of the City's festivities to welcome the return of Charles II in 1660.[4] In or about 1655 he built three houses 'near Moor Ditch', and around the same time he built several houses on two plots leased from the City 'on the postern', which were probably in the street called Basinghall Postern, created after a new passage was made through London Wall there in 1655. These developments were probably not speculative, as they were all on land leased from the City and were sold back to the City.[5]

Jerman's previously unknown project was in the former precinct of the Austin Friars, which had been bounded on three sides by London Wall, Broad Street and Throgmorton Street. After the Dissolution, William

Paulet, later the 1st Marquess of Winchester, acquired most of the northern part of the precinct, including a large area of garden, a double cloister and the choir of the friars' church (the nave became the Dutch Church). He converted the cloisters into a mansion that became known as Winchester House. Archaeological evidence indicates that he kept the southern cloister largely unchanged, but rebuilt the northern cloister, giving the mansion an H-shape.[6] The remaining parts of it are clearly visible on Ogilby and Morgan's map of 1676 (the heavily stippled structures around the courtyard marked B.21) (Fig. 1). By 1610 there were more houses, now including three 'capital messuages' or mansions: a later Winchester House (discussed below), Cumberland House (the 1st Marquess's mansion) and Shrewsbury House (in Broad Street).[7] The 1st Marquess's mansion may have been divided into several parts as early as 1598, and certainly was by 1620.[8] Nevertheless, in the 1640s his great-great-grandson, John, 5th Marquess of Winchester, still held the whole of the estate that the 1st Marquess had assembled in Austin Friars.

The 5th Marquess was both a royalist and a Catholic, and in 1651 an Act of Parliament declared all his lands forfeited. In 1653 the London property (at least) was sold to three men in what appears to have been a collusive sale on behalf of the Marquess, and Daniel Wicherley, who was in fact the Marquess's steward, was given the power to lease it out.[9] The Marquess recovered the property after the Restoration, but sold part of it in 1664 and the rest in 1668.[10]

One of the agreements Wicherley made under the powers he acquired in 1653 was with Edward Jerman. Jerman set out what had happened in a Chancery bill of 1658.[11] He had obtained a lease, dated 20 May 1656, which required him to repair the old houses on the site let to him and to build new ones. The term was fifty-four years, and the rent was £160 a year. Jerman stated that he had built over twenty substantial new houses, and had spent over £6,000 repairing old ones. By 1664 the premises were described as containing twenty-seven houses.[12] The reason for the Chancery bill was that the lease had not been signed by all the parties, so Jerman was unable to let the premises, but this was resolved not later than August 1658.[13]

Jerman's lease described the property as a capital messuage or mansion called Augustine Friars or Winchester House or Place, lately occupied by the Spanish ambassador, abutting north on the street leading by London Wall, east on the capital messuage called 'the glasse house' and its garden, south on gardens occupied by Sir William Hicks and Mr Lant and houses in Austin Friars and west on a garden and tenements of the Carpenters' Company. On Ogilby and Morgan's map of 1676, there is an alley and court west of Winchester Street marked A70, named in the key as the Dog and Bear Inn but on later maps as Carpenters Buildings, and west of that was Carpenters' Hall. Jerman's premises were therefore in the western

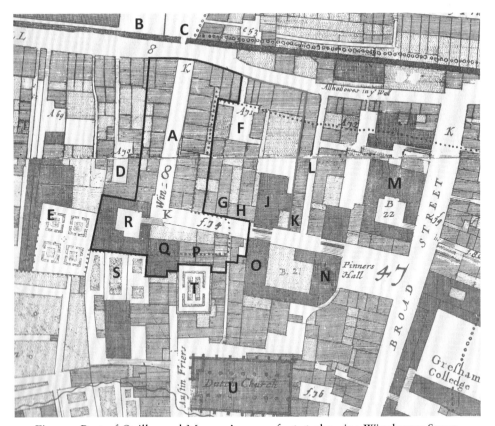

Fig. 1.   Part of Ogilby and Morgan's map of 1676, showing Winchester Street.
The approximate extent of the land in Jerman's lease is outlined in red, and
of Hartopp's in green (except where it adjoined Jerman's). The boundary of
Jerman's land to the south is very uncertain. Key: A, Winchester Street; B,
London Wall; C, postern gate into Moorfields; D, Dog and Bear Inn (later
Carpenters Buildings); E, Carpenters' Hall; F, White Hart Court; G, the
soaphouse; H, Dog Tavern; J, Sir Robert Vyner's mansion, part of the African
House; K, Vyner's goldsmith's shop; L, Little Winchester Street; M, Shrewsbury
House; N, Pinners' Hall; O, part of the African House; P, James Houblon's house;
Q, Sir John Shaw's house, R, part of Winchester House; S, Mr Lant's garden;
T, Sir William Hicks's garden; U, Dutch Church.

part of the Marquess's estate, where Ogilby and Morgan's map shows
the north–south part of Winchester Street (later Great Winchester Street).
In fact the deeds make clear that Jerman created that part of Winchester
Street. In 1675 the name did not yet apply to what became the eastern part
of the street, which was described simply as the way from Broad Street to
Winchester Street.[14]

More evidence is provided by what seems to be a moneylender's note book, recording information obtained in 1677:

> Mr Jarmin's lease for 27 houses on both sides Winchester Streete from the African house on one side & from one house below ye sopehouse on ye other side, & turning at ye posterne gate into Moorefeilds towards Broadstreete as farr as ye White Hart Court worth at least £900 or £1000 pr ann there is 34 yeares to come in ye lease.[15]

These landmarks can be identified using Ogilby and Morgan's map and the surviving deeds.[16] The postern gate into Moorfields was at the north end of Winchester Street, and White Hart Court is A71 on the map. The block of land east of Jerman's was leased in 1675 to Thomas Hartopp, a merchant, and was held by Edward Hawley in 1677, when it was described as 'ye dogtaverne & soape house adjoining with all ye back-buildings belonging to it as far as ye White Hart Court at London-wall into which he hath a backdoore'. This property included at its north end three houses, of which the westernmost abutted west on Jerman's land and was over the entrance to White Hart Court. At the south end of the property were four houses lying together on the north side of Winchester Street, built on a garden that had belonged to the mansion formerly known as the Glasshouse and now as the African House. The two westernmost of these four houses abutted west on Jerman's land, and the easternmost was the Dog Tavern, which itself abutted on part of the Glasshouse known as 'the Long Gallery'. This holding also included the buildings in White Hart Court and the mansion and garden lately occupied by Sir Robert Vyner (evidently part of the Glasshouse or African House).[17] This information gives us the approximate eastern boundary of Jerman's holding north and east of Winchester Street.

Further east, the 1st Marquess's former mansion had been divided into several parts. On the east side in 1675 was 'all that the late greate hall lately called Glasshouse Hall but more late Pinners Hall' (it is labelled as Pinners' Hall on the map). On the west side was another mansion, with 'the great court' and warehouses, known as the African House and occupied by the East India Company. It was said to be part of the Glasshouse, and that name evidently applied to the whole of the 1st Marquess's Winchester House, perhaps referring to an unusually large expanse of windows. The name 'the African House' applied, or had formerly applied, to the whole of the western part of the mansion. Between the African House and the Dutch Church other parts of the 1st Marquess's mansion had been converted into houses. Not only had the mansion been split up, but a new east–west passage had been created, passing under its two wings, and a new north–south street (known later as Little Winchester Street) had been created between those two wings, linking Winchester Street and London Wall. In 1675 this was described as a new way lately made by Thomas Cutler, who had lately built warehouses on both sides of it, together with a building that included Vyner's goldsmith's shop on the south-west corner.[18]

Jerman's properties south of Winchester Street extended to the walls of the Glasshouse, and included one house east of the alley leading to Austin Friars.[19] The occupiers of Jerman's houses, as listed in a deed of 1664, can mostly be identified in the hearth tax list of two years earlier, and this indicates that the houses included two large ones, with twenty-two and seventeen hearths, occupied by Sir John Shaw and James Houblon respectively.[20] These were south of Winchester Street and west of the alley. Jerman also held the courtyard house further west.[21] These three houses were almost certainly Winchester House itself, or the greater part of it, and seem to have been altered rather than rebuilt by Jerman. The houses of Shaw and Houblon survived until 1839, still known as Winchester House, and the drawings of them suggest that Jerman added a storey or storeys (Fig. 2).

WINCHESTER HOUSE, LONDON

Fig. 2. Winchester House in 1839, in a print by George Hollis made just before demolition. The outer wall by the street has already been removed. This was one of the structures refurbished by Jerman and occupied in the 1660s by Sir John Shaw (right) and James Houblon (left). © Trustees of the British Museum, *1880,1113.3979*.

Fig. 3. J. T. Smith's print of the north–south part of Great Winchester Street in May 1804, looking south from near London Wall. At the far end is the part of Winchester House once occupied by Sir John Shaw. © Trustees of the British Museum *Heal, Topography.* 319.

Jerman's new buildings were therefore mainly in the north-south part of Winchester Street. The house on the north-east corner had the date 1656 (the date of Jerman's lease) carved on a bracket.[22] There is good pictorial evidence for these houses, including a photo of those on the east side (Figs 3–5).[23] They were large timber-framed houses with four storeys including garrets, jettied in the first storey. No doubt most of the windows had been altered by the time of the views. On the ward map of 1858 (unlike on Ogilby and Morgan's map), the houses were of similar size on both sides of the street, having a depth of about 36 feet and a width of about 22 feet.[24] In 1662 most of them had nine hearths, apart from several with eight, and nine was one more than the average for merchants' houses.[25] Jerman claimed to have built at least twenty new houses, and Ogilby and Morgan's map shows twenty houses in the north–south part of the street. According to J. T. Smith, writing in 1815, there would have been eighteen gables there (presumably indicating eighteen houses) if some of the houses had not lost their gables, but the difference was probably because the houses at

Fig. 4. Watercolour by Thomas Hosmer Shepherd, *c.* 1841, showing the houses on the east side of Great Winchester Street. On the extreme left of the view, it can be seen that the row did not extend quite as far north as London Wall, but was separated from it by another building, built of brick. © London Metropolitan Archives, City of London *SC/GL/PR/273/GRE/3/q4771094*.

the north end of Great Winchester Street on both sides had been rebuilt at some stage.[26] The development provides a good example of an aristocratic mansion and its gardens in the City giving way to terraces of houses in a new street, and of the scale on which an important carpenter such as Edward Jerman might operate.

Unlike Jerman's developments for the City, this one does seem to have been speculative, and Jerman soon sold the houses. By 1663 he was said to have 'fallen into decay in his estate'; it is not known why. He was buried at St Giles Cripplegate in November 1668, and, despite his exertions after the Great Fire, his widow had to appeal for funds from the companies he had worked for.[27] Jerman's houses on the east side of Winchester Street were demolished in 1865 or 1866. Those on the west side were demolished at around the same time, and certainly not later than 1873.[28]

Fig. 5. Photo of the houses on the east side of Great Winchester Street, apparently shortly before demolition in 1865–66. © London Metropolitan Archives, City of London *SC/PHL/ 01/027/70/6158.*

1. Howard Colvin, *A Biographical Dictionary of British Architects 1600–1840*, 3rd edn (London and New Haven, 1995), pp. 545–46; Helen Collins, *Edward Jerman 1605–1668: The Metamorphosis of a Master Craftsman* (Cambridge, 2004), *passim*.

2. Collins, *Edward Jerman*, pp. 26, 28, 48–51.

3. LMA, City Repertories, vol. 57/2, ff. 67, 135 (mistakenly describing him as Anthony Jerman the younger); LMA, CLA/007/FN/03/017, 12 January 1649/50; Dorian Gerhold, *London Bridge and its Houses, c. 1209–1761*, London Topographical Society publication No. 182 (2019), p. 54.

4. Collins, *Edward Jerman*, pp. 59, 75–76, 82–85, 110–13, 163, 169.

5. Ibid., p. 53; Dorian Gerhold, *London Plotted: Plans of London Buildings c. 1450–1720*, London Topographical Society publication No. 178 (2016), p. 245.

6. Nick Holder, 'The Medieval Friaries of London' (doctoral thesis, Royal Holloway, University of London, 2011), pp. 170–72, 428, 435.

7. LMA, CLC/092/MS20159/015, bundle 4, note of title, bundle 5, lease of 1625.

8. LMA, ACC/1360/16, tables; LMA, ACC/1360/16, lease of 1623.

9. TNA, C 3/449/68.

10. TNA, C 54/4165, No. 26; TNA, C 54/4430, Nos 16, 17, 19.

11. TNA, C 3/449/68. The lease is at LMA, CLC/092/MS20159/003.

12. TNA, C 10/108/85; TNA, C 54/4165, No. 26.

13. TNA, C 5/407/6.

14. LMA, CLC/092/MS20159/001, articles of 1674; TNA, C 54/4430, No. 16.

15. Barnsley Archives, EM 1363, p. 36.

16. TNA, C 54/4430, Nos 16, 17, 19; LMA, CLC/092/MS20159/001 to 015.

17. Barnsley Archives, EM 1363, p. 36; TNA, C 54/4430, No. 17. White Hart Court probably originated as the service wing of Austin Friars (see Holder, 'Medieval Friaries', p. 419).

18. TNA, C 54/4430, Nos 16, 17.

19 . LMA, CLC/092/MS20159/004, deed of 1665.

20. TNA, C 54/4165, No. 26; https://www.british-history.ac.uk/london-hearth-tax/london/1662/broad-street-ward-winchester-street [accessed 4 December 2020].

21. LMA, CLC/092/MS20159/004, deeds of 1658 and 1666.

22. John Thomas Smith, *Ancient Topography of London* (London, 1815), p. 69.

23. Fig. 3 shows all the gables surviving on the left side but two having been replaced on the right side. The houses on the left are therefore those shown in Figs 4 and 5, as the arrangement of windows confirms. The houses east of this part of Great Winchester Street were numbered 11 to 19, from south to north, and those to the west 20 to 27, from north to south (LMA, COL/WD/03/010). Nos 19 and 20, facing London Wall, are not recorded in directories and other documents from the 1840s onwards, and had apparently been rebuilt and renumbered as part of London Wall (LMA, SC/GL/WAK/633/WIN/q4771071). The views provide three clues as to whether the houses shown in Figs 4 and 5 were on the west or east sides. In Fig. 4, the shop on the left of the row is occupied by a stationer and bookseller, with a sign above advertising merchants' account books, and the third from the left is occupied by Mr King, a builder. In Fig. 5, the right-hand shop has a poster advertising the removal elsewhere of an engraver and printer. In the censuses, directories and land tax records, No. 11 is occupied by Henry Haley Collins & Co., stationer and printer or engraver and printer, at least from 1850 to 1865; No. 16 is occupied by Abraham King, carpenter and builder, from at least 1841 to 1860; and No. 18 is occupied by Edward Goodwin and then William R. Goodwin, described at first as cheesemongers, but the latter from 1851 to 1861 as an account book maker. The row shown on the left side of Fig. 3 and in Figs 4 and 5 was therefore Nos 11–18, on the east side of the street.

24. LMA, COL/WD/03/010.

25. https://www.british-history.ac.uk/london-hearth-tax/london/1662/broad-street-ward-winchester-street [accessed 4 December 2020]; M. J. Power, 'The Social Topography of Restoration London', in A. L. Beier and Roger Finlay (eds), *London 1500–1700: The Making of the Metropolis* (London, 1986), p. 214.

26. Smith, *Ancient Topography*, pp. 68–69. See Fig. 4 and LMA, SC/GL/WAK/633/WIN/q4771071 (COLLAGE: The London Picture Archive, ref. 18534). One was rebuilt in 1829 (LMA, CLC/092/MS20159/004, bundle 7, sale catalogue).

27. Collins, *Edward Jerman*, pp. 28, 113.

28. Ancestry, London land taxes, 1865–70 [accessed 29 November 2020]; Ordnance Survey, London large-scale plan 7.66, 1873.

VIII. WHO OWNED THE CITY OF LONDON IN 1666?

By IAN DOOLITTLE

Introduction

THIS investigation is intended to help with the recreation of the City of London at the time of the Great Fire. Some years ago I suggested it should be possible to use the voluminous property records to map and delineate the houses, streets and other features of the pre-Fire City and with the results answer important questions not just about the rebuilding process but also the property market at that time.[1] In this essay I try to create almost literally the building blocks for such an enterprise, by first presenting the evidence for the number of houses and then providing a breakdown of the owners of those houses, distinguishing between 'Institutions' and 'Individuals'. I also use the analysis to make observations about the way property was owned and, in my conclusion, how the leasehold system helped the City respond to the Fire.

I am very conscious that any counting exercise of this kind is fraught with risks. I have done my best to mitigate or at least highlight those risks. My figures are based on the research described in the volume of Supporting Evidence I will deposit with both the London Metropolitan Archives and the Guildhall Library (and which is available via email from me).[2] Notwithstanding the assistance of Derek Keene and Vanessa Harding's marvellous *Survey of Documentary Sources for Property Holding in London before the Great Fire*,[3] I may have missed some records and I am sure I have misread an archival convention or misunderstood an administrative arrangement. That is why I have set out both my methodology and the results in the Supporting Evidence. I see this as simply a starting point, with its figures and therefore its conclusions to be corrected in future years. I will try to contribute to that work, with my continuation of the calendar of the Fire Court decrees and related studies,[4] but this will have to be a long term, collaborative exercise if it is to succeed. In the meantime I hope readers will kindly focus on the transparency rather than the gaps and uncertainties.

Specific methodological challenges are discussed in the volume of Supporting Evidence, but three points warrant rehearsal here. The first is 'the City'. I am mindful of Vanessa Harding's wise words on this issue,[5] and I have decided to confine myself to what contemporaries called the Liberty of the City, including the liberties or precincts within it.[6] In other words, my area is that covered by the twenty-five wards north of the river (i.e. excluding Bridge Ward Without in Southwark).[7] The City included 108 parishes, but six of them extended into Middlesex. Those areas have been excluded.

The second issue concerns the term 'house'. This is my focus, to help with cross-references to those lists of houses and householders which were compiled at this time (including the total of 13,200 said to have been destroyed in the Fire).[8] I have chosen to omit obviously non-residential properties (such halls, warehouses and so on), conscious that by doing so I am excluding some households (in taverns, for example). I do, however, want expressly to address the 'house/shop' conundrum — illustrated strikingly in the case of the Royal Exchange[9] — and I have therefore noted all identified shops.[10] The term 'house' was certainly used frequently by contemporaries, but the usual term in the legal or financial records was messuage or tenement. There was a tendency to use messuage for larger properties (as in 'capital messuage'), while small properties, especially those in back alleys or courts, were usually called tenements (or 'rents'), but there was no consistent distinction.[11] And though taverns and shops can sometimes be identified in other ways, they could well be 'lost' as 'messuages' or 'tenements'. It is important therefore not to read too much into such terms, and lists or totals of 'houses' might well have referred to the larger properties *on* the streets or lanes and ignored the clusters of tenements *behind* them. As Bill Baer commented to me, these terms are indeed 'slippery'. The point is significant because if we take the figures too literally there is scope for getting it badly wrong, especially outside the walls where large numbers of poorer tenants were clustered in subdivided, 'inter-mixed' or otherwise makeshift properties. Indeed, it is always worth bearing in mind the contrast between the number and type of properties in the core (and settled) intra-mural area and those in the populous (and expanding) areas beyond the walls.

The final point is related to the second. Some records refer to 'divers' properties. This could mean anything from two adjacent messuages to a large cluster of tenements. I have done my best, but apart from the obvious uncertainty there is the odd-sounding but real risk of over-analysis — that is, digging deeper than those who compiled the well-known lists of houses.[12] Except where there are obvious and major groups of small houses,[13] I have simply treated all these 'multiples' as comprising three houses. If I have erred on the low side it is because of the distribution effect; I think most will be two or three, at least in the core of the City. In the populous parishes, where there were more and larger clusters, a higher multiplier might be appropriate. It is, of course, a simple matter — and I have done so below — to see what results from applying four or five. Or to guess at what an entry for a mere 'tenant' means. It would also be possible to differentiate between areas or landlords. I want, however, to provide data that has not been over-interpreted, allowing others to apply their own techniques to the figures.

The Number of Houses — from the Hearth Tax

The obvious source for the number of houses in what I term (and have defined) as the City is the Hearth Tax of 1666, not least because there is now a splendid edition published by the Roehampton team.[14] The editors, however, discourage counting. There are two particular reasons for this. The first is the simple omission of some householders. In some returns those exempt from the tax were noted (in a few cases in clusters at the end) but in many instances they were not. The collectors differed in their approach. And that is the second problem. Each collection book needs to be treated as almost *sui generis*. The editors pointedly do not attempt to aggregate the totals. I understand the need for caution but I decided to carry out my own analysis, identify obvious difficulties and tabulate the results. My workings are set out in the volume of Supporting Evidence, but it is worth explaining here that I believe I have found a way of filling the gaps in the 1666 records (based on parishes) with totals from the 1662–63 Hearth Tax and other returns (based on wards).[15] It is also to be noted that, while the Roehampton editors prefer 'householders', I am comfortable with 'houses', not only because that is the term used by the collectors and/or constables themselves but partly because (as explained above) I want to adhere to contemporary usage.

The 1666 data, especially now that it has been so expertly collated, is a unique resource, but the effects of the Plague and the Fire have to be taken into account. The editors draw readers' attention to the many references to burnt properties and so on, and it is obviously important to consider the 1665–66 context. In the case of the Plague it is worth appreciating that the Hearth Tax was a tax on property: if the occupier/tenant could not pay then the owner/landlord had to, and in the case of the Fire occupiers/tenants were still recorded (from old assessment lists), even though their properties has been destroyed. In short, the returns retain at least their basic value and, at the risk of belabouring my point, I want future discussions to be based on clear data — evidential warts and all.

The results of my analysis, by parish, are in Table 1. The order and style of parishes follow the contemporary Bills of Mortality. The total is 24,260 or so. I believe most historians will find this plausible, with Mark Jenner suggesting 19,000 for 1638, Jacob Field 25,000 for 1675, and Craig Spence 21,000 for 1693–94.[16] There are three detailed *house* lists in the early part of the eighteenth century,[17] but the effects of the Fire itself and London's volatile growth makes comparison hazardous. This is especially true of the large extra-mural parishes, where 'new buildings' proliferated.[18] By far the largest house numbers are at the end of the list, where the Bills for the 'fringe' parishes appear. St Bride, St Giles Cripplegate, St Dunstan in the West, St Sepulchre (Newgate) and the three St Botolph parishes (Aldersgate, Aldgate and Bishopsgate) together accounted for nearly 40% of the total. Certainly, the closest attention must be paid to these totals when assessing the reliability of my calculations. And it is not just the large numbers of houses that matter; it is also their nature. The so-called 'rents' in alleys and courts may not always have been captured. As already noted, there are indications that this could make a significant difference to the totals. (It is for this reason that I have noted when the 'poor' or equivalent categories were identified.[19]) Nevertheless, it is worth noting that the overall total and, for the most part, the individual parish totals are either in line with the other lists (or, if not, there are post-Fire or passage-of-time reasons for major discrepancies).[20]

The next step was to analyse house *ownership* to see how this fits within the overall house numbers calculated from the Hearth Tax.

Institutions — from Estate Records

For obvious reasons it is much easier to trace property ownership by Institutions than Individuals. In doing so, and by making use of the rich archives for this period, we can hope to assess how 24,260 houses were 'split'. It is, of course, important to appreciate that the split is somewhat artificial: Institutions owned some properties through individual trustees and they also were themselves trustees for properties left to them for specified, often charitable, purposes.[21] And though I have done my best to identify individual 'units' to help with the comparison between estate records and tax lists, the latter are principally concerned with tax-paying occupiers and the former with rent-paying tenants (whether occupiers or not). Nevertheless, the distinction is interesting; it certainly has implications for the way the property market worked, both in its steady state and for the post-Fire rebuilding process. As the remarks in this essay suggest, and as more detailed work on different Institutions is carried out, we will be able to see the role the City, the Livery Companies and so on played in shaping not just the reconstruction and growth of the Square Mile but also the market that underlay that growth and reconstruction. And, in turn, since property was so important to these Institutions, the vicissitudes of that property market had a major impact on their own fortunes.

Crown (see Table 2) — it is well known that the Crown's estate had been heavily eroded and that the Crown anyway owned little property in the City, but the house numbers are still strikingly small.

The City (see Table 2) — the 'Corporation' alone was the largest owner in my lists, with some 700-odd houses. The City also administered the Bridge House Trust,[22] which with 250 or more takes the City's aggregate to over 950. The Trust's income was devoted to the maintenance of the Bridge.

Livery Companies (see Table 3) — they were collectively the largest owner, with over 2,400 houses (some 10% of the total). It is important to appreciate that these are simply houses owned by the Companies, whether in their corporate or trust accounts. Properties were often 'labelled' to indicate the benefactor and to show the obligations attached to them, but the overall private/charitable distinction was rarely laid bare.[23] I am also conscious that some mortgage/trust arrangements were adopted in the 1650s to appease or avoid creditors and I hope I have not missed any properties. Predictably, the Great Twelve accounted for many of the houses: about 1,900 or nearly 80% of the 2,400 or so. The Goldsmiths had 500 (bolstered by recent, small-unit developments); they were followed at a distance by the Drapers, Mercers and Merchant Taylors with 200 or more each.

Churches (Table 4) — the collective holdings of Deans and Chapters, Bishops and others amounted to 730 or more houses. The St Paul's records are not easy and the personal leases of 'officials' are elusive, but it is clear that the Cathedral, in this wider sense, was by far the most important owner in this category: it accounted for well over half the total. Next came Westminster Abbey, benefiting (so to speak) from the development of St Martin le Grand. The Bishop of London's houses are not easy to count, given the somewhat messy records, the split between the rents committed to St Paul's and those for his personal benefit, and the redevelopment of the old Palace; but the total was probably only sixty or so. The holdings of other 'Cathedrals' were mainly small, but the Chichester (i.e. Dean and Chapter) estate comprised forty houses.

Parishes (Table 5) — parishes *together* were quite significant house owners in 1666, with a total of some 740 houses, depending on the number of houses owned by clergymen in their own name. Individual parish holdings, however, were small: most parishes had fewer than ten properties, and only seven exceeded twenty. (This makes the absence of property records for twelve of the 108 parishes less problematic.)

Hospitals (Table 6) — St Bartholomew's accounted for much the largest 'share' of the total of 670 or so; Christ's, St Thomas's, Bridewell and Bethlem (in that order) had somewhere between 125 and sixty-ish each.

Oxford and Cambridge (Table 7) — the Colleges' holdings were not large: 140 or so in total and none much exceeding twenty.

Schools (Table 8) — aside from Eton College, the totals were negligible, and the overall total was only twenty or so.

Others (Table 9) — this, too, is a small category, with possibly seventy houses in all. More 'Institutional' owners may be found in future, but it is unlikely that in size or nature they will affect the general findings.

The overall results appear in Table 2. I calculate that nearly 5,770 houses were owned by what I am calling Institutions. As already indicated, the City and the Livery Companies accounted for most of the houses, perhaps 3,370 in all (or approaching 60%). The Church (i.e. 'Cathedrals' really), Parishes and the Hospitals owned much of the rest.

A comparison of the 5,770 with the 24,260 must take account of the sources on which the two totals are based. Both have deficiencies, but they are different deficiencies. How many non-payers were not included in the Hearth Tax returns? And have I under-estimated the number of tenements in the alleys, courts and so on? It is one thing to rely on the use contemporaries made of tax and similar listings to claim at least consistency of comparison; it is another to rely on the accuracy of the property records themselves, which do not just require adjustment to deal with multiples (or plain lessees, too?) but might occasionally take you into those alleys and courts whose poor occupiers the tax collector ignored. And the records of at least one large Institution — the Goldsmiths' Company — uses the term 'room' (which I usually ignore) as synonymous with house.[24] The 'multiple' issue can at least be reconsidered by increasing the factor (three), which I have applied. Using five would increase the total by 340 or more,[25] thus taking the percentage of houses from twenty-three to twenty-five. Tenants, being more numerous, are more difficult: if (say) half of them were assumed to have two houses,[26] this adds 475 or so and increases the percentage to twenty-seven. This guesswork is hardly sensitivity testing, but it does seem to indicate that 25–27% as an upper limit is a fair conclusion from my work.

This is substantially lower than the only other detailed assessment. Bill Baer used the Fire Court decrees to suggest a minimum of 39%,[27] but as he appreciated this is awkward evidence to use in this way, not least because of the difficulty of distinguishing between 'real' owners and landlords (an issue I address for Individuals later in this essay). Some Institutions were clearly under-represented. The largest owner of them all, the City, rarely needed or was required to accept a decree — there were 'barely a dozen' petitioners 'from' the 300 tenancies affected by the Fire[28] — while others (including the Church, I believe) were over-represented (needing or wanting the sanction of the Court to endorse agreements and/or grant long rebuilding leases). My percentage is even lower than the (maximum) 30% (at least for the City Corporation, the Hospitals and Livery Companies) suggested many years ago by D. W. Jones.[29] It is difficult to trace his archival footsteps and he did not include some owners, but since he was probably the only other person to attempt to count properties in the rental accounts it is interesting that, like me, he concluded that Institutional ownership was lower than hitherto assumed.[30] The weakness in my calculation is the use it makes of data derived from occupation on the one hand and ownership on the other; its strength derives from the rehearsal of a great deal of archival evidence and the basis this provides for future work.

Individuals — from the Fire Court Evidence

If Institutions really accounted for only 25% of City houses in 1666, it is correspondingly important to understand the role Individuals — that is, the owners of the 18,500 or so other houses — played in the property market.

The first question is, how many owners? My instinct is that they had only a few properties each, and then not frequently,[31] but this is difficult to quantify. Bill Baer drew similar conclusions (about *landlords*) from an assessment for St Margaret, Westminster, in the 1690s (as well as some confirmatory data from the 1630s),[32] but I have found no equivalent assessment for the City. There are tantalizing references to owners but the lists are essentially of occupiers or at least tenants. There is, however, no obvious reason why the City should have been different. Indeed, there may have been (even) fewer opportunities for accumulating significant private holdings, whether single sites or multiple ones. I have analysed the register of 'foundations' for which post-Fire rebuilders were required to pay. Of course, this is not a list of owners: the foundations may have 'belonged' to X and Y,[33] but the rebuilders were frequently tenants and some who got/paid for foundations did not in fact rebuild. And whether and how the 8,100 odd foundations 'replaced' the possible 13,200 burnt houses is difficult to assess.[34] Nevertheless, the results suggest that the landlords of those sites had small-scale, scattered property holdings.[35]

It is tempting to go on to ask how many of these owners were also occupiers, but the evidence does not help us much. Here, too, the assessments get us close — with columns of 'inhabitants' and 'landlords' — but not close enough. Baer indicates that at least 75% of houses may have been rented, not owned, but he acknowledges the lack of data.[36] Only if some of the assessments can be made to yield owner (not just landlord) — as well as occupier — information or if chance survivals (such as the sixty-odd post-Fire claims at St Bride's[37]) can be augmented will the picture become clearer. And even if it does, we need to recognize that owners of (say) three or four houses may have occupied one and leased the others.

A full account of this multitude of Individual property owners will clearly take a very long time and a very large team to compile; but if it is not practicable to identify *who* they were it *is* possible to find out, so to speak, *what* they were — that is, types or categories of Individuals, including the various capacities in which they held or had a property interest in their houses. Information is, of course, available from the voluminous deeds of these years but for analytical purposes I need a database. I believe the best available to be the decrees of the Fire Court, which settled disputes, or recorded agreements, between landlords and tenants as to the terms for rebuilding.[38] I have analysed the 1,170 or so cases that have been calendared so far.[39] I have explained elsewhere how the decrees can be used in this way,[40] but it is worth emphasizing the risks inherent in any editorial judgements. Jones was an expert guide but he summarized rather than rehearsed, and for volume F (and for the future volumes I am working on) I have decided to set out the petitions and the hearings in full to ensure no details are missed. It is certainly a good-sized sample, with multiple-property cases meaning that even the 690 or so where Individuals are owners accounts for over 1,300 of their assumed 18,000 or so houses.[41] Reassurance as to the decrees' reliability principally derives from the party-to-party challenge inherent in the process, as well as the Court's readiness to intervene and verify the evidence. And though the cases obviously concern only the burnt areas of the City (and it would certainly be interesting to look at more extra-mural areas), there is a reasonable 'spread' of property types and values.[42] More difficult is the fact that cases involved landlords and tenants, not owners and occupiers. For the analysis that follows I am pragmatically treating as owners those who as freeholder or head landlord treated the property as a source of income. The Court was not concerned with such distinctions and so my approach could potentially produce an inconsistency, with an 'owner' in one decree being an 'occupier' in another. This is untidy, but the decrees provide a remarkable opportunity to lift the lid, so to speak, on landlord-tenant relationships on the eve of the Fire. Here again I hope that my imperfect but visible approach (documented in the volume of Supporting Evidence) will be regarded as creating a sensible framework and useful preliminary findings for future researchers.

Given this 'ownership' issue — and before looking at the different types of 'owner' the decrees indubitably reveal — it is worth highlighting how difficult it is to identify what might be called degrees of ownership. This is rarely an issue for Institutions, who usually owned property free of 'superior' interests (save for quit rents and other nominal payments): that at any rate is a fair assumption.[43] For Individuals it is different. How many were freeholders? I have used that convenient term already, but its infrequency in the decrees is interesting.[44] The more formal 'fee simple' is rare, too.[45] 'Seised' appears regularly, but not often in what lawyers regarded as the fullest extent, that is, 'seised in his demesne as of fee'.[46] Usually 'owners' were simply 'seised of the fee *or* inheritance'. This was a conveniently vague phrase — the legal term would have included 'and' not 'or' — and can be seen as just a general statement of ownership or perhaps a reflection of the long-held right to hold and dispose of City property.

This terminological haziness (a reminder that legal history can be too wedded to categories, especially 'feudal' categories) means or shows that some of my 'owners' will have been leaseholders. There are clear references to leasehold interests in only twenty-three cases, but, while there may well have been more, all the cases demonstrate the distinction between landlords and tenants and explain the owner/occupier relationship. Very occasionally (as already noted) this means that the same individual can be owner for the purposes of one decree and occupier for the purposes of another. There are one or two other overlaps, including appeals (which were usually unsuccessful). Overall, however, the Fire Court evidence is broad in scope and rich in detail — and unique in its accessibility.

Each category of 'owner' that follows presents the results of an analysis of all the calendared Fire Court decrees (i.e. volumes A–F). Details are provided in Section 3 of the volume of Supporting Evidence to enable readers to see the judgements that have been formed where there is uncertainty. The totals are given by volume, with first the number of instances of that category and then the number of cases involving Individual owners.

The total number of cases involving *Individuals* is 700 or so. By each analysed volume the totals are A: 141 (192); B: 101 (140); C: 111 (191); D: 129 (240); E: 109 (230); F: 109 (178).[47] For obvious reasons the numbers in the categories exceed the numbers of cases and where there is more than one person in the same category *per property* in a case that counts as one for my total: that is, I generally treat multiple owners (with the same legal title) as one owner. (I am focusing here on *types* of ownership.) And I have sometimes been pragmatic about the distinction between legal and beneficial ownership. Please bear in mind that my own calendaring — for F — is fuller than Jones's and deliberately records the details important for the analysis presented here. So if the results from F differ from those for the other volumes that could be significant.[48] For this and other reasons please therefore look at the totals per volume as well as the aggregate ones.

I need also to emphasize that the categories analysed below are not exclusive — in particular, they are not designed to 'split' Men and Women. I highlight what I believe are the most important and interesting types of ownership and I have tried to provide enough information to allow readers to create other statistics.

Men — these are male owners who are not also identified as *Husbands* (including widowers), *Infants*, *Trustees*, *Partners* and *Mortgagees* in those other categories. Despite those 'exclusions', the numbers are large:

A: 93 (66%); B: 71 (70%); C: 49 (44%); D: 74 (57%); E: 60 (55%); F: 44 (40%) = 391 (56%)

The totals reflect not just society's expectation that men would own property, whether for business or personal purposes, but also the legal entitlement arising from even the qualified fem(m)e covert regime which applied in the City. But it is becoming clear — and the Fire Court evidence supports this — that, in whatever capacity men held property, personal loyalty and affection as well as contractual requirements constrained their use and disposal of that property. They rarely considered themselves free agents — and often were not.

Women — these are (adult) female owners who are not also identified as *Wives* (i.e. with *Husbands*), *Widows* (who were not remarried) and *Infants*. (Executrices have not been counted.) The numbers range from small to smallish:

A: 13 (9%); B: 8 (8%); C: 9 (8%); D: 16 (12%); E: 15 (14%);
F: 11 (6%) = 72 (10%)

Here we see the obverse of the *Men* total. Only as *Wives* and (especially) *Widows* did women feature significantly as owners; but as joint or prospective owners (especially as a result of marriage settlements) they were certainly important, quite apart from the personal/informal commitment of their propertied fathers and husbands.

Husbands and wives — these cases include husbands owning property 'in the right of' their wives (i.e. their interest determined when they died); others are simply instances of apparent joint ownership (including life interests). The numbers, though small (especially in A and B), are perhaps somewhat larger than might have been expected from the application of the (qualified) fem(m)e covert rule:

A: 5 (4%); B: 2 (2%); C: 9 (8%); D: 9 (7%); E: 9 (8%);
F: 11 (10%) = 45 (6%)

It could well be that we see here some practical responses to fem(m)e covert, with wives wanting or being encouraged to 'join in' the agreements which the Court endorsed or imposed. The benefits were obvious and this perhaps should discourage us from assuming that the legal niceties of fem(m)e covert (and sole) were followed in practice?[49]

Infants — the cases seem to have usually identified all technically minors — not necessarily 'children'.[50] They were usually *prospective* owners, with future interests, so it is interesting that the figures, at least in the later volumes, are not small.

A: 4 (3%); B: 2 (2%); C: 12 (11%); D: 15 (12%); E: 15 (14%);
F: 26 (24%) = 74 (11%)

The later totals reflect the number of family arrangements revealed in the decrees.

Widows — they appear in their own right here and below as *Life tenants*. Those who had remarried are excluded. Those designated dames are included if they are clearly widows. Those (still) acting as executrices are excluded. The bare totals are modest but certainly not insignificant:

A: 18 (13%); B: 17 (17%); C: 24 (22%); D: 19 (15%); E: 13 (12%);
F: 13 (12%) = 104 (15%)

Women brought some of their own family's assets into marriage and resumed control when widowed, and their husbands often accorded them life or other interests, either pursuant to marriage settlements or through love-and-affection arrangements of various kinds. Property was clearly seen as an asset belonging to the 'family' in the widest sense.

Life tenants — it is not always easy to trace life interests; I have assumed some where there are settlements.[51] The totals are significant — second only to *Men*:

> A: 25 (18%); B: 30 (30%); C: 41 (37%); D: 51 (40%); E: 37 (34%);
> F: 28 (26%) = 212 (30%)

There could be some over-representation here because there was a need to go to Court for agreements to be sanctioned, but the numbers are still large, reflecting the fact that property was used to extract an income for individuals or families — and especially, in the short term, to protect surviving spouses: see *Widows*. By creating family arrangements the settlor was ensuring long-term support for surviving family members. (Life interests could certainly be 'traded', but only within the life of the grantor.) There were many modest family settlements, at the other end of the spectrum from the landed estate settlements on which historians' attention has been lavished. They might also explain the otherwise surprising leases granted by husbands *and* wives, that is, 'joining in' the future life tenant?

Trustees — this category covers those empowered to administer Individuals' trusts and settlements (as opposed to mere covenantees enforcing promises); it excludes executors/rices of wills, who though they certainly 'owned' and could deal with property during the period of administration are generally disregarded, not least because they could be beneficiaries, too (and thus be *Inheritors*). In almost all cases the trusts were family ones. Trustees are counted collectively (i.e. as one) and only where mentioned expressly (i.e. not just inferred from the existence of a trust). Their role generally fell away over time;[52] I have taken a view whether trustees were still active. The numbers are small to smallish:

> A: 6 (5%); B: 9 (9%); C: 10 (9%); D: 15 (12%); E: 10 (9%);
> F: 14 (13%) = 64 (9%)

It may be that their role was not significant. The simple family trusts identified through the decrees afforded, expressly or by default, a good deal of power to the *Life tenant* (often the settlor's *Widow*), even when they were limited to twenty-one-year terms.[53] The Fire Court often decreed terms extending after death to facilitate rebuilding.

Inheritors — here I include devisees but otherwise exclude beneficiaries of formal settlements (acknowledging that the distinctions are not straightforward — and devises of life interests are included). Care has been taken with the 'inheritance came to …', 'had the inheritance', and similar descriptions: these could mean 'purchaser', too, but references to 'heir' or similar are followed in the absence of contrary evidence. And, as already noted, I ignore executors as owners. This is the third largest category — not far behind *Life tenants*:

A: 29 (21%); B: 16 (16%); C: 39 (35%); D: 40 (31%); E: 37 (34%); F: 32 (30%) = 193 (28%)

Inheritance of property in this straightforward form was clearly common — and needs to be 'read' alongside family settlements (see *Life tenants*): the aggregate totals are very substantial. The right to pass on City property had a long tradition, and leases — including those long leases akin to 'outright' ownership — were chattels that could be bequeathed by will. Property was not often allowed to leave the family, at least not by default on death.[54]

Purchasers — for this category I have obviously looked for 'sales', but given that some of my 'owners' were lessors I have not excluded assignments. I have generally excluded intra-family 'sales' and conveyances — but included cases where the 'inheritance had come' from an unrelated individual. The overall numbers are small, especially given the inclusion of some assignments:

A: 17 (12%); B: 10 (10%); C: 12 (11%); D: 3 (2%); E: 5 (5%); F: 4 (4%) = 51 (7%)

Perpetual or long-term interests in property were only sold occasionally. The flexibility of the property market was perhaps such that most needs, financial or otherwise, could be met without 'selling'. It is true that there were manuals providing guidance for investors/purchasers,[55] but the evidence of that activity is hard to find and, though this may be remedied by further research into individuals' records,[56] those who have looked at property investment as an economic activity have not reported much urban activity, at least not in the City.[57] And there also seems to have been only a modest amount of site acquisition or aggregation by developers (as opposed to consolidating owners). My current belief is that most purchases for this purpose were opportunistic. The still-to-be-developed West End presumably offered better scope.

Partners — here I have tried to identify joint investors or business partners, but recognizing that different surnames do not rule out family relationships.[58] My aim is to identify property that was not bought or used for domestic purposes. Both are difficult to trace. Joint investment can only be surmised and joint use is even more problematic: shops or other commercial premises were often on the ground floor and personal accommodation above, but the category connects with my focus on 'houses' (as explained in the Introduction). It would also be interesting to look at joint ownership generally, but the legal status of the partners (joint tenants or tenants in common, for example), if mentioned, is not always clear. The totals are very small:

A: 5 (4%); B: 5 (5%); C: 5 (5%); D: 1 (1%); E: 2 (2%);
F: 2 (2%) = 20 (3%)

The figures reinforce the impression that property ownership was a family-wide enterprise and much accommodation was a combination of personal and commercial. Whether the Fire Court decrees evidence can be easily supplemented from elsewhere is unfortunately doubtful. Certainly, the Hearth Tax and other assessment information present similar difficulties, as the volume of Supporting Evidence (in Section 1) demonstrates.

Mortgagors/mortgagees — this category is confined to formal charges on property to secure repayment of loans, often by long lease. It does not include annuities or rent charges, i.e. regular payments to a third party. I have counted mortgagors (including those who owned properties subject to an existing mortgage) and also mortgagees. Even the combined totals are very small:

A: 6 (4%) and 0 (0%): 5 (4%); B: 4 (4%) and 3 (3%): 7 (7%);
C: 1 (1%) and 0 (0%): 1 (1%); D: 6 (5%) and 1 (1%): 7 (5%);
E: 5 (5%) and 0 (0%): 5 (5%); F: 6 (6%) and 0 (0%): 6 (6%)
= 28 (4%) and 4 (1%): 32 (5%).

By themselves they indicate that mortgages were rarely enforced, at least to the point of converting a mortgagee into an owner, but they also reflect the overall use of mortgages by City property owners. I am reasonably confident that the petition and/or the decree will have either made a mortgagee a party or at least referred to the mortgage. And given that there was evidently no in-principle difficulty in charging a lease, I have probably not missed any mortgages by including lessee 'owners' here. The figures appear to confirm that most property was held for income, not speculation, and certainly rebuilding costs were not generally such as to require loan finance, at least not secured against the property. Most mortgages were required for other, specific purposes. Whether the (newish) right to redeem,[59] had any impact is difficult to say: it may have encouraged prospective mortgagors, but did it make enforcement less frequent? These Fire Court decree figures are too small to interpret for that purpose — but for our ownership purposes therein lies their interest.

Citizens — here I count those freemen, shown as 'citizen and [*member of a livery company*]' and some other cases where citizenship is indicated. There may be some under-recording here, but it seems to have been regular if not invariable practice to identify at least petitioners and defendants like this (and Jones seems to have included details in 'his' volumes).

A: 8 (6%); 11 (11%); C: 6 (5%); D: 7 (5%); E: 6 (6%);
F: 7 (6%) = 45 (6%)

The numbers are smaller than might have been expected, even for owners as opposed to occupiers. It might be supposed that citizens did not *own* City property as well as trading from it. A reliable answer depends on the owner-occupation issue discussed in the Introduction to this section. Many of the more senior citizens (Aldermen and Common Council men) recorded in J. R. Woodhead's *The Rulers of London 1660–88* (1965) left or referred to City property in their wills, but this information will often relate to leases (which, as chattels, could be devised) and has various other problems attached, not least the time-span.[60] Taken with the evidence of other categories I believe we can conclude that citizens — even the increasing numbers who were not freemen-traders — did not *own* a great deal of property in 1666. Perhaps control of City property had passed from previous generations of citizens to others, including their own families?

Gentlemen and esquires — these terms certainly meant something at this time and potentially offer at least a crude way of assessing status,[61] but the petitions and/or the decrees were not consistent,[62] and Jones was not consistent either and indeed sometimes omitted the terms altogether. The totals below therefore need to be treated with care, particularly those for A–E.

A: 21 (16%); B: 23 (23%); C: 31 (28%); D: 26 (20%); E: 16 (15%);
F: 31 (28%) = 148 (21%)

The figures do, however, confirm, as might be expected, that a significant proportion of property owners were accorded, or accorded themselves, some social status.[63]

The 'titled' — this is a crude shorthand for knights, baronets and (a few) others. I have included 'dames' on the assumption that they are indeed wives/widows of knights and baronets. There appears to be less risk of omissions than for 'gent.' and 'esq'.

A: 21 (16%); B: 21 (21%); C: 17 (15%); D: 22 (17%); E: 19 (17%);
F: 11 (10%) = 111 (16%)

The totals are certainly not as large as 'gent.'s and 'esq.'s but interestingly they are markedly larger than 'citizen's.[64] It might be surmised that either these were owners who acquired their lands and titles many years earlier (in the aftermath of the Dissolution?) or simply happened to become titled later. Family records might exist in some of these cases to test the hypothesis.

What, then, can we surmise about these Individuals who 'owned', say, 75% of the City's houses? They were often long-term, passive owners, looking for a 'return' — giving their tenants free rein, whether they were themselves lessees or 'real' owners. Property ownership was family-based, with women/ widows playing a central part, notwithstanding the formal legal constraints, and it passed where possible from generation to generation. And ownership was small scale — with no large blocs of property and no need or desire to sell and thus allow speculators or developers to consolidate.

Conclusion

The ownership analysis presented here suggests ways of understanding the property market in 1666 — and in particular explaining its resilience in response to the disastrous Fire. The fact — if fact it is — that three-quarters of the City's houses were owned by Individuals might lead to assumptions about the volatile, personal nature of the market, but the collective profile presented in the previous section indicates that this would be wrong. My findings point to the similarities rather than the differences between Institutions and Individuals. Property ownership for Individuals was usually long-term, like Institutions. Property — even if 'only' leasehold — was not really an Individual's own property. It may technically have been 'personal' but it was subject to family commitments, not so far removed from the charitable and other obligations assumed by Institutions. And this was true of owners *and* 'sub-owners' (i.e. long lessees, with the 'fee or inheritance') or at least freeholders and long lessees. The pervasive tiered leasehold structure blurred distinctions at this higher, ownership level. Individuals and Institutions therefore reacted to the Fire in much the same way. They all wanted *income* again and quickly — and so were ready to come to agreements with their tenant-occupiers who, in turn, wanted to resume trading as soon as they could. Some required the help of the Fire Court to do so but most were able and willing to find a compromise that suited both parties. The City's owners, both Institutions and Individuals, thus responded effectively to the massive challenge of the Fire.

Appendix — How Many Houses Destroyed in the Great Fire?

In the London Topographical Society's *Newsletter* no. 83 (2016) I examined the contemporary total of 13,200 houses destroyed in the Fire. This derived from an issue of the *London Gazette* dated 3–10 September 1666 (which in its original form was Issue 85). I speculated about the well-known list of destruction in which the house total appeared. This was included in a section headed *A Farthur Account of this Lamentable Fire*. The work for this essay prompted further investigation. This made me realize that, contrary to the general assumption so far, the list of Fire damage did not appear in Issue 85 at all. That Issue was drafted straight after the Fire by Joseph Williamson (see TNA, SP 29/170 no. 151) and it was published as quickly as possible. *A Farthur Account of this Lamentable Fire* only appeared as an insert in a subsequent, unnumbered version of Issue 85. The fact that the 13,200 total was not 'produced' immediately after the Fire brings into play other possible sources. There is an interesting set of fourteen Fire damage returns in the so-called Alchin collection in the LMA, COL/AC/06/006. These came from various ward beadles. Only one (for Vintry) is dated — 25 September. Is this too late for the expanded Issue 85? Certainly, the use of ward lists was an obvious way of compiling totals of destroyed houses, and in some instances (of presumably complete devastation) the beadles did so by simply providing a list of pre-Fire inhabitants. (This is redolent of the practice of some Hearth Tax collectors: Roehampton edition, p. 69.) The surviving ward records afford no clues, but unless we establish that the revised Issue appeared before 25 September (and I have tried, in vain, to find out) there are reasonable grounds for thinking that 13,200 was no guess: it was based on the same Assessments as I have used to support my 24,260 total and, given that two-thirds or so of the City was destroyed in the Fire, 13,200 has at least some credibility.

Acknowledgements

I am very grateful to Vanessa Harding for her generous help with both methodology and detail, to Dorian Gerhold and Bill Baer for kindly providing comments and advice, and to Amy Erickson for suggesting ways of improving the presentation of Individuals' ownership status. I also thank a large number of institutions, especially the London Metropolitan Archives and the Guildhall Library, for facilitating my research. Particular acknowledgements appear in the volume of Supporting Evidence.

1. Ian Doolittle, 'Recreating London in 1666', *London Topographical Society Newsletter*, no. 78 (2014).
2. Email: idoolittle@btinternet.com. The LTS is investigating whether a link can be provided on its website. Please note that when the text of this article was finalized some points in the volume of Supporting Evidence had not been checked, due to COVID circumstances. The points are not likely to make a material difference to the figures in the Tables here, save for the uncertainty attached to the National Archives' reconstruction of the St Giles Cripplegate Hearth Tax return. This might mean that the overall house total is 190 or so too high.
3. Derek Keene and Vanessa Harding, *Survey of Documentary Sources for Property Holding in London before the Great Fire*, London Record Society, vol. 22 (1985).
4. Volumes I and II were calendared and published by P. E. Jones as *The Fire Court* (London, 1966 and 1970). I have recently published Vol. III with the City Corporation's support in the same style and format. A previous analysis appeared in I. Doolittle, 'Property Law and Practice in 17th-Century London', *Urban History*, 42 (2015), pp. 204–24.
5. Vanessa Harding, 'The Population of London, 1550–1700: A Review of the Published Evidence', *London Journal*, 15 (1990), pp. 111–25. Despite her warning and eschewing her

alternative terms (ibid., p. 123), I have used 'City and Liberties' below.

6. Notably Blackfriars, Bridewell, St Martin le Grand and Whitefriars. The principal liberties adjacent to but outside the City were St Katharine by the Tower, the Rolls and the Tower itself.

7. Dorian Gerhold has kindly explained that St Olave Southwark included a few houses in Bridge Ward Within (i.e. the first precinct of London Bridge).

8. See the Appendix.

9. See the Mercers entry in the volume of Supporting Evidence. There is also a telling reference description of a set of tenements belonging to Westminster Abbey: half of them were 'under tenements and so go in the name of shops'. Volume of Supporting Evidence.

10. I have noted, in passing (for other purposes), that when the City at the end of the nineteenth century gave a breakdown of the Bridge House estates properties it listed houses, shops and offices, wharves, etc., warehouses and stables: *Statement as to the Origin, Position, Powers, Duties and Finance of the Corporation of London* (London, 1893), p. 123.

11. FCD A514 (in Jones, *Fire Court*, vol. I) refers to eight tenements divided into sixteen messuages.

12. See the Westminster Abbey analysis in the volume of Supporting Evidence.

13. For example, the development of the Goldsmiths' property in the 1650s.

14. *London and Middlesex Hearth Tax*, ed. by M. Davies et al., 2 vols, British Record Society, 129 (2014). I refer to this as the Roehampton edition/editors hereafter.

15. *London Topographical Society Newsletter*, no. 86 (2018).

16. M. Jenner, 'From Conduit Community to Commercial Network? Water in London, 1500–1725', in *Londinopolis*, ed. by P. Griffith and M. Jenner (Manchester, 2000), p. 269, n. 74 (extrapolating from the tithe returns); J. Field, *London, Londoners and the Great Fire of 1666* (London, 2018), table 3.1, deducting Suburbs and Southwark (65–66), preferred to table 1.1 (29), showing a net 21,000; C. Spence, *London in the 1690s* (London, 2000), p. 176. There are other analyses, but most concern inhabitants not houses, and parish-based ones do not correlate with the City and its Liberties. One house list by ward, in 1641, has been ignored; its total of 13,313 (deducting the estimate for Bridge Ward Without) seems unreliably low, especially by comparison with Jenner's 1638 calculation: see N. Brett-James, *The Growth of Stuart London* (London, 1935), pp. 500–01. (The extra-mural areas seem particularly under-recorded.)

17. E. Hatton, *New View of London*, 2 vols (1708); *New Remarks of London* (1732), including figures collected by the Parish Clerks; J. Smart, *A Short Account of the Wards, Precincts, Parishes etc. in London* (1741/2), based on 1735 totals.

18. See the irregular returns in *A Particular of the New Buildings from the Year 1656 to 1677* (1678). The 'original' figures for one parish, St Bride's, are at LMA, P69/BRI/B/012/MS06570/001.

19. 'Poor' appear in just over half of the parishes, including some of the largest and poorest ones. (It is to be noted that there was no requirement to list those exempt in 1662–63.)

20. I have cross-referred my totals with those derived from the 1638 tithe returns by R. Finlay in *Population and Metropolis* (Cambridge, 1981), appendix 3. There is reassuring degree of compatibility for most parishes but I am reluctant to make assumptions about the significant differences. There are particular difficulties with 'tenements', especially in the large extra-mural parishes. Note also Catherine Ferguson's parish register work which casts doubt on the total for St Bartholomew the Great: Roehampton edition, p. 5. I was also tempted to cross-check against Derek Keene and Vanessa Harding's *Cheapside Gazetteer* (available through British History Online); but the parishes are central and small, and much of the 1666 information is (naturally) taken from the Hearth Tax returns.

21. For parishes, but not usually (I think) for other Institutions, the use of feoffees/trustees could cause difficulty: see e.g. FCD C125, 128, 129v and 135v (St Stephen Walbrook), all in

Jones, *Fire Court*, vol. II.

22. It also provided Governors of the Royal Hospitals.
23. See the headings added later to the Haberdashers' 1657 'State': Guildhall Library, MS 15876.
24. For my attempt to address this problem, see the entry in the volume of Supporting Evidence.
25. Ignoring the extra fifty for Westminster Abbey.
26. A review of the estates of St Bart's and St Thomas's Hospitals and the Bridge House in the eighteenth century found an overall ratio of 421:765 (55%) for leases and houses: B. A. S. Swann, 'A Study of Some London Estates in the 18th Century' (doctoral thesis, University of London, 1964), p. 9.
27. W. C. Baer, 'Landlords and Tenants in London, 1550–1700', *Urban History*, 38 (2011), p. 246.
28. Jones, *Fire Court*, II, p. iii.
29. D. W. Jones, 'London Merchants and the Crisis of the 1690s', in *Crisis and Order in English Towns, 1500–1700*, ed. by P. Clark and P. Slack (London, 1972), pp. 336–37.
30. Perhaps a focus on the intra-mural area has encouraged a belief in a high level of Institutional ownership?
31. Jones thought blocs of more than five to be rare: ibid.
32. Baer, 'Landlords and Tenants', pp. 246–52. Baer's conclusions about categories of 'owners' are interesting but his data may 'miss' head landlords.
33. This is the word used by Mills: see Peter Mills and John Oliver, *The Survey of Building Sites in the City of London after the Great Fire of 1666* (London Topographical Society publications, Nos 97–99, 101, 103 (1962, 1964, 1967), vols 2–3 (i.e. Nos 101 and 97), *passim*.
34. Gerhold rehearses the evidence against consolidation in *London Plotted* (London Topographical Society publication No. 178, 2016), p. 298, n. 196, referring to evasion of the requirement for a survey. I personally find *widespread* evasion implausible. For the answer we need comparable and reliable pre- and post-Fire Hearth Tax totals: Field's table 3.1 in *London, Londoners and the Great Fire* is inconclusive. 8,097 is Jones's total for the foundations up to 31 December 1673: *Survey of Building Sites*, I, p. xxix.
35. I will rehearse the figures in a supplementary article — in a future *Record* perhaps? — on 'Who "Owned" and Who Occupied the City of London in 1666?'.
36. Baer, 'Landlords and Tenants', pp. 253–54.
37. LMA, P69/BRI/B/012/MS6570/001, ff. 124 + (typescript calendar in MS6570A). The claims were taken across into a contemporary list of householders in MS14819, ff. 7 +: this seems to be the only surviving product of the City's short-lived requirement that title interests be recorded in anticipation of wholesale re-configuration. What a record a complete register would have been!
38. I carried out an analysis of some parishes in Keene and Harding's *Cheapside Gazetteer* but concluded that the title documents used by them did not provide the same depth and 'colour' as the Fire Court petitions/hearings.
39. I.e. vols A–F in the City's engrossed versions, taken from Jones's published calendars of A–D and my own publication of E–F (comprising Jones's unpublished calendar of E and my own fuller calendar of F).
40. In Doolittle, 'Property Law and Practice'.
41. The total is taken from the descriptions I give in Section 3 of the Volume of Evidence. There are thirty-six multiples. I have only counted properties which were the subject of the decree — i.e. ignoring the frequent references to adjoining properties, to avoid double-counting.
42. There is, of course, still scope for future parish-by-parish or similarly detailed comparisons. (Please note that I have not attempted to exclude those (few) cases which related to properties (just) outside the City's boundary.)
43. It will be noted from the volume of Supporting Evidence I have looked hard for signs of leasehold interests: they are infrequent.
44. I have found only three instances in the fully rehearsed cases in vol. F, i.e. 61v, 104 and 227v.

45. Eight in F: 11v, 104, 158, 171v, 196v, 219, 266 and 282; in one case the owners were feoffees (i.e. trustees) and in another the description was 'fee or fee simple'.

46. Four in F: 7, 31, 40 and 59. (By this time and in the somewhat informal context of the Fire Court seisin can be taken as merely meaning owned.)

47. Each volume has a few quirks — C has a batch of Bishop of London cases — which could distort the figures a little, but the use of six volumes and the generally similar percentages which emerge (see below) is reassuring.

48. There is of course the additional possibility that these later cases were different from the earlier ones. I will try to test for this in my later calendaring work.

49. The basic principle, that a married woman had no separate legal personality while married, did not apply if she was 'fem(m)e sole'. There is a good deal of London information in M. K. McIntosh's 'The Benefits and Drawbacks of Femme Sole Status in England, 1300–1630', *Journal of British Studies*, 14 (2005), pp. 410–38. For the later period London information is best obtained from the customs and cases rehearsed in the legal treatises of the period, the best known of which is William Bohun's *Privilegia Londini* (1702).

50. E115 refers to a married infant.

51. It will be understood that I am concerned with *current* owners, so future interests — remainders and such like — are excluded.

52. C206 seems to be unusual.

53. For example, E80 (one of a number of cases involving Lord Robartes) and E280 (no fine, as well).

54. It is worth noting here that the Custom of London which prescribed shares of estates for widows and children only applied to goods/chattels - and therefore to leasehold, not freehold interests.

55. W. C. Baer, 'The Institution of Residential Investment in Seventeenth-Century London', *The Business History Review*, 76 (2002), pp. 515–51.

56. One of the best models is still A. Simpson, *The Wealth of the Gentry* (Cambridge, 1961): see pp. 131–32 (Thomas Cullum).

57. The main discussions appear still to be P. Earle, *The Making of the English Middle Class* (London, 1989), pp. 152–57, and R. Grassby, *The Business Community in Seventeenth-Century England* (Cambridge, 1995), pp. 373–78.

58. And of course some family members might carry on business together as individuals (and not just as families, as it were).

59. R. W. Turner, *The Equity of Redemption* (Cambridge, 1931). The mortgage (by lease) in B631 included a power of redemption.

60. My crude analysis is as follows. Out of 1,400, 314 left City property. Of 219 Common Councilmen who left property, 78 (over 36%) left only City property; *cf.* Aldermen: 14 out of 95 (less than 15%). Strikingly, therefore, 141 + 81 (222) also left property outside City. (NB I included the many short-term Aldermen on grounds that wealth not status is important here.) 'Left' seems to be right: Woodhead invariably takes his property information from wills.

61. The terms were interchanged in E306v.

62. In three decrees involving the same owner he was 'esq.' in two only: E188-92.

63. Cf. Baer's somewhat higher % for 'gentry' ownership in 'Landlords and Tenants', pp. 245–46.

64. And they are much higher than Baer's ownership percentage: ibid.

TABLE 1

No. of 'houses' in the City in 1666 (by parish)

	Parishes (in contemporary order)	'Houses'
1	Alban Wood Street	135
2	All Hallows Barking	453
3	All Hallows Bread Street	81
4	All Hallows the Great	347
5	All Hallows Honey Lane	38
6	All Hallows the Less	173
7	All Hallows Lombard Street	101
8	All Hallows Staining	159
9	All Hallows London Wall	302
10	Alphage	169
11	Andrew Hubbard	110
12	Andrew Undershaft	216
13	Andrew Wardrobe	166
14	Anne Aldersgate	158
15	Anne Blackfriars	296
16	Antholin	87
17	Augustine by St Paul	105
18	Bartholomew Exchange	119
19	Benet Fink	117
20	Benet Gracechurch	64
21	Benet Paul's Wharf	170
22	Benet Sherehog	35
23	Botolph Billingsgate	106
24	Christ Church, Newgate	457
25	Christopher le Stocks	85
26	Clement Eastcheap	64
27	Dionis Backchurch	132
28	Dunstan in the East	371
29	Edmund Lombard Street	98

30	Ethelburga	125
31	Faith	173
32	Foster (i.e. Vedast)	134
33	Gabriel Fenchurch	81
34	George Botolph Lane	46
35	Gregory St Paul's	358
36	Helen Bishopsgate	125
37	James Duke's Place	174
38	James Garlickhithe	177
39	John Walbrook	108
40	John Evangelist	26
41	John Zachary	86
42	Katherine Coleman	199
43	Katherine Creechurch	366
44	Lawrence Jewry	164
45	Lawrence Pountney	116
46	Leonard Eastcheap	126
47	Leonard Foster Lane	196
48	Magnus	118
49	Margaret Lothbury	146
50	Margaret Moses	66
51	Margaret New Fish Street	107
52	Margaret Pattens	63
53	Mary Abchurch	108
54	Mary Aldermanbury	151
55	Mary Aldermary	109
56	Mary le Bow	105
57	Mary Bothaw	59
58	Mary Colechurch	53
59	Mary at Hill	144
60	Mary Mounthaw	54
61	Mary Somerset	228
62	Mary Staining	38

63	Mary Woolchurch	99
64	Mary Woolnoth	103½
65	Martin Ironmonger Lane	49½
66	Martin Ludgate	235
67	Martin Orgar	126
68	Martin Outwich	76
69	Martin Vintry	291
70	Matthew Friday Street	47
71	Mary Magdalen Milk Street	61
72	Mary Magdalen Old Fish Street	127
73	Michael Bassishaw	157
74	Michael Cornhill	159
75	Michael Crooked Lane	132
76	Michael Queenhithe	226
77	Michael le Querne	88
78	Michael Paternoster Royal	100
79	Michael Wood Street	110
80	Mildred Bread Street	63
81	Mildred Poultry	105
82	Nicholas Acon	66
83	Nicholas Cole Abbey	83
84	Nicholas Olave	75
85	Olave Hart Street	245
86	Olave Old Jewry	58
87	Olave Silver Street	126
88	Pancras Soper Lane	48
89	Peter West Cheap	80
90	Peter Cornhill	159
91	Peter Paul's Wharf	126
92	Peter le Poor	114
93	Stephen Coleman Street	487
94	Stephen Walbrook	64
95	Swithin	104½

96	Thomas the Apostle	175
97	Holy Trinity (the Less)	89
98	Andrew Holborn	486
99	Bartholomew the Great	287
100	Bartholomew the Less	123
101	Bride	1,614
102	Bridewell Precinct	(See 101 above)
103	Botolph Aldersgate*	500
104	Botolph Aldgate*	1,914
105	Botolph Bishopsgate*	1,842
106	Dunstan in the West	703
107	Giles Cripplegate*	2,100
108	Sepulchre	994
	Total	24,260½

Sources: Hearth Tax returns for 1666, supplemented by those for 1662–63, chiefly from *London and Middlesex Hearth Tax*, ed. by M. Davies et al., 2 vols, British Record Society, 129 (2014), and supplemented where necessary from other tax assessments. Details are set out in Section 1 of the volume of Supporting Evidence.

Note: Methodology is described in the volume of Supporting Evidence, where detailed calculations are given and caveats explained.

* These parishes extended beyond the City boundary — only houses within the City are included. For reconciliations of parish and ward boundaries and other issues, see the volume of Supporting Evidence.

TABLE 2

No. of 'houses' in the City in 1666 owned by 'Institutions' (grouped)

	'Houses'	Tenants	Multiples	Total?
The Crown	17	–	–	17
City of London	576	–	43 (129)	705
Bridge House	247	–	3 (9)	256
Livery Companies	1,988½	223	66 (198)	2,409½
The Church	637	–	15 (95)*	732
Parishes	354½	320	22 (66)	740½
Hospitals	209	404½	19 (57)	670½
Oxford & Cambridge	136½	3	1 (3)	142½
Schools	16	–	2 (6)	22
Others	66	4	–	70
Totals	4,247½	954½	171 (563)	5,765

Sources: See Tables 3–9 below and the detailed information in Section 2 of the volume of Supporting Evidence.

Note: Methodology is described in detail in the volume of Supporting Evidence where uncertainties are discussed. 'Houses' and 'Tenants' do not overlap.

'Houses' include messuages or tenements unless otherwise designated. ('Shops' are identified in the volume of Supporting Evidence.)

'Multiples' refer to 'several' etc. houses. 'Totals' derive from the application of a multiplier of 3 or higher where appropriate — or otherwise for reasons explained in the volume of Supporting Evidence.

* Includes 50 for Westminster Abbey.

TABLE 3

No. of 'houses' in the City in 1666 owned by Livery Companies

	'Houses'	Tenants	Multiples	Total?
Apothecaries	–	3	–	3
Armourers & Braziers	76	–	–	76
Bakers	6	–	1 (3)	9
Barber Surgeons	6	1	2 (6)	13
Blacksmiths	7	–	–	7
Brewers	3	30	–	33
Broderers	17	–	–	17
Butchers	3	–	–	3
Carpenters	17½	–	1 (3)	20½
Clothworkers	156½	–	3 (9)	165½
Cooks	7	–	–	7
Coopers	7	2	1 (3)	12
Cordwainers	10	–	3 (9)	19
Curriers	1	4	1 (3)	8
Cutlers	20	11	2 (6)	37
Drapers	200	–	–	200
Dyers	–	7	–	7
Fishmongers	102½	–	4 (12)	114½
Girdlers	10	2	–	12
Goldsmiths	500	–	–	500
Grocers	49	12	4 (12)	73
Haberdashers	63	1	7 (21)	85
Innholders	–	5	–	5
Ironmongers	–	32	1 (3)	35
Joiners	–	–	1 (3)	3
Leathersellers	–	27	–	27
Masons	–	1	–	1
Mercers	155	22	9 (27)	204
Merchant Taylors	203	–	4 (12)	215

Parish Clerks	1			1
Pewterers	5	20	–	25
Plumbers	–	4	–	4
Poulters	–	2	–	2
Saddlers	58	–	1 (3)	61
Salters	30	–	5 (15)	45
Scriveners	5	–	–	5
Skinners	135	15	9 (27)	177
Stationers	12	–	1 (3)	15
Tallow Chandlers	41	–	2 (6)	47
Turners	–	1	–	1
Tylers & Bricklayers	2	3	–	5
Vintners	79	1	4 (12)	92
Wax Chandlers	–	16	–	16
Weavers	1	–	–	1
Woolmen	–	1	–	1
Totals	1,988½	223	66 (198)	2409½

Sources: Renter wardens' accounts and other records detailed in Section 2 of the volume of Supporting Evidence.

Note: See Table 2 for methodology, terms and important caveats.
The Great Twelve (i.e. most senior) Companies are shown in italics.

TABLE 4

No. of 'houses' in the City in 1666 owned by the Church

	'Houses'	Tenants	Multiples	Total?
St Paul's	400	–	–	400
Bishop of London	61	–	1 (3)	64
Westminster Abbey	41	–	13 (= 89*)	130
Canterbury	3	–	–	3
Chichester	40	–	–	40
Colchester	32	–	–	32
Ely	4	–	–	4
Hereford	5	–	–	5
Peterborough	12	–	1 (3)	15
Rochester	13	–	–	13
Windsor	21	–	–	21
Worcester	3	–	–	3
York	2	–	–	2
Totals	637	–	15 (95*)	732

Sources: As detailed in the volume of Supporting Evidence.

Note: See Table 2 for methodology, terms and important caveats.

NB: The properties were owned variously by the Bishop, Dean & Chapter, Dean and Canons, Prebendaries (and other office-holders) and Archdeacons. See the Volume of Evidence.

(* total includes the special addition of 50 for Westminster Abbey.)

TABLE 5

No. of 'houses' in the City in 1666 owned by parishes

		'Houses'	Tenants	Multiples	Total?
1	Alban Wood Street	4	–	–	4
2	All Hallows Barking	4½	–	–	4½
3	All Hallows Bread Street	1	–	–	1
4	All Hallows the Great	8	4	–	12
6	All Hallows the Less	1	–	–	1
7	All Hallows Lombard Street	–	6	–	6
8	All Hallows Staining	–	3	–	3
9	All Hallows London Wall	1	–	–	1
10	Alphage	4	6	–	10
11	Andrew Hubbard	–	3	–	3
12	Andrew Undershaft	1	–	–	1
13	Andrew Wardrobe	2	–	–	2
14	Anne Aldersgate	–	17	–	17
15	Anne Blackfriars	1	–	–	1
16	Antholin	2	–	–	2
17	Augustine by St Paul	4	–	1 (3)	7
18	Bartholomew Exchange	–	8	–	8
19	Benet Fink	–	3	–	3
20	Benet Gracechurch	–	9	–	9
21	Benet Paul's Wharf	–	4	1 (3)	7
23	Botolph Billingsgate	1	–	–	1
24	Christ Church, Newgate	1	–	–	1
25	Christopher le Stocks	4	–	–	4
26	Clement Eastcheap	–	18	–	18
27	Dionis Backchurch	3	2	–	5
28	Dunstan in the East	29½	–	–	29½
29	Edmund Lombard Street	9	–	–	9
31	Faith**	?	?	?	?
32	Foster (i.e. Vedast)**	?	?	?	?

33	Gabriel Fenchurch**	?	?	?	?
34	George Botolph Lane	–	3	–	3
36	Helen Bishopsgate	3	–	–	3
37	James Duke's Place**	?	?	?	?
38	James Garlickhithe	41	1	3 (9)	51
39	John Walbrook	–	9	–	9
40	John Evangelist**	?	?	?	?
41	John Zachary	5½	–	–	5½
43	Katherine Creechurch	–	1	1 (3)	4
44	Lawrence Jewry	14	–	3 (9)	23
45	Lawrence Pountney	3	–	–	3
46	Leonard Eastcheap	3	–	–	3
48	Magnus	10	–	–	10
49	Margaret Lothbury	2	–	–	2
51	Margaret New Fish Street	1	6	–	7
52	Margaret Pattens	9	–	–	9
53	Mary Abchurch	13	–	–	13
54	Mary Aldermanbury	–	5	–	5
55	Mary Aldermary	–	8	–	8
56	Mary le Bow	4	–	–	4
57	Mary Bothaw	4	–	–	4
58	Mary Colechurch	1	–	–	1
59	Mary at Hill	3	–	1 (3)	6
60	Mary Mounthaw**	?	?	?	?
61	Mary Somerset	–	3	–	3
63	Mary Woolchurch	1	4	–	5
65	Martin Ironmonger Lane**	?	?	?	?
66	Martin Ludgate	3	2	–	5
67	Martin Orgar	4	6	1 (3)	13
69	Martin Vintry**	?	?	?	?
70	Matthew Friday Street	–	1	–	1
71	Mary Magdalen Milk Street	3	1	–	4

72	Mary Magdalen Old Fish Street	–	3	–	3
73	Michael Bassishaw	10	–	–	10
74	Michael Cornhill	2	18	–	20
75	Michael Crooked Lane	–	12	–	12
76	Michael Queenhithe	2	16	–	18
77	Michael le Querne	–	12	–	12
78	Michael Paternoster Royal**	?	?	?	?
79	Michael Wood Street	1	8	–	9
80	Mildred Bread Street	4	–	–	4
81	Mildred Poultry	1	–	1 (3)	4
82	Nicholas Acon	1	–	–	1
83	Nicholas Cole Abbey	2	–	–	2
85	Olave Hart Street	8½	–	–	8½
86	Olave Old Jewry	4	–	–	4
87	Olave Silver Street	–	1	–	1
88	Pancras Soper Lane	3	–	–	3
89	Peter West Cheap	2	–	–	2
90	Peter Cornhill	1	10	–	11
91	Peter Paul's Wharf**	?	?	?	?
92	Peter le Poor**	?	?	?	?
93	Stephen Coleman Street	4	–	1 (3)	7
94	Stephen Walbrook	6	11	–	17
95	Swithin	11	–	–	11
96	Thomas the Apostle	24	–	–	24
98	Andrew Holborn	–	15	–	15
99	Bartholomew the Great	–	1	–	1
100	Bartholomew the Less**	?	?	?	?
101	Bride	16½	–	3 (9)	25½
102	Bridewell Precinct (see 101 above)	–	–	–	–
103	Botolph Aldersgate*	9	–	2 (6)	15
104	Botolph Aldgate*	12	1	–	13

105	Botolph Bishopsgate*	–	12	–	12
106	Dunstan in the West	10	–	–	10
107	Giles Cripplegate*	12	20	4 (12)	44
108	Sepulchre	–	47	–	47
	Total	354½	320	22 (66)	740½

Sources: As detailed in the Section 2 of the volume of Supporting Evidence — chiefly churchwardens' accounts.

Note: See Table 2 for methodology, terms and important caveats.

    * These parishes extended beyond the City boundary — only houses within the City are included (for assumptions, see the volume of Supporting Evidence)

    ** No (worthwhile) surviving records. (Parishes with no property are omitted.)

TABLE 6

No. of 'houses' in the City in 1666 owned by Hospitals

	'Houses'	Tenants	Multiples	Total?
St Bart's	–	299½	–	299½
Bethlem	47	–	4 (12)	59
Bridewell	78	–	1 (3)	81
Christ's	84	–	14 (42)	126
St Thomas's	–	105	–	105
Totals	209	404½	19 (57)	670½

Sources: As detailed in Section 2 of the volume of Supporting Evidence.

Note: See Table 2 for methodology, terms and important caveats.

TABLE 7

No. of 'houses' in the City in 1666 owned by
Oxford and Cambridge Colleges etc.

	'Houses'	Tenants	Multiples	Total?
Oxford				
The University	12	–	–	12
Balliol	10	–	–	10
Brasenose	5	2	–	7
Christ Church	10	–	–	10
Merton	4	–	–	4
New	15	–	–	15
St John's	4	1	–	5
Cambridge				
Emmanuel	21½	–	–	21½
Gonville & Caius	3	–	–	3
Jesus	17	–	1(3)	20
King's	4	–	–	4
Pembroke	11	–	–	11
St John's	14	–	–	14
Trinity (College)	6	–	–	6
Totals	136½	3	1 (3)	142½

Sources: College rentals etc. and other sources detailed in Section 2 of the volume of
          Supporting Evidence.

Note: See Table 2 for methodology, terms and important caveats.

TABLE 8

No. of 'houses' in the City in 1666 owned by Schools

	'Houses'	Tenants	Multiples	Total?
Eton College	8	–	1 (3)	11
Newport Grammar School	3	–	–	3
Nottingham Free School	3	–	–	3
Winchester College	2	–	1 (3)	5
Totals	16	–	2 (6)	22

Sources: As detailed in Section 2 of the Volume of Evidence.

Note: See Table 2 for methodology, terms and important caveats.

TABLE 9

No. of 'houses' in the City in 1666 owned by 'other' institutions

	'Houses'	Tenants	Multiples	Total?
Dutch Church, Austin Friars	1	–	–	1
Master of the Rolls	16	–	–	16
New England Company	6	–	–	6
Rochester Bridge Trust	17	–	–	17
Royal College of Physicians	1	–	–	1
St Katharine's Hospital	13	–	–	13
Salisbury	3	–	–	3
Sheffield	2	–	–	2
Sion College	–	4	–	4
Steelyard	6	–	–	6
Temple Hospital, Bristol	1	–	–	1
Totals	66	4	–	70

Sources: As detailed in Section 2 of the volume of Supporting Evidence.

Note: See Table 2 for methodology, terms and important caveats.

IX. JAN KIP'S BIRD'S-EYE PROSPECT OF WESTMINSTER AND LONDON

By RICHARD STEPHENS

A PROSPECT *of the City of London, Westminster and St James's Park* by the Dutch engraver Jan Kip (1653–1722) (Fig. 1) occupies a special place not only in the iconography of London — as perhaps the largest-ever engraved prospect of the city — but also in the history of the London Topographical Society, which has issued two facsimiles, in 1903 and 2003 (LTS publication Nos 14 and 161). A legal complaint that Kip filed in the Court of Chancery in 1721 has come to light, which provides a detailed first-hand account of the difficulties the engraver faced in working on his magnum opus.[1] It explains why, though Kip advertised proposals for the *Prospect* in 1715, he did not announce its completion until 1720. It is also sheds light on the insecure circumstances faced by engravers such as Kip, and the difficulties they nevertheless overcame, to produce work of great skill and ambition.

Details of Kip's life are few.[2] He was born in 1652 or 1653 in Amsterdam, where he learned engraving from Bastiaen Stopendael (1637–before 1707). He produced many plates there from the early 1670s onwards, and in 1680 he married Elizabeth Breda, daughter of Elizabeth Asselijn of Amsterdam.[3] By the end of the 1680s, though, Kip had relocated to London, where he engraved birds after Francis Barlow, in a set published by the printseller Pierce Tempest (1653–1717), five of whose plates were engraved in 1686 by Kip's Amsterdam contemporary, Jan Griffier (*c.* 1646–1718), who was by then long-established in the London art trade and had perhaps helped Kip find work on his arrival.[4] From 1701 onwards, Kip (or Keep) appears in the rate books for St John Street in the parish of St Margaret, Westminster, and several Kipp/Kipps/Kips appear in the St Margaret parish records, such as the baptism on 27 July 1703 of Hariott, daughter of 'Hanah Kep wife [of] Jan [the] younger', who was presumably Kip's son.

Kip's first dated English view was a 1690 print of Chelsea Hospital, and it was as an engraver of views that he was to specialize.[5] In his 1721 legal complaint, he narrated that he had 'for divers years followed and used the Art and profession of an engraver and of drawing and preparing by the pen and pencill fitting and proper draughts and representations of cities towns houses seats of noble men and other Buildings and of their respective views and situations'. In the late 1690s and early 1700s, Kip engraved many views for the Haarlem-born painter and picture-seller Leonard Knyff (1650–1722) who launched an ambitious project to create a collection of one hundred

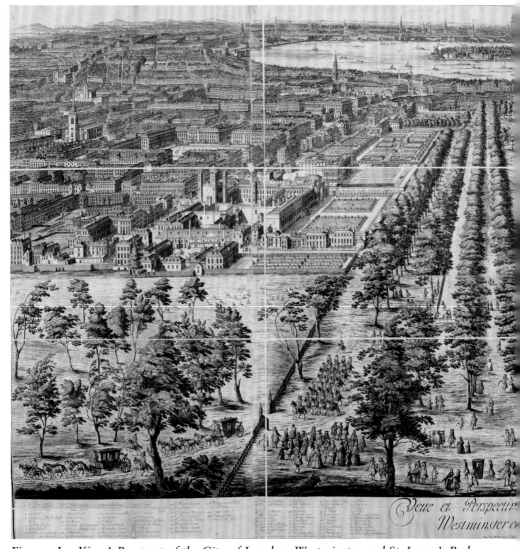

Fig. 1.   Jan Kip, *A Prospect of the City of London, Westminster and St. James's Park*,
etching and engraving, edition of *c.* 1728. © The British Library Board *Maps*
* *3518.(9.).* For the original 1720 edition, see British Museum *1880,1113.1181*,
reproduced as *Jan Kip's Prospect of London 1720*, London Topographical
Society publication No. 161, 2003.

views of English country seats in 1698.[6] Unfortunately, subscribers proved
difficult to find, despite the promising situation of Knyff's house, in Old
Palace Yard next door to the entrance to the House of Lords. By the middle
of 1701, sixty views had been finished,[7] and Kip engraved a further nine

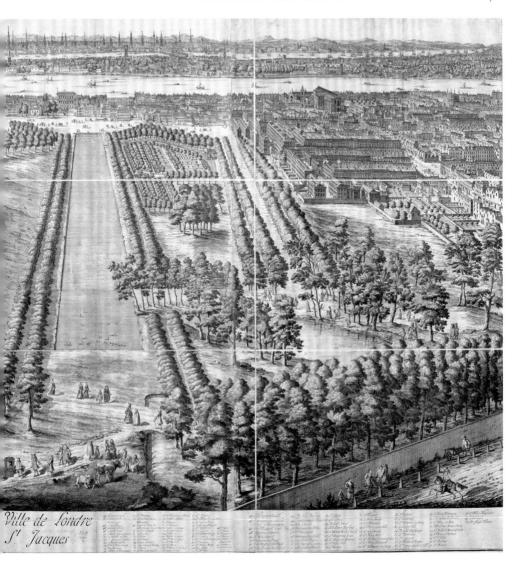

Ville de Londre
St Jacques

plates by the end of the following year.[8] Eventually eighty views were completed, but in 1707 Knyff abandoned the project, announcing that

> for want of subscriptions, and on account of his health, (the time first propos'd being long since expir'd) [he] is oblig'd to desist ... [and] designing to withdraw himself from this into his native Country for the Recovery of his Health: In the meantime he intends to dispose of by Auction his curious Collection of Original Paintings, also his Plates, Prints, House, and Houshold Goods.[9]

Knyff probably sold his rolling press, too, as in 1708 one was offered for sale in the coffee house directly below his house.[10] The plates went to

David Mortier, a book- and printseller at the sign of Erasmus's Head in the Strand, who published a bound collection of Kip's engravings with the title *Britannia Illustrata* and, in the years to come, repackaged them in various formats, including with a title page aimed at the French market.[11]

After the end of his work for Knyff, Kip drew and engraved eighty views for Atkyns's *History of Gloucestershire* (1712), whose plates made up a second volume of *Britannia Illustrata* that was sold by Joseph Smith at Exeter Exchange in 1716.[12] Kip's major project, though, was the great *Prospect of the City of London, Westminster and St James's Park*: a huge bird's-eye view of the city, seen from the western end of The Mall. Kip had made bird's-eye views of London during his time working for Knyff, such as a view of St James's Palace from a similar vantage point as the *Prospect*, with the spires of the City of London churches on the distant horizon much as they are in the larger print (Fig. 2).[13] Kip had also engraved a multi-sheet view of Westminster and the City of London seen from south of the river, published around 1710 not long after the completion of the new dome of St Paul's Cathedral.[14] The *Prospect*, though, was not merely much larger, it boldly reoriented the London city view genre.[15] Whereas earlier large-scale London views by Visscher and Hollar had focused on the City of London from a viewpoint on the south bank of the River Thames, Kip put the fashionable Westminster district of St James in the foreground, leaving St Paul's Cathedral and the City of London in the far distance. Kip's was the first great prospect of London to acknowledge the westwards shift in London's centre of gravity following the destruction of the City of London in 1666 and the subsequent development of Westminster. Thus it stands at the beginning of a long tradition of eastward views looking from

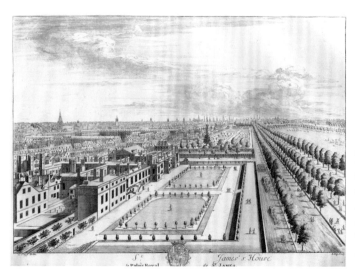

Fig. 2. Jan Kip, after Leonard Knyff, *St James's Palace, London*, etching, *c.* 1709. © Trustees of the British Museum, *1880, 1113.2260.*

Westminster towards St Paul's, whose most famous exponent was Antonio Canaletto.[16]

Kip announced the project in the *Daily Courant* on 29 November 1715:

For Engraving by Subscription, A large Prospect of St. James's-Park, the Cities of London and Westminster, and the River of Thames, from the farthest part of Westminster to Limehouse, drawn in a perfect (tho' uncommon) Manner. Giving a splendid View of those Magnificent Cities, in their most Beautiful Appearances. This Prospect is above 7-Foot long, and about 4 Foot and half deep, and is approved by several Noblemen and Gentlemen, who have already subscribed. The Proposals, as also the Original Drawing, are to be seen at Mr. Tho. Taylor's, Printseller, at the Golden Lyon in Fleetstreet, where Subscriptions are taken; as also at Mr. John Kip's, the Designer and Engraver, in St. John's-street, Westminster, (who is actually Engraving the same.) And likewise at Mrs. Ellerd's at the Rainbow Coffee-house at Westminster-Hall-Gate; Mr. Moll, Geographer, against Devereux-Court in the Strand; Mrs. Wilcox at the Temple-Change Coffee-house against St. Dunstan's Church in Fleet-street; Mr. Squire's Coffee-house in Fuller's-Rents in Holborn; Mr. Jellicoe's at his Coffee house (call'd Hamlin's Coffee-house) in Swithings-Alley near the Royal-Exchange; and at Mr. Ive's at Tom's Coffee-house in Cornhil.

The appeal for subscribers appeared about ten weeks after Kip had agreed terms with two partners in the venture, John Bulfinch (*c*. 1654–1729) (Fig. 3) and Thomas Taylor (fl. 1685–1726). In his legal complaint, Kip was to argue that both of these partners had defaulted on their agreements with him, but because Taylor settled his differences with Kip at an earlier stage, Bulfinch was the sole defendant in the Chancery suit and the principal target of Kip's ire. Kip's financial situation was modest, and the partnership was a marriage of convenience. As he put it in his Chancery complaint,

had not your Orator [Kip] wholly depended on such their Assistance therein, he must and would have entred into such or the like Agreemt: with some other person or persons in that behalfe, to have enabled him to have provided[?] therein, He then being unable to have carryed on such work and undertaking at his own ... charge and expence, as was and is well known to the said John Bulfinch and Thomas Taylor.

Kip's working arrangement with Knyff during the previous decade is unclear, but he might have made a more suitable partner had his own projects not failed by this point.

Thomas Taylor was a map- and printseller (Fig. 4).[17] He was a member of the Goldsmiths' Company and can probably be identified with the son of Thomas Taylor, scrivener of Worcester, who was bound in 1685 as apprentice to Landor Smith (fl. 1674–93). In turn, Taylor himself registered apprentices in 1698, 1702 and 1705.[18] Between *c*. 1711 and 1726 Taylor traded from the sign of the Golden Lyon on Fleet Street, 'near the Horn Tavern' and 'over against Serjeant's Inn'.[19] Taylor sold 'all sorts of fine French and Dutch

Fig. 3. David Loggan, *John Bulfinch*, engraving, 1680s–90s. © Trustees of the British Museum, *Heal, Portraits.285*.

Prints and Maps, and Indian Pictures of all Sizes, Framed or Unframed', 'great Variety of Maps and Prints for furnishing Halls, Stair Cases, and Parlours, at very reasonable Rates, with good Allowance to those who buy to sell again'.[20] No advertisements naming Taylor in Fleet Street have been found later than 1726, and in 1725 Mr Stokes, a stationer, was at the Golden Lyon in Fleet Street; succeeded in 1728 by Timothy Jerdan, a printseller; and from 1739 to 1754 by John Tinney.[21] These later premises may not have been the same as Taylor's, but it is unlikely that Stokes, Jerden and Tinney would have invited confusion by adopting Taylor's sign if he was still trading under it.

Befitting his shadowy role in Kip's project, Bulfinch's trade is not as easy to define. In the words of Kip's complaint, Bulfinch 'stiled himself bookseller and Citizen and Draper of London but had then taken upon himself to draw and engross writings as a scrivener'. At his death one newspaper called him 'an Auctioneer', another 'formerly a Bookseller, but late a Dealer in Pictures'.[22] He was the son of Grizella and John Bulfinch, a yeoman from Chatham in Kent, and in 1668 was apprenticed to the Wapping shipbuilder and prominent Anabaptist Sir William Warren (fl. 1652–90).[23] Warren served as Master of the Drapers' Company in 1668–69 and was Samuel Pepys's closest business advisor. Bulfinch was to become a fixture of the London art trade. He was one of George Vertue's informants, who noted that he 'Bought all Mr. [Thomas] Bettertons Pictures amongst which were a great many Crayon pictures of famous Playereses these he sold to Mr. [William] Sykes'.[24] Bulfinch was a buyer at the Robert Streeter sale of 1711 and was a customer of the printseller Edward Cooper (fl. 1682, d. 1725), to whom he owed at £2 15s. 6d. at the latter's death.[25] Bulfinch's memorandum book, now in the British Library, conveys the range of his business dealings: in 1701, buying pictures at auction; in 1705, holding book auctions at two coffee houses; and in the 1720s, compiling and selling extra-illustrated copies of books to order.[26] In his legal complaint, Kip referred to 'so unjust and litigious a person as the said Bulfinch', which is borne out by surviving legal records. In 1698 Bulfinch and two others who organized picture auctions at the Palace of Westminster sued two painters, Thomas Murray and Edward Roberts, over a business arrangement that had gone wrong. With his brothers Thomas and Adino, Bulfinch went to court in 1703 over a property in Chatham, Kent, probably their mother's former home. He sued William Gaunt over money in 1704 and in 1710 he was suing his landlord over property in Wapping.[27] Bulfinch is noted at several addresses throughout his career: 'in St. James's-street near St. James's House' (1707–09); 'under the South Portico of the Royal Exchange' (1714); 'at Bird Coffee House new Palace yard' (probably later 1710s); and at Bennetts Court, off Drury Lane between King's Head Alley and White Horse Yard (from 1721 until his death).[28] Bulfinch lived until his mid-seventies, when a newspaper reported that he

Fig. 4. Trade card of Thomas Taylor. © Trustees of the British Museum, *Heal, 100.75+.*

'dropt down dead, as he was walking along Fleet-street' in February 1729.[29]

Under the agreement that Kip made with his two shareholders, Taylor and Bulfinch were each liable for one quarter of the ongoing production costs, which Kip described as including the purchase of

> plates of copper whereon the said view or prospect was to be engraved and etched, which plates were to be twelve in number for the whole view or prospect, (vizt) every plate proporconable to an Elephant Sheet of paper which when printed and pasted together would make one entire Impression of the said view or prospect … the charge of fitting the said plates for engraving and of buying and paying for the paper, printing the same off by the Rolling press printer, and of all other incident charges of or about the promoting carrying on and finishing the said work.

Furthermore, Bulfinch and Taylor were each to pay Kip 20s. for every plate the engraver completed, for 'his Art workmanship and Time' and in order 'to enable him to proceed in the work'. The plan was that Kip, his 'Servants workmen or assignes' (though realistically it was Kip alone) could complete all twelve plates within six months, by 16 March 1716. To execute the agreement, Bulfinch and Taylor were each to pay Kip two guineas or 43s., in recognition of 'the great study Labour and pains he had before been in drawing modeling and composing the said draught of the said view or prospect'. A penalty clause was also agreed, whereby if any of the three partners defaulted on the agreement then they would be liable to pay a penalty of £100; additionally, if Bulfinch and Taylor did not make their contributions towards the costs of the project, they would lose their quarter share of the income from sales of the print. For, as Kip was keen to emphasize in his complaint, their 'agreeing to assist him with money in manner aforesaid for his Carrying on and finishing his said work in that behalfe ... [was] the sole Inducemt and consideracon of and for his Admitting them to be copartners with him therein'.

The agreement was made orally between Kip, Bulfinch and Taylor shortly before 16 September 1715, and Kip's intention was to have it written up in contracts for the shareholders to sign. But

> being wholly Ignorant in all matters relating to the forms of Law whereof the said Bulfinch was likewise very sensible, He the said John Bulfinch insinuated to your Orator that as he was well experienced in drawing and engrossing of writings, your Orator could not employ or entrust any person to prepare the Articles of such Agreemt between your orator and them the said Bulfinch and Taylor who would be more careful to draw the same fairly and according to their reall Agreemt: than he the said Bulfinch would be, And which matter he often repeated to your Orator with many Solem promises and asseveracons of his Honesty and fidelity to your Orator therein, untill he prevailed with your Orator to give his Consent that he the said John Bulfinch should draw and prepare the Articles of such Agreemt between your Orator and them.

Shortly afterwards, at a meeting of the partners Bulfinch brought documents for everyone to sign in front of witnesses. Kip and Taylor signed and exchanged two copies of their agreement, and each of them kept a copy for their records. But when it came to Kip's agreement with Bulfinch, there was only one copy for Kip to sign: Bulfinch claimed that he had left the other one at home 'as not being then fully finished'. Bulfinch asked if he could take Kip's copy away with him to help him complete the other copy. Kip agreed, 'not having any friend present either to peruse the said Articles for him before his sealing thereof or to give him any Advice in the matter'. We can probably see where this is going, for, when afterwards Kip asked a friend to peruse his copy of the agreement signed with Taylor, they 'found thereby that he the said John Bulfinch (who both drew and engrossed the same as aforesaid) had not inserted any Date of or in such Counterpart, but had left the same un-dated'. This was when Kip came to believe that

> the whole Contrivance Acting and proceeding of the said John Bulfinch in the premises was an entire fraudulent contrivence of him the said Bulfinch (from

the Beginning to the End) to Introduce Himself and the said Thomas Taylor into the said agreemt with your orator, and Intitle them to such shares of the profits as aforesaid of [such your] Orator's Art Labour and Expences without their being obliged by the said Articles to pay your Orator any propoconable value for the same.

In the meantime, since both of Kip's partners had paid their initial two guineas to initiate the agreement, Kip began the task of engraving. Once he had completed the first plate, he printed off some proofs and let Taylor and Bulfinch know, asking them for the first payment of 20s. that was due on the completion of each plate, 'And also to pay your Orator (each of them) one fourth part of his reall disbursmts. out of purse in buying the said copper and getting the same fitted for engraving.' Neither paid up, of course, but while Kip had easy access to Taylor, 'Bulfinch continued to Abscond and secret himself from your Orator, and also to refuse or neglect the sending your Orator his Counterpart of the said Articles'. Kip had little room for manoeuvre, because he had already given his partners 'blank Receipts in writing under your Orator's Hand to the Amount or value of the sume of Eighteen pounds and upwards on account of such the then intended co-partnership'. By this point, of course, Kip was beginning to realize Bulfinch had stitched him up: he had signed Bulfinch's contract before witnesses without even reading it, and now he could not even procure a copy. So Kip was careful not 'to give either the said Bulfinch or Taylor any the least cause or reason to charge your orator with the breach or non-performance of any Covenant', and even tried returning Bulfinch's two guineas to him as a way of ending his involvement in the enterprise.

Without the financial support of his business partners, Kip proceeded with the engraving as best he could. He found the money to purchase two further copper plates, which he engraved and proofed. By May 1716, with three of the twelve sheets now complete, Kip found an opportunity 'to shew such proofs of the said fourth part both to the said John Bulfinch and Thomas Taylor respectively, and then personally demanded of them the moneys so payable from them to yor Orator'. Kip's pleas fell on deaf ears and he maintained in the complaint that neither of his partners ever contributed any money beyond the initial two guineas. Far from facilitating his work,

> John Bulfinch hind[e]red and obstructed your orator for the space of several years of and in the finishing the engraving of his said view or prospect, and carrying on other his Business and employm[en]t: aforementioned to his reall Loss and damage of the full sume of one hundred pounds and upwards as your Orator doubts not to prove.

At some point Taylor seems to have got cold feet and he 'freely cancelled and delivered his said Articles unto your Orator'. In doing so, he explained to Kip that had Bulfinch stuck by the terms of the partnership then he, Taylor, would have done so too, but that when he realized that Bulfinch intended to take a share of the profits without contributing towards the costs, 'he thought it very unreasonable for your orator and him the said Taylor to carry on the work only at their own Charge for the Joynt Benefit of the said Bulfinch therein, and that he therefore refused payment as aforesaid'. Kip tried to attract other partners to be involved in the publication, but found that 'divers honest and un-contentious persons refused afterwards to enter into any co-partnership with your Orator in an Affair wherein so unjust and litigious a person as the said Bulfinch had any pretence of being concerned with him'.

In the end, Kip had to rely on 'some worthy friends (after a Considerable space of time) [who] assisted your orator with money to go on with and finish the engraving of such his view or prospect and bringing his work therein to perfection'. So it was that, almost five years after beginning it, in June 1720 Kip was able to announce to the public that he 'has finished his beautiful Prospect of London and Westminster, and St. James's Park, engraven on 12 large Plates, 7 Foot long, and 5 Foot broad'. They were available for sale 'neatly pasted on Cloth and Rowles, at one Guinea each, at his House in St. John-street, No4 over the Door, near Story's Passage, Westminster'.[30] In his advertisement Kip mentioned that the print was 'dedicated to Her Royal Highness the Princess of Wales', and the Prince and Princess of Wales appear prominently in the foreground. This led Ralph Hyde to suggest that the delay in its publication was caused by the Prince and Princess of Wales's difficult relationship with George I. Shortly after Kip had begun his work, the Prince and Princess had been forced to leave St James's Palace for Leicester House. However, in 1720 there was a rapprochement, which saw their return to St James's Palace.

Kip could not disentangle himself from the partnership, even in mid-1721, a year after he launched the *Prospect* for sale. Bulfinch was now threatening to arrest him and put him in prison, and had lately filed a suit in the Court of Common Pleas to recover £100. Bulfinch and his lawyers

> have continued such their endeavours from time to time to the very great Injury and oppression of your orator in the hindering and obstructing him in the following his aforesaid lawfull employmt: for the support of himselfe and his family, when he the said Bulfinch and his confederates well know that such his Action at Law against your Orator wholly unjust And groundless.

Unfortunately, Bulfinch's version of events has not survived, nor is the Court's judgment known; it is doubtful whether a judge would have looked kindly on a man who had freely signed a contract without reading it. Either way, a few weeks after making his complaint in the Court of Chancery, Kip 'dropt down dead suddenly, at his House'. He was buried at St Margaret's, Westminster, on 12 August 1721.[31]

Kip's Chancery suit is a reminder of the critical role that financing and contractual arrangements played in facilitating artistic production. Originally, Kip had planned to engrave all twelve plates in the six months between 16 September 1715 and 16 March 1716: a fortnight per plate. During this time his partners would supply his living expenses, which (at 20s. or £1 per plate per partner) were a meagre £4 per month, or about £50 per year. The contract committed Kip's partners to each meet one quarter of the actual production costs and, as Kip had written out receipts to Bulfinch to the value of £18, he must have anticipated these would be about £24 in total, or £2 per plate.[32] Kip did commit to finding £12 for half of these costs, but the precariousness of his situation is clear from the fact that, with no support from the partners, he only managed to complete three plates by himself in the eight months to May 1716, and it was another four years before the remaining nine plates were finished. Doubtless Kip spent much of that time on other work, such as the many country house views after Thomas Badeslade's drawings that he engraved for a *History of Kent* by John Harris, published in 1719. He also made a further view of St James's Palace for John Stow's *Survey of London* (London, 1720).[33]

Kip's situation, in which his lack of credit forced him into the arms of unscrupulous business partners, was not unique to the print trade, but it was a characteristic of it in early eighteenth-century London. When in the following decade Hogarth complained to the House of Commons about the exploitation suffered by engravers, in a petition that led to the Copyright Act of 1735, he was concerned with a different issue, of piracy.[34] But his 'overgrown shopkeeper', whom 'the Artist, though at first he may complain of him wherever he comes, and stand out in Opposition against him, must of necesity at last fall into his unmerciful Hands', is recognizably the central villain in Kip's story, too.[35]

1. TNA, C 11/42/20. A full transcript of Kip's complaint appears on *The Art World in Britain 1660–1735*, ed. by Richard Stephens <artworld.york.ac.uk> [accessed on 6 August 2020].

2. The account here relies on Nicholas Grindle, 'Kip, Johannes (b. before 1653, d. 1721?)', *ODNB* <https://www.oxforddnb.com/view> [accessed on 6 August 2020]. See also Laurence Worms and Ashley Baynton-Williams, *British Map Engravers* (London, 2011), p. 373.

3. Elizabeth Breda was the daughter of Elizabeth Asselijn of Amsterdam. A. D. de Vries Azn., 'Biografische aanteekeningen betreffende voornamelijk Amsterdamsche schilders, plaatsnijders, enz. en hunne verwanten', *Oud Holland*, 3 (1885), p. 77.

4. British Museum, 1850,0223.857; see Antony Griffiths, *The Print in Stuart Britain*, exhibition catalogue, London, British Museum (London, 1998), cat. no. 89.

5. Kip's earliest dated London plate may be *Ierusalem* (1689) for Nicolas Fontaine, *The history of the New Testament* (1688), see Worms and Baynton-Williams, p. 373.

6. *Post Man*, 10 May 1698.

7. From 1701 Knyff was also offering the prints invidually at 2s. each from his house in Old Palace Yard. *Post Man*, 31 May 1701.

8. Letters from Leonard Knyff, dated 4 December 1702 and 9 January 1703, West Yorkshire

Archives Service, transcribed in Hugh Honour, 'Leonard Knyff', *Burlington Magazine*, 96, no. 620 (November 1954), pp. 337–38; and Hugh Honour, 'Leonard Knyff: Painter and Picture Dealer', *Leeds Arts Calendar*, 7, no. 23 (Autumn 1953), pp. 20–25.

9. *Daily Courant*, 1 February 1707.

10. *Daily Courant*, 1 February 1707; *Post Man*, 23 November 1708.

11. *Britannia Illustrata, or views of several of the Queen's palaces and principal seats of the nobility and gentry of Great Britain*, 2 vols (London, 1707); *Nouveau Theatre de la Grande Bretagne* (London, 1708). Kip's work for Knyff was also extensively pirated by Pierre van der Aa, whose engravings appeared in James Beeverell's *Les Delices de la Grand' Bretagne & de l'Irelande*, published in Leiden from 1707. For an account of its bibliographic history, see Eileen Harris and Nicholas Savage, *British Architectural Books and Writers 1556–1785* (Cambridge, 1990), p. 145, n. 9. A facsimile edition was published by Paradigm Press in 1984, ed. by John Harris and Gervase Jackson-Stops. See also Hilary McKee, 'The Bird's-Eye Views of L. Knyff and J. Kip, as Published in Britannia Illustrata, and The Use for Understanding Historic Landscapes' (doctoral thesis, Oxford Brookes University, 2004).

12. *Daily Courant*, 15 March 1716.

13. British Museum, 1880,1113.2260.

14. Kee Il Choi Jr, '"Partly Copies from European Prints": Johannes Kip and the Invention of Export Landscape Painting in Eighteenth-Century Canton', *The Rijksmuseum Bulletin*, 66, no. 2 (2018), pp. 130–34, fig. 17, proposes Kip's view from the south as the source for the decoration of a Cantonese plate, c. 1735–40 (Metropolitan Museum of Art, New York, inv. 62.1872). Choi dated the print to c. 1710, but the Metropolitan Museum of Art gives a date of 1720 (acc. no. 2017.128a,b).

15. Ralph Hyde, 'Jan Kip's Prospect of London', in Ralph Hyde and Peter Jackson, *Jan Kip's Prospect of London, Westminster & St. James's Park 1720*, London Topographical Society publication No. 161 (London, 2003), p. 3. Hyde also outlines the later history of Kip's plates.

16. For instance, *The River Thames with St Paul's Cathedral on Lord Mayor's Day*, c. 1747–48, Lobkowicz Collections, Czech Republic (see p. 16), and *The Thames from Somerset House Terrace towards the City*, c. 1750–51, Royal Collection Trust (RCIN 400504).

17. Sarah Tyacke, *London Map-Sellers 1660–1720* (London, 1978), p. 144.

18. Goldsmiths' Company apprenticeship records <www.londonroll.org> [accessed on 6 August 2020]. Landor Smith had previously taken Taylor's older brother John as apprentice in 1674. If this identification is correct, then he cannot have been the map-seller who was trading on London Bridge in the 1670s, as proposed by Thomas Chubb, *The Printed Maps in the Atlases of Great Britain and Ireland: A Bibliography, 1579–1870* (London, 1927). Taylor's own apprentices were Benjamin Innes (1698), Orelabar Wilson (1702) and Nathaniel Fleckno (1705).

19. *Post Boy*, 1 January 1712; *Daily Courant*, 30 April 1718.

20. *British Apollo*, 26 January 1711; *Daily Courant*, 30 April 1718.

21. *London Journal*, 6 March 1725; *Daily Journal*, 11 May 1726; *Daily Journal*, 22 January 1728; *London Evening Post*, 24 November 1739; *Whitehall Evening Post*, 18 April 1754.

22. *Daily Journal*, 18 February 1729; *Flying Post*, 22 February 1729.

23. Drapers' Company apprenticeship records <www.londonroll.org> [accessed on 6 August 2020]. Bulfinch only gained his freedom by servitude in 1712, shortly before taking on an apprentice, Francis Coke; another, Charles Smith, was bound in 1714. In 1640 Bulfinch's father was living at Salem, Massachusetts, but he returned to England in 1653 and died at Chatham, Kent, in 1679/80 (Edward F. Johnson, *A Genealogy of the Descendants of John Bulfilnch of Boston, Massachusetts, 1700–1895* (Woburn, 1895), p. 4). Grizella Bulfinch made her will in 1677 but it was not proved until 1692 following a lawsuit (TNA, PROB 11/22/55, PROB 11/412/38, PROB 11/410/391, PROB 5/1252, PROB 5/1253). Grizella bequeathed her house to her children, whom she named as Thomas, Adino, Mary and John. Adino Bulfinch

was a sail-maker who emigrated to Boston, Massachusetts, *c.* 1700 (Zachariah G. Whitman, *The History of the Ancient and Honorable Artillery Company*, 2nd edn (Boston, 1842), p. 247; Ellen Susan Bulfinch ed., *The Life and Letters of Charles Bulfinch, Architect* (Boston, 1896), p. 12).

24. George Vertue, 'Notebook A.j', *The Walpole Society: Vertue 1*, vol. 18 (1929–30), p. 52. For Betterton, see *ODNB* https://www.oxforddnb.com/view [accessed 29 September 2020]; William Sykes (*c.* 1659–1724) of Lincoln's Inn Fields, was an art dealer and member of the Virtuosi of St Luke's.

25. TNA, PROB 3/24/190, Probate Inventory of Edward Cooper, 14 October 1725.

26. British Library, London, Add. MS 19929, Memorandum Book of John Bulfinch, early eighteenth century. One of the book auctions was advertised in *Post Man*, 25 September 1705.

27. All of these suits were filed in the Court of Chancery, whose records are held at TNA: C 6/309/16 (1698); C 8/609/27; C 8/363/6, C 8/591/63 (1703); C 8/599/8, C 8/466/50 (1704); C 10/315/10 (1710).

28. *Daily Courant*, 16 October 1707, 1 June 1714; British Library, London, Add. MSS 23095, Address book of George Vertue (Notebook E.2), 1715–51; St Clement Dane Rate Books <www.findmypast.com> [accessed 6 August 2020].

29. *Daily Journal*, 18 February 1729; *Flying Post*, 22 February 1729, gave the cause of death as apoplexy. Bulfinch was buried at Stepney on 21 February.

30. *Daily Courant*, 8 June 1720.

31. *Daily Journal*, 15 August 1721. Maybe Kip collapsed at hearing the outcome of his case?

32. Bulfinch's quarter share was £6; the remaining £12 of his £18 receipts would have been for the twelve £1 fees paid to Kip for each engraved plate.

33. British Museum, 1880,1113.2256.

34. Kip's view was pirated in Amsterdam by 'van Hove' (British Museum, 1880,1113.1182.1–4).

35. *The Case of Designers, Engravers, Etchers, &c.* (London, 1735), p. 3; L. Bently and M. Kretschmer eds, *Primary Sources on Copyright (1450–1900)* <www.copyrighthistory.org> [accessed on 30 January 2017].

X. AFTER THE WAR …

By ANN SAUNDERS

L AMBETH PALACE, the London home of the Archbishop of Canterbury, with its Library lies on the south bank of the River Thames, about a quarter of a mile upstream of the Houses of Parliament. Thus any wartime aerial attack on Parliament stood an equal chance of damaging Lambeth Palace with its precious books, the manuscripts having been evacuated out of London. This is precisely what happened on the night of 10 May 1941, when a bomb hit the Library, going through the roof and setting the books on fire. As much damage was caused by the hoses of the firemen quenching the flames. Then, on 21 July 1944, a flying bomb came through the central lantern[1] and did even more damage.

In 1952, I saw the post of Deputy Librarian advertised in *The Times*, applied for it and to my surprise got it. Thirty years later, I asked Reg (C. Reginald Dodwell, Lambeth Librarian from 1953 to 1958) why he chose

Fig. 1.   The Great Hall of Lambeth Palace after bombing in May 1941.
By permission of Lambeth Palace Library *C-2013-4_LP_5*.

me. He replied, 'Because you looked mad, and you needed to be mad to have taken on that job'. He was quite right — you did need to be mad.[2]

Clad in stout dark green cotton overalls, we started work on 1 January 1953. My salary was £400, rising later to £415. On that first day, we just wandered around looking at the desolation before our eyes. The dust that never ceased falling, volumes in fragments — a careless false move could jerk one volume into a pile of similarly disintegrating pieces. In the end, we went home early — Reg across the yard to houses where outbuildings had been converted into nice little dwellings for back-up staff such as chaplains and librarians, and me on a long train journey out to Pinner, beyond Harrow — got into baths, and came back the next day feeling (on my part) plain bloody-minded.

Apart from those first two days, the rest becomes a blur of cleaning, lifting and arranging volumes, or sets of volumes, on shelves. Clerics and bishops came in and out; they took no notice of me save for one bishop — Bishop George Bell of Chichester, who always spoke kindly. I remember he seemed particularly joyful when the *Patrologia Latina* and the *Graeca* were back on the Reading Room shelves.

Paper only burns at very high temperatures, but other parts of books disintegrate. The stitching holding the quires together melts easily; therefore if you have — let us say — a set of twelve volumes of *St Thomas of Aquinas* near a set of fourteen volumes of *Sayings of King Alphonso the Wise of Spain*, and you happen to stumble or fall against the volumes, *St Thomas* gets finely mixed with *King Alphonso* and it can take a full hour to get them in order again. Moral: tread warily in a bombed library. Before long, I had a rash covering my hands, something like eczema, soon reaching up to my elbows. I tried a thick layer of a pink barrier cream called Swarfega and carried on — it held it at bay.

The first thing to do was to recruit a team of bookbinders capable of realizing how precise the stitching needed to be. Frank Francis (later Sir Frank) sent his head binder with a team from the British Museum and we employed several independent binders. I became particularly fond of a Mr Hodge, and was very sad when he died, probably from overwork. His widow tried to take the work on, but she could not sew the damaged books well and precisely enough.

While we were casting around for the best way to organize the work, Reg came across two crates of blue laundry slips that could be paired together with carbon paper in between. I would list an author and abbreviated title on each pair and the binder would letter the spine in gold. By such primitive methods was order re-established. What would we not have given for the sophisticated techniques available today!

One day I was on my knees in Juxon's Great Hall — I forget what I was doing — and something fell down the back of my neck. I started to scream

Fig. 2.   Wartime damage to the seventeenth-century hammer-beam roof of the Great
Hall. By permission of Lambeth Palace Library C-2013-4_LP_4.

uncontrollably, so loudly that Reg left his study to see why I was hysterical.
It was a huge cockroach or beetle, fallen from the roof. In restoration,
unseasoned wood had been used to repair the old wood in the pendants; it
was lucky for the cockroach that I was there to break his fall. Reg put him
in a large matchbox, which he took to the Natural History Museum. I heard
no more of the poor insect. We made an extra pot of tea that afternoon. Tea
was made in a primitive and highly dangerous manner. We had a single tiny
electric fire for warmth, which we laid on its back to boil the kettle — there
was no other way to do it.

Just before Christmas 1953, when three cataloguers had been appointed,
we opened to readers who were petitioning Archbishop Fisher. We opened
all day Tuesday to Saturday and were closed on Sunday and Monday.
Reading Room duties became my particular preserve.

The Reading Room was arranged with a small dais on which I sat, ready
to spot a raised hand signalling the need for another volume or help with
something, trying to type up handwritten cards with a so-called silent
typewriter. You needed to be watchful. One day two German students came

in and sat very close together, her arm around his shoulders. I judged this to be out of affection — how wrong I was. He was tracing a map. Reg came in and, being on his feet, spotted this at once. The tracing stopped, the map was confiscated and restored to the strongroom and within a few weeks we found a charming French lady to take care of photography. Such service cost a few shillings a sheet.

Other incidents occurred from time to time. An elderly retired Classics teacher realized we held the Latin grammar book composed by William Lily, illuminated by an excellent scribe, and bound with stiff board covered in crimson silk.[3] The book is so beautiful that it makes you want to learn. Miss Archibald came in several times a week. She christened the volume 'Little Edward'. All went well for at least a year until one day she sprang up onto the dais with such eagerness, took hold of Little Edward, and leapt off again, falling on the book and tearing off the front cover. The binders soon repaired the damage, but after this Miss Archibald came less often. She had received a proposal of marriage from a gentleman a little older than herself, after which we saw her no more. Clearly, a living husband was more fun than Little Edward.

The next incident was more sinister. We had just appointed three cataloguers, so it must have been in late 1953. The most precious material was kept in the strongroom. This included the medieval manuscripts that had been catalogued by Dr M. R. James, author of many learned works as well as *Ghost Stories of an Antiquary*. If one got hold of the catalogue, which had been published in 1932, it revealed what was in the strongroom, which was built on two levels. At that time, since we knew and trusted many of our readers, we would take them into the strongroom, which was still fairly chaotic, and, *never taking our eyes off them*, let them select what they required. Of course, this was a risky business, but these were desperate times and we were there to serve readers.

One day a stranger came in. I was on duty. I looked him up and down and questioned him. He seemed respectable and said that he came from a good American university, so I took him into the strongroom. He wanted a first edition of Roger Bacon's *Essays*, a presentation copy for the Archbishop of Canterbury, a tiny book (a 16°) bound in white vellum decorated with gold tooling.[4] My eyes were fixed on the man. He found it on the far side, turned and asked: 'What would it cost for you to blink long enough for me to slip this into my pocket?'. I continued to stare at him for a full half-minute. Then I took him by the sleeve, holding that as if it were a foul tarantula spider, and said: 'I think we will go down now'. Never letting go of his sleeve, I led him out of the strongroom, down the stairs, locked the door ostentatiously without letting him go, and — still holding him — back to his place. Then I dusted my hands and remained standing. He gathered his notebooks and slunk out.

At lunch break, I gathered everyone together and told them what had happened. After that, we never admitted anyone to the strongroom again.

One further reader deserves mention. He was Mr Blore. He came almost every day. He seemed such a lonely old man that I — perhaps foolishly — invited him to join us for tea. This made him happy. Sometimes he would hold forth, occasionally usefully. Perhaps I should not have done it, for when I eventually left Lambeth in 1955, Mr Blore was told by Susan Hare that he was unwelcome in the future and Mr Blore ceased coming to the Library at all. I hope he transferred himself to the British Museum Reading Room, which has always seemed a friendly place, especially in the old building.

It is time to turn from readers to Archbishops. Though ordained, Dr Fisher had never served as a parson working with parishioners and ordinary humans; instead, he had been Headmaster of Repton, teaching mathematics and presumably religious studies there, for eighteen years.[5] He never remembered your name correctly. My maiden name was Cox-Johnson. As soon as he entered the Library, he would shout — or bawl — 'Miss Brox-Bonson ... Miss Scott-Thompson ... come here, you!'

*　　*　　*

After much interviewing, three cataloguers had been appointed in late 1953. They were Gwenda Thomas, Susan Hare[6] and Rosemary Burdett.[7] When Gwenda left to get married in the summer of 1954, her place was taken by Julian Roberts, who later worked at the British Museum, and then moved back to the Bodleian at Oxford where he spent the rest of his working life, first as Keeper of Printed Books and, eventually, Deputy Librarian.[8]

Reg was now concocting his own classification system. Doctrinal theology was separated from moral theology and so on. Otherwise the original collection was kept by itself. Not very surprisingly, the staff who took over when he had left for Trinity College Library at Cambridge, which he did promptly at the end of this contract with the Church Commissioners,[9] had a higher opinion of Dewey.

Early in 1954, just after the cataloguers arrived, we acquired Clem. Archbishop Fisher could endure Mr Clements, his secretary, no longer, so he sent him down to the Library to be Reg's secretary and shorthand typist. He was a strange, tubby, very short-legged little man who, at coffee- or tea-time, would perch on his chair, tipping it up backwards, kicking his short, fat legs in the air, chortling at the memory of long-dead archbishops who were always 'funny men' or even 'very funny men'. Rosemary, ever gentle and discreet, would try to prise out in what their 'funniness' lay, but Clem would never give a definition, so we remained unenlightened.

Reg now made two decisions — there must be special tables in the Reading Room, and we must get rid of all books not relevant to the historical or theological substance of the collection. For example, novelists or poets, even historians who were friends of archbishops, would send copies of their works as gifts. There were sackloads of these, so sacks were filled — probably about three or four hundred books — and smuggled out, usually when the Archbishop was in Canterbury. Each had the Library's bookplate in it, which made the volumes the more valuable. They went to Hodgson's auction rooms in Chancery Lane and sold well, which helped the Library's funds, for this was money that did not need to be accounted for to the Church Commissioners.

The books had to be loaded onto a red metal trolley that had to be dragged round three sides of the cloisters to reach the point where they could be stacked up for action.[10] Gwenda Thomas announced she could not do such heavy work, and, anyway, she was leaving to get married. Rosemary was too frail, Susan Hare would lend a hand sometimes. One day, I felt the inner lining of my stomach wall tearing apart. I stopped work

Fig. 3.   The Great Hall, housing most of the library, in chaos after bombing.
By permission of Lambeth Palace Library C-2013-4_LP_8.

and took things gently for a few days, and my stomach righted itself. But now, in old age, I am incontinent, which is very boring.

Let us turn to Reg's table-designing, in which I was not involved. Reg was not a furniture designer, but he always thought he could do anything. He designed a beautiful table with battleship linoleum sunk into the top. The man he had picked to build it could not have known much either, for within a few weeks the legs began to splay outwards and the top to sink towards the floor. After some costly attempts at repairs, individual tables for readers were the choice.

At some time before Reg and I began work, a vast mass of coverless, split, torn, broken books had been heaped in piles along the way round the cloisters, making it impossible to drag the trolleys laden with books for the cataloguers. All were post-1700. In sheer desperation, someone had pushed the lot down into the unrestored crypt chapel and so cleared a way. One year Reg took his leave in a three-week lump, and went to Italy with his friend, George Zarnecki, another art historian.[11] No sooner was Reg out of the Library and across the Channel than Sir Frank Francis and his friend, Professor William Jackson of Harvard University, swooped down on Lambeth and saw the books in the crypt. We explained with one voice why they were there. They would have none of that. Somewhere in the heap was an account of the flooding of Lisbon in 1755. Carry the books up immediately! I toiled away. Months later, when Francis had gone about his affairs and Jackson was back in America, the cataloguers and I found the fragments that made up the three volumes describing the Lisbon earthquake and flood. It was something that today would be called a tsunami.

*   *   *

One evening Reg and I were sitting together after work. He confided that he intended to leave before long. He had been offered the post of Librarian at Trinity College in Cambridge.[12] A day or two later, Frank Francis asked if I would come to the British Museum for two years whilst someone was doing their military service. After careful thought, I accepted.

I was set to work learning how to catalogue under Anna Simoni.[13] Anyone who ever met Anna never forgot her — she was strict and dogmatic, but we got on well enough. I learned how to catalogue, though by British Museum rules, which are unlike any other.

What Happened Next

Reg stayed eight years at Trinity (1958–1966). He was offered a chair in Manchester and the directorship of the Whitworth Art Gallery, where he remained until he retired in 1989. He and Sheila remained in Manchester, which she detested, Reg still concerned with the Gallery and its postgraduate students. Before long, he had a bad stroke, which rendered him part-blind. Sheila announced that they were now going south, so that she could be near her daughter, Jane, and her two granddaughters. Reg's son, David, had become a psychiatrist, and saw little of his parents.

I served my two years at the Museum, and then came up before a selection board for a permanent post — all men. As soon as they saw me, they began to laugh. They asked me what I would have if I could have one object in the whole Museum. It was a silly question, and I gave an unwise reply — I said I wanted the Aztec crystal skull in what was the Main Gallery where treasures were displayed.[14] The next morning, Robert Wilson, the Keeper of Printed Books, told me to get out as soon as I could — I knew he hated me because I was Francis's protégé and he and Francis were enemies. The Museum was *not* a happy place in which to work. I wonder what it is like now. I gave the Department the best leaving party I could — they all got happily drunk. They presented me with the first two volumes of *Remembrance of Things Past*, Marcel Proust's *A la Récherche du Temps Perdu*, the first of which everyone signed.

*   *   *

In 2018 Ann was interviewed by Krzysztof Adamiec of Lambeth Palace Library about her memories of the 1950s, and the following excerpts add some detail to her article.

AS: It was horrifying to see. There were books in piles on the floor, and the first thing to realize is that when a bomb falls on a building, and there are books (the manuscripts had mostly been evacuated to Aberystwyth and elsewhere, so thank God the Lambeth Bible and the blessed Macdurnan Gospels were safe and alright — but the books were not) what happens is not so much, excepting by a direct hit ...

KA: *When did you see this?*

AS: I think that it was the year 1952 or 1953, and the terrifying thing was the dust which was lying everywhere. And it never stopped. You dusted a shelf, you brought water and a cleaning cloth, and washed the shelf. The next morning when you looked at the same shelf again, the dust was as thick as ever. It went on forming for the first nine months or so and it was quite, quite distressing. The covers were loose on everything, we had absolutely no facilities at all ... The attitude was — and possibly I am not being fair — but the attitude generally was that the library could jolly well manage without any money and I really think that Archbishop Fisher would have got rid of it, if he could possibly have done so.

Fig. 4. Books damaged by fire and water, piled in the thirteenth-century crypt of Lambeth Palace. By permission of Lambeth Palace Library C-2013-4_LP_3.

He was a very strange man, he had been a headmaster most of his life and he ruled in a way a certain type of teacher rules. He never remembered your name correctly ... And you said, 'Yes, Archbishop', very respectfully, all the while not feeling very loving toward him. We felt very, very sorry for the Queen, when it came to her coronation, to be crowned by a man as objectionable as that. I think it must have been a terrible experience for her.[15]

We had two trusted helpers, one was called Lambert, and I can't remember the name of the second one, but they were absolutely dab hands with an electric floor polisher and they polished the floor every single day, so even though the dust never stopped falling the floor always looked shiny and beautiful. Later we had a pair called Warburton and Trinder. Warburton had been a ship's purser. His hands were exquisite — he often sat admiring his nails — and he very carefully treated the leather bindings, because we had got them restored by then. Trinder was a glorious Cockney. He had no wife, [but] two little girls, he called them names like Scruff. Every so often he would come back on a Monday morning or a Tuesday, 'I've been around the market, Miss, here this is for you, here is a keyring, I nicked it'. And you would gratefully accept it, because it was so kind of him to trouble to nick it for you. But they were a pair of treasures ...

KA: *What was your daily job? What were you doing every single day?*

AS: ... [as well as sorting the books] I had to run the reading room too because there was only me. I had to answer the telephone and take care of everything.

KA: *And did you also do cataloguing of the books and manuscripts?*

AS: Scarcely at that time, the manuscripts had come back in perfect order, and they were stowed in the strongroom. I tried to sit when I could in the reading room, when there was a reader, and there weren't very many at the beginning, I had to invigilate it ... we managed to get a splendid French lady, with a camera, and she provided the camerawork for anyone who wanted it. We tried to save the requests and get her to do five or six at a time. And she always came, and kept accounts terribly carefully, down to the last single halfpenny, because of course it was old money, sensible twelve pennies to the shilling, instead of revolting decimal money which is absolutely impossible.

Bruce Saunders: Well, you've only got ten fingers?

AS: No, you've got two big toes!

Bruce: Alright, OK!

AS: When it came to the autumn, I think somewhere about October, we recruited three cataloguers. They had all had proper library training, or archive training, which I had not had. It was just coming in at UCL and I suppose I could have had it, had I been able to stay on for another year. But I couldn't because my brother was coming after me, and mother couldn't possibly afford two of us being students, so I had to go out and get a job. My first job was as a hire purchase agent. I was not a good hire purchase agent. I carefully resigned, when I heard about Lambeth Palace, and although I couldn't hope that I would get it, I still terribly wanted that job. Our first cataloguers were Susan Hare, Rosemary Burdett and Gwenda Thomas who endlessly said, 'Oh, no, it's too hard for me! I can't do it'. And Reg's answer to that was, 'Ann, work harder!'. And I endeavoured to make up for it ... The Laudian Room[16] had above it, or adjacent to it, a lavatory, and up the stairs, two rooms. One became Reg's office, the other became a staff room where we congregated to have a cup of coffee mid-morning, or whoever was not on duty in the reading room.

Reg had a very stressful time with the Committee because Canon Jenkins refused to leave. He had been the librarian before the war. He never did any work, he was a very odd gentleman indeed.[17] He had Dr Irene Churchill[18] who was an amazingly learned lady as his dogsbody — i.e., she did absolutely everything, and she left a written account which is in the Church of England archives, of the state she found the library in, after the war. One always felt that probably she went on holding the job because she was in love with Canon Jenkins, but he never took any notice at all of her. He just used her as a dogsbody and she toiled away and struggled and quite obviously hadn't got a hope in hell of getting the place to any sorts of rights. You needed to be young and very strong in order to do it ...

Reg was married to a very interesting woman — I am still in touch with her. We will still have a gossip after all these years because we like having a gossip. Sheila is ten years older than me, so as I am eighty-five, she is ninety-five, but she is still absolutely coherent, and she is a very fine pianist. And she has a magnificent harpsichord in her front hall, and when we go there she and Bruce, my husband, rush to the harpsichord and start playing duets as hard as they can. She was frequently asked to play before the Queen or any important visitor who came to Lambeth Palace, which she did exquisitely. She really should have continued a musical career, and also she wrote, and I think possibly still writes, rather good poetry and rather good stories. Sheila is quite a girl. She had two children, Jane and David, Jane designs clothes and has a shop in Bath making the sort of evening clothes that people want to wear that are different from everybody else's. And David is a psychiatrist.

Reg was having to do a lot of negotiating with the Church Commissioners, who didn't want to spend a penny on the library. But luckily we got the Pilgrim Trust — they gave us the enormous sum of £10,000, which would probably be £10 million today, with the inflation we have had. And we managed to get almost all the rebinding done with that money. We had about five or six either full-time or part-time binders. They would come in, take a consignment of books, match up the binding with any previous ones — because of course you never knew what was coming to the top first — and bring it back about a fortnight later, rebound, and one could put them on the shelves, think, oh, they are beginning to look proper, and one was filled with joy.

The Archbishop was very strictly teetotal. Unfortunately, Reg was not teetotal at all, so on the odd occasion when he became, let's say, not drunk, but he had taken drink, if he ran into the Archbishop it tended to be very unfortunate. The Archbishop did not approve of that at all.

Reg moved subsequently, first to Cambridge, where Sheila had a rotten time of it because all the academic wives didn't seem to want to speak to her so she was left out of everything and she was miserable. And then he moved up to Manchester where he was in charge of the Whitworth Art

Gallery. She thought that was even worse. She was very lonely. We went to visit them both in Cambridge and on one manic occasion in Manchester when we had a son, Matthew, and a daughter, Katherine, a baby, and a wheel came off the Volkswagen. It had been badly serviced. I still don't know how Bruce managed to hold it steady on the road, we skidded to a halt and he contrived — he is an engineer, thank goodness — to get the car jacked up and put the wheel on after a fashion. We said quite a lot of things to the garage when eventually we got home to London.

Canon Jenkins was firmly refusing to retire. He was a very odd person. He made every committee meeting absolute hell for everyone else. He stole the Archbishop's bananas. Now, there were no bananas available after the war, but the Archbishop managed to get some, and Canon Jenkins would quietly steal them, eat them in the churchyard outside, stick the banana skins into the hedge, and then he would gather harebells from somewhere or other, and stick them all around the band of his hat. He really was a very odd librarian indeed. But there was one amazing thing about him. To say anything at all in the Great Hall, your voice disappears into the lantern, so if you have a visiting group of students and you are trying to tell them about the Library, you have to gather them round you very, very closely and tell them. He could stand anywhere in the Great Hall and he would speak in his sermon voice — although he was so old, he still had a sermon voice — and he would speak and deliver his sermon and he would be audible everywhere. I couldn't do it myself. I mean, I am quite used to lecturing, but I can't do that in the Great Hall …

To be on the receiving end of a heavy bombing raid is unimaginable. And the dust never seemed to stop pouring down at first. The thought of quitting never occurred to me. Was I mad? Reg rightly thought so. And the other thing that was very noticeable was that lots of things that we would have today simply hadn't been invented, or if they had they were so dear that we didn't get them. There were no computers — or rather, there were computers in the world, but they were enormous things that filled a whole room and you certainly didn't have one at the Library. All we had were our hands and our brains, and lots of dusters and scrubbing brushes.

One felt with Archbishop Fisher that he should have been the head of ICI — rather than the Church of England. He would, I am sure, have been very much better at that. His wife was equally strange. I never had any experience of her, but Sheila Dodwell had a lot of experience. She would never greet you, she would never say hello or goodbye. She would just come up, say something completely irrelevant and then walk away from you. They seemed a very odd pair together.

When people ask you about the Library, there are things that had not yet been invented. People presume, 'Oh, you were on your knees scrubbing. Can I see a photograph of it?' Well, people didn't have the sort of cameras that could photograph like that. So, no, you can't see a photograph of me scrubbing the floors because there weren't those sort of cameras. It was filthy dirty. I was talking to someone who had been a reader, and with whom I am still friends. She is an English historian, who was married to a Japanese gentleman, the Japanese correspondent for *The Times*, and I say to her, and it's perfectly true, that I had outbreaks of eczema all up my hands and my arms, all because of the extreme dirt in the Library.

I left largely because one of my three cataloguers, Susan Hare, said that she ought to be in charge of everything because she was qualified and I was not. I got very sore about this and it was a factor when the British Museum's Sir Frank Francis, as he later became, said, 'There's a temporary job coming up if you think you want to work in the British Museum and the Library, then why don't you take the temporary job?'. I was being rather nettled with the remarks that I was getting, and I thought, yes, I will take the temporary job. He said he would be at the interview, but he wasn't, and at the interview — I think I was the only woman interviewed — the whole committee laughed at me, they didn't ask me any questions about Lambeth Palace ... I didn't get the job.[19] But never mind, when I left I got the best job I ever had in my life. I became local history librarian and archivist for Marylebone Public Library and we still more than nearly fifty years on have regular meetings, quite often in this house which is very large. Well, we've stopped them now because at the last one nobody turned up. But we've stuck together as a team, in the public library, for nearly half a century. And I think that's nearly all I've got to say.

We had terrible thieving and damage. I don't know the name of the man who committed the crimes in 1974, but they've had an awful lot of restoration to do. And it's been very ugly indeed. He left a will, confessing what he had done, saying where the books could be found, and they've just about got them all back and got them restored.[20]

KA: *Yes, they are in the process of restoration. There are quite a lot of books being repaired now.*

AS: Yes, there certainly are. He hacked the coats of arms out with a knife, and it was pity he wasn't hanged for it, he should have been. There are some cases where I think that a death sentence is justified if people mess up books and manuscripts. My husband would not agree, but I don't care. I do feel very strongly about it. At any rate, I think that's just about all I've got to say.

KA: *Were you interviewed to get the job at Lambeth Palace Library?*

AS: Yes, I was. I was interviewed. The job I had after I was a hire purchase agent was in York Art Gallery, and the whole staff was Hans Hess,[21] myself, a secretary, a carpenter and three very good men, stout-hearted, hard-working, who did the shifting round of the pictures. The trouble with Hess

was, he could not keep his hands to himself, and so when it came to the
end of my six months I was to be sacked, got rid of. What he didn't realize
was that I had joined a trade union. I may be highly Tory in my views,
but I believe in trade unions. So I fought him, I fought him solidly for
the next two months. I would sometimes wake almost vomiting, because I
couldn't stand the set up any more. But I went in and did my work every
day, and Hess insisted that I should be sacked. Eventually, the Organizing
Committee, all of whom were borough councillors and volunteers, said
they would give me the option of being sacked or I might be permitted to
resign. I said that there was no choice, was there? I resigned. And so I had
to go back to London effectively having been sacked but allowed to resign.
I am not at all surprised that when the Lambeth Palace job came up, I did
look mad when I came to the interview, completely mad — I felt it.

KA: *Just one more question. What is your best memory from Lambeth
Palace Library?*

AS: Books coming back from the binders and looking glorious on the
shelves. And looking beautifully bound — they resonated glory. Yes, I was
very happy.

I have written a lot of books since, I'm never quite sure how many I've
written, but it certainly is twelve, and it could be fourteen. There were
some I did for Phaidon and I have written one or two books that I am
actually curiously proud of, but compared with Lambeth Palace? The sense
of achievement, restoring that place, I always feel, it's the one good thing I
have ever done in my life.

KA: *I think there are a lot of things you can be proud of, but as you say, it
is a great achievement.*

AS: It really was something that I am proud of.

KA: *Thank you very, very much.*

Giles Mandelbrote, Librarian and Archivist of Lambeth Palace Library, has kindly read this
article and suggested clarifications as well as amplifying notes.

1. This originally carried smoke away when Juxon's Great Hall was warmed in winter by a
    central hearth. Presumably the floor was then of stone.
2. For some background to this period in the history of Lambeth Palace Library (LPL),
    see Richard Palmer, *Catalogues, Shelf Marks and other Evidence for the History of the
    Collection 1785–1952* (Lambeth Palace Library Research Guide, 2017).
3. LPL [ZZ]1540.5 (formerly MS 1368) William Lily, *Institutio compendiaria totius
    grammaticae* (London, 1540), printed on vellum and illuminated, with the hand-coloured
    device of Edward VI. The binding, heavily repaired, retains its crimson silk.
4. Giles Mandelbrote notes: this is a puzzle. LPL [ZZ]1597.11 is the first edition of Francis Bacon,
    Essayes (London, 1597), bound in plain vellum. LPL [ZZ]1590.12 is Roger Bacon, *Libellus
    ... de retardandis senectutis* (Oxford, 1590), bound in vellum with gilt decoration. Both are

small octavos, but neither is 'tiny' and neither appears to be a presentation copy. Another possible candidate is LPL [ZZ]1617.22 Francis Bacon, *De sapientia veterum* (London, 1617), which is a duodecimo in a vellum binding with gilt decoration (slightly smaller, though still not tiny and not a presentation copy).

5. Judging from the entry in the Oxford *DNB*, Dr Fisher was a far nicer person than he seemed to be to us in the Library. In retirement, in Trent Rectory near Sherborne in Dorset, he played chess with the boys in the village, but at the same time he bombarded his successor, Dr Ramsey, who had been his pupil, with letters on how the diocese should be run. Dr Ramsey wrote forgivingly and with affection of him. Dr Fisher's sons and grandsons spoke to their pupils as he had spoken to us at Lambeth (private information). The Hon. Editor's grandfather, who was a physical training instructor at Repton School in the 1920s, would have been more inclined to agree with Ann's original opinion of Dr Fisher; he was shocked to see the injuries inflicted on boys by the headmaster's beatings.

6. Susan Hare became Librarian of the Goldsmiths' Company in 1958.

7. Rosemary Burdett succeeded Ann as Assistant Librarian at Lambeth Palace in 1955.

8. Julian Roberts was an Assistant Keeper at the British Museum Library from 1958 to 1974 before moving to the Bodleian Library as Keeper of Printed Books (1974–97) and later Deputy Librarian (1986–97).

9. Reg (Charles Reginald Dodwell, 1922–94) left Cambridge after a comparatively short time; he was Professor of History of Art at the University of Manchester and Director of the Whitworth Art Gallery from 1966 to 1989. See Richard Palmer, 'Reginald Dodwell, Lambeth Librarian 1953–1958', in *Medieval Art: Recent Perspectives. A Memorial Tribute to C.R. Dodwell*, ed. Gale Owen-Crocker and Timothy Graham (Manchester, 1998), pp. 224–30.

10. Reg shouted, 'Work harder, Ann!'.

11. In his memoir of Dodwell, Zarnecki recalled frequent travels together 'to study buildings, their decoration, museums and libraries' (*Proceedings of the British Academy*, 105 (Oxford, 2000), pp. 389–94).

12. Although Dodwell did not take up the post of Librarian at Trinity College, Cambridge, until 1958, his predecessor H. M. Adams was considering retirement in 1955 and Dodwell would have been approached in that year (information from Dr Nicolas Bell).

13. Anna Simoni (1916–2007), a native of Leipzig, came to Britain as a refugee in 1938. She joined the British Museum Library in 1950 and became head of the Dutch section.

14. The rock crystal skull, bought by the British Museum (Am1898.1) from Tiffany of New York in the 1890s, is of uncertain origin, but is now thought to be a nineteenth-century fake, or possibly an example of colonial Mexican art.

15. Archbishop Fisher's spiritual advice to Princess Elizabeth was collected in a small privately printed volume: *For the Queen: a little book of private devotions in preparation for Her Majesty's coronation* (1953; LPL KA113 1953 (**)).

16. The Laudian Room, to the north-west of the Great Hall, was later converted into the Library's staff room.

17. Claude Jenkins (1877–1959) was Lambeth Librarian from 1910 until 1952, but held the Librarianship in an increasingly honorary capacity from 1929, drawing no salary. He combined this with a chair in ecclesiastical history at King's College, London, and in 1934 he moved to Oxford as Regius Professor of Ecclesiastical History and a Canon of Christ Church. Renowned for both his learning and his eccentricity, he retained the title of Honorary Librarian and a place on the Library Advisory Committee despite the appointment of Reg Dodwell as his successor in 1952: see his biography by E. G. W. Bill in the *Oxford Dictionary of National Biography*.

18. Irene Churchill (1887–1961) worked at the Library from 1918 until 1952 as an assistant to Jenkins; in 1929 she was given the title Assistant Lambeth Librarian. Her account of the war years at Lambeth is in the Library records: LPL LR/J/10/9.

19. Ann must be referring to a permanent job which she applied for as her temporary contract was coming to an end.

20. Ann is referring to some 1,400 books, mostly printed in the sixteenth and seventeenth centuries and from the personal libraries of Archbishops Whitgift, Bancroft and Abbot, which were stolen from Lambeth Palace Library in 1974 and found only after the thief's death in 2011. See *Lambeth Palace Library Annual Review* for 2012, pp. 7–10.

21. Hans Hess (1907–75), a German refugee, was curator of York Art Gallery from 1948 until 1967, when he became reader in the History of Art at the University of Sussex.

XI. IAIN STUART BAIN

6 February 1934–20 April 2018

Iain Stuart Bain was a Vice-President of the London Topographical Society. He had been a member since the 1960s and was involved in the production of a number of the Society's publications. He was a Fellow of the Society of Antiquaries and of the Royal Society of Arts; President of the Printing Historical Society; President of the Bewick Society; President of the Private Libraries Association; Trustee of the Thomas Bewick Birthplace Trust; Trustee of the

Iain Bain in Venice, 2007.
Courtesy of Christina Anderson.

Wordsworth Trust; Freeman of the City of London; and Honorary Doctor of Letters of Civil Law, University of Northumbria. The proud representative of a family that was Scottish to the core, it was one of life's little ironies that Iain, through no fault of his own, was born in Edgbaston. His excuse was that his mother was en route to the north by the night train, hoping that Iain would be born in the land of his ancestors, only for Fate to ordain otherwise. In fact, his maternal grandfather was a physician in Birmingham and his mother's arrival (and indeed his own) was entirely expected. That said, much in Iain's early life defied expectation.

His early childhood was spent in Penang, in the old Straits Settlements, where his father, having been badly knocked about in the 1914–18 war, had been appointed Superintendent of Education. These were idyllic days but they were not to last. December 1941 found the Japanese invading forces sweeping south through Malaya towards Singapore. The Bain family were barely one step ahead and took passage for Australia on the overcrowded Blue Funnel steamship *Ulysses*, one of the last ships to leave Singapore, spending Christmas at sea before disembarking at Fremantle. However, Iain's father, having won the MC in the first war, stayed behind and joined the ill-fated civilian defence force but rid himself of the uniform on the fall of Singapore and presented himself as a civilian. Internment followed, which was no picnic but not the virtual death sentence of the Burma railway.

There followed three years of schooling near Perth for Iain before the family was reunited in Scotland and Iain departed for Fettes College. Tall for his age and mature beyond his years, Iain gained a reputation as academically and musically gifted. He also made his mark in the school's cadet force as the Company Sergeant Major and Pipe Major (piping, especially the Northumbrian small pipes, remained a passion for the rest of his life). But where he truly excelled was as an athlete, especially throwing the hammer, where strength, rhythm, balance and precision are vital; Iain became the AAA Junior Champion two years in a row and the Scottish Junior Champion in 1952. (As an adult, Iain went on to become a three-time Scottish champion, in 1956, 1957 and 1959.)

National Service found him commissioned as a first lieutenant into his father's old regiment, the Seaforth Highlanders, first in Germany and Egypt, followed by a short spell on active service with the Black Watch in Kenya during the height of the Mau Mau uprising. Despite his clear ability to lead, a soldiering life held little appeal; the dreaming spires of Oxford were far more enticing. In the autumn of 1955 he went up to St Edmund's Hall to read English, largely thanks to his hammer-throwing skills, for Teddy Hall looked favourably on undergraduates who excelled at 'manly sports'. Nor did Iain disappoint them, winning the British Universities title with a record throw and competing in the World University Games in Paris in 1957.

Balancing tutorials and training (and an active social life — Iain possessed an imposing presence and considerable charm) stretched his abilities to the limit. Alas, St Edmund Hall proved not to have the patience of a saint and sent him down at the end of his first year. He found employment in London selling advertising space on business calendars, modest employment, perhaps, but a first step towards developing a growing interest in print as a physical process and publishing in general. By the time he arrived at printers Unwins of Woking as a sales rep (later being promoted to production) he was fully conversant in all aspects of the 'black arts' and had founded a private press of his own. In October 1966 he joined the publishers Bodley Head as production manager, working with the legendary typographer and inspirational book designer John Ryder. One of their responsibilities was the fine printing subsidiary Nattali and Maurice. Here the die was unexpectedly cast. Iain first saw *Bewick to Dovaston: Letters 1824–1828* through the press (which sparked a lifelong interest in the work of the wood engraver Thomas Bewick, leading to numerous books and exhibitions and Iain's unrivalled pre-eminence in that field) and then produced a facsimile edition of Tallis's *London Street Views* for the London Topographical Society (the start of another lifelong involvement).

Although a congenial place of employment, Bodley Head paid poorly, all the more regrettably as Iain now had a young family. A chance remark by a friend, Leslie Parris, art historian and curator at the Tate, encouraged Iain to apply to the Gallery for the vacant position of publications manager. His application was successful and in 1972 Iain shouldered the responsibility for the production of all Tate Gallery publications, major and minor. Blessed with the capacity to 'power nap', Iain could work half the night on his own books and still be up with the lark the following morning, ready to devote all his energies to the Tate's demanding schedule. He remained at his post for twenty-two immensely rewarding years, only leaving (reluctantly) when he reached the statutory retirement age of sixty.

During his final years at Millbank he had introduced computerization into the publishing office and the knowledge he had gained thereby paid dividends in his so-called retirement. Having installed his own computer at home, he immediately set about designing a series of titles for the short-lived imprint of Bain and Williams. Following its dissolution he became a sought-after freelance designer with numerous books to his credit, all characterized by careful attention to detail, sympathetic typography and a sureness of touch rarely encountered in modern publishing. Whether designing a Christmas card for his personal use or the two elephant folios, *A Highgrove Florilegium* (2008) and *The Transylvania Florilegium* (2018) for the Prince of Wales, Iain was in his element. More than half a century on, strength, rhythm, balance and precision were yet abundantly in evidence.

Iain is survived by his wife Susan (née Forbes), daughters Kirsty Anderson and Nina Bain, son-in-law Alasdair Anderson and grandchildren Donald and Alice Anderson.

NIGEL TATTERSFIELD

XII. DENISE SILVESTER CARR

1 April 1939–6 September 2016

Denise was the eldest of seven sisters. Her father was the owner of a chain of cinemas throughout Ireland, and also worked for Warner Brothers. The family were comfortably off. She was educated as a boarder at the Ursuline Convent in Waterford where she did well, eventually graduating with honours. Her best friend at school was Rosemary Smith, who was later well known as a racing driver. After graduating Denise worked for an advertising company in Dublin before leaving for London in the 1960s. She lived in Hither Green until 1988 when she moved to Sidcup.

Her professional work was as a journalist and she developed an intense interest in the city's past and present. She was editor of the *London Weekly Diary of Social Events* for many years from 1975. She wrote more than 4,000 reviews for a range of magazines and was a member of the Critics' Circle; in 2014 she contributed to the history of the Circle, *A Critical Century*. Her books included *A Tribute to Nash, Architect and Planner*, published in 1975 to accompany an exhibition at Austin Reed on the 150th anniversary of Regent Street, and European Heritage Year; *Crime and Scandal : The Black Plaque Guide to London* (with Felix Barker, 1987; revised edition, 1995); *London*, with photographs by Andrew Butler (1991; paperback edition, 1993); *Greenwich: A History and Celebration of the Town* (2005). In retirement Denise worked for a tourist information bureau in Greenwich and was an active member of the Greenwich and Lewisham Historical Society.

Through her work she formed close friendships with the writer Felix Barker and the historian Peter Jackson, the London Topographical Society's former chairman. She helped with the preparation and editing of *The Pleasures of London*, published in 2008 as a celebration of their contributions to London history (London Topographical Society publication No. 167). As a member of the Society's Council Denise's journalistic experience meant she was able to help with publicizing our publications by press releases and articles in periodicals. Between 2003 and 2007 she edited the *Newsletter*.

A party was something which Denise loved. At such gatherings, she displayed her wicked sense of humour. One party in 1992 lasted for three

Ardmore, 16 June 2014, photograph by Vadrefjord. Ann Saunders was especially keen to include this view of the town where Denise was buried and that meant so much to her. *Creative Commons Attribution-Share Alike 4.0 Internationallicense.*

days when she organized a long weekend in Essen for six of us to go to the *London World City* exhibition at Villa Huegel (the catalogue by Celina Fox is worth searching out).

In spite of living in London for the greater part of her working life, Denise thought of herself as Irish, never English. Each summer she returned to Ardmore, whither her family also gathered. There she was reunited with her sisters and schoolfriends, and there she chose to be buried. The funeral service in St Declan's Church was conducted by the Reverend Father John Kiely; the organist was Dina Welshe. The arrangements for the burial were made by Messrs Leverton of London, the Royal Funeral Directors; Denise would have appreciated — and enjoyed — that. I only wish that I could have been there.

Denise left a bequest of £5,000 to the Society, which was used to support the publication of *London Parish Maps to 1900* by her friend Ralph Hyde.

ANN SAUNDERS WITH ROGER CLINE

Jeannette Hyde (Ralph's daughter) has added the following tribute:

It warmed my heart when I heard that Denise bequeathed £5,000 to the Society, which was used to publish dad's book *London Parish Maps to 1900* posthumously. I think he had been writing this book ever since I was a babe in arms. I'm now almost fifty-three! So you can see it took rather a long time to make it into print.

If dad knew Denise enabled his book to be published after his death I think he'd be chuckling in his grave while Denise would be scowling. They liked each other very much, hung out together and loved a good long conversation involving the words 'maps' and 'prints'. But there was always this funny tension between them — Denise scowling and telling him how stupid he was (usually criticizing his — to be fair — bad driving), and he laughing because she was so edgy and opinionated.

As a child growing up in the 1970s, I remember her as one one of the few women our family had close contact with at that time who had her own profession. She bypassed housewifery and children, and used her sharp wit, intelligence and pithy writing to have what was at that time more of an unconventional life. She was independent and had her own journalist career — which inspired me later to go into that profession. Women in journalism were still pretty trailblazing in the 1970s.

She was also the official and very public mistress of Felix Barker, the even cooler and wittier journalist at the now-defunct *Evening News*. He would drive his red MG sports car down the motorway, the lid off, a few drinks under his belt, to Benenden in Kent for weekends. We would meet him and his wife Anthea there when invited *en famille* — my dad, mum and siblings — to the fifteenth-century country house with own duck pond you could row a small boat on. Anthea would entertain my mum and me with wonderful stories, a fag and wine glass in each hand while something cooked in the oven, while Felix, Denise and dad would sit around the open fire (with more wine) in another room having endless maps and prints conversations. Everybody got on well and would have a jolly weekend. Even Anthea and Denise seemed to get on.

Denise was generous in giving me an insight into journalism. When I was a teen (I can't remember the exact age) she let me spend a day with her at *London Weekly Diary of Social Events* and showed me how to write tightly and get all the punctuation exact, to publishing quality standard. It was a good insight into what the craft of journalism looked like. She was a role model showing that a woman could be a journalist — and you didn't have to be a middle-aged man to be one.

She could be ratty at times. She would arrive at my parents' Christmas party each year with a bottle of wine. If I came near her trying to fill up her drink with sparkling Cava she would snap my head off. No bubbles, just wine for Denise! She would get annoyed if anyone failed to remember this detail. I think she was really sad when Felix died and missed his wit and company terribly. I think she'd be secretly delighted about her money helping dad's book see the light of day, but she'd be having a go at him for taking so long to write it and leaving this earth with the manuscript unfinished so his colleagues at the Society had to finish it!

XIII. STEPHEN CROAD

17 March 1946–12 September 2017

Ann Saunders drafted this obituary in 2017 shortly before her own death.

> Stephen Croad died on 12 September. He served on the London Topographical Society's Council for fifteen years.
>
> He was born on 17 March 1946, the only child of Lionel Croad, a golf-club groundsman, and Dorothy (née Stephens), a school secretary. He attended Dr Morgan's grammar school in Bridgwater where he forged a lifelong friendship with Paul Upton, as dedicated to cycling as Stephen was. The two boys explored the countryside around Taunton and, as they grew older, further afield. The young men were interested in buildings.
>
> Stephen gained a place in the Courtauld Institute of Art; he left in 1967 with an exceptionally strong Masters' degree. A year later, he joined the buildings section of the National Monuments Record in the Royal Commission on the Historical Monuments of England. Public access was given to its Reading Room, where a myriad of photographs were stored in red boxes. Stephen knew them all — his visual memory was, in my experience, unique.
>
> Little more than a year later he was involved in a road accident from which he was not expected to live but, owing to the care he received at Lodge Moor Hospital in Sheffield and his own determination, he returned to work in 1971 and was soon put in charge of the department.

Stephen Croad © Tony Rumsey.

I will add that Stephen was Head of the Architectural Record for the RCHME from 1981 to 1994. In those years he was often to be found among the red boxes in the Reading Room on the first floor of the Commission's headquarters at Fortress House, 23 Savile Row. He had a keen curiosity to help to the point of nosiness, wheeling (he always used a manual wheelchair) hither and thither in that long room to ask what it was you were investigating. He did indeed have an extraordinary visual memory.

More than once he looked at the pictures of the building I had out and said something along the lines of 'Oh that looks like X [obscure building elsewhere], have you looked at that?', which of course I hadn't. Until and unless face recognition software is architectural, computers can't match that.

Ann continued:

> In 1994 the department was moved to Swindon and Stephen took early retirement in 1996. He moved back to Taunton where he bought a flat on the ground floor in Bridge Street. He bought it before it was built, off the plan, and so was able to adapt it to his particular, personal needs. He soon became a familiar sight, steering his way along and across the streets of Taunton. When my husband and I came to Taunton to stay with Sheila Dodwell whom I knew well from Lambeth Palace days (see pp. 281–96) — we usually came at least twice a year — we all went out together for dinner — we could just squeeze the wheelchair up two steps and through the restaurant's door.
>
> He was the bravest, most cheerful, patient, and wisest man I have ever known. I weep, but not for him — he was in grievous pain every hour of the day and night — but for myself and all his other friends, Paul and Vivienne Upton in particular.

Stephen Croad co-wrote with Peter Fowler, then RCHME Secretary, an account of the first seventy-five years of the Commission for its *Annual Review* (1983–84), and a catalogue with an introduction by Sir John Summerson, *50 Years of the National Buildings Record* (1991), to accompany an exhibition at the V&A. He published books on the river, *London's Bridges* (1983) and *Liquid History: The Thames through Time* (2003), republished and retitled in 2016 as *The Thames through Time: Liquid History*. From 1994 to 2011 he was the assistant and book review editor of the *Transactions of the Ancient Monuments Society*, in which journal he published several articles. Later on, he was active with the Somerset Vernacular Buildings Research Group (Chairman 2005–07). He was a member of the Committee of the National Inventory of War Memorials (from 1989), a Fellow of the Royal Geographical Society (2000) and was appointed MBE in 1997. In his memory, the Ancient Monuments Society instituted the Stephen Croad Essay Prize in 2018.

PETER GUILLERY

XIV. RALPH HYDE

25 March 1939–2 June 2015

There was probably no one who knew more about the maps and views of London than Ralph Hyde, who died on 2 June 2015 at the age of seventy-six. His knowledge found expression in authoritative bibliographies, introductions and notes to facsimiles of the more important historic maps both printed but latterly also electronic. Equally importantly and just as lastingly, this knowledge underpinned the acquisitions that he made for the Guildhall Library where he was Keeper of Prints and Maps from 1975 to 1999. Undoubtedly, the item for which he will be best remembered is the 'Rhinebeck Panorama', an aerial watercolour view of London on four sheets, three metres in length, dating from about 1809, which he identified after it had been found in a house in New York State. He wrote a detailed commentary when a facsimile was published by the London Topographical Society in 1981. It is now owned by the Museum of London.

Though born in the London suburb of Uxbridge, Ralph grew up in Somerset and only returned to London for military service with the RAF and then to train as a librarian — initially at Marylebone Library. Here he worked with people such as Ann Saunders and Peter Clayton, who went on to distinguish themselves in the worlds of scholarship, libraries and museums. While at Marylebone he met and married his wife Ruth. It was through her that his interest in maps and carto-bibliography may have been awakened: at the time Ruth was working as secretary to R. V. Tooley, at Francis Edwards, around the corner from the Library in Marylebone High Street. Tooley was the effective founder of the British antiquarian map trade

Ralph and colleagues in the Guildhall Library in the 1990s. On the computer screen can be seen the home page of *Collage* (now the *London Picture Archive*), the image database that Ralph was rightly proud to have created. Courtesy of Jeannette Hyde.

307

and a distinguished carto-bibliographer in his own right. Tony Campbell, who was also working at Francis Edwards at the time, remembers that Ralph was particularly interested in the bibliography section there, while in his turn Ralph had happy memories of its antiquated lift in which part of his courtship was conducted!

Ralph joined the Guildhall Library as an Assistant Librarian in 1965, eventually working under James Howgego, whom he was to succeed in 1975. Under the supervision of Ida Darlington, with whom Howgego had compiled the first edition of the published bibliography of maps of London up to 1850, he wrote a thesis for the Fellowship of the Library Association, on the printed maps of London from 1851 to 1900. He received a mark of distinction on completion in 1971. Much of the typing of the text was, his family recalled, done in the early hours before he went to work, on an ancient typewriter at the foot of the matrimonial bed. It was published as *Printed Maps of Victorian London* in 1974 and remains the standard work on the subject.

Over the following decades, Ralph's enthusiasm led him down several other cartographic paths. He searched out and catalogued the ward and parish maps of London. The catalogue of the ward maps was published by the London Topographical Society in 1999. The catalogue of parish maps had to wait. It was only in 2015 that Ralph revived the project, but decided to hand over its revision and completion to others. A meeting between Ralph, Simon Morris and myself just two weeks before his death paved the way to the publication of the catalogue by the London Topographical Society in 2020. Though the final product owes much to the perseverance and enthusiasm of Simon Morris, Laurence Worms and a team of eager volunteers, and many maps have been discovered (and a few lost) in the intervening years, the core of the catalogue represents Ralph's hard work.

From the 1970s, Ralph, in collaboration with Guildhall Library, Harry Margary and the London Topographical Society, collectively and separately, also contributed scholarly introductions and notes to facsimiles of the great seventeenth-century maps of London by Ogilby and Morgan and to the *A to Z of Victorian London* (1987). In retirement Ralph continued this type of work, providing an introduction to the *A–Z of Charles II's London 1682* (2013) and, in electronic form, introductions to the digital versions of Stanford's, the Greenwoods' and Horwood's maps of London (2002, 2005, 2006) for Motco.

From the late 1970s, however, Ralph's primary passions had moved on to panoramas and optical toys: phenomena that reached their apogee in the early nineteenth century and ranged from enormous painted panoramas in purpose-made buildings to small paper peepshows and to playing cards. He became a world authority on panoramas, and was responsible for two major exhibitions on them: *Gilded Scenes and Shining Prospects. Panoramic View of British Towns 1575–1900* (Yale Center for British Art,

New Haven, Connecticut, 1985) and the wider-reaching *Panoramania: The Art and Entertainment of the 'All-embracing' View* (1988), an exhibition in the Barbican Art Gallery in London (1988–89), which introduced the phenomenon to the general public. Both exhibitions were accompanied by authoritative catalogues written entirely by him. A stream of scholarly articles, particularly in *Print Quarterly*, and introductions to facsimiles appeared in the same years. All were distinguished by meticulous, in-depth research. *Paper Peepshows*: *The Collection of Jacqueline and Jonathan Gestetner* was published in May 2015, just weeks before Ralph's death. The fruit of several years' work, the book won widespread acclaim and has become yet another standard work. At the time of his death Ralph was working on a biographical dictionary of panoramists.

While his energies were focused on panoramas, and he continued to work on maps of London, Ralph also found time to collaborate with Felix Barker on *London As It Might Have Been* (1982; reprint 1995), a book on plans and elevations of proposed London buildings and developments that had never got off the drawing board. He also selected and wrote accompanying texts to H. E. Tidmarsh's evocative watercolours of the streets of late nineteenth-century London (1992), *A Prospect of Britain: The Town Panoramas of Samuel and Nathaniel Buck* (1994) and, another London Topographical Society publication, *London Displayed: Headpieces from the Stationers' Almanacks* (2010).

Ralph's activities were not confined to researching and writing. He acted as a consultant to several exhibitions, notably *Sehsucht. Das Panorama als Massenunterhaltung des 19. Jahrhunderts* (Bonn, 1993) and was a very active member of the councils of several societies in the fields in which he was interested — not only the London Topographical Society, on which he served from 1977 until his death, but also the Ephemera Society and particularly the International Panorama Council.

Ruth Hyde predeceased her husband by several years. He is survived by two daughters, a son and seven grandchildren.

That Ralph achieved so much was down to hard work but it was spurred on by the unquenchable and boyish enthusiasm that he displayed to the last. There was a *joie de vivre*, modesty and humour about him that made it rewarding to know and to work with him. There was also an empathy, kindness and human understanding that provided comfort to others at times of need. As the numbers who attended Ralph's funeral attested, he had many friends and is sorely missed.

PETER BARBER

Adapted from the obituary in *Imago Mundi: The International Journal for the History of Cartography*, vol. 68, issue 1 (2016), pp. 99–100, with permission of Taylor & Francis. doi: 10.1080/03085694.2016.1107388

XV. STEPHEN POWYS MARKS

24 April 1932–8 June 2020

Stephen Powys Marks, Vice President of the London Topographical Society since 1989, died aged eighty-eight in June 2020. He became involved with the Society from the 1960s and he did much to establish the Society in the form it is today. He was a highly efficient Secretary from 1966 to 1983, encouraging new members (including our Treasurer Roger Cline), attracting them by the sale of older LTS material, and

Stephen Marks, 2019. © Dawn Collins.

organizing satisfactory storage of the Society's publications. He established the *Newsletter* in 1975 — the first issue (called the preliminary issue, now no. 00 on our website), announced the appointment of Ann Saunders as Editor of the Society's publications — and he continued as the Newsletter Editor until 1989. The early *Newsletters* are all available on the Society's website, as is his history of the Society, published in volume 24 of the *Record* (1980). He lived in Camberwell Grove, and was very active in the Camberwell Society, editing a facsimile reprint of Blanch's *History of Camberwell* in 1976. He became a Fellow of the Society of Antiquaries in 1979. His own notable collection of London topographical material is now held by Texas A & M University. After he moved with his family to Somerset in 1978 he concerned himself with local conservation and green issues and also with Powys family history, acting as publication manager of the Powys Society that promotes the appreciation and enjoyment of the writings of John Cowper, Theodore (T. F.) and Llewelyn Powys.

Historical topography was only one aspect of his activities. His grandfather was the architect Albert Powys, secretary to the Society for the Protection of Ancient Buildings; his mother trained as an architect under Clough Williams Ellis, and, following the family tradition, Stephen trained at the Bartlett School of Architecture, developing a strong interest in conservation. In the 1980s, when he was a much-respected planning inspector, his most famous case was the celebrated inquiry into Lord Palumbo's proposal for a building on Mansion House Square by the modernist architect Mies van der Rohe; his recommendation of refusal was accepted by the government. Earlier, he was an influential Conservation officer for Westminster City Council and was responsible for many of the reports on the newly formed conservation areas created after the Civic Amenities Act. This marked the shift from the post-war belief in wholescale rebuilding to the desire to preserve the best of the past. One outcome was the formation of ASCHB (Association for Studies in the Conservation of Historic Buildings) whose *Transactions* Stephen edited from its inception in 1976.

BRIDGET CHERRY

Patrick Frazer, Hon. Secretary of the Society from 1983 to 2011, added the following memories of working with Stephen:

Stephen Marks was one of the four heroes of the Society who put it back on its feet after the death of Marjorie Honeybourne at the end of 1974. She had combined the roles of Editor, Treasurer, Membership Secretary and Publications Secretary, but left its affairs in some confusion. Stephen, together with Ann Saunders as Hon Editor, Peter Jackson as Chairman and Anthony Cooper as Hon Treasurer, got to grips with the problem.

Stephen launched the *Newsletter* the following February, as a way of keeping closer contact with members, reporting that he and Anthony Cooper had been hard at work on the Society's accounts and management, and had consolidated the stock of publications in a single safe location. In addition, Stephen initiated a publicity campaign to recruit more members and increase sales of publications.

It worked. I joined on the strength of a most attractive flyer for Milne's Land Use Map, picked up in a local library. Membership numbers increased from just over 400 when Marjorie Honeybourne died to nearly 700 ten years later when Anthony Cooper was the first of the officers to retire.

Attending my first AGM in 1978, I was the only volunteer to take over the vacant role of the Publications Secretary. Stephen initiated me in the mysteries of the job, essentially packing and sending out publications, which were stored in a basement at the Bishopsgate Institute.

Stephen was the ideal Hon. Secretary, calm, good-humoured, conscientious and precise. Meetings ran smoothly and the minutes were always accurate and up to date. For the *Newsletter*, he did the typesetting and pasted it up ready for printing. He was always active in running the AGMs, which were attended by ever-increasing numbers of satisfied members. When I once complained that I had no time to enjoy them, he happily pointed out that was not why we were there.

Eventually Stephen relinquished his direct involvement with the Society, first after seventeen years as secretary in 1983, then after fourteen years as Newsletter Editor in 1989.

XVI. ANN SAUNDERS, MBE, PhD, FSA

23 May 1930–13 February 2019

Ann Saunders was a remarkable woman who made her mark in many fields but, perhaps, the London Topographical Society was her lode star.

Ann was born on 23 May 1930, the daughter and first child of George Cox-Johnson and his much-younger wife Joan Loreille Clowser. Her father was a company director and her mother a teacher. They lived in St John's Wood at 20 Wellington Road near Lord's Cricket ground but after her father died in 1941, the family moved to Hampstead Garden Suburb which was to be Ann's home, off and on, for the rest of her life. She went to Henrietta Barnet School, then to Queen's College, Harley Street, followed by a History degree at University College.

Ann Saunders at the Regent's Park Villas exhibition at Bedford College explaining the model of the Park, 1981.

Her first job in 1951 was as an assistant in the City of York Art Gallery, followed, in 1952, by a post as a librarian at Lambeth Palace where she helped to excavate for books which had landed in the cellars when the Library was bombed. This was followed by two years as an assistant keeper in the Library of the British Museum. [Ann's personal recollections of her time in these early jobs can be found on pp. 283–98 of this volume of the *Record.*] Then in 1956 she was appointed, at the remarkably young age of twenty-six, as the archivist to Marylebone Borough Council, where she remained for the next seven years. Here she made her mark by cataloguing the remarkable Ashbridge Collection on the history of St Marylebone, as well as hand lists and guides to other collections in the Library. But she had other interests: in June 1960 she married Bruce Saunders, a budding engineer, at Hampstead Parish Church and she also embarked on research for a doctorate at Leicester University under the supervision of the notable local historian, H. P. R. Finberg. She left Marylebone in 1963, perhaps for family reasons. Her son Matthew was born in 1964 and Katherine, three years later. But Ann was always able to do many things at once and in 1965 she was awarded her doctorate on the subject of the Manor of Tyburn and the Regent's Park over a remarkably long period, from 1086 to 1965.

From this date until the end of her long life Ann was an energetic, resourceful, compassionate and encouraging editor and scholar. She continued to produce scholarly books and articles on many aspects of the history of London and her remarkable guide to the *Art and Architecture of London*, published in 1984, was a tour de force and went into three editions. The bibliography which is attached to this obituary testifies to

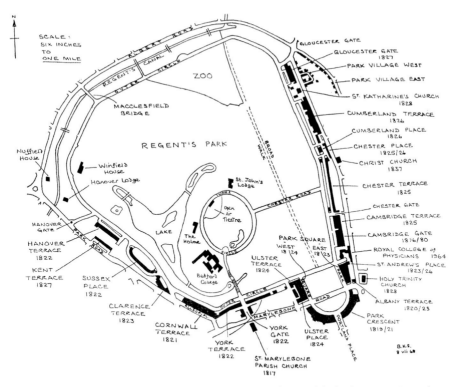

Plan of Regent's Park in 1968 by Bruce Saunders first published in Ann Saunders, *Regent's Park: A Study of the Development of the Area from 1086 to the Present Day* (Newton Abbot, 1969).

the extent of her interests and scholarship ranging from 'popular' books to detailed examinations of particular places or images. And alongside her own research and writing, Ann taught American students at Richmond College where she took them on bracing walks around the City of London and fed them on home-made cakes back in the Garden Suburb. But perhaps Ann's many talents found their fullest expression in her work as an editor: in particular, shaping and encouraging the work of younger scholars. She took on the editorship of the Journal of the Costume Society in 1967 (the tributes to Ann paid by members of that Society can be found in *Costume*, volumes 44 and 53) and ran that in parallel with her work for the London Topographical Society, and she managed to make both societies believe that they were the more important!

When Marjorie Honeybourne died in 1974 Ann took over as the Honorary Editor of the LTS and only resigned in 2015 when ill health and her lack of familiarity with computer technology made it impossible for her to continue. It was one of the quirks of Ann's personality that she resolutely refused to master typing or to embrace the advantages of computers, perhaps because when she began work as a woman in the early 1950s she was determined not to be considered as a typist. As Honorary Editor of the LTS she oversaw the publication of over forty annual volumes and eight volumes of the Society's quinquennial *Record*. The edited annual volumes ranged in date from *The London Surveys of Ralph Treswell* in the early seventeenth century to Cecil Brown's drawings of the bombed city in 1945. And it was Ann who realized the potential of the *A–Z of Elizabethan London* based on the 'Agas' map, to be followed by six more A–Zs volumes covering different periods up to the *A–Z of Edwardian London*. From my own experience I know that Ann's editorial style was creative, engaged, challenging and constructive. She liked to make things happen and rose to the challenges posed by inexperienced authors or stubborn printers. She enjoyed engaging with authors, discussing their work and helping to improve it and to see it published. During her time as the Honorary Editor the LTS took on new life: the number of members grew from just under 500 in 1972 to over 1,000 in 2015, and they valued the contacts and friendships which Ann fostered and encouraged. The Annual General Meeting became a notable event in the London calendar: for weeks in advance Ann would organize local members (who could not escape) to bring cakes and other goodies to the festival tea which was always sumptuous and a telling testimony to Ann's persuasive skills. In this way the LTS developed as a forum for scholarly friendship.

It is impossible to do justice to Ann's many achievements in a single obituary: she was a person with many different facets and a range of talents from cartography to cooking. But her life had its difficulties and sadness: her daughter Katherine died tragically in 1985 and in the last years of her life

Ann had physical setbacks which made travelling difficult and so her world began to shrink. But she and Bruce remained close and companionable and he cared for her at home until she died. Hers was a rich life, lived to the full, in which she wove together her scholarship, her love for her family and her desire to make things happen for other people. Ann Saunders was, in every way, a life enhancer: she used her considerable gifts and talents to help others to be happy and successful. I shall end this tribute with an anecdote (one of the many generated by Ann) which I learned only recently. When Ann published her book on Regent's Park in 1969 she decided to publicize it by placing leaflets under the windscreen wipers of every car parked in the Inner Circle. It was this combination of imagination and energy that made Ann so exceptional.

CAROLINE BARRON

BIBLIOGRAPHY OF PUBLISHED WORK

BOOKS

Handlist to the Ashbridge Collection on the History and Topography of Saint Marylebone (London, 1959).

John Bacon R.A. 1740–1799 (London, 1961).

Handlist of Painters, Sculptors & Architects Associated with St. Marylebone, 1760–1960 (London, 1963).

The King's England Series: London North of the Thames Except the City and Westminster, by Arthur Mee (full revision; London 1972).

The King's England Series: London, the City and Westminster, by Arthur Mee (full revision; London 1975).

Regent's Park: A Study of the Development of the Area from 1086 to the Present Day (Newton Abbot, 1969; revised edn, London, 1981).

The Regent's Park Villas (London, 1981).

St Martin in the Fields: A Short History and Guide (London, 1990).

The Art and Architecture of London: An Illustrated Guide (Oxford, 1984; 2nd edn, 1988; 3rd edn, 1992).

The Royal Exchange (London, 1991).

St Paul's: The Story of the Cathedral (London, 2001).

The History of the Merchant Taylors' Company (with Matthew Davies; Leeds, 2004).

Historic Views of London: Photographs from the Collection of B. E. C. Howarth-Loomes (Swindon, 2008).

St Paul's Cathedral: 1400 Years at the Heart of London (London, 2012).

ARTICLES, ESSAYS AND CONTRIBUTIONS TO VOLUMES

'Lambeth Palace Library, 1610–1664', *Transactions of the Cambridge Bibliographical Society*, 2 (1955), pp. 105–26.

'Gentlemen's Agreement', *Burlington Magazine*, 101 (1959), pp. 236–42.

'The Regent's Park', *Geographical Magazine*, 33.12 (1961), pp. 664–75.

Diary of William Tayler, Footman, 1837, ed. by Dorothy Wise (London 1962; 2nd edn, 1998).

'Tilbury's: The First Storage Warehouse', *Archives*, 5 (1962), pp. 217–23.

'A Gentleman's Servant's Journal', *History Today*, 13 (1963), pp. 102–07.

'Marylebone Park', *Transactions of the London and Middlesex Archaeological Society*, 21 (1968), 178–88.

'The Four Seasons by Wenceslas Hollar' (topographical notes following an introduction by J. L. Nevinson), *Costume Society* (1979).

'Samuel Johnson's Funeral Monument', *Journal of the Royal Society of Arts*, 133 (1985), pp. 632–36.

'Westminster Hall: A Sixteenth Century Drawing?', *London Journal*, 12.1 (1986), pp. 29–35 (see p. 7 of this volume, Fig. 3).

'Forbes House, Halkin Street, SW1', *London Topographical Record*, 27 (1995), pp. 281–90.

'Lord Harley and his Friends', *Westminster History Review*, 1 (1997), pp. 27–32.

'The Stationers' Hall', in *The Stationers' Company and the Book Trade 1550–1990*, ed. by Robin Myers and Michael Harris (1997).

'Reconstructing London: Sir Thomas Gresham in Bishopsgate', in *Sir Thomas Gresham and Gresham College*, ed. by Francis Ames-Lewis (Farnham, 1999).

'St Paul's in Wartime' (with Noel Mander) in *London Topographical Record*, 28 (2001), pp. 187–90.

'"A Cloke Not Made so Orderly": The Sixteenth-Century Minutes of the Merchant Taylors' Company', *The Ricardian*, 13 (2003), pp. 415–19.

'A Day in the Life of a Merchant Taylor', in *City Merchants and the Arts, 1670–1720*, ed. by Mireille Galinou (Wetherby, 2004).

'The Post-Reformation Monuments of St Paul's' (with Roger Bowdler) in *St Paul's: The Cathedral Church of London 604–2004*, ed. by Derek Keene, R. Arthur Burns and Andrew Saint (New Haven and London, 2004), pp. 269–92.

'Temple Bar', *Goldsmiths' Review* (2005), pp. 14–15.

'Arches of Triumph: James VI and I's (Unfortunate) Ceremonial Entry in the City of London, 1604', *London Topographical Record*, 31 (2015), pp. 79–105.

'Willan's Farm — In Memoriam', *London Topographical Record*, 31 (2015), pp. 151–53.

EDITED VOLUMES IN ADDITION TO THOSE PUBLISHED BY THE LONDON
TOPOGRAPHICAL SOCIETY

*La Belle Epoque: Costume 1890–1914: Proceedings of the First Annual Conference
of the Costume Society* (1968).

*High Victorian Costume: 1860–90: Proceedings of the Second Annual Conference
of the Costume Society* (1969).

Ian Doolittle with an introduction by Peter Nailor, *The Mercers' Company 1579–
1959* (London, 1994).

Emma Bashforth, Daniel Beagles and Sally Robbins (ed. with Henry S. Cobb),
Handlist of the Hampstead Garden Suburb Archive: A User's Guide (London,
2001)

THESIS

'The Manor of Tyburn and the Regent's Park, 1086–1965' (doctoral thesis,
University of Leicester, 1965).

XVII. ELSPETH VEALE

6 May 1916–2 April 2015

Elspeth Veale who died in April 2015 was born on 6 May 1916 in the middle of the Great War. Her father was a Methodist minister and she and her sister went to Newland High School in Hull which she remembered with affection. From there she went on to King's College London to read history and was awarded her BA in 1937. After a year's training course Elspeth taught in girls' grammar schools in St Albans and West Yorkshire but returned to London in 1946 when she was appointed to a post at the Skinners' Company's School for Girls in Stamford Hill.

This appointment was significant in determining Elspeth's later career because she became interested in the Skinners' Company, taught the girls about medieval skinners and began herself to explore the rich archive of the Skinners' Company kept at their hall. Encouraged by the award of a one-year research fellowship at the Institute of Historical Research in 1950, Elspeth developed her research on the English fur trade in the medieval period into a doctorate which she was awarded by London University in 1953. Her ground-breaking book on this topic (published by the Oxford University Press) followed in 1971. Elspeth was one of the first historians to write a company history which looked not simply at the governing structures and

Elspeth Veale holding a copy of her collection of essays, *Wimbledon's Belvedere Estate*, published in 2012.

physical environs of the company but rather at the ways in which medieval skinners actually worked in importing, preparing and stitching the furs. Her focus was on the craft and not the company, but in spite of this the company acknowledged her scholarship, paid her fee when she took up the Freedom of the City, escorted Elspeth to the Guildhall and gave her, she recalled, 'a splendid lunch'.

In 1953 Elspeth had taken up a post at City of London School for Girls where she is remembered fondly by those she taught — not only for her historical insights but also for her stylish outfits in bright colours. Elspeth's final move was to Goldsmiths College, University of London, where she became, in due course, the Dean of the School of Humanities. She continued with her scholarly publications, which included an Historical Association pamphlet on *Teaching the History of London*. She always maintained her interest in London history and in dress and clothing, although after her retirement in 1977 she extended her scholarly work to include studies on the history of Wimbledon where she lived.

Elspeth was a great supporter of London history, not only by her excellent scholarly publications, but by serving as Treasurer of the London Record Society for many years. She also unobtrusively subsidised a number of London research activities. She was a regular attender at the medieval London seminars at the Institute of Historical Research. She joined the London Topographical Society in 1957, and in 1980 played an important part in organising the Society's 80th anniversary celebrations. In the same year she was elected to the Council. She was appointed Vice President in 1991 and made an honorary member in 2008. Her intellectual powers remained sharp until the end of her life and she never lapsed into sentimentality. On occasion she could be bracing, or forthright, but she was always kind, encouraged younger scholars and was willing to share her knowledge, and to learn from them. Elspeth had a wide circle of friends and a cluster of cousins and godchildren many of whom spoke with warmth and humour about their friendships with her at the service held to celebrate her life. The study of medieval London history and medieval London historians have benefited immeasurably from Elspeth's purposeful scholarship and supportive friendship. She was an admirable scholar and an admirable person.

CAROLINE BARRON

XVIII. DAVID WEBB

14 May 1939–30 December 2017

When Rachel Lichtenstein needed to know where to start researching her book on Spitalfields mystic David Rodinsky, she asked Professor Bill Fishman. 'Call at the Bishopsgate Institute', he said, 'and ask for David Webb'. This she did and, as recorded in her book, David Webb gave her not only a file of cuttings, but also regaled her with anecdotes and a great deal more on what she was looking for.[1] This is the David we recall — a man who combined learning with enthusiasm, and who was ever willing to assist with some untapped source, unpublished illustration or tangential anecdote on a London-related topic.

David was born in 1939 in Worcester Park, a new 1930s suburb between Epsom and Wimbledon. He was educated at Kingston Grammar School and from there won a County Major Scholarship to Oxford University where he entered what was then St Catherine's Society, later St Catherine's College. Here he studied French and Spanish, graduating in 1961 with a degree in modern languages. He was in good company at the University; preserved among his papers at the Bishopsgate Institute is the menu for an Oxford Old Kingstonians dinner that he attended in November 1960, signed by him and nineteen others who had come from his old school to study at Oxford.

On graduation he went into librarianship and was appointed a Library Assistant at City of Westminster Libraries. Five years later he attained the important position of Reference Librarian at the Bishopsgate Institute. A unique London foundation, the Institute was formed in 1895 from an amalgamation of parochial charities and occupies a striking Art Nouveau building on Bishopsgate. It houses a notable collection of London material ranging from history and topography to a large archive of early London socialism, including the manuscript minutes of the First Internationale.[2] David was the Institute's first Reference Librarian; before him there had been a Librarian to the Institute, the most prominent being Charles Goss (from 1897 to 1941) who had built up the Library's London collection. The position was split in 1966 when the lending library was passed to the City of London, with the Institute retaining the reference library and archival collections.

David held this post from 1966 until his retirement thirty-three years later in 1999. During this period he was instrumental in increasing and consolidating the Institute's London collections, notable additions being the archives of London historian Raphael Samuel and of the London Cooperative Society. The acknowledgements he received from authors of books as diverse as histories of London, of French Marxism and of Trade

Union legislation show how his knowledge and commitment extended to all of the Institute's collections.[3]

David was especially interested in London history. Having qualified as an Associate of the Library Association in 1967, he was elected a Fellow three years later with a thesis on 'Guide Books to London before 1900: A History and Bibliography'. Drawing on the Institute's large collection of London material, this topic reflected David's interests in local history and bibliography; guidebooks were one of David's enduring interests, and he wrote on them in both the *London Journal* and the *London Topographical Record*.[4]

David's association with the Society as a member and, later, a member of the Council, began around 1975 when the Council started meeting at the Institute. Prior to that the Institute had agreed to house the Society's stock of publications, an arrangement that lasted from 1961 to after his retirement. David enabled the Society to benefit from the Institute's holdings, providing the original for a number of publications, including Mylne's *Map of the Geology and Contours of London* (publication No. 146, 1993) and

David Webb at the Bishopsgate Institute in 1967.

Lockie's *Topography of London* (publication No. 148, 1994), for which he additionally wrote the introduction.

In addition to his involvement with the Society David was also Honorary Librarian of, and later a Vice President of, the London and Middlesex Archaeological Society, and he was Vice President of the East of London Family History Society. A further interest was the photographers and photographic studios of Victorian London; some of his research is available on the photoLondon.org website, while much further unpublished material is contained in his papers held at the Bishopsgate Institute.[5]

Alongside these achievements sit countless acts of courtesy, consideration and generosity extended to thousands of enquirers who called at the Library seeking his assistance on a gamut of subjects, and it is for this that David will principally be remembered. The last words belong to Raphael Samuel: 'Mr Webb, the Chief Librarian, knows his collection very well indeed, and is available for consultation at the counter at all times. You would be well advised to introduce yourself when you arrive, and tell him what you are looking for, because apart from helping you to find it he will probably have suggestions of his own'.[6]

SIMON MORRIS

1. Rachel Lichtenstein and Iain Sinclair, *Rodinsky's Room* (London, 1999).
2. Raphael Samuel, 'The Bishopsgate Institute', in *History Workshop*, 5 (Spring 1978), pp. 163–72.
3. John Marriott, *Beyond the Tower — A History of East London* (New Haven and London, 2011); Leslie Derfler, *Paul Lafargue and the Founding of French Marxism 1842–1882* (Cambridge, Mass., and London, 1991); Mark Curthoys, *Governments, Labour and the Law in Mid-Victorian Britain* (Oxford, 2004).
4. David Webb, 'For Inns a Hint, for Routes a Chart: The Nineteenth-Century London Guide Book', in *London Journal*, 6 (1980), pp. 207–14; David Webb, 'Guide Books to London before 1800: A Survey', in *London Topographical Record*, 26, London Topographical Society publication No. 141 (1990).
5. David Webb, 'The Photographic Studios of Regent Street 1850–1875', in *London Topographical Record*, 28, London Topographical Society publication No. 57 (2001).
6. Samuel, 'The Bishopsgate Institute'.

LONDON TOPOGRAPHICAL SOCIETY

The London Topographical Society, founded as the Topographical Society of London in 1880, is mainly a publishing society and is registered as a charity (no. 271590). Its purpose is to make available facsimiles of maps, plans and views illustrating the history and topography of London, and to publish research.

Over the years, the Society has produced facsimiles of most of the important large-scale maps of London, as well as plans of many individual parishes and buildings. Reproductions of views include panoramas by Wyngaerde, Visscher, Hollar, Kip, Barker, Girtin, Lawrence Wright, the Rhinebeck Panorama, and sets of drawings by E. W. Cooke, William Capon, Philip Norman and Sir George Scharf.

The Society has published thirty-two volumes of its journal, the *London Topographical Record*, which contains articles relating to London topography. There are also seven volumes in the *A–Z of London* series, covering *Elizabethan, Restoration, Charles II, Georgian, Regency, Victorian* and *Edwardian London*. Other books include major works on *Mercers' Hall, Royal Exchange, Somerset House, John Tallis's London Street Views, The Pleasures of London, London Bomb Damage Maps* and *London Bridge and its Houses*.

The annual subscription, currently £20 in the UK and £30 abroad (reduced to £18 and £28 respectively for members paying by standing order), entitles members to receive one or more publications for the year. Members can obtain earlier publications at a preferential rate. A newsletter is issued twice a year.

Further information about the Society, its Council and its publications can be found online at www.londontopsoc.org.

LONDON TOPOGRAPHICAL SOCIETY

Officers and Members of the Council, 31 December 2020

Patron	His Royal Highness the Duke of Edinburgh, KG, KT
Vice-Presidents	Iain Bain, FSA (died 2018)
	Ann Saunders, MBE, PhD, FSA (died 2019)
	Stephen Marks, MA, FSA, RIBA (died 2020)
Chairman	Penelope Hunting, PhD, FSA
Hon. Treasurer	Roger Cline, MA, LLB, FSA
Hon. Editor	Ann Saunders, MBE, PhD, FSA (until 2015)
	Sheila O'Connell, BA, FSA (from 2016)
Hon. Newsletter Editor	Bridget Cherry, OBE, BA, FSA, Hon FRIBA
Hon. Publications Secretary	Simon Morris, MA, PhD, FRGS
Hon. Secretary	Mike Wicksteed
Hon. Membership Secretary	John Bowman, JP, MA, PhD, MCLIP, FSA
Hon. Auditor	Hugh Cleaver, MA, ACA
Members of Council	Peter Barber, OBE, MA, FSA, FRHistS
	Caroline Barron, OBE, PhD, FSA
	(from 2017)
	Dorian Gerhold, MA, DLitt, FSA, FRHistS
	(from 2016)
	Peter Guillery, BA, FRHistS (from 2016)
	Robin Michaelson, MA, FIA (until 2018)
	Michael Port, MA, BLitt, FSA (until 2017)
	Anne Ramon, BA, FRGS (from 2019)
	Peter Ross, MA, PhD, DipLib, MCLIP
	Denise Silvester Carr (until 2016)
	Andrew Thorp, BA, ACG (2017–20)
	Geoffrey Tyack, MA, MLitt, PhD, FSA, FRHistS (from 2016)
	David Webb, MA, FCLIP (until 2016)
	Rosemary Weinstein, BA, PhD, FSA, FSA(Scot)
	Laurence Worms, FRBS

RULES

I.   The London Topographical Society is a publishing Society: its purpose is to assist the study and appreciation of London's history and topography by making available facsimiles of maps, plans and views and by publishing research.

II.   The affairs of the Society shall be conducted by a Council, consisting of a Chairman, Hon. Treasurer, Hon. Secretary, and not more than twenty-one elected Members of the Society.

III.   The Subscription shall be not less than one guinea, payable in advance on the 1st January.

IV.   The names of those wishing to become Members shall be submitted to the Council for approval.

V.   There shall be each year a General Meeting of the Society, at which the Council elected for the preceding year shall report upon the work of the Society during that year.

VI.   At each Annual Meeting all the members of the Council retire from office and shall be eligible for re-election.

VII.   No Member whose subscription for the preceding year remains unpaid shall be eligible for election to the Council.

VIII.   A certified Cash Statement shall be issued to all Members with the Annual Report of the Council.

IX.   The Council shall have power to fill up occasional vacancies in their number during the year, and to elect any Member of the Society to serve on any Committee or Sub-Committee of the Council.

X.   A publication of the Society shall be issued each year to all members whose subscriptions have been paid. No Member whose subscription is in arrears shall be entitled to receive such publication. Occasional additional publications may be issued at a reduced rate to paid-up Members.

XI.   No alteration shall be made in these Rules except at an Annual General Meeting, or at a Special General Meeting called upon the requisition of at least five Members. One month's previous notice of the change to be proposed shall be given in writing to the Secretary, and the alteration proposed must be approved by at least three-fourths of the Members present at such Meeting.

London Topographical Society

REPORT FOR THE YEARS 2015–2020

The Council's annual reports were carried in the May *Newsletter* each year along with the Accounts. During the period of this Report the Society issued eight publications, recorded as the final eight items in the List of Publications on page 338. The *Newsletter* continued to be published twice a year in May and November and paper copies are sent to members, and appear subsequently on the Society's website.

In July 2019 a new version of the Society's website (www.londontopsoc. org) was launched with useful information for members and others. Publications, including those for sale, are listed. Access is available, through the Hathi Trust Digital Library, to digitized versions of the *London Topographical Record* from 1898 to volume XXIX published in 2006. In addition, all copies of the *Newsletter* may be read, from the first edition published in 1975 up to the latest.

As of 31 December 2020, there were 1,351 paid up and 2 honorary members compared with 1,221 paid up and five honorary members at the time of the last Report. The Society's annual subscription has remained at £20 for UK members since 1992 (reduced to £18 for those paying by standing order) and at £30 for overseas members, unchanged since 2012 (reduced to £28 for those paying by standing order). Although the Society has made a 7% net deficit over the period in review, this has been amply covered by its reserves and during the period the Society has continued to assist organizations with financial grants for London-related projects with a topographical focus.

2015:   £11,356 to the Guildhall Library for conservation of the library's set of John Tallis's *London Street Views 1838–40* in the original coloured wrappers, and £10,000 to the British Film Institute (BFI), the first of three annual grants for the digitization and cataloguing of short historical films about London.

2016:   the second annual grant of £10,000 to the BFI, and £1,756 to the London Metropolitan Archives (LMA) for assistance in conserving Claes Jansz. Visscher's 1616 panorama of London.

2017:   the last of three grants of £10,000 to the BFI.

2018:   £8,000 to the Historic Towns Trust towards the publication of a map of Tudor London in *c.* 1520; copies of the map were provided to members of the Society.

2019:   £1,472 to the London Metropolitan Archive (LMA) for conservation of drawings by William Alistair MacDonald (1861–1948). £8,234 was also spent on the Society's new website.

2020: £500 to the Survey of London for the digitization of first-edition Ordnance Survey maps of Whitechapel to be used in the Survey's two volumes on Whitechapel.

Annual General Meetings were held at the Cadogan Hall in Chelsea (2015), the Great Hall at St Bartholomew's Hospital (2016), the Octagon at Queen Mary University of London (2017), the Senate House at the University of London (2018) and St Andrew Holborn (2019). Generally, attendance continued to be strong with around 250–300 members and guests turning up for each meeting. Sadly, the 2020 AGM, which was to have been held in the Great Hall of King's College, had to be cancelled due to the Covid-19 pandemic.

The Council continued to meet three times a year: as a result of the pandemic, the meeting in September 2020 was held online via Zoom. The Society's Hon. Editor of forty years, Ann Saunders, formally stood down at the 2015 AGM to be succeeded by Sheila O'Connell, Mrs Saunders being appointed as a Vice-President. Other Council officers remained in post throughout the reporting period, although in mid-2020 Roger Cline announced he would be resigning as the Society's Hon. Treasurer, a post he had held since 1985, and would be handing over his duties to Council Member Anne Ramon. This change was to have been ratified at the 2020 AGM, which was cancelled, and remains to be formally ratified by members at the 2021 AGM.

MIKE WICKSTEED
Hon. Secretary

LIST OF PUBLICATIONS

Dimensions are given in inches to the nearest eighth of an inch, with centimetres in brackets to the nearest half-centimetre; height precedes width. In the case of items in several sheets dimensions may be approximate only. Borders, original titles, and other wording are included in the dimensions but added titles are excluded.

Dates in brackets are those of publication and do not necessarily coincide with the year for which the publication was issued.

1. Van den Wyngaerde's View of London, *c.* 1550 (Topographical Society of London), 1881–82: 20¾ × 116¼ in. (52.5 × 295.5 cm), on 7 sheets 31½ × 23⅜ in. (80 × 59.5 cm), with sheet of text. (See No. 151.)
2. Plan of London, *c.* 1560, attributed to Hoefnagel (T.S.L. 1882–83): from Braun and Hogenberg's *Civitates Orbis Terrarum,* second state showing Royal Exchange, 13¼ × 19⅜ in. (35.5 × 49 cm), on sheet 22¼ × 29¼ in. (56.6 × 74.5 cm).
3. *Illustrated Topographical Record of London,* first series (1898), drawings by J. P. Emslie of changes and demolitions, 1880–87: 11½ × 8⅞ in. (29 × 22.5 cm), sewn, paper wrapper.
4. Visscher's View of London, 1616 (T.S.L. 1883–85): 16⅝ × 85⅛ in. (42 × 216.5 cm), on 4 sheets 23¼ × 31¾ in. (59 × 78 cm). (See 'Notes on Visscher's View of London, 1616', by T. F. Ordish, *L.T.R.,* VI, 39.)
5. Porter's 'Newest and Exactest Mapp of London and Westminster', *c.* 1660 (1898): 11¼ × 30¼ in. (28.5 × 77 cm), on 2 sheets 22¼ × 29¼ in. (56.5 × 74.5 cm).
6. *Illustrated Topographical Record of London,* second series (1899), drawings by J. P. Emslie of changes and demolitions, 1886–87: 11½ × 8⅞ in. (29 × 22.5 cm), sewn, paper wrapper.
7. Norden's Maps of London and Westminster, 1593, from the *Speculum Britanniae* (1899): 6¾ × 9⅝ in. (17 × 24.5 cm) and 6⅛ × 9⅞ in. (15.5 × 25 cm), on one sheet 29¼ × 22⅛ in. (74.5 × 56 cm). (See 'Notes on Norden and his Map of London', by H. B. Wheatley, *L.T.R.,* II, 42.)
8. Kensington Turnpike Trust Plans, 1811, by Salway, of the road from Hyde Park Corner to Counter's Bridge (1899–1903): 20⅝ in. × 56 ft 1⅝ in. (52.5 × 1711 cm), in colour, 30 sheets and title–page 24 × 27 in. (61 × 69 cm). (See 'Notes on Salway's Plan', by W. F. Prideaux, *L.T.R.,* III, 21, and v, 138.)
9. *Illustrated Topographical Record of London,* third series (1900), drawings by J. P. Emslie of changes and demolitions, 1888–90: 11½ × 8⅞ in. (29 × 22.5 cm), sewn, paper wrapper.
10. Comparative Plan of Whitehall, 1680/1896: modern ground plan superimposed on Fisher's plan of 1680 as engraved by Vertue (1900): one sheet 26⅜ × 22 in. (67.5 × 56 cm).
11. *Annual Record,* I, ed. by T. F. Ordish (1901): 8¾ × 5⅞ in. (22.5 × 15 cm), quarter cloth; continued as *London Topographical Record.*
12. Hollar's West-Central London, *c.* 1658, a bird's-eye-view (1902): 13⅛ × 17¼ in. (33.5 × 44 cm) on 17 × 23¼ in. (43 × 59 cm). (See 'Hollar's Map', by W. R. Lethaby and R. Jenkins, *L.T.R.,* II, 109.)

13.   *London Topographical Record*, II, ed. by T. R. Ordish (1903); 9 × 5⅞ in. (23 × 15 cm), quarter cloth.

14.   Kip's View of London, Westminster and St James's Park, 1710 (1903): *c.* 53 × 82 in. (134 × 208 cm) on 12 sheets 22⅛ × 24 in. (56 × 61 cm). (See No. 161.)

15.   Morden and Lea's Plan of London, 1682, also known as Ogilby and Morgan's Plan (1904): 300 ft to 1 in., 59¼ × 93¾ in. (150.5 × 238 cm) on 9 sheets 22 × 30⅛ in. (56 × 76.5 cm) and 3 sheets 22 × 15⅛ in. (56 × 38.5 cm). (See 'Morden and Lea's Plan of London', by W. L. Spiers, *L.T.R.*, V, 117.)

16.   *London Topographical Record*, III, ed. by T. F. Ordish (1906): 9 × 5⅞ in. (23 × 15 cm), quarter cloth.

17.   Map of Elizabethan London, formerly attributed to Ralph Agas (1905): 28⅛ × 72 in. (71.5 × 183 cm) on 8 sheets 23½ × 17¼ in. (59.5 × 44 cm).

18.   Faithorne and Newcourt's Map of London, 1658 (1905): map *c.* 32½ × 71 in. (82.5 × 180.5 cm) on 6 sheets 20 × 25¼ in. (51 × 64 cm) and 2 sheets 20 × 12½ in. (51 × 31.5 cm), and title on 4 pieces.

19.   Hollar's Long View of London, 1647 (1906–07): 18 × 92 in. (46 × 233.5 cm) in 7 pieces on 6 sheets 25⅜ × 19 in. (64.5 × 48.5 cm).

20.   *London Topographical Record*, IV (1907): 9 × 5⅞ in. (23 × 15 cm), quarter cloth.

21.   Wren's Drawings of Old St Paul's (1908): (i) plan of old cathedral before the Great Fire, 18⅞ × 14½ in. (48 × 37 cm); (ii) section of Wren's Scheme for rebuilding, 18½ × 12 in. (47 × 30.5 cm); on 2 sheets 29⅜ × 22½ in. (74.5 × 57 cm). (See 'Wren's Drawings of Old St Paul's …', by W. R. Lethaby, *L.T.R.*, V, 136.)

22 and 26.   Hollar's 'Exact Surveigh', 1667 (1908, 1909): 21⅜ × 32½ in. (54.5 × 82.5 cm) on 2 sheets 25⅜ × 19 in. (64.5 × 48.5 cm).

23.   *London Topographical Record*, V (1908): 9 × 5⅞ in. (23 × 15 cm), quarter cloth.

24.   The Palace of Whitehall, View from the River, 1683 (1909): 14 × 24½ in. (35.5 × 62.5 cm) on sheet 24 × 35 in. (61 × 89 cm). (See 'View of the Palace of Whitehall', by W. L. Spiers, *L.T.R.*, VII, 26.)

25.   *London Topographical Record*, VI (1909): 9 × 5⅞ in. (23 × 15 cm), quarter cloth.

26.   See No. 22.

27.   *Seven London Views by Deceased Artists* (1910): 14 × 11 in. (35.5 × 28 cm). (See 'Notes on London Views', by P. Norman, *L.T.R.*, VIII, 94.)

28.   *London Topographical Record*, VII, ed. by H. G. Head (1912): 9 × 5⅞ in. (23 × 15 cm), quarter cloth.

29.   Seven More London Views by Deceased Artists (1911): 14 × 11 in. (35.5 × 28 cm). (See 'Notes on London Views', by P. Norman, *L.T.R.*, VIII, 94.)

30.   Roads out of London, from Ogilby's *Britannia*, 1675, with descriptive letterpress (1911): 15⅛ × 11⅜ in. (38.5 × 29 cm), sewn, paper wrapper.

31.   Jonas Moore's Map of the River Thames from Westminster to the Sea, 1662 (1912): part only, 20⅞ × 23⅝ in. (53 × 60 cm) on one sheet 23¼ × 33 in. (59 × 84 cm). (See 'A Seventeenth Century Map of London and the Thames', by M. Holmes, *L.T.R.*, XX, 26.)

32.   *London Topographical Record*, VIII, ed. by H. G. Head (1913): 9 × 5⅞ in. (23 × 15 cm), quarter cloth.

33. Seven Drawings of London Bridge by E. W. Cooke (1913): 14 × 11 in. (35.5 × 28 cm). (See 'Drawings of Old and New London Bridge by E. W. Cooke', by P. Norman, *L.T.R.*, IX, 1; see also No. 113.)

34, 36, 37, 41, 42, 43 and 44.   Rocque's Plan of London, 1746 (1913–19): 6 ft 8 in. × 12 ft 8½ in. (203 × 387.5 cm), with key, on 49 sheets 17 × 22½ in. (43 × 57 cm). (See 'Rocque's Plan of London', by H. B. Wheatley, *L.T.R.*, IX, 15.)

35. *London Topographical Record*, IX, ed. by H. G. Head (1914): 9 × 5⅞ in. (23 × 15 cm), quarter cloth.

36. See No. 34.

37. See No. 34.

38. *London Topographical Record*, X, ed. by H. G. Head (1916): 9 × 5⅞ in. (23 × 15 cm), quarter cloth.

39. A Plan of Ebury Manor, *c.* 1663–70 (1915): in colour, one sheet 30⅛ × 19⅞ in. (76.5 × 50.5 cm), and sheet of text.

40. *London Topographical Record*, XI, ed. by H. G. Head (1917): 9 × 5⅞ in. (23 × 15 cm), quarter cloth.

41. See No. 34.

42. See No. 34.

43. See No. 34.

44. See No. 34.

45. A View of London Bridge by John Norden, 1597 (1919): 15¼ × 20⅛ in. (38.5 × 51 cm) on one sheet 18⅞ × 25¼ in. (48 × 64 cm).

46. *London Topographical Record*, XII, ed. by H. G. Head (1920): 9 × 5⅞ in. (23 × 15 cm), quarter cloth.

47. A View of London Bridge from both sides, by Sutton Nicholls, *c.* 1710 (1921): 11 × 17¼ in. (28 × 44 cm) on sheet 14⅞ × 22 in. (37.5 × 56 cm).

48. Tallis's Plan of Bond Street (1921): 12 pages 5¾ × 9 in. (14.5 × 23 cm). (See 'Tallis's Street Views of London', by E. B. Chancellor, *L.T.R.*, XII, 67; see also No. 110.)

49. Matthew Merian's View of London, 1638 (1922): 8¾ × 27½ in. (22 × 70 cm) on sheet 13½ × 31½ in. (34.5 × 80 cm), folded.

50. Seven Unpublished Drawings by Hollar: from the Pepysian Library, Cambridge (1922): 4 sheets 14 × 11 in. (35.5 × 28 cm).

51. *London Topographical Record*, XIII, ed. by H. G. Head (1923): 8⅞ × 5⅞ in. (22.5 × 15 cm), quarter cloth.

52 and 53.   Views of Westminster, 1801–15, by William Capon, with Capon's descriptions annotated by P. Norman (1923–24): 16 views, 1 in colour, and map, 5 sewn sections 14 × 11 in. (35.5 × 28 cm).

53. See No. 52.

54. A London Plan of 1585 (1925): 22½ × 31 in. (57 × 98 cm) on sheet 25⅛ × 35⅞ in. (63.5 × 91 cm), folded. (See No. 55.)

55. *The Early History of Piccadilly, Leicester Square, Soho and their Neighbourhood*, by C. L. Kingsford (1925): written to explain the map of 1585 (see No. 54.) 8⅞ × 5⅞ in. (22.5 × 15 cm), quarter cloth, uniform with the *Record*.

56. Drawings of Buildings in the Area described in *The Early History of Piccadilly* … (1926): 11 drawings on 7 sheets 14 × 11 in. (35.5 × 28 cm), and plan of West London, *c.* 1710, on double sheet folded. (See No. 55.)

57. *London Topographical Record*, XIV, ed. by W. H. Godfrey (1928): 8⅞ × 5⅞ in. (22.5 × 15 cm), quarter cloth.

58. Plan of Nevill's Alley, Fetter Lane, 1670 (1928): 20¼ × 25 in. (51.5 × 63.5 cm). (See 'Nevill's Court, Fetter Lane', by W. G. Bell, *L.T.R.*, xv, 87.)

59. Seven Views of the Inns of Court and Chancery, with notes by J. B. Williamson (1928): 14 × 11 in. (35.5 × 28 cm), 2 sewn sections.

60. *London Topographical Record*, xv, ed. by W. H. Godfrey (1931): 8⅞ × 5⅞ in. (22.5 × 15 cm), quarter cloth.

61. Area east of St Katherine's Dock, *c.* 1550, from a tracing by M. B. Honeybourne of a plan in the Public Record Office (1929): 27¼ × 21¼ in. (69 × 54 cm) on sheet 29¼ × 23⅜ in. (74 × 59.5 cm), folded.

62. *London Topographical Record*, xvi, ed. by W. H. Godfrey (1932): 8⅞ × 5⅞ in. (22.5 × 15 cm), quarter cloth.

63. Hollar's View of Greenwich, 1637 (1930): 5¾ × 33 in. (14.5 × 84 cm) on sheet 7¾ × 35¾ in. (19.5 × 90.5 cm), folded.

64. A Plan in the Public Record Office of property on the south-east side of Charing Cross, 1610 (1930): 19 × 26 in. (48 × 66 cm) on sheet 22⅝ × 29⅛ in. (57.5 × 74 cm).

65. Plan of the Manor of Walworth and Parish of Newington, Surrey, 1681 (1932): two–thirds scale, 13¾ × 18 in. (35 × 45.5 cm) on sheet 18⅛ × 23 in. (46 × 58 cm). (See 'Thomas Hill's Maps …', by I. Darlington, *L.T.R.*, xxi, 37.)

66. Plan of the Duke of Bedford's Estates, 1795 (1933), from Bloomsbury to the river: 23⅛ × 40⅞ in. (59 × 103.5 cm) on sheet 28⅜ × 43⅛ in. (72 × 109.5 cm), folded. (See 'Duke of Bedford's Estate Map, 1795', by E. Jeffries Davis, *L.T.R.*, xviii, 134.)

67. Plan of the Parish of St Mary, Kensington, 1822 (1934): 28 × 34⅝ in. (71 × 88 cm) on sheet 31⅝ × 37¼ in. (81.5 × 94.5 cm), folded, with sheet of notes.

68. Eight Views of Kensington, from originals in Kensington Public Library (1934): 8 sheets 11 × 14 in. (28 × 35.5 cm).

69. *London Topographical Record*, xvii, ed. by W. H. Godfrey (1936): 8⅞ × 5⅞ in. (22.5 × 15 cm), quarter cloth.

70. Four drawings by Philip Norman (1936): (i) Vine Tavern, Mile End; (ii) Nos 5 and 7, Aldgate; (iii) Nos 10 and 11, Austin Friars; (iv) St Magnus' Church, London Bridge: 4 sheets 14 × 11 in. (35.5 × 28 cm), in folder.

71. A further four drawings by Philip Norman (1937): (v) No. 13, Leather Lane; (vi) Staircase in the Old Bell Inn, Holborn; (vii) Old houses, Chelsea; (viii) Backs of old houses, Cheyne Walk: 4 sheets 14 × 11 in. (35.5 × 28 cm), in folder with No. 70.

72. Clothworkers' Company, Survey of Properties in 1612 and 1728 (1938): (i) Clothworkers' Hall, 1612; (ii) St James's in the Wall, 1612; (iii) St James's in the Wall, 1728: 3 sheets 22½ × 17½ in. (57 × 44.5 cm) in folder. (See 'The Clothworkers' Company: Book of Plans …', by W. H. Godfrey, *L.T.R.*, xviii, 51.)

73. Clothworkers' Survey (1939): (iv) Neighbourhood of the Fleet Prison, 1612: (v) Neighbourhood of the Fleet Prison, 1728, 2 sheets 22½ × 17½ in. (57 × 44.5 cm), in folder.

74. Clothworkers' Survey (1940): (vi) Richard Fishburne's House, Throgmorton Street, 1612: 22½ × 35 in. (57 × 89 cm), folded; (vii) Fox Court, Nicholas Lane, 1612: 22½ × 17½ in. (57 × 44.5 cm), in folder.

75. Clothworkers' Survey (1941): (viii) Sir Edward Darcy's House, Billiter Street, 1612: 22½ × 34⅞ in. (57 × 88.5 cm), folded; (ix) Fox Court, Nicholas Lane, 1728: 22½ × 17½ in. (57 × 44.5 cm), in folder.

76. *London Topographical Record*, XVIII, ed. by W. H. Godfrey (1942): 8⅞ × 5⅞ in. (22.5 × 15 cm), quarter cloth.

77. Van den Wyngaerde's View of the City of London between Fleet River and London Bridge, *c.* 1550 (1944): 5⅛ × 50⅛ in. (13 × 127.5 cm) in 3 sections on 1 sheet 23⅛ × 18⅝ in. (58.5 × 47 cm).

78. View of London from Southwark, attributed to Thomas Wyck (1616–77), at Chatsworth House (1945): original size 20¼ × 30½ in. (51.5 × 87.5 cm), reproduced 15⅛ × 22¾ in. (38.5 × 57.5 cm) on sheet 20 × 30 in. (51 × 76.5 cm).

79. *Survey of Building Sites in the City of London after the Great Fire of 1666*, by Mills and Oliver, vol. 1: (i.e. part i of Mills 1) (1946, extra publication): reduced facsimile, 8⅞ × 5⅝ in. (22.5 × 14.5 cm), quarter cloth, uniform with the *Record*.

80. *London Topographical Record*, XIX, ed. by W. H. Godfrey (1947): 8⅞ × 5⅞ in. (22.5 × 15 cm), quarter cloth.

81. Whitehall Palace, a seventeenth-century painting at Kensington Palace (1948): original size 16 × 37 in. (40.5 × 94 cm) reproduced 9½ × 22¼ in. (24 × 56.5 cm) on sheet 20 × 30 in. (51 × 76.5 cm).

82. A Prospect of the City of London from the South-east, 1945, by Cecil Brown (1949): original size 9 ft × 6 ft 6 in. (274.5 × 183 cm) reproduced 14⅞ × 20⅞ in. (37.5 × 53 cm) on sheet 16⅝ × 23 in. (42 × 58.5 cm). (See No. 142.)

83. *Le Guide de Londres*, 1693, by F. Colsoni, edited by W. H. Godfrey (1951): 8⅞ × 5⅞ in. (22.5 × 15 cm), quarter cloth, uniform with the *Record*.

84. Seventeenth-century Plans of the Properties belonging to St Bartholomew's Hospital (1950–51): (i) The Grey Friars, *c.* 1617 (see 'The Precinct of the Greyfriars', by M. B. Honeybourne, *L.T.R.*, XVI, 9); (ii) Properties adjoining Hosier Lane; (iii) St Nicholas Flesh Shambles: on 2 sheets 19½ × 29 in. (49.5 × 74 cm) folded, in folder.

85. *London Topographical Record*, XX, ed. by W. H. Godfrey (1952): 8⅞ × 5⅞ in. (22.5 × 15 cm), quarter cloth.

86. *Berkeley Square to Bond Street, The Early History of the Neighbourhood*, by B. H. Johnson (1952): 8⅞ × 5⅞ in. (22.5 × 15 cm), full cloth, published by John Murray in association with the London Topographical Society.

87. Seventeenth-century Plans of Properties belonging to St Bartholomew's Hospital (1953–54): (iv) south-west portion of the hospital adjoining the City Wall Ditch; (v) north portion adjoining Smithfield from Duck Lane to the Hospital Church; (vi) south portion adjoining Little Britain and the City Wall and Ditch; (vii) property north of Chick Lane: on 2 sheets 19½ × 29 in. (49.5 × 74 cm), folded in folder with 84.

88. Plan of the precinct of St Bartholomew's Hospital, *c.* 1617 (1955): in colour, 15⅞ × 10¼ in. (40.5 × 26 cm) on sheet 19½ × 14½ in. (49.5 × 37 cm), in folder with 84.

(See 'The Fire of London and St Bartholomew's Hospital', by G. Whitteridge, *L.T.R.*, xx, 47.)

89. *Survey of Building Sites in the City of London after the Great Fire of 1666*, by Mills and Oliver, vol. II (i.e., part ii of Mills I) (1956, extra publication): reduced facsimile, 8⅞ × 5⅞ in. (22.5 × 14.5 cm), quarter cloth, uniform with the *Record*.

90. Plan of the precinct (eastern part) of the Hospital of St Katherine by the Tower, 1685, part of a survey by John Ogilby (1957): 1 sheet 28 × 25 in. (71.5 × 63.5 cm).

91. *London Topographical Record*, XXI, ed. by W. H. Godfrey (1958): 8⅞ × 5⅞ in. (22.5 × 15 cm), quarter cloth.

92. The City of London, showing Parish Boundaries prior to the Union of Parishes Act, 1907, on the 1:2,500 Ordnance Survey Map, 1st edition, 1876 (1959): in colour, 24¾ × 44⅛ in. (63 × 112 cm) on sheet 27 × 46 in. (68.5 × 117 cm).

93. A Map of London under Richard II, from original sources, by M. B. Honeybourne (1960): 27⅜ × 41 in. (69.5 × 104 cm) on sheet 31⅞ × 45 in. (81 × 114.5 cm).

94. A View of London, 1600, by John Norden, from the engraving in the de la Gardie Collection in the Royal Library, Stockholm (1961): 18⅛ × 47⅞ in. (46 × 121.5 cm) on sheet 24⅛ × 50 in. (61 × 127 cm).

95 and 96. A Survey of the Parliamentary Borough of St Marylebone, including Paddington and St Pancras, 1834, engraved by B. R. Davis (1962–63): slightly reduced scale, 40½ × 34⅛ in. (103 × 86.5 cm) on 2 sheets 22 × 36½ in. (50.5 × 92.5 cm).

96. See No. 95.

97, 98 and 99. *Survey of Building Sites in the City of London after the Great Fire of 1666*, by Mills and Oliver, vols III, IV and V (i.e., Mills II and Oliver I and II) (1963, extra publication): reduced facsimile, 9½ × 6⅛ in. (24 × 15.5 cm), quarter cloth.

98. See No. 97.

99. See No. 97.

100. *The Map of Mid-Sixteenth Century London: An Investigation into the Relationship Between a Copper-Engraved Map and its Derivatives,* by S. P. Marks (1964): 11½ × 8⅞ in. (29 × 22.5 cm), quarter cloth.

101. *Survey of Building Sites in the City of London after the Great Fire of 1666*, by Mills and Oliver, vol. II (i.e., Mills I) (1965, extra publication): reduced facsimile, 9½ × 6⅛ in. (24 × 15.5 cm), quarter cloth, uniform with 97, 98 and 99: a new edition of 79 and 89.

102. *London Topographical Record*, XXII, ed. by M. B. Honeybourne (1965): 8⅞ × 5⅞ in. (22.5 × 15 cm), quarter cloth.

103. *Survey of Building Sites in the City of London after the Great Fire of 1666*, by Mills and Oliver, vol. I, Introduction and Indexes (1967, extra publication): 9½ × 6¼ in. (24 × 16 cm), quarter cloth, uniform with Nos 97, 98, 99 and 101.

104. Hollar's 'Exact Surveigh', 1667 (1966, extra publication): 21½ × 32½ in. (54.5 × 82.5 cm) on sheet 25 × 34¾ in. (63.5 × 88 cm), replacing Nos 22 and 26.

105. Grand Architectural Panorama of London, Regent Street to Westminster, by R. Sandeman, 1849 (1966): 4¾ in. × 22 ft 6 in. (12 × 686 cm) in a small case 6 × 7⅛ in. (15 × 18 cm).

106. Horwood's Plan of London, 1792–99 (1966, extra publication, a memorial to the work of the London Survey Committee): 7 ft 3 in. × 13 ft 4 in. (221 × 406 cm), iv + 32 sheets 24½ × 23 in. (62.5 × 58.5 cm); includes variant plates from sheets A1 and B1.

107. The Banqueting House with the Whitehall and Holbein Gates, by Inigo Jones, for a masque by Ben Jonson performed in 1623 (1967): 14 × 24¼ in. (37 × 61.5 cm) on sheet 19 × 26⅞ in. (48 × 68 cm); with 'A Prospect of Whitehall by Inigo Jones', by J. Harris, offprint from *The Burlington Magazine*, February 1967.

108. *Index to Rocque's Plan of the Cities of London and Westminster and the Borough of Southwark*, 1747 (1968, extra publication): facsimile, 11½ × 8⅞ in. (29 × 22.5 cm), full cloth, uniform with 100.

109. *The London Panoramas of Robert Barker and Thomas Girtin, c. 1800*, by H. J. Pragnell (1968): 11½ × 8⅞ in. (29 × 22.5 cm), quarter cloth, uniform with No. 100. (See also No. 139.)

110. *John Tallis's London Street Views*, 1838–1840 and 1847, with introduction by Peter Jackson (1969, extra publication): 8 × 11¼ in. (20 × 28.5 cm), full cloth; published by Nattali and Maurice in association with the London Topographical Society. (See Nos 48 and 160.)

111. Map of Chelsea by F. P. Thompson, 1836 (1969): 27¾ × 41⅝ in. (70.5 × 104.5 cm), on 2 sheets 29⅞ × 22½ in. (76 × 57.5 cm).

112. Hollar's Long View of London from Bankside, 1647 (1970, extra publication): 18½ × 93 in. (47 × 236.5 cm) on 7 sheets 25 × 19 in. (63.5 × 48 cm), replacing No. 19.

113. A Selection of Drawings of Old and New London Bridge, c. 1830, by E. W. Cooke (1970): 14 × 11 in. (35.5 × 28 cm) in folder.

114. Langley and Belch's 'New Map of London', 1812 (1971): in colour, 20¾ × 30¾ in. (52.5 × 78 cm) on sheet 25 × 35 in. (63.5 × 89 cm).

115. *London Topographical Record*, XXIII, ed. by M. B. Honeybourne (1972): 8¾ × 5¾ in. (22 × 14.5 cm), quarter cloth.

116. *Map of the Railways proposed by the Bills of the Session of 1863 in the Metropolis and its vicinity* (1973): 24¼ × 23⅞ in. (61.5 × 60.5 cm) on sheet 28 × 24⅞ in. (71 × 63 cm). (See 'Parliament and the Railways', by David J. Johnson, *L.T.R.*, XXIV, 147.)

117. *The Public Markets of the City of London surveyed by William Leybourne in 1677*, by Betty R. Masters (1974): 11½ × 8⅞ in. (29 × 22.5 cm), quarter cloth.

118 and 119. Thomas Milne's Land Use Map of London and Environs in 1800, with an introduction by Dr G. B. G. Bull (1975–6): north and south sections each 20⅛ × 40½ in. (51 × 103 cm) on 3 sheets, iii + 6 sheets 24 × 16½ in. (61 × 42 cm) in folder, available in colour and in black and white.

119. See No. 118.

120. *The Artillery Ground and Fields in Finsbury*, two maps of 1641 and 1703 reproduced with a commentary by James R. Sewell (1977): 14¾ × 11⅜ in. (37.5 × 29 cm), sewn in card wrapper.

121. *The Park Town Estate and the Battersea Tangle, A peculiar piece of Victorian London property development and its background*, by Priscilla Metcalf (1978): 11⅛ × 9 in. (28 × 22.5 cm), Linson.

122. *The A to Z of Elizabethan London*, compiled by Adrian Prockter and Robert Taylor with introductory notes by John Fisher (1979): 12⅛ × 8⅝ in. (31 × 22 cm), Linson, published concurrently by the Society and by Harry Margary in association with Guildhall Library.

123. *London Topographical Record*, XXIV, ed. by Ann Saunders (1980, centenary volume): 8¾ × 5¾ in. (22 × 14.5 cm), quarter cloth.

124. London from the North, by J. Swertner, 1789 (1980, extra centenary publication): 19 × 31½ in. (48.5 × 80 cm) on sheet 23 × 32¾ in. (58.5 × 83 cm).

125. The 'Rhinebeck' Panorama of London, c. 1810, with an introduction by Ralph Hyde and keys by Peter Jackson (1981): in colour, reduced, 18¾ × 107¼ in. (47.5 × 272.5 cm) on iii + 4 sheets 24⅝ × 18¾ in. (62.5 × 47.5 cm) in folder. (See 'A London Panorama, c. 1800 Resurrected', by Ralph Hyde, *L.T.R.*, XXIV, 211.)

126. *The A to Z of Georgian London*, with introductory notes by Ralph Hyde (1982): 12 × 8⅝ in. (30.5 × 22 cm), Linson, uniform with 122, published concurrently by the Society and by Harry Margary in association with Guildhall Library.

127. *Robert Baker of Piccadilly Hall and his Heirs*, by Francis Sheppard (1982, extra publication): 11⅛ × 8¾ in. (28 × 22 cm), Linson, uniform with No. 121.

128. A Survey of Hatton Garden by Abraham Arlidge 1694 (1983): in colour, 31¼ × 26 in. (79.5 × 66 cm) on sheet 36⅜ × 27¾ in. (92.5 × 70.5 cm) with sheet of text. (See 'The Survey of Hatton Garden in 1694 by Abraham Arlidge', by Dr Penelope Hunting, *L.T.R.*, XXV, 83.)

129. A Plan of the Tower of London in 1682 (1983): in colour, 25¾ × 25¾ in. (63 × 63 cm) on sheet 30 × 27½ in. (76 × 70 cm) with sheet of text. (See 'Five Seventeenth-Century Plans of the Tower of London', by Geoffrey Parnell, *L.T.R.*, XXV, 63.)

130. Charles Booth's Descriptive Map of London Poverty 1889, with an introduction by Dr David A. Reeder (1984): in colour, 36½ × 46¼ in. (93 × 117.5 cm) on ii + 4 sheets averaging 20 × 25 in. (51 × 64 cm) in folder.

131. *The A to Z of Regency London*, with introduction by Paul Laxton and index by Joseph Wisdom (1985, extra publication): 12 × 8⅝ in. (30.5 × 22 cm), Linson, uniform with No. 122, published concurrently by the Society and by Harry Margary in association with Guildhall Library.

132. *London Topographical Record*, XXV, ed. by Ann Saunders (1985): 8¾ × 5¾ in. (22 × 14.5 cm), quarter cloth.

133. The Kentish Town Panorama, by James Frederick King c. 1850, with explanatory booklet by John Richardson (1986): 6 in. × 39 ft 8 in. (15.5 × 1209 cm) on 26 sheets 9⅜ × 23½ in. (24 × 59.5 cm) in folder.

134. Satellite View of London, taken by Landsat on 21 October 1984 (1986, extra publication): in colour, 20¼ × 23½ in. (51.5 × 59.9 cm) on sheet.

135. *The London Surveys of Ralph Treswell*, ed. by John Schofield, illustrated with Treswell's London plans, several in colour (1987): 11⅛ × 9 in. (28 × 23 cm).

136. *The A to Z of Victorian London*, with notes by Ralph Hyde (1987, extra publication): 12⅛ × 8¾ in. (31 × 22 cm), Linson, uniform with No. 122, published concurrently by the Society and Harry Margary in association with Guildhall Library.

137. *Hugh Alley's Caveat — The Markets of London in 1598*, ed. by Ian Archer, Caroline Barron and Vanessa Harding (1988): 9½ × 10¼ in. (24 × 26 cm).

138. Hollar's Prospect of London and Westminster taken from Lambeth in 2 versions *c.* 1665 and *c.* 1707 (1988, extra publication): 12¾ in. × 10 ft 6½ in. (32.5 × 322.4 cm) on 8 sheets 14 in. × 11 ft (35.6 × 336 cm) in folder. (See 'Some Notes on Hollar's *Prospect* …', by Peter Jackson, *L.T.R.*, XXVI, 134.)

139. Barker's Panorama of London from the Roof of the Albion Mills, 1792, with an introduction by Ralph Hyde and keys by Peter Jackson (1988, extra publication): in colour, 16¾ × 130½ in. (42.5 × 343 cm) on iii + 6 sheets 19¼ × 23½ in. (49 × 59.5 cm) in folder, published concurrently by the Society and Guildhall Library. (See No. 109.)

140. *Good and Proper Materials, the Fabric of London since the Great Fire*, papers given at a conference organized by the Survey of London, ed. by Hermione Hobhouse and Ann Saunders (1989): paperback, 70 pp., 10¾ × 8¾ in. (27.5 × 22 cm).

141. *London Topographical Record*, XXVI, ed. by Ann Saunders (1990): 8¾ × 5¾ in. (22 × 14.5 cm), quarter cloth.

142. *Devastated London* (The Bombed City 1945), drawn by Cecil Brown, with notes by Ralph Hyde (1990): on sheet 33⅛ × 46½ in. (84 × 188 cm), available flat or folded. (See No. 82.)

143. *The Mercers' Hall*, by Jean Imray, with an introduction by Derek Keene (1991, extra publication): 11⅛ × 9⅛ in. (28 × 23 cm).

144. Facsimile of the Ordnance Surveyors' Drawings of the London Area 1799–1808, with an introduction by Yolande Hodson (1991): in colour, on iii + 6 sheets 35 × 25⅛ in. (89 × 64 cm) in folder.

145. *The A to Z of Restoration London (The City of London, 1676)*, with introductory notes by Ralph Hyde and index by John Fisher and Roger Cline (1992): 12 × 8⅝ in. (30.5 × 22 cm), Linson, uniform with 122, published concurrently by the Society and Harry Margary in association with Guildhall Library.

146. Map of the Geology and Contours of London and its Environs, by R. W. Mylne (1856), with an introduction by Eric Robinson and topographical notes by Simon Morris (1993): in colour, on vi + 4 sheets 23¼ × 17¼ in. (59 × 44 cm) in folder.

147. *Drawings of Westminster* by Sir George Scharf (1859–74), with text by Peter Jackson (1994): 11⅛ × 9 in. (28.5 × 23 cm).

148. *Topography of London*, facsimile of John Lockie's *Gazetteer* (2nd edition, 1813) with introduction by David Webb (1994): 7⅛ × 4½ in. (18 × 11.5 cm).

149. *London Topographical Record*, XXVII, ed. by Ann Saunders (1995): 8¾ × 5¾ in. (22 × 14.5 cm), quarter cloth.

150. *Joel Gascoyne's Engraved Maps of Stepney*, 1702–04, with an introduction by W. Ravenhill and D. Johnson (1995); eight sheets 21½ × 24½ in. (54.5 × 62.5 cm) in folder + an explanatory booklet.

151. *The Panorama of London circa 1544*, by Anthonis van den Wyngaerde, ed. by Howard Colvin and Susan Foister (1996): 13⅜ × 19¼ in. (34 × 48.5 cm).

152. *The Royal Exchange*, ed. by Ann Saunders (1997): hardback, 444 pp., 11¼ × 8⅞ in. (28.5 × 22.5 cm).

153. *The Whitehall Palace Plan of 1670*, by Simon Thurley (1998): hardback, 55 pp., 12⅛ × 9 in. (31 × 23 cm).

154. *Ward Maps of the City of London*, by Ralph Hyde (1999): 12 × 9⅞ in. (30.5 × 25 cm).
155. A Map of the Ecclesiastical Divisions within the County of London 1903, with introductory notes by Simon Morris (1999): on sheet 26½ × 39 in. (67 × 99 cm), folded.
156. *Two Thousand Years of London*, by Andrew Ingamells (2000): screenprint in colour 15¾ × 25 in. (40 × 63.5 cm) on sheet 21½ × 29¾ in. (54 × 75.5 cm).
157. *London Topographical Record*, XXVIII, ed. by Ann Saunders (2001): 8¾ × 5¾ in. (22 × 14.5 cm), quarter cloth.
158. *The Elizabethan Tower of London: The Haiward and Gascoyne Plan of 1597*, by Anna Keay (2001): 11⅞ × 8⅝ in. (30 × 22 cm).
159. *Tudor London — A Map and a View*, ed. by Ann Saunders and John Schofield (2001): paperback, 57 pp., 11⅞ × 8⅝ in. (30 × 22 cm).
160. *John Tallis's London Street Views 1838–1840*, with the revised and enlarged views of 1847. Introduction and biographical essay by Peter Jackson (2002): hardback, 305 pp., 8 × 11½ in. (20 × 29 cm). (See Nos 48 and 110.)
161. Jan Kip's View of London, Westminster and St James's Park 1720, with an introduction by Ralph Hyde and keys by Peter Jackson (2003): 51⅝ × 75½ in. (131 × 192 cm) on 12 map sheets each *c.* 20 × 27 in. (51 × 69 cm). (See No. 14.)
162. Charles Robert Cockerell's Tribute to Sir Christopher Wren, with an introduction by John Schofield and key by Tracy Wellman (2003): 19½ × 22¼ in. (50 × 57 cm).
163. *'Old St Paul's': The Society of Antiquaries' Diptych, 1616*, by Pamela Tudor–Craig with Christopher Whittick, published in association with The Society of Antiquaries (2004): 67 pp., 11⅞ × 8¾ in. (30 × 22 cm).
164. *The London County Council Bomb Damage Maps 1939–1945*, with an introduction by Robin Woolven, ed. by Ann Saunders, published in association with London Metropolitan Archives (2005): 215 pp., 14⅝ × 10¾ in. (37 × 27 cm).
165. *London Topographical Record*, XXIX, ed. by Ann Saunders (2006): 236 pp., 10 × 7 in. (25.5 × 18 cm).
166. *The A to Z of Edwardian London*, with an introduction by M. H. Port, ed. by Ann Saunders (2007): in colour, hardback, 169 pp., 14¼ × 10¾ in. (36 × 27.5 cm).
167. *The Pleasures of London*, by Felix Barker and Peter Jackson, ed. by Ann Saunders and Denise Silvester Carr (2008): hardback, 249 pp., 11⅞ × 8¾ in. (30 × 22 cm).
168. *Somerset House: The Palace of England's Queens 1551–1692*, by Simon Thurley with contributions by Patricia Croot and Claire Gapper, ed. by Ann Saunders and Roger Cline (2009): hardback, 144 pp., 12 × 9 in. (30.5 × 23 cm).
169. *London Topographical Record*, XXX, ed. by Ann Saunders (2010): hardback, 276 pp., 10 × 7 in. (25.5 × 18 cm).
170. *London Displayed — Headpieces from the Stationers' Company Almanacks*, by Ralph Hyde (2010): hardback, 88 pp., 11¾ × 9½ in. (30 × 22 cm).
171. *The Palace of Westminster — Surveyed on the Eve of Conflagration, 1834*, by H. M. Port (2011): set of seven large sheets with accompanying booklet, in folder. 10½ × 7⅝ in. (26.8 × 19.5 cm).

172. *The London Letters of Samuel Molyneux, 1712–13*, with an Introduction and Commentary by Paul Holden, ed. by Ann Saunders (2011): hardback, 182 pp., 9¾ × 6⅞ in. (24.7 × 17.6 cm).

173. *London — A History in Maps*, by Peter Barber with notes on the engravers by Laurence Worms, ed. by Roger Cline and Ann Saunders, published in association with the British Library (2012): hardback, 388 pp., 9½ × 12 in. (24 × 30.6 cm).

174. *The A to Z of Charles II's London, 1682*, with introductory notes by Peter Barber and Ralph Hyde; an index compiled by Robert Thompson, ed. by Ann Saunders (2013): hardback, 158 pp., 11¾ × 8⅜ in. (30 × 21.3 cm).

175. *The Singularities of London, 1578*, by L. Grenade (Biblioteca Apostolica Vaticana MS Reg. Lat. 672), ed. by Derek Keene and Ian Archer (2014): hardback, 296 pp., 9¾ × 6⅞ in. (24.7 × 17.4 cm).

176. *London Topographical Record*, xxxi, ed. by Ann Saunders (2015): hardback, 218 pp., 10 × 7 in. (25.5 × 18 cm).

177. *Two Early Panoramas of The Regent's Park: The Panoramas of Richard Morris and John Mortimer*, by Geoffrey Tyack (2015): hardback, 46 pp., 11¾ × 8¾ in. (29.5 × 22 cm).

178. *London Plotted: Plans of London Buildings c. 1450–1720*, by Dorian Gerhold (2016): hardback, 320 pp., 12 × 9 in. (30.5 × 22.5 cm).

179. *London: Prints & Drawings before 1800*, by Bernard Nurse, published in association with the Bodleian Library, University of Oxford (2017): hardback, 226 pp., 9¾ × 11¼ in. (24.5 × 28.5 cm).

180. *A 'Connoisseur's Panorama': Thomas Girtin's* Eidometropolis *and Other London Views, c. 1796–1802*, by Greg Smith (2018): hardback, 72 pp., 12 × 9 in. (30.5 × 22.5 cm).

181. *The Stone Gallery Panorama: Lawrence Wright's View of the City of London from St Paul's Cathedral, c.1948–56*, by Hubert Pragnell, Patricia Hardy and Elain Harwood: hardback, 50 pp., 12 × 9 in. (30.5 × 22.5 cm).

182. *London Bridge and its Houses, c. 1209–1761*, by Dorian Gerhold (2019): hardback, 168 pp., 9 ½ × 12 in. (24 × 30 cm).

183. *London Parish Maps to 1900: A Catalogue of Maps of London Parishes within the Original London County Council Area*, by Ralph Hyde, augmented and completed by Simon Morris and Members of the Society; Biographical Notes and Supplementary Material by Laurence Worms; Introduction by Peter Barber (2020): hardback, 470 pp., 12 × 9 in. (30.5 × 22.5 cm).

LIST OF MEMBERS 2021
(prepared 1 March 2021)

His Royal Highness the Duke of Edinburgh, KG, KT, *Patron*

Personal members

This list aims to show members who have expressed a wish to be included, in many cases with address omitted. Some seventy wished to be excluded, and about another sixty did not reply and so are omitted.

2010   Adams, Mr A   29 Dunbar Road, London N22 5BG

2010   Adams, Dr R, *MA*

2013   Adshead, Mr D J, *MA MLitt FSA*

1987   Aickin, Dr R M   69 Lauriston Road, London E9 7HA

1991   Aitchison, Mr J S, *BEng*   9a Wilbury Road, Hove, East Sussex BN3 3JJ

2008   Alderman, Mrs M, *LLB*

1980   Aldous, Mr A M   12 The Priory, London SE3 9XA

2020   Allen, Mr C   Grove House, Bangors Road South, Iver SL0 0AD

1984   Allen, Mr G R

2013   Allen, Mr M   17 Heather Close, St Leonards, Ringwood, Hampshire BH24 2QJ

1990   Allen, Professor M E, *PhD*   533 Nova Way, Madison WI 53704, USA

1996   Allen, Mr W J C, *AADipl*   76 Half Moon Lane, London SE24 9JE

1988   Allin, Mr P V, *MSc*   7 Pontymason Rise, Rogerstone, Newport NP10 9GJ

2004   Ambler, Dr R W, *FSA*   Oxfordshire

2019   Anderson, Miss C

2021   Anderson, Mr C   51 Festing Road, London SW15 1LW

1999   Anderson, Mr P   47 Wood Lodge Lane, West Wickham, Kent BR4 9LY

2021   Anderson, Mr P   24 New Jubilee Court, Grange Avenue, Woodford Green IG8 8JU

2020   Andrews, Dr M, *BSc MA PhD*   The Old Cider Mill, Drake Street, Welland, Malvern, Worcestershire WR13 6LN

2017   Aramaki-Jones, Ms S

1987   Archer, Dr I W, *MA*   Keble College, Oxford OX1 3PG

2010   Archer, Mr Q D R, *MA LLM*

2020   Armstrong-Fox, Mr M   21 Broomhill Road, Woodford Green IG8 9HA

2001   Arthurs, Mr W M, *MA FRSA*   Pentlands, 5 The Leys, Chesham Bois, Amersham HP6 5NP

1967   Ash, Mr H J, *BA(Hons)*   6 Holly Brooke Close, Shanklin, Isle of Wight PO37 7PD

2001   Ashby, Mr A   4 Forsyte Crescent, London SE19 2QN

1986   Ashdown, Mr J H, *FSA*   5 Hall Farm Paddocks, Springhill Road, Begbroke, Kidlington OX5 1FW

2018   Ashton, Professor R D, *OBE FRSL FBA*   7 Carver Road, London SE24 9LS

1990   Askey, Dr M K, *BA(Hons)*   6 Burch Place, Eyam, Hope Valley S32 5QE

2019   Atkins, Mr M   97 Rannoch Road, London W6 9SX

2016   Averby, Ms K, *BA MA*

2008   Axford, Mr M E   33 Langley Way, Watford, Hertfordshire WD17 3EH

1980   Aylward, Mr R   85 West Lane, London SE16 4PA

2013   Ayres, Mrs S   39 Savernake Road, London NW3 2JU

2012   Ayton, Mr R   32 Pentney Road, London SW12 0NX

2004   Ayton, Mrs V H, *CertEd*   70 Trinity Road, Billericay, Essex CM11 2RY

1972   Backman, Mr P R   6A The Avenue, London N3 2LB

2013   Bacon, Miss S J   16 Slade End, Theydon Bois, Essex CM16 7EP

1977   Bacon, Mr T R   Ramsden Farm, Stone-cum-Ebony, Tenterden, Kent TN30 7JB

2007   Badcock, Mr A J   59 Felsham Road, London SW15 1AZ

2012   Badcock, Mr D   59 Felsham Road, London SW15 1AZ

2001   Badham, Mr P E   59 Salthill Road, Fishbourne, Chichester PO19 3QD

1993   Bailey, Mr S   27 Toot Baldon, Oxford OX44 9NE

2016   Baker, Ms H, *MA PGDip*

1997   Baker, Mr J J, *MA FRGS*   27 Carson Road, London SE21 8HT

1990   Baker, Professor Sir John H, *LLD FBA*   St Catharine's College, Cambridge CB2 1RL

2001   Baker, Dr P   2 Maclise House, Marsham Street, London SW1P 4JJ

2002   Baldwin, Mr R H, *BSc MSc*   Kester, Cotmans Ash Lane, Kemsing, Sevenoaks, Kent TN15 6XD

1990   Bamji, Dr A N, *MB FRCP*   Norman House, West Street, Rye, East Sussex TN31 7ES

1982   Bankes, Mr A G K   24 Willifield Way, London NW11 7XT

1999   Banks, Miss S   Via Regina Margherita 47, 96016 Lentini (SR), Italy

1985   Bar, Mr N C

1980   Barber, Mr P M, *OBE Member of Council*   16 Tivoli Road, London N8 8RE

2010   Barends, Mr C J, *BA(Hons) LLB*   69 Woodplace Lane, Coulsdon CR5 1NE

2002   Barker, Mrs J, *BA(Hons)*   Woodway House, 30 Woodway Road, Teignmouth, Devon TQ14 8QY

2005   Barker, Mr K   Watermill House, Mill Street, Iden Green, Cranbrook TN17 4HL

1995   Barratt, Mr S A B, *MA*

1989   Barriff, Mr S J   Quackers, 13 Canal Walk, Hungerford, Berkshire RG17 0EQ

1979   Barron, Dr C *Member of Council*   9 Boundary Road, London NW8 0HE

1991   Bartlett, Mr R K   5 Aldersgrove, East Molesey, Surrey KT8 0AB

1991 Bate, Mr G, *CEng MICE FICD*   4 Blackthorn Close, Newport, Brough, East Yorkshire HU15 2QJ

1991 Baty, Mr P R   47 Haldon Road, London SW18 1QF

1983 Baxter, Mr A, *CBE*   Alan Baxter Ltd, 75 Cowcross Street, London EC1M 6EL

2013 Bayliss, Mr C   Flat 25 Kings College Court, 55 Primrose Hill Road, London NW3 3EA

1992 Bayman, Mr R E, *MCIT*   109 Park Road, New Barnet, Barnet EN4 9QR

2020 Baynes, Miss N

2010 Bazely, Mr R, *BA MSc*

1984 Beacham, Mr J W   Abbotsford, Elmstead Road, West Byfleet, Surrey KT14 6JB

2004 Beard, Mr A T   58 Perry Street, Billericay, Essex CM12 0NA

2021 Beardsell, Mr H J   27 Old Gloucester Street, London WC1N 3AX

1997 Beautyman, Dr A C, *PhD CEng*   Upper Maisonette, 200B Hammersmith Grove, London W6 7HG

1981 Beecroft, Mrs A J   1 Dalton Close, Orpington, Kent BR6 9QY

2021 Beer, Mr D   76 Ridgeway Avenue, Barnet EN4 8TN

1967 Belcher, Mr V R, *MA*   55 Gore Road, London E9 7HN

1995 Bell, Mr N D J, *BA*   7 Thornton Street, St Albans, Hertfordshire AL3 5JW

2008 Bell, Mr P W R   2 The Court, Cascade Avenue, London N10 3PS

2005 Bell, Mr T A P

2018 Bellamy, Mr D   Homestead Lodge, Wigsley Road, Harby, Newark NG23 7EF

1990 Bellamy, Mrs J

1990 Bellenie, Mrs L F G   14 Collard Drive, Willesborough, Ashford, Kent TN24 0JR

2020 Bellwood, Mr B, *BSc MSc*

1990 Bendall, Dr S, *MA PhD MCLIP*   Emmanuel College, Cambridge CB2 3AP

2003 Bennett, Mr H F   9 Howard Road, Dorking RH4 3HR

2016 Bennett, Mr J   48 Perrers Road, London W6 0EZ

2002 Bennett-Richards, Dr P, *MB BS BSc MRCGP*   14 Storers Quay, London E14 3BZ

2019 Benson, Dr A   Brynderi, Wainfield Lane, Gwehelog, Usk, Monmouthshire NP15 1RG

2004 Bentley, Mr L   Ascot, Randolph Lane, Iden, Rye, East Sussex TN31 7PR

1990 Berry, Mr I M   2 Ivy Place, Hove, East Sussex BN3 1AP

2013 Bestavachvili, Miss M, *BSc LRAM*   11 Micheldever Road, London SE12 8LX

2004 Bevan, Mr I, *MA*   130 Aylesford Avenue, Beckenham, Kent BR3 3RY

2010 Bill, The Revd A, *BA AKC*   13 Wilmington Close, Newcastle upon Tyne NE3 2SF

1964 Bimson, Miss Mavis, *FSA*

2009 Bird, Mr P D   48 Margravine Gardens, London w6 8rj
2007 Birney, Mrs I J   Kelmscott House, 26 Upper Mall, London w6 9ta
2013 Blaber, Mr R G   Knockenden, Woodchurch Road, Tenterden, Kent
TN30 6AE
2021 Black, Dr I   43 Peggys Walk, Littlebury, Saffron Walden CB11 4TG
2020 Black, Mr MC, *BSc ARCS CPhys MInstP*   Hardknott, Chadwell, Ware,
Hertfordshire SG12 9JY
2012 Blades, Mr D   52 Carlisle Road, Hove, East Sussex BN3 4FS
2017 Blake, Mr P   18 Rosevine Road, London sw20 8rb
2018 Blake, Mr R   50 The Glade, Stoneleigh, Epsom, Surrey KT17 2HB
2019 Blaxall, Mr K   12 Harsnett Road, Colchester CO1 2HY
2012 Blight, Mr I   129 Epsom Road, Guildford, Surrey GU1 2PP
1993 Blurton, Mr R   39 Narbonne Avenue, London sw4 9JP
1993 Board, Dr C, *OBE*   36 Wakefield Gardens, London SE19 2NR
1989 Bodnar, Mr A   8 Robinson Court, Pickering, North Yorkshire YO18 8EG
2012 Boon, Mr M C M, *BA MSt FCA FCMI*   Hill House, 5 Addison Road,
Gorleston, Great Yarmouth NR31 0PA
1975 Booth, Mr P A   4 Ventnor Place, Sheffield s7 1LA
2001 Booth, Mr S J, *FRGS*   2b North Road, Stevenage, Hertfordshire SG1 4AT
1999 Borchard, Mr J D   Coburg House, 5 Gloucester Road, Teddington,
Middlesex TW11 0NS
2012 Boris, Mr B B   Flat 2, 19 Normanton Road, South Croydon CR2 7JU
2005 Bovill, Mr P J, *BSc MA MRICS FRGS*   Lemon Tree House, Main Street,
Wentworth, Ely, Cambridgeshire CB6 3QG
1995 Bowden, Mr R A, *MA DAA*   4 Ascott Avenue, London w5 5QB
1994 Bowers Isaacson, Dr L   62 Breton House, Barbican, London EC2Y 8DQ
2012 Bowley, Mrs J   10 Church Crescent, London N10 3ND
1988 Bowlt, Mrs E M, *BA*   7 Croft Gardens, Ruislip, Middlesex HA4 8EY
1997 Bowman, Dr J H, *JP MA PhD FSA Hon. Membership Secretary*   17 Park
Road, London w7 1EN
2014 Bowsher, Mr D, *MA FSA*
2019 Bowsher, Ms E A   Lichfield
2004 Boylan, Mr H T   Liniskyle, Claycastle, Haselbury Plucknett, Crewkerne,
Somerset TA18 7PE
2021 Boys, Mr P   14 Loxley Road, London sw18 3LJ
2002 Bradley, Mr G   Greentree Cottage, Town End, Broadclyst, Exeter EX5 3HW
2014 Bradley, Mr P   110A Haverstock Hill, London NW3 2BD
2012 Brady, Mr D
2013 Braham, Mrs M F   9 Chestnut Avenue, Tunbridge Wells, Kent TN4 0BS
2021 Brian, Miss J   Apartment 1305, 9 Churchyard Row, London SE11 4FF
2020 Bricusse, Mr G   6 Latham Road, Twickenham TW1 1BN
2015 Brighty, Ms Catherine   8 Wynyatt Street, London EC1V 7HU
1990 Brill, Mr M J   Well Cottage, Abbess Roding, Ongar, Essex CM5 0PB

1988	Britten, Mr N W, *FCA* 19 College Gardens, London SE21 7BE
2007	Brodie, Mrs L, *BA(Hons)* Penthouse E, St John's Wood Court, St John's Wood Road, London NW8 8QT
1993	Brook, Mr C A 27 Ormsby Lodge, The Avenue, London W4 1HS
2010	Brooker, Mr P H, *FRICS LLB(Hons)* 137 Goddard Way, Saffron Walden, Essex CB10 2ED
2021	Brooks, Ms M 70 Hyde Road, South Croydon CR2 9NQ
1998	Brooks, Miss M M, *MA DipTexCons* 51 Westwood Terrace, South Bank, York YO23 1HJ
2020	Brophy, Miss J, *MA FCA* 32 Lauderdale Tower, Barbican, London EC2Y 8BY
1989	Brown, Mr D G 44 King Henry's Road, London NW3 3RP
1990	Brown, Mr J W 316 Green Lane, London SW16 3AS
2010	Brown, Dr N Flat 2, 2 Dalebury Road, London SW17 7HH
2007	Brown, Mr P 54 Mentmore Road, Linslade, Leighton Buzzard, Bedfordshire LU7 2NZ
2002	Brown, Mr R E 21 Fir Tree Close, Hemel Hempstead HP3 8NG
2001	Brown, Mr S 8 Loxton Road, London SE23 2ET
1992	Brown, Miss S F 25 Homecroft Drive, Packington, Ashby de la Zouch, Leicestershire LE65 1WG
2000	Brushfield, Mr J N, *MCAM*
2012	Bryars, Mr T Bryars & Bryars, 7 Cecil Court, London WC2N 4EZ
2020	Bull, Mr S 46 Roupell Street, London SE1 8TB
1999	Burgess, Mr M S Stoke Cottage, Stoke St Mary, Taunton, Somerset TA3 5BZ
1991	Burgess, Mr V 224 Priests Lane, Shenfield, Essex CM15 8LG
2011	Burke, Ms M
2013	Burley, Mr P R Draper House, 161 Jerningham Road, London SE14 5NJ
1991	Burrell, Mr A B 14 Leybourne Road, London NW9 9QE
2003	Burt, Mr H C 12A Coinagehall Street, Helston, Cornwall TR13 8EB
2007	Burton, Mr N H, *BA FSA* 14 High Street, Tisbury, Salisbury SP3 6HG
1993	Butcher, Mr D C, *BSc(Hons)* Vine Cottage, 23 Hollybush Hill, London E11 1PP
2007	Buxton, Mr E B, *MA* 26 Dodson Vale, Kesgrave, Ipswich, Suffolk IP5 2GT
2015	Byrne, Mr R 6 Copperways, 80 Palatine Road, Manchester M20 3JZ
2010	Caistor, Ms M E, *MA* 13 Studd Street, London N1 0QJ
1989	Caplin, Miss E T, *MA* 15 Edward Bond House, Cromer Street, London WC1H 8DT
2018	Carey, Mr P 56A Woodville Road, New Barnet, Hertfordshire EN5 5NG
1980	Carlin, Dr M History Department, PO Box 413, University of Wisconsin, Milwaukee WI 53201, USA
1981	Carnaby, Mr J J, *EngTech MIP* 3 Lakeside Crescent, Barnet EN4 8QH
2021	Carolan-Taylor, Ms C 3 Duncan Terrace, London N1 8BZ

2019   Carr, Mr D

1980   Carter, Mr N R W, *FRICS DipTP*   9 Cannock Mill Rise, Colchester, Essex CO2 8YY

2001   Carvagal, Mr F P   14 Brading Terrace, London W12 8ES

1978   Catford, Mr K E   17 The Looms, Parkgate, Neston, Cheshire CH64 6RE

2005   Causer, Mr J C   9 Oakcroft Road, London SE13 7ED

2014   Cerasano, Professor S P   English–Colgate University, 13 Oak Lane, Hamilton NY 13346, USA

2020   Chaddock, Mr S, *BA MA AMA*

2011   Chafer, Mr P   26 Milton Abbas, Blandford Forum, Dorset DT11 0BL

1960   Chaffin, Mr D E   11 Abercromby Place, Stirling FK8 2QP

2011   Chandler, Miss J

2005   Chapple, Mrs E G

2018   Charles, Ms K J

1996   Charlish, Mrs D M   132 Park Lane, Carshalton, Surrey SM5 3DT

1983   Charlton, Mr S A   Flat 1, 7 Riverdale Road, Twickenham TW1 2BT

1988   Cherry, Mrs B K, *OBE FSA Hon. Newsletter Editor*   Bitterley House, Cleestanton Road, Bitterley, Ludlow, Shropshire SY8 3HJ

2018   Child, Mr G D   London W11

2019   Chippendale, Mr N   71 Riviera Avenue, Terrigal NSW 2260 Australia

2017   Chivers, Mr D, *BA FSA*   Flat 2, 28 Lofting Road, London N1 1ET

2019   Chubb, Mr R

2001   Chweidan, Dr C D, *BA BDS*   92 Brim Hill, London N2 0EY

2021   Clark, Mr C J   34 Gainsborough Avenue, St Albans AL1 4NL

1992   Clark, Miss J E, *BA MCLIP*   Flat 8, 2 Trinity Church Square, London SE1 4HU

2020   Clarke, Dr C, *BA MA DPhil*

2014   Clarke, Mr P D   36 Eldred Drive, Orpington, Kent BR5 4PF

2013   Clarke, Ms S   29 Longfield Road, Tring, Hertfordshire HP23 4DG

2003   Claxton Stevens, Mr C P   24 Shandon Road, London SW4 9HR

2018   Clay, Mr A

1990   Claydon, Mr K   9 Hawthorn Road, Ripley, Woking, Surrey GU23 6LH

1988   Cleaver, Mr H *Hon. Auditor (to 2020)*

1989   Clifton, Dr G C, *BA PhD*   55 The Ridgeway, Sutton, Surrey SM2 5JX

1983   Cline, Mr R L, *MA LLB FSA Hon. Treasurer*   Flat 13, 13 Tavistock Place, London WC1H 9SH

1989   Clute, Mrs J L   221 Camden High Street, London NW1 7BU

2020   Coakley, Mr S   105 Hightown Road, Ringwood, Hampshire BH24 1NL

2021   Coates, Mr S   Antique Beat, 122 Crimsworth Road, London SW8 4RL

1989   Cockings, Mr J H, *BA MSc*   8 Ardilaun Road, London N5 2QR

2014   Coggin, Mr R   Pipkins, Lake Lane, Barnham, Bognor Regis, West Sussex PO22 0AJ

1990   Cohen, Mr M A, *LLB*   3 Grays Inn Square, Grays Inn, London WC1R 5HP

2017 Coke, Mr D E, *FSA* 6 Whistler Avenue, Roussillon Park, Chichester, West Sussex PO19 6DL

2020 Collins, Mr B 1 Ormanton Road, London SE26 6RB

2003 Collins, Dr M, *MSc PhD* 15 Talacre Road, London NW5 3PH

1990 Collins, Mr P H, *BA* 19 Wentworth House, Irving Mews, London N1 2FP

2018 Colson, Dr J 125 Turnpike Link, Croydon, Surrey CR0 5NU

2005 Conlin, Mr S W, *MA* The Limes, Hextol Terrace, Hexham, Northumberland NE46 2DF

2021 Constable, Dr C 71 Isobel Place, London N15 4FP

2021 Constantine, Mrs R 6 Ormond Road, Richmond, Surrey TW10 6TH

2013 Cook, Mr D 56 Clerkenwell Road, London EC1M 5PX

1999 Cook, Mr T 15 Royal Oak Lane, Middleton Cheney, Banbury, Oxfordshire OX17 2LX

1998 Cookson, Mr B D, *BA*

1984 Coombes, Mr A J 43 Church Street, Dorking, Surrey RH4 1DJ

1995 Cooper-Smith, Mr M The Coach House, Tokens Green Lane, Kidmore End, Reading RG4 9EE

2013 Coote, Mr N A 20A New Quebec Street, London W1H 7RZ

2014 Cope, Mr P F, *BSc* Cameley, 17 Broadwater Rise, Tunbridge Wells, Kent TN2 5UE

2018 Cormack, Dr A E, *PhD FSA FRHistS* 36 Ebbisham Road, Worcester Park KT4 8NE

1993 Cornes, Mr C N 80 Coombe Road, Croydon, Surrey CR0 5RA

2014 Cornish, Mr S M, *MA BSc* 16 Gatehill Road, Northwood, Middlesex HA6 3QD

2013 Costin, Mr R C Kilronan, Polmorla, Wadebridge, Cornwall PL27 7JU

2021 Cottam, Mr G 16 Dartmouth Street, London SW1H 9BL

1991 Coughlin, Mr P M, *BSc*

2010 Coupe, Mr M J, *BSc DipTP MRICS FRSA* 48 Rosendale Road, London SE21 8DP

1998 Cousins, Mr B T

2021 Cousins, Mr E 37 Roderick Road, London NW3 2NP

2004 Cowe, Mrs M, *MA* 12 Nettlecroft, Boxmoor, Hemel Hempstead HP1 1PQ

1994 Cox-Johnson, Mr N 8 Blenkarne Road, London SW11 6JD

2011 Crane, Mr P Meadowbank, Old Mill Road, Denham UB9 5AW

2009 Craven, Mrs A-M 19 Albany Street, London NW1 4DX

1980 Crawford, Mr D L, *BA, MCIJ* 24 Fitzgerald Road, Framingham Earl, Norwich NR14 7TJ

2002 Crawshay Jones, Mr N 2 Cossor Road, Pewsey, Wiltshire SN9 5HX

1999 Croft, Mr R J 3 Westbourne Road, London SE26 5NJ

1990 Crook, Mr A J 11 Deep Lane, Basingstoke, Hampshire RG21 7RY

2004 Crouch, Mr D Daniel Crouch Rare Books, 4 Bury Street, St James's, London SW1Y 6AB

1993 Crowe, Mr N G, *BSc ARICS* 11 Stanley Terrace, Douglas, Isle of Man IM2 4EP

1990 Cudby, Mr B E Homefield, White Hill, Pitton, Salisbury SP5 1DU

2007 Cumming, Mr G, *MA MSc*

2011 Cumming, Mr J L, *BA MSc FCIPD* 7 Frere Street, London SW11 2JA

1994 Cundy, Dr P J, *MBBS FRACS* Memorial Hospital, 1 Kermode Street, North Adelaide 5006 South Australia, Australia

2004 Curling, Mr M D Cherokee, Lower Wokingham Road, Crowthorne RG45 6DB

2012 Currell, Mrs J

2008 Cutbill, Mr C D, *LLB(Hons)* 4 Lower Barn Road, Purley, Surrey CR8 1HQ

1997 Dack, Mr E G 70 Palace View, Shirley, Croydon CR0 8QN

1991 Daley, Mr P, *BSc MSc* 37 Aylesbury Road, Bromley, Kent BR2 0QP

1994 Dalton, Mrs C M 34 Westfield Road, Wheatley, Oxford OX33 1NG

2006 Daniels, Mr P J 35 Benthal Road, London N16 7AR

2020 Darley, Mr P, *MA MSc MICE* Camden Railway Heritage Trust, 21 Oppidans Road, London NW3 3AG

1987 Davidge, Mr I

1990 Davie, Mr R J, *BA FCA* 196 Princess Park Manor, Royal Drive, London N11 3FR

2020 Davies, Mr B

2021 Davies, Ms S 2 St Paul's House, 2 Market Yard, London SE8 4BX

2020 Davis, Mr M

2001 Davis, Dr M I M, *BA MB BChir* 106 All Saints Street, Hastings, East Sussex TN34 3BE

2005 Day, Mr N C 6 Rose Cottages, Uppertown Lane, Bonsall, Matlock, Derbyshire DE4 2AW

1981 De'Ath, Mr D A 32 Queensway, Caversham Park Village, Reading RG4 6SQ

1994 Dean, Mr C, *MA* 3 St Hilda's Road, London SW13 9JG

2017 Dedman, Mr J Timbers, Old Perry Street, Chislehurst, Kent BR7 6PL

1987 Dell, Mr D J 66 Vallance Road, London N22 7UB

2018 Dempsey, Mr S

2007 Denning, Mr I, *BA(Hons)* 3 Wilmington Square, London WC1X 0ES

1996 Dennison, Mr P R 4 Betula Close, Kenley, Surrey CR8 5ET

2000 Densem, Mr R G, *FSA* The Dell, 210 Hertfordingbury Road, off Old Thieves Lane, Hertford SG14 2LA

2021 Derry, Dr C 201 Glanville Grove, London SE8 4BT

2018 Dew, Miss C Goldsmiths' Centre, 42 Britton Street, London EC1M 5AD

2021 Dewick, Mr T Flat 12 Stamford Mansions, Stamford Grove East, London N16 6LT

2018 Dibiase, Mrs S A 28 Arnison Road, East Molesey, Surrey KT8 9JP

2020	Dick, Mr Andrew J, *BA FRGS FITG*
2008	Dickson, Mr M E, *BA(Hons) BArch* 6 Fletcher House, 122 Nuttall Street, London N1 5LL
2021	Dillon, Mr R Flat 5, 92 Burnt Ash Hill, London SE12 0HT
2020	Dimancescu, Ms K 5 Edmonds Road, Concord MA 01742, USA
1995	Dimen, Mr S T 10 West 16 Street, Apartment 1NS, New York NY 10011, USA
1997	Dixon, Mr P J, *BSc* 33 Tredegar Square, London E3 5AE
2011	Dobby, Mr S 39 Chester Road, Winsford, Cheshire CW7 2NG
2021	Dobson, Mrs J Falconcroft, 17 Station Road, Wilmcote, Stratford-upon-Avon CV37 9UN
2014	Dodd, Dr A 53 Radley Road, Abingdon OX14 3PN
2017	Dodge, Mr P Radcliffe Chambers, 11 New Square, London WC2A 3QB
1994	Doolittle, Dr I G, *MA DPhil* Trantlebeg, 1 Derby Road, Haslemere, Surrey GU27 1BS
2018	Doolittle, Mr R 27 Harefield, Esher, Surrey KT10 9TG
2014	Dore, Ms S 31 Longfield Road, Bristol BS7 9AG
2017	Dover, Mr M Jasmine House, 190 New Kings Road, London SW6 4NF
2010	Dowley, Dr T E, *PhD BA(Hons)* 44 Carson Road, London SE21 8HU
2017	Down, Mr J, *FRGS* 9 Marsden Road, London SE15 4EE
2006	Doyle, Mr R 219 Sternhold Avenue, London SW2 4PG
1993	Drake, Mr A D G, *BA MA PGCE* 3/6 Bedford Avenue, Bexhill-on-Sea, East Sussex TN40 1NE
1991	Drew, Miss A M, *BA*
2001	Duggan, Mr S J 34 Wantage Road, Reading RG30 2SF
2006	Duncan, Dr A I M 19 Boileau Road, London SW13 9BJ
1968	Duncan, Mr D H S 116 Fairlawn Drive, Berkeley CA 94708-2108, USA
2004	Dunn, Mr M J, *BA FCII* Flat 32, 129 Park Street, London W1K 7JB
2014	Dunning, Mr R Flat 1 Walmer Castle Court, 102 Peckham Road, London SE15 5BE
1990	Durne, Mr M E, *BA* Fir Bank Cottage, Warren Lane, Cross in Hand, Heathfield, East Sussex TN21 0TE
2005	Durne, Mrs V M, *BA(Hons)* Fir Bank Cottage, Warren Lane, Cross in Hand, Heathfield, East Sussex TN21 0TE
2011	Duthie, Mr R 5 Levyne Court, Pine Street, London EC1R 0JQ
1970	Earl, Mr J 60 Balcaskie Road, London SE9 1HQ
1986	Eastment, Mr M J 301 Woodstock Road, Oxford OX2 7NY
1977	Edwards, Mr H G 34 Capstan Square, London E14 9EU
2021	Efstathiou, Mr M 42 Buryholme, Broxbourne, Hertfordshire EN10 6PE
2020	Einck, Ms N
1987	Elam, Mr R A 31 Loxley Road, London SW18 3LL
2015	Eley, Ms J
1999	Eliot, Professor S J 1 Highview, Upper Oldfield Park, Bath BA2 3JT

2016   Elis-Williams, Mr D   Twrcelyn, 22 Ffordd Ffriddoedd, Bangor, Gwynedd LL57 2TW

2004   Ellis, Mr R, *BSc MSc*   50 Shakespeare Drive, Upper Caldecote, Biggleswade SG18 9DD

2015   Ellis, Mrs R   Twin Barns, High House Farm Lane, Colton, Norwich NR9 5DG

1991   Elliston, Mr M F, *BSc CEng*   96 Sparrows Herne, Basildon, Essex SS16 5EX

2020   Elwall, Mrs C

2015   Emery, Mr C   367 Chartridge Lane, Chesham HP5 2SL

1985   Epstein, Mr J A   Flat 2, 23 Holly Park, London N3 3JB

2017   Erickson, Dr A   Kyverdale Road, London N16 6PH

2014   Evans, Mr J C   10 Mount Hermon Close, Woking, Surrey GU22 7TU

1994   Evans, Mr M V   Bramleys, Woodlands Lane, Holcombe, Radstock BA3 5DE

2019   Evans, Mr R

2004   Everett, Mr C M   56 Inchmery Road, London SE6 2NE

2003   Everitt, Mr K D, *BSc RIBA*   4 St Albans Crescent, Woodford Green IG8 9EH

2013   Everson, Mr T F J, *MA MPhil DipLib*   40 Woodlands Avenue, New Malden, Surrey KT3 3UQ

2020   Ewles, Ms R J, *BA*   105 Greenway Avenue, London E17 3QL

2011   Eyton, Mr L   Flat 1 Ames House, 44 Mortimer Street, London W1W 7RJ

2021   Fairbairn, Mr G   201 Hillbury Road, Warlingham, Surrey CR6 9TJ

2021   Fairbank, Mr G   48 Ernest Gardens, London W4 3QJ

2018   Farr, Mr P

2021   Fathers, Mr D   9 Fenstanton Avenue, London N12 9HA

1993   Fearnley, Mrs Y   2 Woodlea Close, Winchester SO22 6DW

1991   Feltham, Mr I, *MA CEng MICE*   5 Fergus Road, London N5 1JS

1982   Fenwick, Mr P H   78 Herald Walk, Knight's Manor, Temple Hill, Dartford, Kent DA1 5SS

1975   Field, Mr E F   165 Raeburn Avenue, Surbiton, Surrey KT5 9DG

2005   Fielding, Mr A   27 Forton Road, Newport, Shropshire TF10 7JR

2018   Finch, Ms J

2016   Finn, Mr J   23 Groombridge Road, London E9 7DP

2002   Flaxman, Mr R H   10 Sandgate Lane, London SW18 3JP

1996   Fleming, Mr W B, *MA BCL*   268 Latymer Court, Hammersmith Road, London W6 7LB

2017   Fletcher, Dr D H

2018   Flockton, Mrs S, *MPhil*   73 Brookside, East Barnet, Barnet EN4 8TS

2021   Foley, Professor N   44A Yilgarn Street, Shenton Park, Western Australia 6008, Australia

2019   Foord, Mr A   171 Melrose Avenue, Willesden Green, London NW2 4NA

2017	Ford, Mr A, *FSA* PO Box 767, Ocean Grove, Victoria 3226, Australia
1978	Ford, Mr T T, *FRSCM ARAM ARSCM HonRCO* 17 Blake Apartments, New River Avenue, London N8 7QF
1980	Forrest, Mr J A 2 Mayfield Lodge, 28 Brackley Road, Beckenham BR3 1RQ
2002	Forrester, Mr R G, *LLM* 84 Litchfield Road, London E3 5AL
2005	Fosdal, Ms C E H, *BA MA* 70 Engadine Street, London SW18 5DA
2010	Foster, Mrs H 16 Pellor Fields, Breage, Helston, Cornwall TR13 9UL
2006	Fowler, Mr J A 6 George Street, Bridlington, East Yorkshire YO15 3PG
2014	Fowler, Mr S 254A Kew Road, Richmond, Surrey TW9 3EG
1986	Fox, Mr H, *MA FCA* 3 Shakespeare Gardens, London N2 9LJ
2006	Foxell, Mr S M, *BA* 23 Beacon Hill, London N7 9LY
1990	Frankland, Mr C J, *FCA* 29 Montalt Road, Woodford Green IG8 9RS
2020	Fraser-Fleming, Mr C 18 Anglesey Avenue, Farnborough, Hampshire GU14 8SF
1977	Frazer, Dr P A T, *MA MSc PhD* 6 The Avenue, Richmond, North Yorkshire DL10 7AZ
1990	Freestone, Ms T M Flat C, 33 Windsor Road, London W5 3UL
2013	French, Mrs A Keepers Cottage, 5 Langton Road, Great Bowden LE16 7EZ
1987	French, Mrs J R
1997	Frost, Mr A 17 Hazelwood Avenue, Eastbourne, East Sussex BN22 0SE
2014	Frost, Ms E Flat 2, 161 Clapham Road, London SW9 0PU
1992	Frost, Mr P M, *BDS* 178 Peckham Rye, London SE22 9QA
2016	Frow, Mr A Y Byddwn, Llanhamlach, Brecon LD3 7SU
2010	Fuller, Mr G W
1978	Fulwell, Miss S 26 Avenue Road, Leigh-on-Sea, Essex SS9 1AX
1983	Gale, Mr L T 216 Sailfish Court, Durham NC 27703-8373, USA
2005	Galer, Mr B R, *RIBA* 37 Victoria Park Road, Malvern, Worcestershire WR14 2JK
1996	Galer, Mr D W, *BPharm* 507 Hurst Road, Bexley, Kent DA5 3JX
2000	Galinou, Miss M 8 Green Court, 27 Beckenham Grove, Bromley, Kent BR2 0XS
1980	Gan, Mr R L, *JP BA BSc MEd* The Beeches, Sands Lane, Carlton-le-Moorland, Lincoln LN5 9HJ
2014	Gapper, Dr C, *BA PhD FSA* 12 Officers' Terrace, The Historic Dockyard, Chatham, Kent ME4 4LJ
1995	Gatford, Mr K The Ridge House, 2c Kemerton Road, Beckenham, Kent BR3 6NJ
2021	Gay, Ms O 4 Nightingale Lane, London N8 7QU
2002	Gaylard, Mr D, *FRGS FBCS* 7 Woodland Drive, St Albans, Hertfordshire AL4 0EL
2016	Geall, Mr D 42 Overhill Road, London SE22 0PH

1991   Gerhold, Mr D J, *MA Member of Council*   19 Montserrat Rd, London SW15 2LD

1972   Gestetner, Mr J

2003   Gibbons, Mr S J D   83 Hewitt Avenue, St Helens, Lancashire WA10 4EF

2002   Gibbs, Mr P M E, *BA*   75 Arlington Road, London NW1 7ES

2021   Gilbert, Mr M   14 Melrose Avenue, London SW16 4QU

2004   Gilbody, Mr J P, *BA(Hons)*   Sevenoaks

2020   Gilburt, Mr J

1993   Giles, Mrs K D, *BA*

2016   Gillingham, Mr S   3 Blagden Close, London N14 6DE

2013   Gilmore, Mr D

2008   Glennie, Mr D   Winter's Grace, Tonbridge Road, Ightham, Kent TN15 9AN

2013   Glews, Mr D   90 Cleveland Gardens, London SW13 0AH

2011   Glithero, Mrs B J, *BA(Hons)*   15 Chestnut Close, Witney, Oxfordshire OX28 1PD

2009   Glover, Mr G E   228 Malpas Road, Brockley, London SE4 1DH

1980   Glover, Mrs J J   48 Hermitage Lane, London NW2 2HG

1990   Gloyn, Mr W J, *FRICS*

2000   Goddard, Mr R A, *BA ACA*   Mockbridge Cottage, Brighton Road, Shermanbury, Horsham, West Sussex RH13 8HD

2010   Gold, Mr R M F   Courtfield, Stoke Trister, Wincanton, Somerset BA9 9PG

2003   Goldfinch, Mr J   63 The Quadrant, London SW20 8SW

2005   Goodison, Mrs K

2020   Goodwin, Mr D, *MPS MA CMLI FLS*

2018   Gordon, Mr I   16 Bayle Court, The Parade, Folkestone, Kent CT20 1SN

1990   Gordon-Smith, Mr B   36 Munster Road, Teddington, Middlesex TW11 9LL

2019   Gornall, Mr M

1984   Gotlop, Mr P F, *MA MRTPI*   32 Walmington Fold, London N12 7LR

1990   Gough, Mrs W

2020   Gowers, Dr K, *BSc MSc PhD MRSC*   8 Edinburgh Way, Chester CH4 7AS

1998   Graham, Mr D A M, *FRICS*   May Cottage, Fragnall Lane, Winchmore Hill HP7 0PG

2000   Grange, Mrs E K C, *BA(Hons)*   9 Peacemarsh Farm Close, Gillingham, Dorset SP8 4XQ

2016   Gray, Mr E L, *MA*   The Rill, 118 Church Way, Iffley, Oxford OX4 4EG

2020   Green, Mrs A

2014   Green, Mr C, *BA MBA*   Noddyshall, Rockshaw Road, Merstham, Surrey RH1 3DB

2000   Green, Dr D R, *BA PhD*   Department of Geography, King's College, Strand, London WC2R 2LS

2019   Green, Mr P

1998   Greggains, Miss R   23 Avenue Road, Wallington SM6 9QF

1990	Grice, Mr R I 198 Sandbed Lane, Belper, Derbyshire DE56 0SN
2001	Groom, Ms S 15 High Park Road, Kew, Richmond, Surrey TW9 4BL
1992	Grynberg, Mr W
2021	Gubbins, Mr S 162 Richmond Road, London E8 3HN
2010	Guillery, Mr P *Member of Council* 13 Swallowfield Road, Charlton, London SE7 7NS
2021	Gunning, Mr M 4 Aquarius, Eel Pie Island, Twickenham TW1 3EA
2018	Guy, Mr A 14 Church Hill, Luddenden, Halifax HX2 6PZ
2012	Hadley, Mrs S J
2013	Hahn, Ms S 17 Highbury Hill, London N5 1SU
1991	Hall, Mr D A, *DipCart* Coombe House, Chapel Street, Axmouth, Seaton, Devon EX12 4AU
1978	Hall, Mr J M 8 Woodside Road, Woodford Green IG8 0TR
2003	Hall, Mrs J M 10 Elsworthy, Thames Ditton, Surrey KT7 0YP
2021	Hall, Mr M 6 Pilley Crescent, Cheltenham GL53 9ET
2014	Hall, Mr P J 178 Albert Road, London E10 6PD
2021	Hallam-Smith, Dr E M, *CB FSA FRHistS* 8 Gaston Bell Close, Richmond, Surrey TW9 2DR
2002	Hallett, Mrs A M H, *BA MA* 6 George Lane, Lichfield, Staffordshire WS13 6DX
2003	Hallett, Dr D, *BSc PhD FGS* 13 York House, Courtlands, Sheen Road, Richmond, Surrey TW10 5BD
2014	Halligan, Mr J 36 Hayes Garden, Bromley, Kent BR2 7DG
1990	Halpin, Dr D M G, *MA DPhil* 373 Topsham Road, Exeter EX2 6HB
2011	Hamilton, Mr A P, *BA* Flat 1, 123 Fore Street, Exeter EX4 3JQ
1996	Hamilton, Mr H R B 2 Wild Hatch, London NW11 7LD
2005	Hammond, Mrs L, *MSc* 17 Chemin de Hajau, 32170 Mielan, France
1965	Hammond, Mr P W 3 Smithie Close, New Earswick, York YO32 4DG
2018	Hampshire, Mr J A 19 Chapel Street, Chichester PO19 1BU
2007	Hansell, Mr B P 43 Graham Road, London N15 3NH
2015	Hanson, Dr K W
2004	Harding, Mr J J, *MBE MA* 29 Aylward Road, Merton Park, London SW20 9AJ
1979	Harding, Dr V A Birkbeck, University of London, Malet Street, London WC1E 7HX
2021	Hardy, Mr D 5 West End Road, Silsoe, Bedford MK45 4DU
2001	Hardy, Ms S 32 Whiteadder Way, London E14 9UR
2013	Harper, Mr T 80 Belmont Road, Beckenham, Kent BR3 4HL
1981	Harris, Mr Michael 135 Anson Road, London NW2 4AH
2021	Harrison, Mr B 68 Bushey Hall Road, Bushey, Hertfordshire WD23 2EQ
2016	Harrison, Mr D
2020	Harrison, Mr R S C 9 Enmore Road, London SW15 6LL
1997	Harrod, Mrs J, *BA* 15 Berry Close, Hornchurch RM12 6UB

1990   Harry, Mr C D   54 Oakmere Lane, Potters Bar, Hertfordshire EN6 5LT

2021   Harry, Mr D   10 Nutbrook Street, London SE15 4LE

2006   Hart, Ms V   19 Norman Road, East Ham, London E6 6HN

1980   Harte, Mrs C   21 Dumbreck Road, Eltham, London SE9 1XG

1982   Harte, Dr N B, *BSc FRHistS FSA*   St Aldhelm's Cottage, 5 Stokes Road, Corsham, Wiltshire SN13 9AA

2017   Harvey, Mr C

2014   Harward, Mr C, *BA MifA*   2 Slad View, Gaineys Well, Stroud, Gloucestershire GL5 1LQ

2002   Hathway, Mr N   30 Shirlock Road, London NW3 3HS

2003   Hawgood, Mr D, *MA FBCS FSG*   26 Cloister Road, London W3 0DE

2021   Hawkins, Ms B *Hon. Auditor (2021–)*   100 Beechwood Road, South Croydon CR2 0AB

2005   Hayes, Mrs A B   7 Speed House, Barbican, London EC2Y 8AT

1991   Hazeldine, Mrs R   52 Jacksons Lane, London N6 5SX

2017   Hearn, Professor K   22B Digby Mansions, Rutland Grove, London W6 9DE

2005   Hebbert, Mr C   85 Windus Road, London N16 6UR

2000   Hedgecock, Ms D   Bruce Castle Museum, Lordship Lane, London N17 8NU

2005   Heller, Mr B, *MPhil*

2018   Helston, Mr M J C   33 Colveston Crescent, London E8 2LG

2008   Helyer, Mr J

2010   Henderson, Dr P, *MA PhD FSA*   The Old Mill, Upper Swell, Cheltenham, Gloucestershire GL54 1EW

1987   Hendy, Lord, *QC*   75 Hillway, London N6 6AB

2013   Henry, Mr J, *BA DipITC FGS FRGS*   71A Oxford Gardens, London W10 5UJ

1992   Hepher, Mr R A, *BA MTP FRICS*   105 Andrewes House, Barbican, London EC2Y 8AY

2020   Heppinstall, Mr A, *MA*   Henderson Chambers, 2 Harcourt Buildings, Temple, London EC4Y 9DB

1997   Herbert, Mr F, *HonFRGS*   46 Chilcombe House, Fontley Way, London SW15 4NB

2005   Hewett, Mr D, *MRICS*   44 Heathhurst Road, South Croydon CR2 0BA

1989   Hewett, Mr P G, *MA*   White Cottage, Church Road, Milford, Surrey GU8 5JD

2005   Heyking, Baroness G   Hamilton Cottage, Waterloo Road, Cranbrook, Kent TN17 3JJ

1994   Hibberdine, Mr S, *BSc FRICS*   38 Alleyn Road, London SE21 8AL

1984   Hidson, Mr R, *DipArch FCLIP*   117 St Thomas's Road, London N4 2QJ

2013   Higgott, Dr G   17 Windermere Avenue, London NW6 6LP

2013   Higgs, Ms G, *RIBA*   53 Balcombe Street, London NW1 6HD

1993   Higham, Mr G A   32 East Saint Helen Street, Abingdon, Oxfordshire OX14 5EB

2018   Higham, Mr N   81 Aden Grove, London N16 9NP

2018   Hill, Professor T   8 Victoria Place, Larkhall, Bath BA1 6RW

1967   Hillier, The Revd J F   70 Royal Way, Trumpington, Cambridge CB2 9AX

1995   Hillier, Mr M J S   71 Haydon Park Road, London SW19 8JH

1993   Hilling, Dr D, *MSc PhD*   4 Torrington Road, Berkhamsted HP4 3DD

1995   Hills, Mrs C M   Tile House, 36 Wansunt Road, Bexley, Kent DA5 2DQ

2019   Hills, Mr J   12 The Cedars, Milford, Godalming, Surrey GU8 5DH

1991   Hilson, Dr A J W, *MA MB BChir MSc FRCP*   62 Ossulton Way, London N2 0LB

2006   Hina, Mr R P J

1986   Hinchliffe, Mrs C L   221 Tring Road, Aylesbury HP20 1JH

2013   Hinks, Dr J   52 Fairefield Crescent, Glenfield, Leicester LE3 8EH

2007   Hinshelwood, Mr J   9 Umfreville Road, London N4 1RY

1983   Hird, Mr R L   25 Rozel Road, London SW4 0EY

1991   Hitchcock, Dr T, *DPhil*   19A Cecil Road, London N10 2BU

2007   Hobson, Mrs A M R   77 Onslow Road, Richmond, Surrey TW10 6QA

2005   Holder, Mr N   25 Monmouth Street, Topsham, Exeter EX3 0AJ

2004   Hollamby, Mr K, *BSc FSA(Scot) FRGS FEI*   2 Queensway, Lincoln LN2 4AH

2004   Holland, Mr T E, *BSIM MBA*   315 South Royal Street, Alexandria VA 22314, USA

1991   Holloway, Professor R G, *MA PhD*   Gonville & Caius College, Cambridge CB2 1TA

2021   Homewood, Ms A   31 Colebrooke Avenue, London W13 8JZ

1984   Honour, Mr D J   9 Windermere Road, Bacup OL13 9DN

2013   Hook, Mr A   54 Egerton Road, Bristol BS7 8HL

1981   Hornby, Mr J R   The Croft, 9 Lyndon Road, Manton, Oakham LE15 8SR

2014   Horsfall Turner, Dr O, *FSA*

2006   Horton, Mrs J A F   26 The Crescent, Slough, Berkshire SL1 2LQ

2017   Hostler, Mr T   32 Dangan Road, London E11 2RF

2000   Houghton, Mr S J   2 The Maltings, Orpington, Kent BR6 0DH

2005   Howard, Mr M   10 Earlston Grove, London E9 7NE

2021   Howard, Mr T   109 The Chase, Wallington SM6 8LZ

2014   Howcutt, Mr F   22 Thurlestone Road, West Norwood, London SE27 0PD

2004   Howel, Ms S M   21 Wyatt Park Road, London SW2 3TN

2006   Howell, Mr J, *BSc*   Valley Cottage, Laxfield, Woodbridge, Suffolk IP13 8HN

2008   Howse, Ms D, *BSc MSc FRES*   34 Rounton Road, Waltham Abbey EN9 3AR

2017   Hoyle, Mr S, *MA*

1991 Hughes, Mr K J   Worcester Lodge, 35 Forty Hill, Enfield, Middlesex EN2 9EQ

1999 Humm, Ms D   385 Russell Court, Woburn Place, London WC1H 0NH

2013 Hunt, Mr B R   26 Joiners Road, Linton, Cambridge CB21 4NP

1982 Hunting, Dr P S, *PhD Chairman*   40 Smith Street, London SW3 4EP

1983 Hurdley, Mr J R   Jones Farm, Hollington Lane, Woolton Hill, Newbury RG20 9XU

1999 Hutchings, Mr G F   Spruce Wood, Warren Cutting, Kingston-on-Thames, Surrey KT2 7HS

1977 Hutchings, Mrs V   Lesters, Maperton Road, Charlton Horethorne, Sherborne, Dorset DT9 4NT

2020 Hyeyun Chin, Professor, Hannam University, Gangseogu Magokdong Gumho Eullim #101-1306, Seoul 17522, South Korea

2020 Hynynen, Mr T   Flat 2, 54 Trinity Church Square, London SE1 4HT

2016 Inglis, Mr J

1984 Insall, Sir Donald W   73 Kew Green, Richmond, Surrey TW9 3AH

2010 Irving, Mr J   27 Brockenhurst Road, Croydon CR0 7DR

1998 Israel, Mr N B, *FSA*   14 Ryfold Road, London SW19 8BZ

1982 Jackson, Sir Barry, *MS FRCS*   Mapledene, 7 St Matthew's Avenue, Surbiton, Surrey KT6 6JJ

1985 Jackson, Mr D S   65 Longley Road, Harrow, Middlesex HA1 4TQ

2004 Jackson, Mr P   White House, Noon's Folly, Newmarket Road, Royston SG8 7NG

1953 Jackson-Harris, Mrs V   Quadrille, PO Box 327, Northwood, Middlesex HA6 9ES

2006 Javes, Mr G A, *MA*   45 Rushdene Avenue, Barnet EN4 8EN

2006 Jay, Mr P

1999 Jeal, Mr R   48 Malden Green Avenue, Worcester Park, Surrey KT4 7SQ

2013 Jeffery, Dr S   67 Devonshire Road, London W4 2HU

2002 Jeffryes, Mr A   9 Bannerdown Road, Batheaston, Bath, Somerset BA1 7ND

2002 Jelley, Mrs S   Little Oak, 1 Vennings Copse, Budleigh Salterton, Devon EX9 6AX

2012 Jenk, Mr T   4 Hunt Club Lane, Malvern PA 19355-3406, USA

2012 Jenkin, Mr D C   157 Arlington Road, London NW1 7ET

2007 Jenkins, Sir Brian, *GBE*   The Granary, Vale Farm, Battisford, Stowmarket IP14 2HJ

2019 Jenkins, Mr C   E26 Du Cane Court, Balham High Road, London SW17 7JJ

2017 Jennings, Mr J   38 Whittington Court, Aylmer Road, London N2 0BT

2007 Jennings, Mr V, *BA*   24B Kylemore Road, London NW6 2PT

2010 Jeremiah, Mr M G, *CB JP FRSA*   110 Ashley Gardens, Thirleby Road, London SW1P 1HJ

2006	Johnson, Mr I, *BA* Slydersgate, 11 Church Hill, Loughton, Essex IG10 1QP
1979	Johnson, Mr I A Green Tiles, Mill Lane, Chalfont St Giles, Buckinghamshire HP8 4NR
1990	Johnson, Mr K E, *MA CEng* 19 Clarence Road, Redhill, Surrey RH1 6NG
2001	Johnson, Mr P C 22 Burford Road, Chipping Norton OX7 5DZ
2002	Johnson, Mr T, *BSc* 14 Penn Road, London N7 9RD
2019	Jones, Miss C
2007	Jones, Mr D, *BSc MA*
2019	Jones, Mr D
1991	Jones, Mrs E Reay Garth, 39 Woodcroft Road, Wylam, Northumberland NE41 8DH
2012	Jones, Ms L, *BA* The Lodge, Snaresbrook House, Woodford Road, London E18 2UB
2016	Jones, Dr R W, *BSc PhD* 65 Avalon Road, London W13 0BB
2007	Jones, Mr S 17 Cross Road, Tadworth, Surrey KT20 5ST
2015	Jones, Mr S 61B Clinton Road, London N15 5BH
2020	Jutsum, Mr W, *MA MSc* 47 Moreton Place, London SW1V 2NL
2013	Kariya, Mr M 17 Collins Street, London SE3 0UG
2013	Karran, Mr D
2014	Kauder, Ms A
2013	Kaupe, Mr J W 2 Loxley Farm House, Plompton, Knaresborough, North Yorkshire HG5 8NE
1991	Kaye, Mr I F, *CEng BSc MICE* PO Box 2543, New Farm, Queensland 4005, Australia
2017	Keate, Ms D
2010	Keates, Mr J B, *MA FRSL FSA* 5 Houblon Road, Richmond, Surrey TW10 6DB
2019	Keeble, Mr F 2 Angel Yard, Highgate High Street, London N6 5JT
2013	Keegan, Mr V 174 Ashley Gardens, London SW1P 1PD
1994	Kehaya, Mr C A, *BSc CEng MICE* 6 Holne Cross, Ashburton, Devon TQ13 7QU
2006	Kellas, Mrs S H
2021	Kellow, Mr E Flat 2 Slowley House, 12 Hanson Street, London W1W 6UA
2018	Kelly, Mr S 12E Ardgowan Stret, Greenock, Renfrewshire PA16 8LE
1976	Kelsall, Mr A F 4 Woodlands Avenue, London N3 2NR
2020	Kench, Mr A
2008	Kendall, Ms D 115 Howards Road, London E13 8AZ
2013	Kendall, Mr P 20 Ramsbury Road, St Albans, Hertfordshire AL1 1SW
2010	Kennedy, Mrs J L, *JP* 6 Great Spilmans, London SE22 8SZ
2011	Kenny, Mr M G C 3/82 Hailesland Park, Edinburgh EH14 2RG
1997	Kent, Ms E J 103 Friern Road, London SE22 0AZ
2015	Kermath, Ms V 92 Hill Road, Pinner, Middlesex HA5 1LE

1983   Kerry, Mr A

2012   Kewley, Mr J, *MA*   20 Cornwallis Road, London N19 4LT

1989   Keynes, Mr R H, *MA*

2005   Kidd, Mrs F M   3 St Helens Crescent, Sandhurst GU47 9AX

2016   King, Mr A   48 Burnhill Road, Beckenham, Kent BR3 3LA

1979   King, Mr B D

2021   King, Miss D   Flat 19 Kenilworth Court, Lower Richmond Road,
        London SW15 1EW

1995   King, Mr J P   64 Alric Avenue, New Malden, Surrey KT3 4JW

1981   Kinney, Mr L W   9 Old Park Lane, Farnham, Surrey GU9 0AJ

2019   Kirby, Mrs C   24 West Street, Reigate, Surrey RH2 9BX

2003   Kirby, Mr J D   105 Corkland Road, Manchester M21 8XW

2014   Kirby, Mr M J   7 Uplands, Beckenham, Kent BR3 3NB

2019   Klan, Mr C

2006   Knight, Mr L A   19 Howcroft Crescent, London N3 1PA

2008   Knight, Mr R J   Stoneleigh, Dean Lane, Stoke Orchard, Cheltenham,
        Gloucestershire GL52 7RX

2021   Lake, Mr B   Jarndyce Antiquarian Booksellers, 46 Great Russell Street,
        London WC1B 3PA

1988   Lambert, Mr M J   49 Deacon Crescent, Bitterne, Southampton SO19 7BS

2012   Lane, Mr R J   9 Mill View Gardens, Croydon CR0 5HW

2002   Lang, Mrs D M   10 Abbeymead Court, The Old School Place,
        Sherborne, Dorset DT9 3AU

2019   Lang, Mr P H   11 St James Avenue, Epsom, Surrey KT17 1PT

1998   Latey, Mr W N   27 Hospital Bridge Road, Twickenham TW2 5UL

1998   Lathaen, Ms A, *BSc*   9 Boston Road, Henley-on-Thames, Oxfordshire
        RG9 1DY

2020   Laughlin, Mr R   16 Viewforth Place, Pittenweem, Anstruther, Fife
        KY10 2PZ

1998   Laurie, Mr R, *BA(Hons) DipLib*   201 Alberta Avenue, East Kilbride,
        Glasgow G75 8HU

2021   Lawrence, Mr A   7 Waldeck Terrace, London SW14 7HE

2018   Lawrence, Ms S

1990   Laxton, Mr P, *BA*   79 Wellington Road, New Brighton, Merseyside
        CH45 2NE

2003   Lea, Mrs A S, *BA(Hons) DMS*   12 Morell Close, New Barnet EN5 5JU

1985   Leal, Mr D J   56 Micheldever Road, London SE12 8LU

2001   Lear, Mr M   20 Oakland Place, Buckhurst Hill IG9 5JZ

2014   Leary, Mr R   11 Millennium Apartments, Browns Hill, Penryn, Cornwall
        TR10 8GL

1982   Lee, Mr C L   107 Queens Road, Hertford SG13 8BJ

1987   Lee, Mr S, *BSc*   16 Dickens Way, Romford RM1 4GQ

2005 Lefroy-Brooks, Mr S R, *MSc LBH*   12 Little Balmer, Buckingham MK18 1TF

1980 Leith, Mr I   Lilac Cottage, Leigh Street, Leigh upon Mendip, Radstock BA3 5QQ

2005 Lelliott, Mr V J T, *MSc*   47 Debden Road, Saffron Walden, Essex CB11 4AD

1988 Leon, Mr R   Sanchez de Ortega 18, Aracena 21200, Huelva, Spain

2008 Lester, Ms M C   Flat 11, 24 Bartholomew Square, London EC1V 3QT

2003 Letherby, Mrs J E, *DipArch RIBA*   101 Clonmell Road, London N17 6JT

1982 Leverton, Mr A   Leverton & Sons Ltd, 212 Eversholt Street, London NW1 1BD

2005 Levey, Dr B   29 Beatrice Road, Cardiff CF14 1DT

1983 Levy, Mr P L   52 Springfield Road, London NW8 0QN

2007 Liffen, Mr J   71 Burleigh Road, Enfield EN1 1NU

1997 Lillystone, Mr S   Bourne House, Main Road, Otterbourne, Winchester SO21 2EE

1998 Lindsay, Mrs H

2010 Linnell, Mr R F H, *MA FRICS*

1983 Lipton, Sir Stuart   40 Queens Grove, London NW8 6HH

2018 Little, Miss T   2 Montpelier Row, Twickenham TW1 2NQ

1992 Livingston, Dr H J, *BSc*   Orchard Cottage, Wineham Lane, Wineham, West Sussex BN5 9AY

1968 Lloyd, His Honour Judge H J, *QC*   Atkin Chambers, 1 Atkin Building, Gray's Inn, London WC1R 5AT

2003 Lloyd, Dr S, *DPhil*   146 Howard Street, Oxford OX4 3BG

1989 Lockhart, Mr D A, *MA LLB*   Evergreen Lodge, Back Lane, Canonstown, Hayle, Cornwall TR27 6NF

2020 Lockwood, Miss S

1987 Logan, Dr R I   6 Woodnutt Close, Bembridge, Isle of Wight PO35 5YF

2021 Long, Mr D   The Little House, 8 Stone Street, Boxford, Sudbury, Suffolk CO10 5NR

1979 Long, Mr N J

2005 Long, Mr T, *BA DipLib MCLIP*   44 Gabriel House, Odessa Street, London SE16 7HQ

2013 Loost, Mr M J, *BA LLD*   36 Upper Addison Gardens, London W14 8AJ

2004 Loveland, Mr M J S

2001 Luckins, Dr A, *BSc PhD*   Schiehallion, Hill o'Blair, Upper Allan Street, Blairgowrie, Perthshire PH10 6HL

2007 Lund, Mr T   151 Silverdale, London SE26 4SQ

2016 Lyman, Mr S   5 Tomlins Grove, London E3 4NX

1995 Lynch, Ms E K, *MA*   10 Orchard Road, Charlottesville VA 22903 USA

2014 Lynch, Mr M J, *MA LLB*   11 Saberton Close, Waterbeach, Cambridge CB25 9QW

2017   Lyon, Mr D R   1680 Palomino Drive, Henderson NV 89002 USA

2014   Lyon, Mr E, *BA BA MA MA MA*   39A Colyestone Crescent, London
        E8 2LG

1998   Lyster, Miss B   9 Bainton Road, Oxford OX2 7AF

2012   Macarthur, Ms A

2008   Macdonald, Mr C A

2020   Macdonald, Miss M

2018   Mackenzie, Mr D S

2016   Mackin, Miss A   13 Brushwood Close, London E14 6GR

2020   Macnair, Dr A   Church House, 2 Hildolveston Road, Foulsham,
        Dereham, Norfolk NR20 5RX

1964   Maddocks, Dr A C, *BM MRCPath*   The Small House, Willow Grove,
        Chislehurst, Kent BR7 5BS

2013   Major, Mr C T   71 Bromley Common, Bromley, Kent BR2 9LP

2014   Major, Mr I   Guildford

2013   Major, Mr M   Guildford

1990   Makepeace, Mrs M   Bulbarrow, Milton Avenue, Gerrards Cross,
        Buckinghamshire SL9 8QN

2010   Mandelbrote, Mr G H   Flat 1, 137A Gray's Inn Road, London WC1X 8TU

2001   Mann, Dr E

1997   Mannix, Mr P A V, *MA*   The Court House, The Green, Shamley Green,
        Guildford, Surrey GU5 0UB

1971   Marle, Mr W J   Mycroft, 16 Westlea Drive, Bromley, Kent BR1 2TN

2012   Marriner, Miss R   28 Townley Road, Bexleyheath, Kent DA6 7HN

2016   Marriott, Mr M   2 The Drive, Orpington, Kent BR6 9AP

1990   Marsden, Mr P J, *BA MA MSc*   Chequers Cottage, Dunsmore,
        Aylesbury, Buckinghamshire HP22 6QH

2021   Marsh, Dr D   7 Yale Terrace, Mitford Road, London N19 4HL

2016   Marsh, Mr L   62 Fawnbrake Avenue, London SE24 0BZ

2009   Marshall, Mr H R   Roughlands Farm, Goudhurst Road, Marden, Kent
        TN12 9NH

2010   Marshall, Mrs J A, *BSc*   Wildacre, 27 Cedar Road, Farnborough,
        Hampshire GU14 7AU

2008   Marshall, Dr J G, *MA BEd PhD*   25 York Rise, Bideford, Devon EX39 3TN

2021   Marston, Mr T   356 Whitton Avenue East, Greenford UB6 0JP

2011   Martell, Ms V   22 Plashett Road, London E13 0PU

1997   Marter, Mr J S   3 Williams Way, Blandford Forum, Dorset DT11 7YA

2016   Martin, Ms A   c/o Guildhall Library, Aldermanbury, London EC2V 7HH

2020   Martin, Mr D   Shore Books, 20 Gate Hill Court, 166 Notting Hill Gate,
        London W11 3QT

2005   Martin, Mr J   1C Ramillies Road, London W4 1JW

2007   Martin, Mr J E, *CEng MICE*   23 The Drive, Sidcup, Kent DA14 4ER

2020   Martineau, Ms V   20 St Albans Crescent, Wood Green, London N22 5NB

1994 Martin-Ross, Mr C J, *BSc BA MCLIP*   6 Castledown Terrace, Hastings TN34 3RQ

1982 Mason, Mr A D   Finches House, Hiham Green, Winchelsea, East Sussex TN36 4EG

1977 Massil, Mr S W   9A Grove Avenue, Muswell Hill, London N10 2AS

2000 Matthams, Miss J K   113 Ninesprings Way, Hitchin, Hertfordshire SG4 9NX

1985 May, Mr L E   24 Reachview Court, London NW1 0TY

2020 Mayo, Mr C   27 Westhall Road, Warlingham, Surrey CR6 9BJ

2014 McCarthy, Ms S   45 Sandringham Road, London E10 6HJ

2011 McCartney, Mr A   27 Hill Street, St Albans, Hertfordshire AL3 4QS

2014 McEvoy, Mr M   22 The Meadows, Wickhambrook, Newmarket, Suffolk CB8 8GW

2016 McGee, Mr G G   51 Mackie Avenue, Hassocks, West Sussex BN6 8NH

1993 McGrath, Mr M I   11 Regina Drive, Leeds LS7 4LR

1990 McIntosh, Miss F   Oak Farm House, Rue de la Dame, St Saviour, Jersey JE2 7NH

2021 McIntosh, Professor J   Apartment 1602, 251 Southwark Bridge Road, London SE1 6FL

2003 McKellar, Mr T   3 Wellfield Close, Ridgeway, Sheffield S12 3XN

2021 McKernan, Miss M   32 Kirkdale, London SE26 4NQ

1988 McKitterick, Professor D J, *MA LittD FBA*   Trinity College, Cambridge CB2 1TQ

2008 McMaster, Mr A R   35 Cannington Road, Dagenham RM9 4BE

2021 McNamara, Ms S   8 Wiblin Mews, London NW5 1BW

1993 McNie, Mr T M   80 Wharncliffe Road, London SE25 6SL

2003 McRory, Mrs C O   11 North Washington St, #240, Rockville MD 20850-4267, USA

2000 McVeagh, Mr T, *BA MA*

2010 Mead, Mr C W, *FRPSL*   70 Gernons, Basildon, Essex SS16 5TN

1990 Meadway, Dr R J, *MA PhD*   4 Glebe Avenue, Woodford Green IG8 9HB

2015 Mendoza, Lord   Oriel College, Oxford OX1 4EW

2007 Mercer, Mr I

1994 Mernick, Mr P   42 Campbell Road, London E3 4DT

1993 Merrill, Mr A J S, *MA*   5 Woodhall Road, Colinton, Edinburgh EH13 0DQ

1996 Mesquitta, Mr B   81 Harewood Road, Isleworth, Middlesex TW7 5HN

1998 Michaelson, Mr R W, *MA FIA*   6 Oakwood Court, London W14 8JU

1988 Mickleburgh, Mr S P, *BSc MSc*   2 Compass Cottages, Compasses Lane, Staplecross, Robertsbridge, East Sussex TN32 5SE

1985 Middleton, Mr J C   West Poundgate Manor, Chillies Lane, Crowborough, East Sussex TN6 3TB

2020 Miles, Mr J

1993 Miller, Mr D J, *MA*   100 Rosebery Avenue, London EC1R 4TL

2008   Miller, Mr L   102 Brandon Street, London SE17 1AL

2017   Millin, Ms S R, *CertEd FInstT&T*   19 Stannard Court, Culverley Road, London SE6 2LE

2013   Minchinton, Mr P C   396 Erith Road, Northumberland Heath, Erith, Kent DA8 3NJ

2005   Mitchell, Mr A J M   Grey Wings, Sea Road, Fairlight, Hastings TN35 4DR

2003   Mitchell, Mr P K   7 Lakeside Crescent, East Barnet EN4 8QH

2021   Monaghan, Mr I   Flat 4 Rose Court, Islington Green, London N1 2XR

2012   Moncrieff, Miss J

1994   Moore, Mr A P, *BA MBA MCIM*   Old Post Cottage, The Shoe, North Wraxall, Chippenham, Wiltshire SN14 8SA

2020   Moore, Mr J   20 Blinco Grove, Cambridge CB1 7TS

1986   Moore, Mr N H   54 Lord Avenue, Clayhall, Essex IG5 0HN

2014   Morgan, Mrs F

1993   Morgan, Mr G   30 Addison Road, Guildford, Surrey GU1 3QG

2008   Morley, Mr G P, *MSc PCIfA*

1994   Morris, Mr D B, *MSc CGeol*   21 Haddon Court, Shakespeare Road, Harpenden, Hertfordshire AL5 5NB

1981   Morris, Dr S J, *MA PhD Hon. Publications Secretary*   7 Barnsbury Terrace, London N1 1HJ

2013   Morrison, Mr C

2020   Moss, Mr H   35 Manor Road, London N16 5BQ

2017   Mousley, Ms A   4 Elmsdale Road, London E17 6PW

1997   Mullally, The Rt Revd & Rt Hon Dame Sarah, *DBE*   The Old Deanery, Dean's Court, London EC4V 5AA

1975   Mullinger, Mr J P A   5 Parsons Gate, Ansford, Castle Cary, Somerset BA7 7JS

2011   Mundell, Mrs T A, *BA(Hons)*

2012   Munro, Mr E   Flat 51 Hargrave Mansions, Hargrave Road, London N19 5SR

2008   Murphy, Mrs M, *BA*   7 Grove Park, London E11 2DN

2020   Murray, Mr J   Flat 14 John Clifford House, Drylands Road, London N8 9HW

2021   Murray, Ms J

2018   Murtagh, Ms P

1980   Myers, Miss R   302 Hills Road, Cambridge CB2 0QG

2016   Nathaniels, Mrs E A   5 Maze Hill House, 18 Upper Maze Hill, St Leonards TN38 0LG

2018   Naylor, Mr J   36 Lavengro Road, West Norwood, London SE27 9EG

1996   Neville, Miss L   18 Malfort Road, London SE5 8DQ

2004   Newman, Mr M   19 Plover Close, Worle, Weston-super-Mare BS22 8XB

1999   Nicholls, Mr A   33 Heskett Park, Pembury, Kent TN2 4JF

2021   Nichols, Ms S   Apartment B7-2 Arthouse, 1 York Way, London N1C 4AT

2013 Noel, Mr C G   2 Church House, Church Lane, Ledbury, Herefordshire HR8 1DP

2013 Norris, Mr T

1989 Northcott, Mr B J, *FCA*   Langstone Manor Cottage, Brentor, Tavistock PL19 0NE

2001 Norton, Mr H   35 Somerset Road, Brentford TW8 8BT

2014 Nurse, Mr E B, *MA MCLIP FSA*

1999 Nurse, Ms M E, *BA(Hons)*   60 Great Brownings, College Road, London SE21 7HP

2018 Nye, Dr J   3 First Street, London SW3 2LB

2005 O'Brien, Mr C J

2020 O'Connell, Ms M   2 Columbus House, Cinnamon Street, London E1W 3NS

2002 O'Connell, Ms S *Hon. Editor*   312 Russell Court, Woburn Place, London WC1H 0NG

2007 O'Connor, Mr D

1977 Oggins, Dr R S, *PhD FRHS*   412 Pierce Hill Road, Vestal NY 13850, USA

1989 O'Hara, Mr M M, *MA*   London SE1

2002 Olney, Mrs A C M   1 Art School Yard, Victoria Street, St Albans, Hertfordshire AL1 3YS

2005 Olutniks, Mr M, *MITG*   15 Jewel Road, London E17 4QU

2020 Orr, Mr S   49 Enfield Road, Brentford TW8 9PA

1998 Orrell, Mr S J M   139 Earlham Road, Norwich NR2 3RG

2016 Ortolja-Baird, Miss L

1985 Osborne, Dr I

2001 Oska, Mr T H   28 Adolphus Road, London N4 2AY

2013 Ossowski, Mr M   Ossowski, 83 Pimlico Road, London SW1W 8PH

2019 Ovenden, Mrs H S L   2 Loxley Farm House, Plompton, Knaresborough, North Yorkshire HG5 8NE

2010 Owens, Mr P D   5 Hatch Close, Kirtlington, Kidlington, Oxfordshire OX5 3JT

2019 Palmer, Mr B

1993 Palmer, Mr C J   23 Hartington Road, Twickenham TW1 3EL

2013 Palmer, Mr R W   19 Newlands Avenue, Thames Ditton, Surrey KT7 0HD

2005 Palmer, Ms S K C, *MA*   Sir John Soane's Museum, 13 Lincoln's Inn Fields, London WC2A 3RP

2021 Parker, Miss J   70A Sussex Way, London N7 6RR

2008 Parker, Mr S M   Apartment 6, 99 Warwick Park, Tunbridge Wells TN2 5FD

2005 Parrott, Mr B J, *FBEng FIAS MaPS*   95 Chestnut Copse, Hurst Green, Oxted, Surrey RH8 0JJ

2019 Parsons, Mr M   3 Kingswood Avenue, Bromley BR2 0NT

1997 Parsonson, Mr S L, *MA*   The Cottage, Tithe Barn Lane, Briston, Melton Constable, Norfolk NR24 2JB

1979   Pascoe, Dr G   Passaustrasse 18, D-84453 Mühldorf am Inn, Germany

2011   Paterson, Mr M G, *BA(Hons)*   141 Windmill Road, Brentford, Middlesex TW8 9NH

2008   Paton, Mr J   Brookdale, Charlton Road, Tetbury, Gloucestershire GL8 8DY

2007   Payne, Mr M T W, *BA MA*   Keeper of the Muniments, Westminster Abbey, The Chapter Office, 20 Dean's Yard, London SW1P 3PA

2008   Payne, Mr S C, *BSc*   19 Southernhay Avenue, Cliftonwood, Bristol BS8 4TJ

1984   Peacock, Mr J H B   Ravenford Farm, Hamsterley, Bishop Auckland, Co. Durham DL13 3NH

2014   Pearce, Mr P J   1 Heybridge Road, Ingatestone, Essex CM4 9AG

2016   Pearson, Mr F   Rose Cottage, 9 Brookside Road, Breadsall, Derby DE21 5LF

2004   Pearson, Mr J E   64 Scotts Road, London E10 6LW

2021   Pearson, Ms R   91C Mildmay Road, London N1 4PU

1984   Pegg, Mr I   64 Dennis Road, East Molesey, Surrey KT8 9ED

2019   Pendrigh, Mr N   203 Gloucester Road, Cheltenham, Gloucestershire GL51 8NJ

2013   Penney, Mr L   100 Kendrick Road, Reading RG1 5DW

1972   Pepper, Professor S M   21 Warmington Road, London SE24 9LA

1997   Perry, Mr J C, *BSc*   Flat 1, 101 Larkhall Rise, London SW4 6HR

2009   Pessell, Mr M

1991   Petrie, Mr C J

2003   Peverley, Mr J R, *RIBA*   Whitemill, Marston Lane, Frome, Somerset BA11 4DG

2010   Phillips, Miss A J   11 Middleton Close, London E4 8EA

2019   Phillips, Ms H

1995   Phillips, Dr M C   5 Greyfriars Place, Edinburgh EH1 2QQ

1991   Philpotts, Mr R A   3 Brook Meadow, Church Stretton, Shropshire SY6 7EH

1988   Pick, Mr C C, *BA MA*   41 Chestnut Road, London SE27 9EZ

2021   Pickard, Mr M   54 College Road, Isleworth, Middlesex TW7 5DW

1989   Pillinger, Mr R N, *BA FRES*   58 Gadby Road, Sittingbourne, Kent ME10 1TJ

1988   Pinching, Mr A A   Flat 27 Kinnear Apartments, Chadwell Lane, London N8 7RB

1999   Pines, Ms Y

2018   Pinheiro, Mr D   1 Irving Grove, London SW9 9HL

2016   Pink, Dr A

2004   Piper, Mr R J, *BA*   20 Brakespear Road South, Ickenham, Uxbridge UB10 8HE

2021   Plank, Ms C   27 Charlton Road, London SE3 7EU

2004 Plaskett, Mr R D, *MA*   302 Lauderdale Tower, Barbican, London EC2Y 8NA

2012 Pleace, Mr I   141 Burdon Lane, Cheam, Sutton, Surrey SM2 7DB

2004 Pollock, Mr C A E, *CBE*   28 Crooms Hill, London SE10 8ER

2021 Pollock, Mr D   13 Dunsmure Road, London N16 5PU

2017 Pooley, Mr J, *BA DAA FSA*   50 Chesham Road, Kingston-upon-Thames KT1 3AQ

1974 Port, Professor M H, *MA BLitt*   26 Brookfield Park, London NW5 1ER

1981 Porter, Mr N G, *BSc CEng MICE*   2 Eastcote View, Pinner, Middlesex HA5 1AT

1982 Porter, Mr S   12 West End Crescent, Stratford-upon-Avon CV37 6DY

2020 Post, Ms M   16C Tressillian Crescent, London SE4 1QJ

2013 Powell, Mr D M

2008 Powell, Mr K, *MA HonFRIBA*   Flat 1, 78 Nightingale Lane, London SW12 8NR

1997 Powers, Mr G   9a Emu Road, London SW8 3PS

1993 Poynter, Mr D J   17 Neath Abbey, Bedford MK41 0RU

1967 Pragnell, Mr H J, *MA PhD*   12 Meadow Road, Canterbury CT2 8EU

1977 Prebble, Mr T N   105 Old Orchard, Haxby, York YO32 3DS

1981 Prentice, Mrs M   17 Elizabeth Drive, New Mill, Tring HP23 5HL

2019 Prevezer, Ms K   45 Bulwer Road, Barnet EN5 5EU

1997 Price, Mr A, *MA*

1978 Price, Mr R M, *MA MCLIP*   Flat 2, 5/7 Princedale Road, London W11 4NW

2012 Prince, Mr I P, *MRICS MBEng*   Lavender Cottage, Little Top Lane, Lound, Retford, Nottinghamshire DN22 8RH

1991 Prior, Mr C J, *BSc CEng MICE*   18 Boileau Road, London W5 3AH

2017 Prizeman, Mr M   13 Stockwell Park Road, London SW9 0AP

1975 Prockter, Mr A C   21 Queenswood Road, London SE23 2QR

2012 Pulleyn, Dr S

1992 Purcell, Mr T A, *BA(Hons)*   27 West Park Avenue, Kew, Richmond, Surrey TW9 4AN

2021 Putnam, Mr J   43 Gayton Road, London NW3 1TU

1983 Quade, Miss A N M   4 Heathway, Woodford Green IG8 7RG

2002 Quarme, Mr G, *BA DipArch RIBA FRSA*   36 Smith Street, London SW3 4EP

2004 Quartano Brown, Ms K

2018 Quast, Dr T

2005 Quinn, Miss H F   38 Lancaster Road, London NW10 1HA

2012 Rabin, Mr N

1995 Ramon, Mrs A E, *BA(Hons) Member of Council*   63 Ancaster Crescent, New Malden, Surrey KT3 6BD

2020 Rance, Mr C

1995 Raphael, Mr H, *FCA*   Kfar Hittim, PO Box 92, Lower Galilee, Israel

2005 Rastall, Professor G R, *MA MusB PhD FSA*   5 Albert Grove, Leeds LS6 4DA

1992 Rau, Mrs D C, *BA MSc*   38 Fairfax Road, London NW6 4HA

2016 Raven, Mrs D

2003 Raven, Professor J, *LittD FBA FSA*   Magdalene College, Cambridge CB3 0AG

1986 Rawcliffe, Mr J W   9 Copley Deane, Bromley, Kent BR1 2PW

1993 Ray, Mr A L, *BA*   83 Barrons Way, Comberton, Cambridge CB23 7DR

2020 Redding, Dr S, *MA DPhil*   Dept of Economics & WWS, JRRB Bldg, Princeton University, Princeton NJ 08544, USA

1993 Reding, Mr J P, *BA*   18 Winchendon Road, Teddington, Middlesex TW11 0SX

1982 Reed, Miss P H, *MA*   Old Bridge House, 2 Bridge Street, Uffculme, Cullompton, Devon EX15 3AX

2012 Reed, Dr T, *BA(Hons)*   4A Burton Street, London WC1H 9AQ

2013 Rees, Mr D J   Flat 1 St Nicholas House, 33 Glamorgan Road, Kingston upon Thames, Surrey KT1 4HS

2010 Reeves, Dr L H D, *BSc(Hons) PhD*   91 Speed House, Barbican, London EC2Y 8AV

1999 Reid, Dr A M M, *MA*   Highgate

1990 Reid, Dr I, *MA MSc PhD FCIPD*   68 Elizabeth Court, Palgrave Gardens, London NW1 6EJ

2021 Reilly, Mr L   110 Embleton Road, London SE13 7DG

1985 Relf, Sqn Ldr B R F   6 Macdonnell Gardens, Watford WD25 7AG

2005 Renier, Ms H, *BA(Hons)*

2002 Reynolds, Dr P M, *MBBS DO*   15 Great Spilmans, London SE22 8SZ

2000 Rhind, Mr N, *MBE*   8 Dunstable Court, 12 St John's Park, London SE3 7TN

1992 Richards, Ms J E

2013 Richardson, Mr G

1971 Richardson, Mr J C   14 Saddleton Road, Whitstable, Kent CT5 4JD

1982 Ridge, Mr T S   7 Shepton Houses, Welwyn Street, London E2 0JN

2010 Ridgway, Mr P W, *FRGS FRIN*   3 The Green, Ketton, Stamford, Lincolnshire PE9 3RA

2007 Rigby, Mr M S, *BSc*   148 Old Bath Road, Cheltenham, Gloucestershire GL53 7DP

2018 Righiniotis, Mr J   53 South Edwardes Square, London W8 6HP

2016 Rivkin, Ms L, *MA MA*

2017 Roache, Ms A

2003 Roberts, Ms J, *BA*   Flat 1, 9 Grosvenor Road, Marple, Stockport SK6 6PR

1990 Roberts, Mr J R S, *DipTS FRGS*   Bridge House, Wanstrow, Shepton Mallet, Somerset BA4 4TE

2011 Roberts, Mr R A   9 Long Down, Petersfield, Hampshire GU31 4PD

1989 Robinson, Mr D   Flat 2 Chandos House, 27–28 Westgate Buildings, Bath BA1 1EF

2013 Robinson, Mr P   24 Academy Court, 34 Glengall Road, London NW6 7FB

2009 Robson, Mr A L, *BSc RIBA FRSA*   Apartment 1 Belvoir House, 181 Vauxhall Bridge Road, London SW1V 1ER

2017 Roche, Ms A   92B Malden Road, London NW5 4DA

2020 Rodriguez de la Rosa, Mr S

2017 Rogers, Mr N J, *MA MLitt FSA*   The Muniment Room, Sidney Sussex College, Cambridge CB2 3HU

2011 Rogers, Mr R W   20 Montague Road, Richmond, Surrey TW10 6QW

2009 Romani, Mrs J E   The Beams, Udimore Road, Broad Oak, Rye, East Sussex TN31 6DG

2019 Roome, Mr B   Tunbridge Wells

2009 Rooney, Dr D, *PhD*   303 Nevada Building, 40 Blackheath Road, London SE10 8ED

1987 Rose, Mr M T, *MA MPhil*   Ridings, Catmere End, Saffron Walden, Essex CB11 4XG

1996 Ross, Dr P C, *MA PhD DipLib MCLIP Member of Council* 149 Theydon Grove, Epping CM16 4QB

1988 Rosser, Professor A G   St Catherine's College, Manor Road, Oxford OX1 3UJ

2021 Rowles, Mr R   27 Caernarvon Drive, Ilford IG5 0XD

1988 Rowston, Mr G, *MA DipEd*   6 Kenneth Court, 173 Kennington Road, London SE11 6SS

2008 Rubin, Professor Sir Peter C, *MA DM FRCP*

2014 Ruge, Ms Y M   133 Friern Barnet Lane, London N20 0XZ

1981 Ruge-Cope, Mrs C

2008 Rumble, Mr R   19 Parr Crescent, Hemel Hempstead, Hertfordshire HP2 7LJ

2017 Rushmore, Mr P   Hunter Court, 50 High Street, Broadway, Worcestershire WR12 7DT

2009 Russell, Mr T F, *BA PGCE*   94 Hamilton Avenue, Ilford IG6 1AD

1972 Russell-Duff, Mrs J, *JP*   Watch Lane Farm, Moston, Sandbach, Cheshire CW11 9QS

1985 Ruston, Mr A R

1984 Ryan, Miss C   22 Stansfield Place, Headington, Oxford OX3 8QH

2015 Salkeld, Professor D   5 Downland Court, Chichester, West Sussex PO19 6AQ

2008 Sandison, Mr J S, *FCA FRSA*   33 Montagu Road, Highcliffe, Christchurch, Dorset BH23 5JT

2016 Sangster, Dr M

1992   Saunders, Mr M   Spectacle, Unit 25, 99–109 Lavender Hill, London
SW11 5QL

1979   Schofield, Mr J   2 Carthew Villas, London W6 0BS

2004   Scott, Mr F   4 Bayer House, Golden Lane Estate, London EC1Y 0RN

2013   Scott, Dr M

2011   Seaborn, Mr H R, *FRICS*

1999   Selby, Dr J, *MA MSc PhD*   50 Medway Crescent, Leigh-on-Sea, Essex
SS9 2UY

1992   Shalit, Mr D M, *MBE*   8 Staverdale Lodge, Melbury Road, London
W14 8LW

2021   Shaw, Dr N A   16 Torr Lane, Plymouth, Devon PL3 5NY

2017   Sheaf, Mr J C   Feathers Cottage, 4 Thames Street, Hampton, Middlesex
TW12 2EA

2001   Shepherd, Dr A, *PhD*   3 Outwoods Drive, Loughborough, Leicestershire
LE11 3LR

2012   Shepherd, Mr L

2020   Shepherd, Mr R   6 Sion Road, Twickenham TW1 3DR

2010   Sheppard, Mr M L   102 Gloucester Avenue, London NW1 8HX

2021   Sheridan, Mr J   70 Grantham Road, London SW9 9DJ

2008   Sherwood, Mr K R   72a Sedgewick Street, Cambridge CB1 3AL

2020   Shilling, Mrs E   11 Tomlins Grove, Bow, London E3 4NX

1993   Shipley, Dr M E, *MA MD FRCP*   21b Brownlow Mews, London
WC1N 2LA

1995   Shute, Dr J D, *MA MLitt PhD*   70 Bevan Avenue, Ryhope, Sunderland
SR2 0JJ

2003   Shuter, Mr P D   30 Portland Road, Oxford OX2 7EY

2019   Sillis, Mr P J, *MA*

2009   Silverman, Dr L, *PhD*   10 Adams Way, Earley, Reading RG6 5UT

2016   Sim, Mr A I F, *BADA LAPADA*   9 Corner Green, Blackheath, London
SE3 9JJ

2005   Simmonds, Mrs C I   7 Centenary Court, 19 Burton Road, Poole, Dorset
BH13 6DT

2010   Simmons, Dr P D, *MB FRCP*   96 Thomas More House, Barbican,
London EC2Y 8BU

2015   Simmons, Mr R W   121 Worcester Crescent, Woodford Green IG8 0LT

2008   Simpson, Mr E   176 Hadleigh Road, Leigh-on-Sea, Essex SS9 2LP

1996   Simpson, Mr R W   12a Manley Street, London NW1 8LT

2021   Sinton Smith, Mrs S   65 Lichfield Road, London E6 3LQ

2007   Skeet, Mr M E H, *BA(Hons)*   2 St Lukes Mews, London W11 1DF

2002   Skrzypczyk, Mr A   39 Addiscombe Road, Croydon CR0 6SA

1992   Slater, Canon Dr T R, *BA PhD FRGS*   5 Windermere Road, Moseley,
Birmingham B13 9JP

1992	Sleap, Miss S E, *BA DipLib MCLIP* 12 Vernon Avenue, Woodford Green IG8 0AU
2018	Smith, Mr A C 5 Tavistock Terrace, London N19 4BZ
1999	Smith, Mr A N 1 Church Stretton Road, Hounslow TW3 2QP
1980	Smith, Mr B D 227 Ashley Gardens, London SW1P 1PA
1996	Smith, Dr C S, *BSc MA* 61 Cedar Road, Romford RM7 7JS
1994	Smith, Mr D C 3 Bowgrave Copse, Abingdon, Oxfordshire OX14 2NL
2018	Smith, Dr H 194 Rotherhithe New Road, London SE16 2AP
2011	Smith, Ms J E, *MA BA(Hons)* 9 Grange Road, Grays, Essex RM17 6RE
2013	Smith, Mr M P 2 Mill Terrace, Thorpe Thewles, Stockton-on-Tees TS21 3JS
2020	Smith, Mr N
1992	Smith, Mr R G, *BA MSc* 29 Berrymede Road, London W4 5JE
2012	Smith, Mr R S 7 Prospect Road, St Albans, Hertfordshire AL1 2AT
1992	Smith, Mr T L 51 Dunwich Road, Bexleyheath DA7 5EN
2002	Smythe, Mr D 88 Wren Road, Sidcup DA14 4NF
2010	Solomon, Dr D J Quiet Waters, The Street, Ewelme, Wallingford, Oxfordshire OX10 6HQ
2019	Sparkes, Mr M 18 Arcadian Place, London SW18 5JF
2003	Speer, Mr P 32 The Mount, Hailsham BN27 2DT
1988	Spence, Mr C G, *BSc MA MIFA* 52A Spital Street, Lincoln LN1 3EG
2016	Spence, Mr M, *BA MA* 33 Lucas Road, London SE20 7EE
2016	Spencer, Mrs A 70 Sopwell Lane, St Albans, Hertfordshire AL1 1RW
2014	Spencer, Mr H J 24 Park Gate, Somerhill Road, Hove, East Sussex BN3 1RL
2016	Squires, Mrs V, *BA* 18 Conwy Close, Nuneaton, Warwickshire CV11 4FS
1981	Stacey, Miss A 20B Grove Hill, London E18 2JG
2007	Stacpoole, Mr J, *MRICS* 1 Queen's Road, London W5 2SA
2021	Stancomb, Mrs S 41 Woodcotes, Shoeburyness, Southend-on-Sea SS3 8XG
2004	Stanford, Mr A Walsh Associates, 32 Lafone Street, London SE1 2LX
1990	Starkey, Dr D R, *MA PhD* 49 Hamilton Park West, London N5 1AE
2000	Starling, Miss K M 2 Montague Road, London E8 2HW
2021	Steeples, Mr P 38 Handforth Road, London SW9 0LP
2013	Steer, Mr M, *BEng MA*
2004	Stephens, Dr R
2021	Stephenson, Dr J 123 Gleneldon Road, London SW16 2BQ
1983	Stevens, Mr M J 28 Haldon Road, London SW18 1QG
1985	Stevenson, Professor C Courtauld Institute of Art, Somerset House, Strand, London WC2R 0RN
2007	Stevenson, Dr J Merrifield, Down St Mary, Crediton, Devon EX17 6ED
1976	Stewart, Mr A B 26 Payne Road, Wootton, Bedford MK43 9PJ
1997	Stewart, Mr R M 13 Smith Close, London SE16 5PB

1990   Stirling, Mr C R, *BSc CEng MBCS*   3 Meadow Road, Ashtead, Surrey
         KT21 1QR

2020   Stone, Dr I   66A Garthorne Road, London SE23 1EW

2006   Stone, Mr P   82 Myddleton Avenue, London N4 2FH

2007   Storrie, Mr C   129 Balls Pond Road, London N1 4BG

2009   Stott, Mr M R   14 Cyprus Place, Rye, East Sussex TN31 7DR

1990   Strong, Mr J, *FRICS*   53 Watkins Square, Cardiff CF14 4NH

2016   Studman, Mr J   15 Calder Close, Enfield EN1 3TS

2012   Sullivan, Miss A, *BArch MA*   5 Harescombe Court, Penn Road,
         Beaconsfield, Buckinghamshire HP9 2PY

2021   Summers, Miss E   40 Defoe House, Barbican, London EC2Y 8DN

2017   Sumner, Dr G   Springfields, Reading Road, Harwell, Didcot,
         Oxfordshire OX11 0LN

1991   Sunderland, Mr P, *MA CEng*   5 Melplash Avenue, Solihull B91 1LP

2015   Surtees, Mr R A   75 Shalimar Gardens, London W3 9JG

1998   Sury, Dr M R J   61 Arbuthnot Road, London SE14 5NP

2008   Sutherland, Ms S M   10 Narraburra Close, Mount Colah NSW 2079,
         Australia

2009   Swarbrick, The Revd J   18 Latimer Gardens, Pinner HA5 3RA

2013   Swift, Mr P   50 Forde Avenue, Bromley, Kent BR1 3EX

2021   Swinfield, Mrs D   14 Beaconsfield Road, London SE9 4DP

1991   Swinson, Mr C, *MA FCA*   No Ways, Frithsden, Hemel Hempstead
         HP1 3DD

2011   Sykes, Dr S   Glenside, Hindon Lane, Tisbury, Salisbury SP3 6PZ

2010   Talbot, Mr N   Grosvenor Prints, 19 Shelton Street, London WC2H 9JN

1975   Tanner, Mr G C A   107 Camberwell Grove, London SE5 8JH

2008   Tatham, Dr D, *PhD*   329 Westcott Street, Syracuse NY 13210, USA

2013   Tatton-Brown, Mr T   Fisherton Mill House, Mill Road, Salisbury SP2 7RZ

1991   Taylor, Miss A E   30 Almoners' Avenue, Cambridge CB1 8PA

1989   Taylor, Mr A J   35 Chaucer House, Churchill Gardens, London SW1V
         3DW

2006   Taylor, Mr A M, *BA*

1995   Taylor, Mr D F   142 Western Road, Haywards Heath, West Sussex
         RH16 3LQ

2007   Taylor, Mrs D I   41 Fullerton Road, London SW18 1BU

1988   Taylor, Miss J M, *MA*   13e Philbeach Gardens, London SW5 9DY

1987   Taylor, Mr J P   20 Thurnall Close, Baldock, Hertfordshire SG7 6DR

2002   Taylor, Mr K   66–68 Camberwell Road, London SE5 0EG

2016   Taylor, Mr N

2018   Taylor, Mr N A

2007   Taylor, Dr P, *PhD FSA FRHistS*   40 Prince of Wales Road, London
         NW5 3LN

1993   Tennant, Mrs A, *MA BA DipAD*   120 Northcote Road, London E17 7EB

2009	Terroni, Mr J H 51 Brookdale, New Southgate, London N11 1BS
2007	Terry, Mr P M, *BA(Hons) ARCM PGCE*
2015	Thacker, Mr J 39A Old Church Street, London SW3 5BS
1990	Thick, Mr M F, *BSSc* 2 Brookside, Harwell, Oxfordshire OX11 0HG
2021	Thomas, Mrs J 47 Stanhope Avenue, London N3 3LY
1999	Thomas, Mr L H 13 Hurstwood Drive, Bromley, Kent BR1 2JE
1999	Thomas, Mr R G 8 Metropole Court, The Leas, Folkestone, Kent CT20 2LT
1992	Thompson, Mr E J, *CB* 120 Melrose Avenue, London NW2 4JX
2009	Thompson, Mrs L 6 Ufton Grove, London N1 4HG
1991	Thompson, Mr P J, *CEng MSc* 4 Greenways Close, Ipswich, Suffolk IP1 3RB
1991	Thomson, Mr N H, *BSc DipLib* 29 Emlyn Road, London W12 9TF
2002	Thorp, Mr A 45 Stanton Road, London SW20 8RW
1996	Thurley, Dr S J, *CBE* Clifton House, 17 Queen Street, King's Lynn, Norfolk PE30 1HT
2005	Tickell, Ms S 8 Koh-I-Noor Avenue, Bushey, Hertfordshire WD23 3EJ
2017	Tierney, Dr E Top Flat, 44 Adelaide Avenue, London SE4 1YR
1975	Tindall, Ms G 27 Leighton Road, London NW5 2QG
1995	Tiner, Mr R C 24 Thornton Hill, Exeter EX4 4NS
2020	Tomlin, Mr F 43 Palmerston Road, Buckhurst Hill IG9 5PA
1994	Tompkins, Mr P D G, *MA* The Clock Tower, 5.01 St Pancras Chambers, Euston Road, London NW1 2QR
2010	Torrible, Mr C J Ground Floor Flat, 12 Pepys Road, London SE14 5SB
1980	Towey, Mr P J 4 Channel Heights, Bleadon Hill, Weston-super-Mare, Somerset BS24 9LX
2001	Townsend, Mr M J Oak Lodge, 55 Hunstanton Road, Dersingham, King's Lynn, Norfolk PE31 6ND
2012	Traynor, Mr R A 60 Mendip Drive, Frome, Somerset BA11 2HU
1992	Trent, Mr T E, *RVM* Flat 1, 22 Kidbrooke Gardens, London SE3 0PD
2001	Tritton, Mr J A, *BSc* 7 Mace Walk, Chelmsford CM1 2GE
1980	Trueblood, Mr S P 74 Brim Hill, London N2 0HQ
1991	Tubbs, Mr J R, *BA DipArch RIBA* 49 Somerset Road, London SW19 5HT
2011	Tuckey, Mr J L 246 Kilburn Lane, London W10 4BA
1983	Tuley, Mrs I 35 Dane Heights, Dane Close, Seaford, East Sussex BN25 1EA
2013	Turbett, Ms C 87 Brookdale, London N11 1BS
2021	Turner, Mr B 502 Maurer Court, Renaissance Walk, London SE10 0SR
1964	Turner, Mrs P D H, *MA* 40 Stanlake Road, London W12 7HL
2011	Turner, Mr S J, *MA* Belziger str. 28, 10823 Berlin, Germany
2010	Turnor, Mrs A 12 Church Lane Avenue, Hooley, Coulsdon, Surrey CR5 3RT
2020	Turvey, Mr R Flat 4, 107 Rotherhithe Street, London SE16 4NF

2012   Twist, Mr P J, *LLB*   113 Paramount Court, University Street, London
WC1E 6JW

2011   Twort, Mr A, *MA LLB*   35 Frankfurt Road, London SE24 9NX

2013   Tyack, Dr G C, *MA PhD FSA Member of Council*   50 Wytham Street,
Oxford OX1 4TS

2016   Tyacke, Dr S   1A Spencer Rise, London NW5 1AR

1987   Tye, Mr R G   36 Providence Place, Chapel Street, Chichester PO19 1BS

1996   Tyers, Mr N S, *BSc CEng MICE*   6 Aintree Close, Horton Heath,
Eastleigh SO50 7PU

2018   Underhill, Mr M   Flat 14 Cotherstone Court, 25 Mint Street, London
E2 6FZ

1998   Underhill, Sir Nicholas E, *QC*

2019   van der Ree, Mr B

2000   Vander Meulen, Professor D L   Dept of English, University of Virginia,
PO Box 400121, Charlottesville VA 22904-4121, USA

1992   Vaughan, Mrs J M   5 Bishops Court, 180 St Marychurch Road, Torquay
TQ1 3JT

2021   Venning, Miss A   48 Kiver Road, London N19 4PD

1998   Vereker, Mrs J, *BA*

2017   Vile, Miss C   17 Wray Crescent, London N4 3LN

2012   Vince, Mr M, *MA*

1981   Vine, Mr D W   19 Gordon Road, London E11 2RA

2005   Vine, Ms L, *MA*

2011   Wakeham, Ms P M   74 Thorburn Square, London SE1 5QF

2009   Walduck, Mr A G   10 Grove Avenue, London W7 3EP

2014   Walker, Miss R   9 Tilletts Lane, Warnham, Horsham, West Sussex
RH12 3RE

2016   Walker, Dr T

2008   Walkling, Dr A R   28 Davis Street, Binghamton NY 13905, USA

2001   Walton, Miss J   5 Plas Penwern, Johnstown, Carmarthen SA31 3PN

2013   Ward, Mr A C   125 Carmelite Road, Harrow HA3 5LU

1973   Ward, Mr M J   27 Greenglades, West Hunsbury, Northampton NN4 9YW

1992   Warden, Mr C D   Moor Cottage, Higher Chillington, Ilminster TA19 0PT

2006   Warner, Ms C, *MA MBA*

2021   Warren, Mr D   87 Tannsfeld Road, London SE26 5DL

1998   Warren, Mr M J   74 Lancaster Drive, Hornchurch RM12 5ST

2011   Wartnaby, Mr S

2005   Waters, Mr J, *MA*

1985   Watkins, Mr P D   Basement Flat, 127 Camberwell Road, London SE5 0HB

2002   Watson, Mr C H   1 Sadlers Close, Merrow, Guildford, Surrey GU4 7DA

1980   Watson, Ms I M   34 Lodge Road, Alsager, Stoke-on-Trent ST7 2HD

2016   Watson, Mr J   100 Embleton Road, London SE13 7DG

2008   Watson, Ms M S   20 Elmsdale Road, London E17 6PW

1986	Watts, Dr R A, *MA DM* Bury Hill House, Woodbridge, Suffolk IP12 1JD
2021	Watts, Mr W 58 Ravensmede Way, London W4 1TF
2021	Webb, Mr G 75 Teevan Road, Addiscombe, Croydon CR0 6RQ
1996	Webster, Dr P V, *DLitt FSA* 8 Cefn Coed Avenue, Cyncoed, Cardiff CF2 6HE
1990	Weeden, Mr M, *BSc* 21 Avenue Pasteur, L2311 Luxembourg, Luxembourg
2017	Weeks, Mr A The Old Mill, Tracebridge, Ashbrittle, Wellington, Somerset TA21 0HG
2017	Weill, Mr L E T 107 Studland Road, London W7 3QY
1979	Weinstein, Mrs R *Member of Council*
1988	Welch, Mr J J 22 The Park Pale, Tutbury, Burton-on-Trent, Staffordshire DE13 9LB
1996	Wells, Dr E M P 24 Tree Lane, Iffley Village, Oxford OX4 4EY
2000	West, Mr M J 52 Trinity Road, Ware, Hertfordshire SG12 7DD
2006	Whaley, Mr I 46 Brights Avenue, Rainham RM13 9NW
2003	Wheatley, Mr M R, *MA* 12 Dangan Road, London E11 2RF
2019	Wheeler, Mr R
2000	Whetman, Mr P H 38 Burwood Avenue, Pinner, Middlesex HA5 2RZ
1999	White, Professor J
2005	White, Mr R M 10 Victoria Avenue, Shanklin, Isle of Wight PO37 6PJ
1984	Whitehead, Mr J 17A Springcroft Avenue, London N2 9JH
1995	Whitehorn, Mrs A M 4 Woodview, 4 South Hill Road, Bromley, Kent BR2 0RA
2004	Whitehouse, Mr L E 44 Rookery Close, Great Chesterford, Saffron Walden CB10 1QA
2005	Whiting, Mr J P Ground Floor, 117 Old Roar Road, St Leonards on Sea, East Sussex TN37 7HD
2010	Whittaker, Mr A C, *DipTP* 19 Leith Park Road, Windmill Hill, Gravesend, Kent DA12 1LN
2016	Whittaker, Mr D 125 White Horse Road, London E1 0NL
2018	Whittemore, Mr P J 16 Colne Road, London N21 2JD
2010	Whitting, Mr I J 7c Park Hill, Bickley, Bromley, Kent BR1 2JH
2018	Wholey, Mr N 4 High Lane, Haslemere, Surrey GU27 1AZ
1984	Whytehead, Mr R L 27c Colvestone Crescent, London E8 2LG
1983	Wicking, Mr D Field Cottage, Straight Road, Battisford, Stowmarket, Suffolk IP14 2HP
1990	Wicksteed, Mr M R *Hon. Secretary & Website Editor* 103 Harestone Valley Road, Caterham, Surrey CR3 6HR
2016	Wiethege, Dr W
1991	Wilbraham, Mr D L, *BSc CEng MICE* 21 Tennyson Rise, East Grinstead, West Sussex RH19 1SQ
2012	Wilks, Mr K 60 Liverpool Road, Walmer, Deal, Kent CT14 7LG

2021	Willes, Miss M 70 Forest Road, London E8 3BT
2016	Williams, Mr A P, *LLB* 14 Dandridge House, 31 Lamb Street, London E1 6ED
2021	Williams, Ms D 21 East View, Barnet EN5 5TL
2000	Williamson, Mr R D S 13 Ashburn Gardens, London SW7 4DG
2012	Willingale, Mr M Willingale Associates, 2nd Floor, 56 Clerkenwell Road, London EC1M 5PX
1999	Willis, Ms C L, *MA CQSW* Flat 6 Leedham Court, Victoria Road, Hebden Bridge HX7 8DZ
1997	Willsdon, Professor C A P, *MA PhD FSAScot FRHistS FRSA FHEA*
2014	Wilshire, Mr L J Cantley, Hampton Hall Farm Moorings, Moor Lane, Rickmansworth WD3 1LF
2012	Wilson, Mr A 1 Isambard Place, London SE16 7DA
2005	Wilson, Mrs A 22 Crescent Grove, London SW4 7AH
2008	Wilson, Mr D 3 Riverdale Road, East Twickenham TW1 2BT
2005	Wilson, Dr K G, *BA PhD* 74 Glen Avenue, Ottawa, Ontario K1S 2Z9, Canada
2013	Wilson, Mr M 40 Clifford Road, Bentley Heath, Solihull B93 8PF
2004	Wing, Mrs A C PO Box 420, Marion MA 02738, USA
1984	Winkler, Dr K T 4 Impasse des Jardins, F-67220 Dieffenbach-au-Vel, France
1996	Wisdom, Mr J J, *MA FSA* 15 Sutton Square, London E9 6EQ
2016	Withers, Mr S, *BA* 94A Holland Road, London NW10 5AY
1965	Wood, Mr P V Fletcher's Corner, Levens, Kendal, Cumbria LA8 8NL
2017	Woodford, Mr J 36 Huntingdon Road, London N2 9DU
2005	Woodman, Mr J 8 St Aidans, Seahouses NE68 7SR
2014	Woods, Mr B 31 Woodfield Way, London N11 2NR
2016	Woolf, Mr R 2 Berkeley Road, London SW13 9LZ
1978	Woolfenden, Mr A P 18 Beresford Road, Cheam, Surrey SM2 6EP
1984	Woollacott, Mr R J, *MBE FRSA* 185 Gordon Road, London SE15 3RT
2003	Woollard, Mr R A R, *MA DipArch RIBA* 42 Pearman Street, London SE1 7RE
1985	Woolley, Mr J D 107 East Wayne Avenue, Easton PA 18042, USA
2001	Woolstenholmes, Miss M 76 The Mount, Guildford, Surrey GU2 4JB
2002	Woolven, Dr R, *BSc MA PhD* Top House, Camden Lane, Willersey, Broadway, Worcestershire WR12 7PG
1984	Worms, Mr L J *Member of Council* Ash Rare Books, 43 Huron Road, London SW17 8RE
1978	Worrow, Mr A S 2 Provost Kirkpatrick Court, Peebles EH45 8EW
1990	Wright, Mr D H
1995	Wright, Mr D R, *BSc* Lynair, Leatherhead Road, Bookham, Leatherhead KT23 4SJ
2020	Wright, Ms I 2 Holly Bush Hill, London NW3 6SH

2009	Wright, Mr W J, *MA MRICS* The Thatched Cottage, Green Street, Little Hadham, Ware, Hertfordshire SG11 2EE
2013	Wyber, Mr N G Keepers Cottage, Llandewi Rhydderch, Abergavenny NP7 9TP
2009	Wyber, The Revd & Mrs R J 7 Mornington Close, Woodford Green IG8 0TT
1990	Yager, Mrs D C Danehurst Cottage, 1B Parkhill Road, London NW3 2YJ
1990	Yorke, Mr J A, *BA*
2018	Zienkiewicz, Mr A P 10 Rosebury Road, London SW6 2NG
1977	Zierler, Mr G D L 14 Regency Lawn, Croftdown Road, London NW5 1HE

Institutional members

Because the Society's early records are incomplete, some dates of joining before 1932 are approximate.

2012	Altea Antique Maps 35 Saint George Street, London W1S 2FN
1901	The Athenaeum 107 Pall Mall, London SW1Y 5ER
1950	Birmingham, University of, Main Library PO Box 363, Edgbaston, Birmingham B15 2TT
2013	British Museum, Prints & Drawings Library Great Russell Street, London WC1B 3DG
1965	California, University of Print Acquisitions, Box 957230, 621 Charles E. Young Drive South, Los Angeles CA 90095-7230, USA
1971	Camden History Society 46 Southbury Road, Enfield EN1 1YB
1906	Camden, London Borough of, Holborn Library Local Studies 32 Theobalds Road, London WC1X 8PA
1988	Canadian Centre for Architecture Library 1920 Rue Baile, Montréal, Québec H3H 2S6, Canada
2020	Clothworkers' Company Dunster Court, Mincing Lane, London EC3R 7AH
1975	Concordia University Libraries, Sir George Williams Campus PO Box 2650, Montréal, Québec H3G 2P7, Canada
1901	Drapers' Company Throgmorton Avenue, London EC2N 2DQ
1947	Goldsmiths' Company Goldsmiths' Hall, Foster Lane, London EC2V 6BN
1901	Harvard College Library Cambridge MA 02139, USA
1932	Henry E. Huntington Library Acquisitions 1151 Oxford Road, San Marino CA 91108, USA
2019	Heritage of London Trust 34 Grosvenor Gardens, London SW1W 0DH
2004	Historic England The Engine House, Fire Fly Avenue, Swindon SN2 2EH
1936	Institute of Historical Research Senate House, Malet Street, London WC1E 7HU
1901	Inner Temple Library Temple, London EC4Y 7DA
2016	Institution of Civil Engineers 1 Great George Street, London SW1P 3AA

2005 Institution of Structural Engineers   47–58 Bastwick Street, London
 EC1V 3PS

1977 Iowa, University of, Libraries   125 W Washington Street, Iowa City IA
52242-1420, USA

1965 Lambeth Archives   52 Knatchbull Road, London SE5 9QY

1901 The London Library   14 St James's Square, London SW1Y 4LG

1962 Michigan State University Library   366 W Circle Drive, East Lansing
MI 48824-1048, USA

1901 Michigan University Library   1N Harlan Hatcher Graduate Library,
913 S. University Avenue, Ann Arbor MI 48109-1190, USA

1984 Mills Whipp   Finsbury Business Centre, 40 Bowling Green Lane,
London EC1R ONE

1975 Missouri, University of   52 Ellis Library, Columbia MO 65201-5149, USA

1947 Museum of London Library   150 London Wall, London EC2Y 5HN

1938 National Archives, Library   Ruskin Avenue, Kew, Richmond TW9 4DU

1932 National Art Library   V & A South Kensington, Cromwell Road,
London SW7 2RL

1901 New York Public Library, Map Division   11 West 40th Street, New York
NY 10018, USA

1932 Newberry Library   60 West Walton Street, Chicago IL 60610-7324, USA

1932 Oxford & Cambridge Club, Library   71 Pall Mall, London SW1Y 5HD

2007 Pre-Construct Archaeology Unit   54 Brockley Cross Business Centre,
96 Endwell Road, London SE4 2PD

1903 Royal Geographical Society Library   Kensington Gore, London SW7 2AR

1932 Royal Historical Society   University College London, Gower Street,
London WC1E 6BT

1937 Senate House Library   Malet Street, London WC1E 7HU

1901 Society of Antiquaries Library   Burlington House, Piccadilly, London
W1J OBE

1991 Society of Genealogists Library   14 Charterhouse Buildings, London
EC1M 7BA

1974 Survey of London   Bartlett School of Architecture, University College
London, 22 Gordon Street, London WC1H OQB

2017 Thorney Island Society   10 Old Pye Street, London SW1P 2DG

1932 University College London, Library   Gower Street, London WC1E 6BT

1932 Victoria, State Library of   328 Swanston Street, Melbourne, Victoria
3000, Australia

1990 Victoria Studies Centre, Saffron Walden Library   2 King Street, Saffron
Walden, Essex CB10 1ES

1959 Washington, University of   Box 352900, Seattle WA 98195, USA

1967 Watermen & Lightermen, Company of Watermen's Hall,
18 St Mary-at-Hill, London EC3R 8EF

1935 Westminster City Archives   10 St Ann's Street, London SW1P 2DE

SELECT INDEX OF NAMES MENTIONED IN ARTICLES,
pages 1–298

References are to pages; *italics* denote illustrations.